CREATORS TAKE CONTROL

CREATORS TAKE CONTROL

HOW NFTS REVOLUTIONIZE
ART, BUSINESS, *and* ENTERTAINMENT

EDWARD LEE

HARPER
BUSINESS

An Imprint of HarperCollins*Publishers*

HarperCollins books may be purchased for educational, business, or sales promotional use. For information, please email the Special Markets Department at SPsales@harpercollins.com.

FIRST EDITION

Designed by Bonni Leon-Berman

Library of Congress Cataloging-in-Publication Data has been applied for.

ISBN 978-0-06-327677-2

23 24 25 26 27 LBC 5 4 3 2 1

To the creators of the world

The potential of what the Internet is going to do to society,
both good and bad, is unimaginable. . . .
The actual context and state of content is going to be so
different to anything we can really envisage at the moment.
Where the interplay between the user and the provider
will be so in simpatico it's going to crush our ideas of
what mediums are all about. . . .
That gray space in the middle is what the twenty-first
century is going to be about.

—DAVID BOWIE, INTERVIEW WITH BBC IN 1999

CONTENTS

Introduction

Everything you can imagine is real.

—PABLO PICASSO

Pablo Picasso was prolific. In a career spanning eighty years, he produced 50,000 works, including 1,885 paintings.[1] Other estimates put the total at nearly three times that amount. The *Guinness World Records* recognizes Picasso as the most prolific painter of all time.[2] A remarkable achievement of lifelong productivity given how brilliant and influential Picasso's works were. Yet, if he were still living, Picasso would be no match for today's creators. Indeed, he might be considered a slacker.

Digital artists can now produce more works in one year than Picasso produced in his lifetime. Harnessing lines of computer code, digital artists are producing 10,000 works in days, not decades. This generative process starts with some human creation or input that ultimately turns over the task of final creation to a computer program, which uses an algorithm—and sometimes artificial intelligence—to randomly generate the completed artwork. By this generative process, creating a collection of 10,000 artworks is no special feat. Indeed, the 10,000 figure is just by human choice based on the number of unique traits or elements the human creator has added. With a sufficient number of elements, a computer can easily generate billions of unique works—and some projects today, such as the Autoglyphs, are already capable of doing so.[3]

During the pandemic, the market for generative art exploded in sales of digital artwork through a new technology called nonfungible tokens, or NFTs. The NFT is a virtual token created and recorded on blockchain, and is intended to establish the provenance of an item, including purely digital creations. NFTs aren't limited to generative art. They can be used for any artwork, digital or physical—in fact, for *anything* that can be owned.

NFTs created a new market for generative art. Take, for example, Art Blocks, a popular marketplace for generative art created on demand and sold as NFTs. It was founded by Erick Calderon, aka Snowfro, the creator of Chromie Squiggle, a generative-art NFT project. The creative process on Art Blocks involves a "symbiotic relationship" between the artist, who creates the artistic elements and generative script, and the buyer, who makes stylistic selections on the platform, which then uses an algorithm to randomly generate a unique artwork NFT.[4] Six of the ten bestselling NFT artists of all time sell their artworks on Art Blocks, including Tyler Hobbs, a former computer programmer and the creator of Fidenza NFTs.[5] The Fidenza artwork resembles the Mondrian style, but with swirling patterns of colored squares against an off-white background. By April 2022, Hobbs's NFTs had amassed nearly $117 million in sales volume, including for secondary sales. In less than two years, sales of NFTs for generative art on Art Blocks totaled nearly $1.3 billion, placing it in the top five in all-time NFT sales.[6]

Of course, comparing the works of Picasso to computer-generated or generative art may sound insulting, especially when some of the most popular NFTs involve cartoon characters. Picasso is considered one of the most influential artists of the twentieth century. He was a true visionary, who helped to invent a whole style of art, Cubism, which revolutionized modern art by deconstructing subjects into fragmented depictions, offering, simultaneously, multiple perspectives in one artwork. Picasso helped to create a whole new way of viewing art and reality that triggered the movement to modern art and that influenced other fields, including architecture, design, film, and literature. His paintings now typically sell for more than $100 million.

Can the same be said for digital artists—or the computer programs they rely on? Not yet. But just wait. We've seen a glimpse of what the future holds. It's mind-blowing.

Consider Matt Hall and John Watkinson, the self-described "creative technologists" behind Larva Labs, a startup based in New York. Hall is a computer engineer who majored in computer science and math at the University of Toronto. Watkinson is an artist, computer scientist, and software developer, with a PhD in electrical engineering from Columbia. In the past, a STEM background wouldn't be associated with an artist. But today it is. Familiarity with coding comes in handy with generative art and in producing a collection of NFTs. The duo, originally from Canada, met while students at the University of Toronto and then, after graduating, started to develop apps for Android and the iPhone. But in 2017 they turned to blockchain and developed CryptoPunks—with the key insight that a unique token can be created on blockchain to enable virtual ownership. In fewer than five years, CryptoPunks have become legendary—the gold standard of NFTs.

As with any transformative technology, there's always a risk of giving too much credit to one person as being the first. Thomas Edison is often credited as inventing the light bulb, but, in fact, several inventors, including Edison, were responsible for its invention.[7] Recognizing that other NFTs came before CryptoPunks,[8] this book begins with CryptoPunks due to their significance as one of the most successful NFT collections, which helped to spawn the explosion in NFTs. Larva Labs didn't invent the concept of NFTs, but took the technology to a level of public recognition that no prior NFT had attained.

As *Wired* put it, CryptoPunks "launched an NFT revolution."[9] Even today, probably no other collection carries as much prestige within the NFT community as CryptoPunks. Owners of CryptoPunks include Jay-Z, Serena Williams, Odell Beckham, Jr., Snoop Dogg, Steve Aoki, Gary Vaynerchuk, and Logan Paul. And many others who were unknown before they became owners of CryptoPunks have become famous—and influential—within the NFT community, not to mention they have acquired generational wealth simply by owning CryptoPunks.

On June 9, 2017, Hall and Watkinson launched CryptoPunks—

pixelated portraits of 10,000 unique heads, which are tantalizingly retro. The style is more reminiscent of the graphics of an old Atari game than the high-resolution images pervasive today. Hall and Watkinson, who were inspired by the 1970s UK punk movement, characterize CryptoPunks as "a collection of misfits and non-conformists."[10] They viewed the blockchain community in the same way. Watkinson wrote a program to randomly generate the pixelated characters.[11] He added various accessories, such as hats, headbands, cigarettes, pipes, and sunglasses.[12] In explaining the creative process, he told Christie's, "We ran the generator hundreds of times, reviewed the results, and made adjustments."[13]

Most of the CryptoPunks are humans: 3,840 females and 6,039 males. (We'll return to the issue of gender disparity in chapter 11.) Three rarer species exist: 88 zombies, 24 apes, and 9 aliens.[14] CryptoPunk #8348 is the rarest in the collection because it is the only one that has seven different traits.

The launch of CryptoPunks started out slowly. Even though they were offered for free (with a modest gas fee to mint the NFT), only a few CryptoPunks were taken. Then, on June 16, 2017, Mashable published an article titled "This Ethereum-Based Project Could Change How We Think About Digital Art: Yes, You Can Actually Own These Digital Creations," written by Jason Abbruzzese.[15] "It's not inconceivable to envision a future in which CryptoPunks or some other blockchain-tied series of art does become valuable," Abbruzzese concluded. The prescient comment turned out to be an understatement. Within twenty-four hours, the CryptoPunks were all claimed, and soon they were trading on the secondary market with prices escalating.

Hall and Watkinson viewed their CryptoPunks project as an experiment. Indeed, in 2017, the term *NFT* wasn't commonly used—even Larva Labs and Abbruzzese's article didn't use it. The launch didn't go off without a hitch. An error in the code gave the purchase money back to the buyers, instead of the sellers of CryptoPunks, in the secondary market.[16] Watkinson described the snafu as "a complete disaster."[17] Larva Labs also didn't include a written content license for the CryptoPunks, so the owners were left unsure about their rights to use the artworks.[18] Larva Labs fixed both problems (the details of which are complex and not central to our discussion), but the fixes still left some unsatisfied.[19]

Prices for CryptoPunks skyrocketed to astronomical amounts in 2021. Indeed, forty-six of the top sixty sales from the collection (based on ETH) were in 2021, with the remaining fourteen occurring in 2022.[20] Of the top sixty sales, fifty-four were valued at $1 million or more at the time of purchase. Danny Maegaard, a crypto investor and DJ, bought the rarest, Punk #8348, in 2020 for only $18,000.[21] For a short time in August 2021, he offered it for sale at $171.87 million, but later took it off the market.

In just five years, secondary sales of the CryptoPunks NFTs surpassed $2 billion. And that's after Hall and Watkinson gave them all away for free (except one thousand they kept for themselves). In addition to high-priced auctions by Christie's and Sotheby's, galleries in London and Zurich held exhibitions for CryptoPunks.

The most astounding part of CryptoPunks' success is not the astronomical amounts of money people are paying to own a CryptoPunk—the highest sale fetching $23.7 million[22]—it is that the CryptoPunks are all virtual. The NFTs don't exist in a physical form. Even the digital images of the CryptoPunks aren't the same thing as the NFTs. Indeed, anyone can just copy the digital images from the CryptoPunks website. But those copies aren't the NFTs—even though that's what you might think by looking at the display of CryptoPunks online. It's mind-boggling at first. The NFT is more like a figment of the imagination than tangible property.

How can that possibly be? How can a token that exists only virtually have any value, let alone be worth millions of dollars? Or, as Christie's put the question, "Could a few lines of code [in an NFT] translate to a feeling of meaningful ownership?"[23] Hall and Watkinson didn't know for sure—the CryptoPunks were an experiment to test that very question. In an interview in 2019, Hall explained, "When you have a painting on the wall you feel confident you own a piece of art; it wasn't clear the same would be true of ownership of digital art recorded on a blockchain."[24]

Even early buyers of CryptoPunks weren't sure. Dylan Field, the CEO of Figma (a collaboration design company later sold to Adobe for $20 billion, subject to regulatory approval), explained his thinking in buying CryptoPunks NFTs in an interview with David Pierce: "At first I was like, is that art? Is that actually owning anything? I don't know! But then I started to see that other people were believing it was."[25] Field later sold one of his CryptoPunks, a blue alien smoking a pipe, for $7.5 million. Seeing is believing.

This book explains the rise of NFTs and how they are revolutionizing our conceptions of art, ownership, and property. Using key examples in the development of NFTs, I describe the phenomenon, what NFTs are, and how they are transforming the worlds of art, business, entertainment, and beyond. As the pandemic hastened people's shift to teleworking and virtual meetings, which many workers wish to continue post-pandemic,[26] NFTs exploded in popularity, ushering in a new form of virtual ownership of property that is created through a complex arrangement effectuated by computer programs and content licenses. In 2021, NFTs amassed $27 billion in sales.[27] The economic downturn in 2022 rattled all markets, including stocks, real estate, cryptocurrency, and NFTs, but the utility of NFTs has been proven—and will only increase in the future as artists, businesses, and developers build new applications.

I elaborate a new theory called Tokenism to explain this shift in perspective, a change that is every bit as radical as Cubism was at the start of the twentieth century. Cubism transformed the perspective taken in creating and viewing artworks. Tokenism transforms the perspective taken in *owning* artworks or any subject matter. Fitting for the shift to the virtual during the pandemic,[28] Tokenism reconfigures ownership virtually. With NFTs, the physical becomes immaterial—the virtual becomes valuable. People's view of art and ownership—indeed, the world—may never be the same.

A ROAD MAP

Discussing NFTs isn't easy. They defy simple categorization. They are part computer program, part contract, and part property represented by unique virtual tokens recorded on blockchain to identify some other subject matter. Got that? Understanding this new concept requires heavy lifting: it requires some factual discussion to explain how NFTs are already being used by artists, creators, and businesses—the so-called use cases—but also some theory and discussion of the underlying technology to make sense of NFTs.

Four things complicate our task to the nth degree. First, NFTs are rapidly developing—at what feels like warp speed. One of my greatest fears is saying something that becomes obsolete by the time this book is published—a decent possibility. (Indeed, the shocking collapse of the crypto exchange FTX, founded by Sam Bankman-Fried, occurred too late in this book's production to cover it. I expect FTX's demise will affect the cryptocurrency market more than NFTs, and will hasten competing efforts for greater regulation and decentralization.) We're so early. There's still so much being built, somewhat reminiscent of the early Web. Second, 2021 was a year like no other for NFTs, with a big bang of projects, investments, and business development in NFTs across many industries. No book can possibly cover the entire universe of developments. Third, the economic downturn in 2022—during which the markets for stocks, real estate, cryptocurrencies, and NFTs were all down and fears of a recession were up—presented challenges that may slow down investments and business development in NFTs. When I started writing this book, NFTs were booming. When I completed it, they were in a bear market. As we'll discuss, if there was an NFT bubble, it has already burst. The key, though, is focusing on the technological innovation, not the speculation. Finally, NFTs are a disruptive technology, and, as with any major disruption to society, they've sparked a backlash among people who think NFTs are a scam or terrible for the environment, or both.

Recognizing these challenges, this book adopts the following order. Part I provides the factual background to understand how NFTs are already being used by artists and businesses. I have chosen representative examples of artists and businesses using NFTs in creative ways. But I want to emphasize that many other artists and businesses—far too many to mention—are doing innovative work with NFTs. Part II then sets forth my theory of Tokenism, which explains how NFTs create a radical new understanding of ownership for our increasingly virtual world. The ownership is not only virtual, it also is far more interactive—one of the most appealing features of NFTs for businesses. Ownership has added utility. And, because NFTs operate as governance systems, they have also ushered in a new system of decentralized intellectual property—what I call De-IP—by which creators can take control of their artistic fate. Part III addresses some of the major criticisms of NFTs, as well as the challenges to the development of NFTs.

This book is the culmination of my research as a legal scholar. I expect it will be the most controversial thing I ever write. The best way to describe my qualification is that I am a student of the Internet. I became a legal scholar in 1999 to study the Internet. I was so captivated and intrigued by the Internet's transformation of society, I quit my lucrative job at a law firm to go into academia and write about the Internet's disruption to society. My career as a legal scholar has tracked the Internet's evolution, from the days of Napster to the rise of social media and user-generated content, to the controversies over moderating misinformation on social media. In 2021, I wrote several research papers on NFTs and posted them online. To my great surprise, tech and other professionals from around the world started to reach out to me to learn more about my research on NFTs and the theory of De-IP, including some people who kindly offered their enthusiasm and support for my research. This book draws upon the theories from my academic papers, but also offers new theories I develop here.

In the interest of full disclosure, I periodically do paid consulting work for Animoca Brands, a prominent NFT/blockchain gaming company. I also own some NFTs, including a few from collections (including Mutant Ape Yacht Club, Otherdeed, the Flower Girls, and Goopdoods) that I discuss in this book. Because my collection may change, I provide a link to a current list on my website.[29] None of these entities asked me to write about them, much less say anything to promote their business in this book. Indeed, most didn't even respond to my request for an interview. As a legal scholar, I believe strongly in academic integrity. I selected the entities analyzed here for the contributions they add to our understanding of NFTs.

NFTs are global phenomena. I strived to include artists and businesses from around the world to reflect the global scale of these transformations. Yet, due to space constraints, I have undoubtedly omitted many other creators from other countries who are doing amazing work in this area. Moreover, because I am trained as a U.S. legal scholar, the book's legal discussion focuses on U.S. law. Although international intellectual property is one of my areas of expertise, I could only mention the international legal issues in passing. One final caveat: nothing in this book is legal or financial advice.

I'm also a freelance photographer on the side. I have a personal understanding of the many challenges independent artists face. I face those challenges myself. My experience as an artist helped me appreciate why so many artists see NFTs as a revolutionary technology that has sparked a renaissance of creativity.

PART I

THE VIRTUAL RENAISSANCE

CHAPTER 1

MOMENTS

Fantasy. Lunacy. All revolutions are, until they
happen, then they are historical inevitabilities.

—DAVID MITCHELL, *CLOUD ATLAS*

In life there are moments. Events that alter the course of what follows in profound but untold ways. The bigger the moment, the bigger the transformation. For most events, we can't tell how society
will be transformed, if at all, until well after the event—years, if
not decades later. That's typically the job of historians: to explain
the Middle Ages, the Italian Renaissance, or the American Revolution, for example—events that have produced no shortage of history books, even ones published recently. But sometimes an event
is so big or disruptive that some commentators recognize, in real
time, its profound significance to society. Of course, they might not
appreciate all aspects of the change or future transformation, but
they understand a dramatic alteration of society is afoot, as well as
its significance. And, if a moment is truly revolutionary, history de-
marcates the world before the moment and afterward. The moment
changed the course of history.[1]

"Every once in a while, a revolutionary product comes along that
changes everything," Steve Jobs stated in his Macworld keynote
address to a rapt audience in San Francisco on January 9, 2007.[2]
But the audience didn't fully understand what Jobs meant. He had
to repeat the same slides. "An iPod, a phone—are you getting it?"
he asked. "These are not three separate devices. This is *one* device.

And we are calling it iPhone. Today, Apple is going to reinvent the phone."

Looking back on Jobs's announcement today, it was a moment. It introduced a new technology that would forever change the world. And some people had a sense that it would. Between Jobs's famous unveiling of the first iPhone in January 2007 and its first sales later that summer, media printed 11,000 articles about it, including David Pogue's *New York Times* review that called it revolutionary.[3] That's not to say everyone realized the imminent revolution in smartphones. Then CEO of Microsoft, Steve Ballmer scoffed at the iPhone's lack of a physical keyboard: "[I]t doesn't appeal to business customers . . . which makes it a not very good email machine."[4] At the time, physical keyboards were the industry standard.

But the iPhone's touchscreen was so good, it immediately converted skeptics. The *Wall Street Journal* columnists Walter Mossberg and Katherine Boehret, who professed to being deep skeptics of the lack of a physical keyboard, said it was a "nonissue."[5] Case closed. That assessment validated what Jobs predicted to Marc Andreessen, a venture capitalist, at a dinner in 2006 when Jobs previewed an iPhone prototype. As later recounted to *Forbes*, Andreessen questioned, "Are people really going to be okay typing directly on the screen?" Jobs replied, "They'll get used to it."[6]

They did. Within five years, virtual keyboards became the industry standard. The virtual replaced the physical, in a way that opened up new possibilities, such as a larger display for viewing—and touching. The iPhone revolutionized smartphones.

The iPhone presented an easy case. It's often far more difficult to predict the success, let alone societal significance, of a new technology, especially one being rapidly developed in a decentralized manner by multiple entities.

Just recall all the people—in both media and the tech sector—who said that the Internet itself was just a fad or doomed to fail. There's plenty to choose from, including statements made by very smart people. Robert Metcalfe, the cofounder of Ethernet and the company 3Com, predicted in 1995: "Almost all of the many predictions now being made about 1996 hinge on the Internet's continuing exponential growth. But I predict the Internet . . . will soon go spectacularly supernova and in 1996 catastrophically collapse."[7] Clifford Stoll, an astronomer and technology author, wrote a *Newsweek* article declaring all the hype of how the Internet would transform society "baloney."[8] Stoll even published a book elaborating on his skepticism.[9] Of course, back in 1995, the Internet was clunky and slow. People connected to it through dial-up. Websites were pretty static and didn't do much beyond convey information. Google wasn't invented yet, so it was really hard to find relevant Web pages. Because the technologies for the Internet were still relatively primitive, it was understandable that some people thought it would fail.

But it didn't. The Internet exceeded all expectations. And it hasn't stopped. The design of the Internet, under what's called the end-to-end principle, allows developers anywhere in the world to innovate in a decentralized manner, with new applications added to the end nodes of the network.[10] Under this approach, we don't have to revamp the entire Internet to add new applications or platforms. We just develop the new applications for use on the Internet. Think of it like adding new, state-of-the-art smart appliances to your kitchen and simply plugging them in, instead of having to rewire your entire house. (Of course, advances in connectivity through broadband enabled far greater speeds of Internet access as well as greater functionality, such as streaming of video.)

We're now in the midst of the most important transformation of the Internet since its inception, a transformation that portends revolutionary changes in many sectors and industries. It's being driven by blockchain technology, created by peer-to-peer software that establishes a decentralized system that operates as a kind of public ledger, keeping track of transactions in a permanent record. But blockchain is more than just a public ledger. It is a governance system that can be used by anyone to organize and facilitate numerous interactions among people, including commercial transactions, gaming worlds, community-building, and the formation and operation of organizations, such as businesses and decentralized autonomous organizations (DAOs). And the interactions are all decentralized, meaning that no central authority is needed—or even wanted. This movement to return to a more decentralized Internet, hearkening back to its original ideal,[11] is known as Web3, which we'll study in depth.

Blockchain underlies not only Bitcoin and other cryptocurrencies, it also underlies non-fungible tokens, or NFTs, computer programs that create virtual tokens on blockchain. We'll study the technical elements of NFTs later in the book. For now, it suffices to know that NFTs are computer programs with unique identifiers called token IDs (or, figuratively, virtual tokens), recorded on blockchain to identify or represent things, such as artworks or just about anything. Unlike cryptocurrency, in which each unit is fungible (e.g., all Bitcoins are equivalent), each NFT is unique based on its token ID, hence the name "non-fungible." NFTs create, in effect, what has been likened to a twin of something designated by the NFT creator, such as a painting or artwork. But the twin exists virtually, on blockchain. Like the iPhone did to the keyboard, the NFT uses a virtual embodiment instead of a physical one. And the most mind-boggling part: the virtual twin is property with its own independent value, potentially commanding thousands and sometimes millions of dollars, as with rare CryptoPunks, all without the need for a physical embodiment.

At first, this concept may be hard to grasp. Indeed, it may sound like fantasy, if not lunacy. How can a virtual token of something else have any value at all? Who in their right mind would pay for a token of, let's say, a painting instead of the painting itself? In Part II, we'll devote an entire chapter to understand this shift in perspective—what I call Tokenism, analogous to Cubism's radical shift in artistic perspective at the start of the twentieth century. Trust me, the concept of NFTs or owning a virtual token won't seem foreign for very long. Or, to borrow Steve Jobs's comment, you'll get used to it. And, once you do, a whole new world of possibilities opens up.

In March 2021, NFTs had a big moment. In fact, two big moments. Within the span of five days, two NFT sales showed the vast possibilities they offer. The two moments foreshadowed dramatic change, not just to the world of art, but also to ownership and the Internet as we know it. The metaverse is no longer the stuff of science fiction. It's being built right now.

BEEPLE

Mike Winkelmann is an unassuming family man who lives with his wife and two children in North Charleston. He wears dress shirts, sweaters, and horn-rimmed glasses, which make him look a bit nerdy. Indeed, in a sweater, Winkelmann looks more like Fred Rogers than the avant-garde artist who ushered in a new era for digital art.

Before he did so, Winkelmann's day job was a graphic designer working on corporate and client accounts, including Louis Vuitton, Nike, and Apple. On the side, he was a digital artist, who worked on his own pet projects and was known as Beeple, a nickname he chose in homage to a beeping furry toy from the 1980s. Beeple's client work subsidized his own artistic projects, a common practice for many artists. Beeple created free VJ loops, short videos consisting of animation, such as with neon lights, synchronized with techno music. VJ loops are meant to be played continuously as background entertainment during an event. Beeple offered his VJ loops free for anyone to download and use under Creative Commons licenses.[12] (We'll examine the concept of Creative Commons licenses in Part II.) Sharing the VJ loops this way turned out to be brilliant marketing. Beeple's loops spread among VJs and gave him recognition. His VJ loops were so good, musicians, including Justin Bieber, Eminem, Lady Gaga, One Direction, Nicki Minaj, and Katy Perry, hired him to create the visuals for their concerts and performances, including at the Super Bowl.[13]

Although Beeple's client work achieved both recognition and

success in the music industry, his "Everydays" art project is what made him internationally famous. Beginning on May 1, 2007, when he was twenty-six years old, coincidentally during the same year as the launch of the first iPhone, Beeple started to create one digital artwork a day, every day, no matter what. Inspired by the animator Tom Judd's everyday sketches, Beeple called his daily creations "Everydays."[14] He made no exception for his wedding day, the birth of his two children, or illness. On September 18, 2013, at 5 a.m., he quickly sketched a wire-frame figure, resembling a baby or a teddy bear, right before driving his wife to the hospital for the delivery of their first child.[15]

The point wasn't necessarily to make something good. The point was to create and improve his craft. Or, as Beeple colorfully explained on his website: "By posting the results online, I'm 'less' likely to throw down a big pile of ass-shit even though most of the time I still do because I suck ass."[16] Yes, though he looks like a mild-mannered family man, his comments are often laced with profanity, which gives you a preview of his artistic style. The images Beeple creates, using the 3D animation program Cinema 4D, are graphic and grotesque or downright disturbing—even described by commentators as postapocalyptic. For example, during the 2020 election season, one of Beeple's artworks, titled *Birth of a Nation*, depicted a naked Donald Trump with female breasts, breastfeeding a baby Joe Biden.[17] It's hard to unsee the image once you've viewed it. That's the visceral power of Beeple's work. The artwork received more than 100,000 likes on Instagram. Although many of his Everydays aren't as overtly political, Beeple has likened himself to a political cartoonist.[18] A dystopian political cartoonist is probably more apt, but quite fitting for the chaotic time in which we live.

In 2020, after thirteen straight years of creating Everydays, Beeple assembled five thousand images into a giant collage. The five thousandth artwork depicted a boy drawing, with characters from past Everydays, including Donald Trump, Kim Jong-il, Michael Jackson, Mickey Mouse, Buzz Lightyear, and Mario, looming over the boy.[19] Beeple titled the collage *Everydays: The First 5,000 Days*.

By then, Beeple was thirty-nine years old but still unknown in the traditional art world. He had no gallery representation and was an outsider.[20] Indeed, Beeple openly admitted that he didn't know the traditional art world and had never been to a gallery opening.[21] But he had amassed a following of nearly 2 million people on Instagram, where he posted his Everydays and offered them for free for people to use under a Creative Commons license.[22] Beeple's massive social media following gave him influence—and it would soon give him rabid collectors.

A new breed of artist-influencer was born.

In October 2020, Beeple first learned about NFTs on social media.[23] He later told *The New Yorker* that he consulted Pak, a successful and enigmatic NFT artist, for advice.[24] Beeple was intrigued after seeing other artists making thousands of dollars in cryptocurrency by selling NFTs. Because of his huge following on Instagram, he thought he could do even better than those other artists, who couldn't match his following—or, as he put it to *The New Yorker*: "I would probably make a fucking shitload of money."[25]

Indeed, Beeple did. March 11, 2021, was the Beeple moment.

On that day, Christie's sold Beeple's *Everydays: The First 5,000 Days* for $69.3 million. The bidding started at just $100 on February 25, but the last ten minutes of the auction were intense. A bidding war escalated the price from $22 million to the final sum.[26] In the last minute and eighteen seconds, the price jumped from $27.75 million to $50.75 million to $60.25 million to $69,346,250. If there were more time, the price would have gone even higher. Justin Sun, the founder of Tron, told Christie's that he bid $70 million in the last thirty seconds, but it apparently didn't go through in time.[27]

Beeple recorded the historic moment on video, while he and his family watched from his living room. After the sale, Christie's posted the video on YouTube.[28] It's a hoot to watch. When the price hit $27.75 million with one minute remaining, Jennifer

Winkelmann, Beeple's wife, threw her hands to her face, with her mouth open and eyes wide, in sheer disbelief. Beeple, who was sitting next to her on the couch, had to stand up; the intensity was too much to handle. When the price hit $50 million, most of the family members were chatting in the kitchen. One member alerted the rest, pointing at the TV: "Fifty million!" Beeple can be heard in the background, asking incredulously, "What's going on?!"

The $69.3 million sale didn't come out of nowhere. Beeple had two prior NFT sales, in October and December 2020, that showed the insatiable demand for his work, with the latter sale for The Complete MF Collection consisting of twenty artworks from the "Everydays" project that fetched a total of $3.5 million on Nifty Gateway, at the time a record for the marketplace (later bested by Pak).[29] Beeple's family cracked open the champagne and doused him with it. Noah Davis, the head of digital sales at Christie's, recognized the demand for Beeple's NFTs and seized the opportunity, helping to organize the auction house's first purely digital NFT auction with Beeple's work.[30]

The March 11, 2021, auction took Beeple to a stratospheric level. According to Christie's, *Everydays* was the first purely digital art NFT ever sold by a major auction house. And it wouldn't be the last. Christie's sold a total of $150 million worth of NFTs in 2021, including nine CryptoPunks for nearly $17 million in total.[31] Sotheby's sold $100 million worth of NFTs in the same year, boosted by a new group of younger investors under age forty.[32] *Everydays* was the first artwork that Beeple had ever sold at a major auction house. But the $69.3 million immediately placed Beeple in the upper echelon of the art world: the sale was the third-highest auction sale by a living artist, behind luminaries Jeff Koons ($91 million) and David Hockney ($90 million).[33] Also for the first time, Christie's accepted the payment in cryptocurrency (38,000 ETH) by the winning bidder, Vignesh Sundaresan, a crypto investor and metaverse developer who goes by the name Metakovan.[34] Beeple wasn't a big crypto investor, so he converted the payment into dollars. He candidly described the NFT market as a bubble, similar to the dot-com bubble of the early Web.[35] But he also noted that the bursting of the dot-com bubble didn't end the Internet. For NFTs, Beeple believed "the technology itself is strong enough where I think it's going to outlive that."[36]

The Beeple moment made the world take notice of both NFTs and Beeple. Media widely reported the sale. The CNBC anchor Carl Quintanilla reported it as breaking news, moments afterward.[37] Quintanilla was befuddled. Kelly Crow and Caitlin Ostroff of *The Wall Street Journal* put the sale into historical perspective: it was "more than anyone has ever bid for artwork by Frida Kahlo, Salvador Dalí or Paul Gauguin."[38]

But art critics were utterly unimpressed with Beeple's work. The *New York Times* critic Jason Farago lamented "the violent erasure of human values inherent in the pictures."[39] Blake Gopnik contended that sales of NFTs, including Beeple's, aren't about the quality of art: "artistic brilliance is pretty much beside the point."[40] After reviewing the various styles in all five thousand images in "Everydays," Ben Davis, writing for *Artnet News*, concluded: "None is likely to age well."[41] Davis also questioned Beeple's allegedly "misogynistic treatment" of Hillary Clinton in some images, and depictions of women, Blacks, and Asians.[42] *The Telegraph*'s art critic Alastair Sooke voiced a similar criticism.[43] When Kyle Chayka of *The New Yorker* questioned Beeple about some of his earliest works for "Everydays," which included insensitive comments about "art homos" and "black dildos," Beeple said he wouldn't use that language today.[44] When confronted with the same issue the following year, Beeple reportedly cringed and admitted the captions were "stupid," "gross," and "embarrassing," but said they were from his early work and his approach today is not "so crude."[45] In a joint interview with NVIDIA Studio, Beeple's wife, Jennifer, who is soft-spoken, admitted she's always worried about offending people, but Beeple isn't.[46]

Whether the art establishment fully accepts Beeple's artwork remains to be seen. But, if history is our guide, it will. Many of the most respected artists today faced rejection and great backlash, especially if their styles departed from the orthodoxy of the time, or the content was viewed as too controversial.[47] As we'll discuss in Part II, Picasso, perhaps the most influential artist of the twentieth century, initially faced intense backlash—even protests—for decades in the United States and Europe because critics viewed the Cubist style as degenerate and deranged, which top American physicians even claimed was the product of mental illness.

This isn't to suggest that Beeple will ever reach the level of past artists who are revered today. At least at the moment, Beeple appears to be light-years away from such acceptance. But, being number three on the list of all-time auction sales by a living artist is nothing to scoff at. In less than a year, Beeple put digital art and NFTs into mainstream discussions—and disrupted the entire art market. Christie's has already embraced him. Will galleries, museums, and art critics do so as well? There are some signs of greater recognition of Beeple's works. A year after the historic *Everydays* sale, Beeple had his first solo gallery exhibition in New York City at the Jack Hanley Gallery. (A prior exhibition for a version of *Everydays* occurred at the Northern Contemporary in Ontario in 2019.) Aptly, the NYC exhibition was titled *Uncertain Future*.

A month later, the Castello di Rivoli Museum of Contemporary Art in Turin, Italy, exhibited his *HUMAN ONE* digital sculpture, a generative sculpture that resembled a phone booth with four LED screens depicting an astronaut walking. The sculpture rotates, while the three-dimensional astronaut walks inside the structure, against different backgrounds. The video is dynamic and changes over time. Carolyn Christov-Bakargiev, the museum director, placed Beeple's sculpture at one end of a five-hundred-foot-long wing of the museum, which is a renovated Baroque castle; at the other end, Francis Bacon's painting *Study for Portrait IX* was displayed, facing Beeple's work.[48] Bacon's painting similarly depicts a man within rectangular lines resembling a booth. What Warhol did in creating Pop Art reflecting media consumption in the mid-twentieth century, Beeple is doing today in creating digital art reflecting online consumption in the twenty-first century, according to Christov-Bakargiev.[49]

I have yet to find a very favorable review of Beeple's work by a prominent art critic. Will Gompertz's review for the BBC probably comes closest. Gompertz gave Beeple's *Everydays* three out of five stars, and wrote that the work was good "[i]f you're into the comic book aesthetic, which can be traced back decades."[50] Gompertz even said it wasn't "too much of a stretch" to compare Beeple's style to some of the works of Hieronymus Bosch, Andy Warhol, or Philip Guston. Gompertz recognized the potential: Beeple's *Everydays* "will go down in history either as the moment before the short-lived cryptoart bubble burst, or as the first chapter in a new story of art." (My guess is the latter.)

Outside the traditional art world, Beeple has received more favorable reaction. In an article for *Forbes*, Jesse Damiani noted how Beeple's friends, colleagues, and people familiar with his work described him as "fearless . . . no stranger to vulgarity or twisted humor, and . . . deeply invested in his community."[51] Lady Phe-Onix, an influential digital arts curator and the founder of the online Museum of the Digital Diaspora, told *Forbes* that Beeple is "a very generous artist, first and foremost."[52] And, among the crypto community, Beeple is a rock star.

In terms of the quality of his artwork, Beeple acknowledged receiving pushback from the traditional art world, but he stuck to his artistic vision. "I'm just trying to expand people's idea of what art is a little bit because I think if you look at the artists who have stood the test of time, there are people who expanded the idea of what art is," he explained in an interview with *The Washington Post Magazine*.[53] "Look at Jackson Pollock. It was like, 'That's not art—that's just some splatters,' and then it expanded people's idea of what art is. Warhol with screen prints and Picasso with the way he was drawing."[54] Beeple admitted that he didn't know anything about art history, but, after his *Everydays* sale, he started to study it to become more educated.[55] In an interview with Laurie Segall for

60 Minutes+, Beeple said everyone's opinion of his artwork is valid even if they dislike his work.[56]

As the Christie's auction closed, while sitting with his wife in their living room, Beeple summarized what the moment meant: "Sixty-nine million. I think it means digital art is here to stay."

Then he removed his glasses to wipe away tears of joy.

KRISTA KIM

Krista Kim almost flunked her studies for a master's in fine arts in Singapore because her professors didn't consider her digital art good enough. The school prized painting and sculpture. "They didn't understand [my art]," Kim told me in an interview. "I was creating art on screens . . . [including] manipulated images of light. They didn't think of that as valid art."

Kim passed, but barely. To do so, she fought with the leadership of the school to defend her art. "It wasn't a pleasant experience, but I kept fighting for my art because I believe in my vision—of Zen for the digital age."

Kim's vision emanates from an artistic epiphany she experienced before her master's studies when she lived in Japan. She was meditating in the famous rock garden at Ryōanji Temple in Kyoto. "I just sat there and entered a Zen state of consciousness," Kim recounted. "Then I realized that was facilitated by the environment—that the environment, the way that it was created, was so masterful."

From her enlightenment, Kim developed her vision into an artistic movement that she calls Techism.[57] Kim recognized how she was addicted to her iPhone, and how social media had negative effects on mental health, including depression, obsession with receiving "likes," and narcissism. The business model of social media companies was dehumanizing: it used people as products by selling ads to companies based on tracking people's online behavior and collecting their data—what the Harvard Business School professor Shoshana Zuboff called surveillance capitalism.[58] But, instead of unplugging from our smartphones and technology, Kim came up with the brilliant idea that we can turn technology into a medium for wellness, Zen, and digital humanism.

Influenced by the writings of Marshall McLuhan, who famously recognized in 1964 that "the medium is the message,"[59] Kim's artistic mission is to combat the ill effects of digital technologies by transforming them into an artistic medium.[60] Our digital technologies—our screens, our platforms—can be redesigned or repurposed into channels for artistic creations that foster collaboration, greater consciousness, and our shared humanity. Technology and art are no longer separate, they become one.

So what does this fusion of art and technology look like? The best way to see Kim's unique style is to visit her website.[61] My description won't do it justice. Kim photographs LED lights, a technique she first used while living in Singapore, where LED lights are pervasive, and then manipulates the photographs—what she calls "playing jazz"—using Adobe Creative Suite to accentuate the gradient of colors, in a way that inspires a soothing, sublime, Zen feeling.[62] The gamut of colors in the gradient can be achieved only through light on a digital screen. Kim was influenced by the works of James Turrell and Mark Rothko, but her style and technique are distinctively her own.

"It's all trial and error," she explained. "I make mistakes. . . . I love creating new ways of doing things and making intersections between areas that have not been discovered before."

After her time in Singapore, Kim moved back to Canada, where she was born. In Toronto, she was a full-time digital artist, represented by an agent. During this period, she experienced some recognition in the traditional art world, receiving invitations to art exhibitions and shows in Canada, the United States, Europe, and online. In 2017, she also started to create large-scale public art installations. She was invited to display a public light and sound installation titled *8x8* for display in Paris outside the Palais de Tokyo and the Museum of Modern Art of Paris during Nuit Blanche in 2018.[63] The *8x8* installation later evolved into *Continuum*, a grand meditative installation shown in New York, Miami, Milan, Toronto, and other parts of the world. She also collaborated with the luxury brand Lanvin, which printed five of Kim's artworks for an entire collection of clothing. Kim was a successful artist, but it wasn't easy.

"Trying to make it in the art world is probably one of the hardest things you can possibly do," Kim remarked. "It's a difficult business. Sometimes you don't even get paid." For digital artists, it was even more challenging because, at the time, the art establishment didn't value digital art.

In 2020, Kim had been working on architectural projects to install healing-atmosphere environments for hospitals and hotels. But when the pandemic hit and Canada went into lockdown, Kim started a new art project, Mars House.

Mars House was Kim's dream home. Because of the lockdown, she decided her dream home should be virtual: the house would be virtual and it could be visited in virtual reality. At the time, Kim had envisioned expanding her business to include a lifestyle, architecture brand. The idea was reminiscent of how the leading artists during the Italian Renaissance, including Michelangelo and Raphael, also designed architecture.[64] Mars House would be part of a showcase for Kim's architectural designs.

"I wanted to create a house that heals," Kim elaborated. Mars House was designed for healing based on Zen design, reflecting wellness and a meditative environment. Mars House incorporates the elements of Kim's unique style, using light and the soothing colors of the gradient, accompanied by new-age music composed by her collaborator Jeff Schroeder of the Smashing Pumpkins. Kim designed Mars House—the walls, floor, and furniture—to be constructed all in glass. Yes, Kim intended Mars House to be an actual construction. When I talked with her in summer 2022, she said plans were already underway to build a physical Mars House to make it a destination or retreat for health and wellness, but she wasn't at liberty to disclose where. She's even collaborating with a glassmaking company in Italy, which will construct the structures.

During the pandemic, Kim thought the glass would have an added benefit: an antimicrobial coating could be used to help reduce the spread of viruses.

Mars House is an architectural wonder. Sotheby's described it as "a historic icon of this time" and "the finest example of [a digital house] to ever exist."[65] Kim completed the design for Mars House in 2020. It sat dormant on her computer for the rest of the year, as Kim was waiting for COVID to end so she could launch her new architectural business. But in December 2020 her business plans changed when she learned of NFTs. Kim had been researching Bitcoin and Ether for possible investment. That's when she read more about blockchain. Searching for "blockchain for art" on Google, she discovered NFTs. She immediately applied to the curated marketplace SuperRare and then minted her first NFT, for one of her gradient digital paintings, in February 2021.

Kim soon discovered how NFTs can also be used for the metaverse. Studying what big collectors do with their NFTs, she learned that some display them in metaverse galleries on digital land they've purchased in virtual worlds such as Cryptovoxels, Decentraland, or the Sandbox. That's when Kim recognized NFTs' vast potential for the metaverse.

"NFTs are truly creating real assets in the metaverse," Kim said with conviction. "And therefore are the building blocks and the architecture for the metaverse. This is just the first iteration because NFTs will become 3D digital assets, powered by AI. That's the potential, it can be anything."

With that insight, Kim knew what to do next: "I should offer Mars House as the first [NFT] real estate asset in history. So I minted it. And the rest is history."

March 16, 2021, was the Krista Kim moment. Mars House sold on SuperRare for 288 ETH ($512,712).[66] The purchase included the 3D files to install Mars House on a metaverse platform, plus the NFT owner received the right to commission the manufacture of physical furniture pieces in glass. Later, during the summer, Kim launched Mars House in the metaverse platform Spatial, so people could visit it in virtual reality, using a VR headset. Rebecca Jarvis, a journalist and technology correspondent for ABC News, even interviewed Kim in Mars House, with both appearing as avatars in virtual reality.

The sale of Mars House, which occurred just five days after Beeple's *Everydays* sale, caused quite a stir. Indeed, the sale of Mars House might have been even more confounding than Beeple's sale, which commentators could attempt to understand (incorrectly) as just another high-priced art auction. Mars House defied simple categorization: this NFT digital house was designed to be built in the metaverse *and* in real life. Plus, the all-glass design, with infusion of colors and light, is unlike anything we've seen before. Just as mind-boggling, the virtual Mars House cost more than the median price of a physical house in Chicago, which was $399,000 in 2022.[67] As a *New York Times* article suggested, many people probably scratch their heads "at people paying real money for virtual property in a simulated world."[68] You may, too.

..

The Beeple and Krista Kim moments in March 2021 were historic events that signaled the radical transformation NFTs were effectuating not just in the world of art, but among businesses and industries. The Beeple moment validated the use of NFTs for digital art—as he put it, digital art is here to stay. The Krista Kim moment validated the use of NFTs for virtual property in the emerging metaverse. Or, as *USA Today* described the sale of Mars House, "The digital housing market has officially commenced."[69]

Granted, sales of NFTs in the weeks following these two sales during 2021 were fueled by great speculation, with sales prices of NFTs hitting new heights—which plummeted down to earth in the crypto winter of 2022. It's important, however, to put aside the speculation and focus on the concept of NFTs. The moments involving Beeple and Kim proved how ownership of NFTs is real.

Just as the iPhone showed that people don't need physical keyboards, NFTs show that people don't need physical materials to find value and utility in property that exists only virtually, in tokens on blockchain. What the value is, the market will ultimately decide—just as it does for stocks, real estate, art, luxury goods, and cryptocurrency.

For Beeple and Kim, their lives as artists were forever changed by their respective moments in March 2021. Beeple bought a 50,000-square-foot building in Charleston to serve as his studio and museum for his works, including *Everydays* and more immersive art experiences.[70] Beeple's operations have become a family business, with his brother and once-retired parents involved—all hands on deck to help oversee the sixteen full-time employees. Beeple's second NFT auction at Christie's, in November 2021, involved *HUMAN ONE*. The NFT sold for $28.9 million.[71] In the Hulu documentary *NFTs: Enter the Metaverse*, Beeple explained that he wanted to experiment with screens to "make them feel much more connected and part of the art, and sort of immersive."[72]

In 2022, Kim's *Continuum* installation was acquired by the Los Angeles County Museum of Art (LACMA), as part of its first acquisition in conjunction with a gift by Paris Hilton, an early adopter and supporter of NFTs.[73] Kim also launched, with her partner Peter Martin, a metaverse production studio called 0. Its mission is to build "a human-centered, creative metaverse committed to the highest level of artistic world-building."[74]

I asked Kim how NFTs had changed her life. "Wow," she answered, pausing to reflect. "Completely changed my life. It's empowered me as a creator to be a sovereign creator—and not to rely on intermediaries to be seen or to be heard or to be recognized. I had *immediate* recognition posting my artwork and selling it on SuperRare globally. That never happens in the art world. In the art world, you need to be vetted by gallerists. And it's a heavily gated system, and it's very much about relationships and gatekeeping." NFTs enabled Kim to bypass the gatekeeping and to become an internationally recognized artist on her own. Based on her experience, Kim expressed her ardent belief in decentralization and the promise of Web3 to build a better world.

Sure, there are naysayers who don't believe NFTs are real or meaningful. (We'll examine the skeptics' doubts in depth later in the book.) But, once people shift their perspective from owning something physically to owning something virtually, a new world of possibilities opens up.

If you are a diehard skeptic of NFTs or blockchain, I ask simply to reserve judgment until the end of the book. If you've ever read an online newspaper instead of a paper newspaper, sent an email or text message instead of snail mail or handwritten letter, used a credit card or electronic money instead of paper cash, attended a Zoom meeting instead of an in-person meeting, or used a virtual keyboard instead of physical buttons on a smartphone, I'm confident you'll begin to see the utility of NFTs by the book's end. It requires some outside-the-box thinking—which is why so many artists and creatives are the earliest adopters of NFTs.

Because we're so early into this transformation of society, most people haven't made this shift in perspective yet. But many big businesses have. More than two hundred brands—from Adidas to JP Morgan to HSBC to PwC to Samsung—have already purchased virtual land and are planning for greater interactions online in the emerging metaverse.[75] Big Tech companies, including Apple, Alphabet, Microsoft, Meta (formerly Facebook), Nvidia, and Qualcomm, are investing millions of dollars to develop metaverse-related technologies, including for augmented and virtual reality.[76] And businesses across many industries are developing or have already offered NFTs to their consumers.[77] The economic downturn in 2022 may slow this development, but won't stop it. Businesses see too much potential—and money—in the emerging metaverse.

When the history books are written, the NFT sales in March 2021 by Beeple and Krista Kim will be seen as revolutionary— two moments signaling that NFTs were ushering in a Virtual Renaissance, during which art, ownership, and the Internet forever changed.

CHAPTER 2

LIFE-CHANGING

Change your thinking, change your life.

—ERNEST HOLMES

The starving artist has been romanticized for generations. In 1896, drawing upon Henri Murger's work, the Italian composer Giacomo Puccini featured, in his opera *La Bohème*, four bohemians—a painter, a musician, a poet, and a philosopher—living and struggling together in Paris, with a tragic ending.[1] Ironically, Puccini himself made millions, with a net worth estimated to be $200 million in 1924, equivalent to $3.4 billion in 2022.[2] Despite his own fortune, Puccini's opera helped to popularize the romantic figure of the starving artist, as seen in the Broadway musical *Rent*, inspired by *La Bohème*. Although the starving artist is now enshrined in modern culture, the concept is more disturbing the more one thinks about it: it signals society's acceptance of the devaluing of artists' work. As Neda Ulaby, writing for NPR, put it: "There are very few professions where poverty is romanticized."[3] Indeed, besides religious vocations, it's hard to identify any other.

No matter how romanticized, the starving artist still exists. In 2017, Artfinder, an online marketplace for independent artists, commissioned a survey of artists in the United States and United Kingdom. The income for artists was meager. In the United States, nearly half of independent artists (48.7 percent) earned between $1,000 and $5,000 annually from their artistic work.[4] Also, 47 percent said their art generated less than 25 percent of their income.[5]

Only 21 percent of all artists surveyed generated most of their income (between 75 and 100 percent) from their artistic work.[6] Independent artists spend substantial time each week on marketing and business promotion, operating outside the world of selective galleries, which act as gatekeepers for the art establishment.[7] "The majority of independent artists do not make a full time living from their work, despite identifying themselves as full time artists," the report concluded.[8]

In a similar study of artists from fifty-two countries conducted by the Creative Independent in 2018, the most common sources of income for artists were freelance and contract work (61 percent), income from a job either related or unrelated to their art (both 42 percent), and family support or inheritance (29 percent).[9] Fully 83 percent of artists said they made less than $50,000 annually; 58 percent made less than $30,000.[10] The median annual income was $20,000 to $30,000. Representation by a gallery was "usually not a helpful way for an artist to pursue financial stability."[11] The pandemic worsened the plight for many independent artists. According to a national survey conducted in April 2020, 66 percent of artists in the United States said they were unemployed, and the average respondent expected to earn only $17,000 that year, an amount below the federal poverty threshold for a family of two persons or more.[12]

The Internet and digital technologies have exacerbated the many challenges that artists face. On the one hand, online marketplaces, such as Etsy, and crowdsourced funding platforms, such as Patreon, Buy Me a Coffee, and GoFundMe, offer artists ways to finance and develop their businesses and sell their works. Various vendors, such as Art Storefronts, enable artists to set up their own websites, which include online shopping features, and printing and shipping services. On the other hand, creators still typically must hustle for multiple sources of income to support themselves, such as "a more stable day job to subsidize other projects."[13]

Artists also face the dilemma posed by posting their work online—the Internet dilemma. The Internet is a great way to promote one's work to potentially the widest audience imaginable, the world, but the Internet also makes it easy for people to copy one's work for free. It facilitates both widespread access and widespread copying of artistic works. This dilemma is especially challenging for digital artists whose works are natively digital—there's no difference between the original and copies, so a copy can supplant the original. In my field, the issue of copyright infringement on the Internet, aka "piracy," has dominated policy discussions now for more than two decades—without much progress.

In 2011, in an address at Columbia Law School, Francis Gurry, then the director general of the World Intellectual Property Organization, recognized this problem: the Internet had caused a fundamental change in the dynamics of creative production—making it much easier to both share and copy works of authorship—that required us to reexamine copyright policy.

"How can society make cultural works available to the widest possible audience, while at the same time returning some value to creators and to the business associates who helped the creators to navigate the economic system; and to enable the creators and their business associates to lead a dignified economic existence?" Gurry asked.[14] To answer that question, we must "challenge society," he advised, "to share responsibility" in answering this fundamental question.[15]

Civilizations have always prized art, but how and how much they prize artists have varied. During the Italian Renaissance, the Catholic Church, the rulers, and the wealthy funded artists through a patronage system.[16] Guilds also established artists as a profession, and guild membership was apparently required for commissioned work of any significance.[17] (Back then, people were commonly referred to by their particular craft, such as painter or sculptor, instead of artist.[18]) The artists were employed for work beyond fine art, including architectural and design work for infrastructure. Although a patronage system has its own problems, such as elitism, favoritism, and potential censorship, it instituted a professional system for valuing artists and their works.[19] Under that system, Michelangelo became the highest-paid artist and amassed a fortune (though he tried to conceal it), according to research by the art historian Rab Hatfield.[20] Society viewed artists as central to a city's prosperity. As Bruce Cole described, "Art was not a luxury, but something that society wanted, needed, and used; consequently, there had to be enough artists to satisfy the considerable demand."[21]

The Framers of our Constitution envisaged a different system for the United States. Instead of patronage, the Copyright Clause prioritizes "authors" of creative works by recognizing the power of Congress to grant authors exclusive rights to their works for a limited time.[22] Ultimately, providing authors with financial rewards through copyright—meaning the ability to monetize their works and stop others from freely copying them—is meant to serve the public by incentivizing authors to create and disseminate their works to the public.[23]

That ideal of our copyright system has been lost. Although copyright has often been hailed as superior to patronage, as a way to free authors from the control of and dependence on patrons, the legal scholar Clark Asay points out that our copyright system has never avoided patronage completely—publishers, record labels, and other intermediaries operate as quasi-patrons within our copyright system.[24] Indeed, our copyright laws have long catered to industry distributors, the so-called middlemen—publishers, music labels, movie studios, and now media conglomerates.[25] It's not surprising the copyright system has been distorted to serve industries and intermediaries instead of authors. Legislatures, such as Congress and the European Parliament, are subject to intense lobbying from the major copyright industries, and now also Big Tech companies that depend on ISP safe harbors for immunity from liability based on infringement by their users. Lost in the shuffle are individual artists, who have little, if any, say in the debate—and who, not surprisingly, struggle to find opportunities to showcase their works and survive financially.[26] As the copyright scholar Jane Ginsburg put it: "All too often in fact, authors neither control nor derive substantial benefits from their work."[27] Why? Our copyright system favors distributors. As Jessica Litman noted, "That bias comes at creators' expense."[28] The ease of copying on the Internet made the challenge for artists only harder.

Of course, skeptics may argue that we shouldn't guarantee a living wage to artists. Nothing in the Copyright Clause requires it. If artists have to work three jobs to support their artistic pursuits, so be it. Their art might not be any good. Let the market decide which artists get paid.

The skeptics' critique is misguided. In addressing the challenges presented by the Internet, Ginsburg stressed the need to consider professional authors and provide them with meaningful financial incentives to create.[29] That view comports with the Supreme Court's economic interpretation of the Copyright Clause, in which authors "deserve rewards commensurate with the services rendered."[30] The Court well understood that "[s]acrificial days devoted to creative activities" shouldn't be spent so artists starve. Instead, our copyright system is intended to ensure that authors "secure a fair return for [their] creative labor."[31] The Copyright Clause itself recognizes that if we want "progress" in society, we can't just let the market decide everything. That's why the Framers gave Congress the power to intervene in the market by establishing a copyright system and exclusive rights for authors. The Framers understood that leaving creative production entirely to the market might not work because unauthorized copying of works would dampen creative production.[32] Few artists can afford to create if all of their works can be copied by others for free, with impunity. How will they make a living? The copyright system is meant to address that problem by granting authors exclusive rights to their works for a limited term of copyright. But in the Internet age the ease of sharing unauthorized copies has strained the system, perhaps to its limit. Plus, the concentration of market power in major publishers, labels, and other gatekeepers makes complete reliance on the market dubious at best.[33]

Even putting aside the failings of our copyright system, the low incomes for independent artists suggest that the traditional market for artistic works does not adequately capture the positive externalities that art and culture provide to society. In other words, society is likely benefiting from artists' works without having to pay artists anything close to the full value of their contributions to society. Especially during the turbulent time in which we live, art serves an essential role of reflecting, critiquing, challenging, and contributing to society. For example, studies suggest that exposure to art may help to foster open-mindedness, civic engagement, and tolerance. Kelly LeRoux and Anna Bernadska analyzed data from the 2002 General Social Survey of adults and found that "those individuals who attend arts events at least once a year are more likely to participate in various civic associations, exhibit greater tolerance towards racial minorities and homosexuals, and behave in a manner which regards the interests of others above those of oneself."[34]

Researchers have also found a correlation between education in art and better behavior, better writing, and greater compassion among schoolchildren. In 2019, the Brookings Institution conducted a randomized, controlled study of 10,548 grade school students in forty-two Houston schools, which were a part of the reinvigoration of arts education under the city's Arts Access Initiative.[35] The study found that, compared with the control group, students who were exposed to arts education manifested positive benefits: "a 3.6 percentage point reduction in disciplinary infractions, an improvement of 13 percent of a standard deviation in standardized writing scores, and an increase of 8 percent of a standard deviation in their compassion for others."[36]

These studies are part of a growing body of empirical research on the positive benefits of the arts to society, including health and wellness.[37] Americans already appear to understand intuitively some of these insights identified by researchers. In a random survey of 2,011 adults conducted by Ipsos in 2019, 91 percent of Americans believed "the arts are a vital part of a well-rounded education for K–12 students."[38] In addition, 64 percent believed that, without arts education, students will be less prepared for jobs of the future.[39] Fully 93 percent of Americans said they believed that exposure "to different arts helps broaden one's mind," and 90 percent said it is "a great way to reduce stress."[40] Likewise, 83 percent said that "art is essential to building communities and identities."[41]

Few deny the importance of art to society, yet artists face dim prospects of making a living. The majority of independent artists make less than $30,000 from their art, and the select few who obtain gallery representation are by no means guaranteed financial security. First of all, artists who are represented by a gallery typically get only 50 percent of any sale, with the other half going to the gallery. Moreover, galleries operate on a notoriously bad business model. As one commentator described, "It turns out that the upbeat world of biennials and art fairs and parties is in fact a cutthroat, antiquated, deeply flawed industry hampered by an obsession with keeping up appearances and an often misguided aversion to making money."[42] In 2015, Magnus Resch caused a stir in the art world when he published a book in which he analyzed the flawed business model of art galleries.[43] Resch's expanded study in the second edition of his book included eight thousand galleries in Germany, the United Kingdom, and the United States, the three nations with the highest number of galleries.[44] According to Resch's analysis, galleries congregated in major cities, where rent was the highest expense, and lacked a diversity of offerings, instead targeting a very narrow market of contemporary art collectors.[45] Paying high rent was not economically prudent for many galleries, especially if serious art collectors typically didn't frequent galleries, as one gallery director indicated.[46] Resch concluded: "The almost unanimous, and unquestioned, conviction that central premises in a major city are essential simply cannot be justified with an economic rationale[.]"[47]

What if we can devise a better market for visual artworks? One that has little overhead and requires no rent or physical gallery. One that is decentralized and permissionless, without the need for middlemen or gatekeepers. One that empowers artists to keep most, if not all, of their sales revenue—and even get a royalty for every resale of their art. One that is more diverse and open to all artists. And one that romanticizes the *thriving* artist.

That's what NFTs provide. Within a short time, NFTs have offered a potential solution to centuries of devaluing artists' works. They also offer a potential solution to the Internet dilemma; as we'll examine in Part II, widespread copying doesn't necessarily diminish the value of NFTs. NFTs don't solve all the problems that artists face or all the failings of the copyright system, but they do offer a promising alternative. And the beauty of this alternative is that Congress didn't create it. Blockchain developers and artists did, in a decentralized manner. Artists now have the ability to take control of their own artistic future—through NFTs. This chapter examines how. (Although it focuses on visual artists, as we'll later see, NFTs can be used by artists of all kinds.)

OSINACHI

Prince Jacon Osinachi grew up in Aba, a center for commerce and trade in southeast Nigeria, the most populous country in Africa, where military rule ended just in 1999. Even though Nigeria had one of the largest economies in Africa, the developing country faced many challenges, including one of the lowest per capita incomes ($350).[48] As a kid, Osinachi didn't have Internet access at home. It wasn't until 2003 when he first encountered the Internet as a fourteen-year-old. His father, a businessman, took him to a local Internet café. Sitting in front of a computer, Osinachi sent his first email and visited his first website. He even mistakenly tried to email a website URL. His dad told him that wasn't going to work, but Osinachi insisted, to no avail. The first site Osinachi visited was a website for Azkaban, the Alcatraz of the Harry Potter series. A huge Harry Potter fan, Osinachi found the experience magical, a whole new world.

As a teenager, Osinachi saw the future in the Internet, *his* future. "I saw the Internet as a means through which I could put out my creative works by sending them to literary magazines, and, of course, posting them on websites," Osinachi explained to me in an interview. During his childhood, Osinachi wrote short stories and poems. He also drew Mickey Mouse and cartoon characters, but aspired to be a writer—or so he thought.[49] When his dad brought home a Dell laptop to use for his business in 2007, Osinachi claimed it all to himself. On the laptop, Osinachi began to write on Microsoft Word—which, surprisingly, would turn out to be a key moment in his development as a visual artist. Word became his canvas.

Over the next several years, Osinachi continued to write—and became incredibly proficient in using Word, including during his studies at the University of Nigeria, where he graduated at the top of his class. To take breaks from writing, Osinachi started to fiddle with Word's drawing tools. Yes, Word can be used as a canvas to draw freehand. Who knew?

At first, Osinachi drew simple logos as a diversion. Then he created more abstract artworks. Osinachi thought he would write and illustrate his own books, but he became so adept at drawing art on Word that he started focusing instead on becoming an artist. After completing his national service in 2016, and needing to find a job, he sent many inquiries to galleries in Nigeria to show his digital artwork, but received no interest. Digital art just wasn't a thing in art galleries then. He expanded his search to include galleries around the world. None replied. The only interest Osinachi received was from Artoja, an online marketplace for art, which began selling his abstract artworks as physical prints, which Osinachi signed after traveling several hours to Lagos. The income was modest.

In 2017, Osinachi received an email that changed his life. It was from Google—a Google alert that Osinachi had created for "digital art" and "visual art" to seek out opportunities as an artist. Included in the Google alert was an article about art on blockchain. It drew Osinachi's attention. The article discussed how digital artists were using the technology to sell their artworks. It mentioned a U.S.-based startup, R.A.R.E Art Labs, a platform for digital artists to sell their works by this means.

One of the problems that NFTs solved was how a digital artwork—which can be reproduced infinitely and easily on computers—can have authenticity or any value. For purely digital artworks, the ease of reproducing them and the inherent difficulty of identifying one digital copy as the original or authentic one, such as the Mona Lisa in the Louvre, greatly limited the market for digital artworks. Why would investors buy a digital artwork they could copy for free online? NFTs provided a solution to this problem by creating tokens on blockchain that artists can use to identify their artworks, each as a unique, or non-fungible, item.[50] Blockchain is a public ledger that keeps track of all transactions for NFTs. By this process of tokenization, each digital artwork can be made into a one-of-a-kind.

After reading the article, Osinachi emailed R.A.R.E Art Labs, which, unlike traditional galleries, was happy to sell his works in late 2017. Instead of receiving rejections or no replies as he did with traditional galleries, Osinachi found a market for his art through NFTs, almost immediately.

Osinachi's NFTs soon brought recognition for his art. The 2018 Ethereal Summit in New York City invited Osinachi to exhibit his artwork in a group exhibition. He expanded his sales to other NFT marketplaces, including SuperRare, which launched in 2018. Osinachi felt validation as an artist. That motivated him more. He moved to Lagos, or Èkó, the cultural capital of West Africa, and became a full-time artist.

In 2019, Osinachi's style shifted from abstract art to what is now his unique style: it blends bright, vibrant colors, subtle textures, and engrossing human figures who are Black or, perhaps more accurately, shaded with a textured charcoal coloring. Osinachi's complex style was influenced by Nigerian textiles and fabric. Through remarkable creativity and skill, he creates textured artworks on Word. Within a year, Osinachi developed his own signature style, which he described as figurative portraiture.[51] In late 2019, Osinachi's NFTs began selling for higher prices, jumping from $20 to more than $100 on SuperRare, a price that was substantial for NFTs at the time.

Then the pandemic hit. Nigeria went into full lockdown in late

March 2020. As with other NFT creators I interviewed, the pandemic turned out to be a major catalyst that spurred not only Osinachi's creation of NFTs, but also greater interest in them. During the lockdown, Osinachi had more time to focus on creating. And people who couldn't visit galleries or museums (or anything else), because they were closed, began spending more time online. The world had shifted from IRL (in real life) to virtual. Famous museums around the world, along with Google's Arts and Culture platform, which provides digital access to artworks from hundreds of museums, gave people the ability to take online tours of the art collections owned by the museums.[52] Just as Zoom meetings became standard practice among schools, businesses, and distant family,[53] viewing artwork online became common. The virtual world became the main form of interaction for many people around the world.

Even as lockdowns were lifted, institutions and people were forever changed: virtual interactions became a part of modern living. According to the International Council of Museums' survey of 840 museums in five continents, a majority of the respondents planned to increase their digital offerings.[54] The investment in digital likely marks a permanent shift. As the researchers Tula Giannini and Jonathan Bowen concluded, "Museums will need to be more prepared than ever to adapt to unabated technological advances set in the midst of cultural and social revolution."[55] For example, a foundation for the late CBS founder William Paley planned on auctioning $70 million worth of artworks, including Picasso's Cubist painting *The Guitar on a Table*. The proceeds will be donated to the Museum of Modern Art to expand its digital presence. MoMA's in-person visitors had dropped from 3 million to 1.65 million in 2021, while its online presence, including on YouTube and social media, drew 35 million visitors. Virtual visits are now vital to a museum's reach. Glenn Lowry, MoMA's director, told *The Wall Street Journal* that MoMA aimed to increase its online offerings— and was considering, albeit cautiously, acquiring digital art and its first NFTs.[56]

In 2020, Osinachi had his debut solo exhibition, titled *Existence as Protest*, at the Kate Vasse Galerie in Zurich, Switzerland. The exhibition had a private viewing and then opened online in March 2020, when Zurich was in lockdown. "The entire exhibition is a manifestation of my response to issues like toxic masculinity, gender fluidity, homophobia, sexism, religiosity, climate change, all of which are entwined in the politics of individualism," Osinachi explained in a video for the exhibition.[57] (Nigeria criminalizes same-sex sexual activity and bans gay marriage.[58]) "Through my art, I want to inform citizens that sexual minorities exist and their demonization is just uncalled-for," Osinachi stated.[59]

All ten NFTs for *Existence as Protest* sold out.

Osinachi's star was on the rise. In October 2021, Christie's Europe invited him to be part of its exhibition *First Open: Post-War and Contemporary Art Online*.[60] Osinachi became the first African artist to sell an NFT at a Christie's Europe auction. Inspired by the British artist David Hockney's famous work *Portrait of an Artist (Pool with Two Figures)*,[61] Osinachi created five NFTs with artworks that featured a swimming pool, the subject of many of Hockney's paintings.[62]

Hockney's *Portrait of an Artist* famously depicts a well-dressed man in a pink sports jacket gazing at another man swimming underwater toward him, although it's unclear whether the swimmer is aware of his presence. Both men are white. By contrast, Osinachi's *Pool Day II* depicts two Black men at a swimming pool. One, dressed in a yellow hoodie and swim trunks, gazes at the other man, in a white swim cap, who is swimming away from him.

Christie's sold all five of Osinachi's NFTs in the *Different Shades of Water* collection for a total of more than $213,000.[63] The highest single sale was for $68,850, far eclipsing the income Osinachi had received for a print in the past.

Osinachi's artwork is stunning. That he creates it on Word is mind-boggling. In an interview in 2021, Osinachi explained why he preferred to use Word: "Right now for what I imagine to do in Microsoft Word there is no limit. That is what I enjoy, in fact, the challenge of using this tool that is meant for word processing to create something visually beautiful."[64]

In addition to the beauty of Osinachi's art, NFTs were crucial to his success. "There was no gallery interested in taking on my work because it's digital, and there were issues of provenance and proof of ownership. Those are the issues that, of course, blockchain came to offer a solution to through NFTs," he explained. Before turning to NFTs, Osinachi spent countless hours sending out inquiries to galleries around the world, but none showed interest in his work. One gallery even mistakenly included him in an internal email that skeptically asked, "What does he mean he makes art on Microsoft Word?"

Through NFTs, however, Osinachi has become an internationally recognized artist. In 2022, David Bowie's estate selected Osinachi as one of only nine artists to collaborate in creating the first "Bowie on the Blockchain" NFTs. (The proceeds will be donated to CARE, a nonprofit working to fight world hunger and poverty. Iman, Bowie's wife, is a global advocate for CARE.) In his artwork, titled *The Redemption of Major Tom*, Osinachi reimagined Ziggy Stardust, the early persona Bowie adopted, as Major Tom, the astronaut in several of Bowie's songs.[65] MakersPlace, a curated marketplace, also selected Osinachi to lead its first African Creator Accelerator Program. African artists residing in the continent can submit their artworks to the program. Osinachi will select six artists whose artworks will be a part of the SCOPE Art Show, along with Osinachi's artwork, during Art Week Miami.

Osinachi's making a living as an artist. He described the success he has received from NFTs as "really mind-blowing," especially given that most of his artworks feature Black subjects.[66] "This means I am bringing diversity to cryptoart, and that's important for the space," Osinachi explained to SuperRare. "I also feel like, somehow, I am playing a huge part in history here. I want my success in cryptoart to inspire more African artists to join in the movement, especially those who have authentic stories and are looking for visibility."[67]

LAURA CONNELLY AND THE LURKERS

Laura Connelly was born and grew up in Vilnius, the capital of Lithuania, right after it became independent upon the dissolution of the Soviet Union. (Her family surname is Laurinaityte; for ease of reference, I use her current last name after her marriage.) In an interview with me, Connelly described her childhood as "extremely rough." To help her survive, she turned to art. "The thing that helped me get through my childhood was actually art. I was drawing from as long as I can remember, all the time. . . . That was my biggest escape. I loved it, everything about it."

Her parents, though, discouraged her from pursuing art. They said she wasn't good enough and could never do it for a living, according to Connelly. When she was eleven, her mom left. Later, Gintare Bieliuniene, her cousin (the daughter of her father's half sister), volunteered to adopt Laura when she was thirteen. Bieliuniene was already a single mother of two children and was happy to raise Connelly. From that moment, Connelly's life made a dramatic turn. "She was the number one person who has always supported me," Connelly explained. "She admired every drawing. . . . She said, 'If you really want to do this, you can. Just keeping working at it.'"

With Bieliuniene and her two kids, Connelly moved to Ireland when she was fifteen. It was a difficult transition for a teenager. She had to transfer to a different high school in a new country—and she couldn't speak English. "It was pretty scary," Connelly said. "I went to school but I didn't know what they were saying to me."

Connelly found it easier to express herself through art, a universal language. She took refuge in the mentorship by her art teacher, who recommended that she apply to art schools in Ireland after graduating from high school. Connelly followed her teacher's advice and later studied art and fashion for two years at Coláiste Íde College of Further Education in Dublin. In Ireland, she also fell in love with her future spouse, Patrick. Together, they moved to New York City in 2013 to start a new life. In 2018, after a long hiatus from art due to negativity from others who doubted her ability to make a living as an artist, Connelly started to build her portfolio and to sell her prints of pet sketches on Etsy, while holding a nine-to-five job. The income from her art was modest, below minimum wage, but it was a start.

The pandemic, as dark as it was, turned out to be a major catalyst for Connelly's artistic career. In early 2020, she was living in New York City, the first epicenter of COVID in the United States. Connelly sensed the panic. She decided she needed to do something to help people. On March 17, Connelly posted a photo of herself on Instagram holding one of her dog sketches. In the caption, she recognized that "everybody is in a panic mode," with a lot of negativity swirling on social media.[68] Connelly, who has a Labrador named Lenny, said on Instagram: "To brighten up your day, or if you want to brighten your loved ones day (or even strangers, fuck it, we are in this together) I'm giving away my custom pet illustrations."[69] A couple of days later, after receiving favorable responses, Connelly started a fundraiser for five New York City animal shelters. People who received her free sketches could choose to donate to the shelters.[70]

Connelly didn't have a large following on Instagram, so her initial fundraising goal was only $500. She feared she wouldn't even reach that small amount. But, during the lockdown, her fundraiser went viral on Instagram. Connelly worked all day starting at 5 a.m. and drew 1,262 pet sketches over three weeks—at a pace of about 60 sketches a day. She eclipsed the goal of $500 in two days and, within three weeks, had raised nearly $12,000 from people all over the world. Some of the requests came from doctors and nurses who were on the front lines treating people with COVID. Some told Connelly that her pet sketch was so wonderful to come home to, after a very tough day seeing many COVID cases at the hospital.

The success of the pet fundraiser gave Connelly not only thousands of new followers on Instagram, but also the confidence to start her own art business, Stellar Villa, soon afterward—once she had given her wrist time to recover. Connelly created both pet portraits and art prints; the latter style of artwork would figure into her development of NFTs. She first learned about NFTs in the fall of 2021, when the market was booming, and followed the discussion about them on social media. Several artists whom she followed on Instagram were posting information about the NFTs they launched—and how incredibly successful they were. Connelly recounted how one artist had described how he was no longer taking commissions because he had great success selling NFTs—which were life-changing. Intrigued, Connelly sent him a DM asking, "Is this real?" But he didn't reply.

Although Connelly was initially hesitant about NFTs, she discovered other artists having great success on Solana blockchain. She also found inspiration when she joined the NFT community on Twitter (colloquially called "NFT Twitter") in February 2022, and became captivated. "Twitter really blew me away," she remarked. "Just encouragement alone for artists was incredible."

Connelly decided she was ready to create NFTs. After several months of studying them on social media, she figured out a theme for her NFTs, which would distinguish them from others being sold. Instead of selling a single artwork or a collection of 10,000 cartoon characters, Connelly decided to create a storytelling collection based on suggestions from some buyers; like a comic book or graphic novel, the NFTs tell a story.

She also realized the majority of NFT buyers were men. She knew her story had to appeal to them, so she picked a dark narrative. Reflecting the dark period of the pandemic, Connelly's story "explores the classic struggle of good versus evil and the coming of age decision we face as to which path to follow in life."[71] She titled her collection "The Lurkers," referring to the dark spirits "ever-present in our world."

In March 2022, Connelly, who goes by "iamlaurael" as an artist, launched the first NFT in her series and then each week launched the next one, for a total of twenty-three. Each NFT can stand on its own as an artwork, but collectively they tell a story. The series was completed in summer 2022. Connelly planned on compiling a book for the Lurkers, which each NFT owner will receive. The artworks for the Lurkers are dark, but with splashes of vivid color, such as in depicting a little girl and her dog.

"It's basically a story about the dark spirits that follow children," Connelly explained. "When the full collection is complete, the dark spirit is going to have a change of heart. . . . There will be this one special child who shows him a way to see life in different colors. . . . The color represents hope."

The final two NFTs sold for more than $20,000 in total—an impressive amount during the crypto winter. Looking back on her success with NFTs, Connelly explained how they helped her career as an artist. When she was working on commissioned pieces, her income depended entirely on customers who discovered her work and wanted to hire her. But NFTs enable artists not only to sell on NFT marketplaces, but also to choose to receive royalties for every resale of the NFT. Resale royalties, also called creator royalties, are passive income for artists—and a critical source of financial security. (Resale royalties are discussed in depth later in the book.)

More important, NFTs have created a new market for artists. Connelly was often nickel-and-dimed by customers purchasing her pet sketches on Etsy for $10 a print. Even at that low price, customers wanted a discount. The NFT marketplace was a whole different ball game: there was a lot more money to support artists. Investors routinely bid several thousand dollars (in the cryptocurrency SOL) to own one of Connelly's NFTs. Her collectors, who view the development of NFTs as a digital Renaissance, want to support Connelly and other artists. In March 2022 Connelly reportedly became the first female artist to sell an NFT for more than 100 SOL. Her highest sale so far was for more than $15,000. The Lurkers ranked as the seventh top-selling collection of illustrations of all time on the NFT marketplace Exchange Art in September 2022, generating nearly $100,000 in sales. In just a few months, Connelly had figured out a way to thrive as an artist through NFTs.

"It's been incredible. Sometimes I can't believe this is happening," she told me, reflecting on the past year. "Just the freedom alone to create what you want to create, and there's people interested in buying it, it's incredible."

ELISE SWOPES

Elise Swopes describes herself as a child of the Internet.[72] While growing up in Chicago, she was homeschooled until the third grade and learned a lot on the computer. When she was just ten, she tapped into her love of design by playing around with Kidpix, a drawing program on her mom's blue iMac, the model that Steve Jobs famously launched upon his return to Apple.[73] When she was twelve years old, Swopes convinced her parents to buy a style website called Jazzy Girl, which she loved visiting and converted into her own website.[74] Even at a young age, Swopes loved the Internet and design. She started selling MySpace layouts that she designed, back when MySpace was popular.[75] She taught herself graphic design on Adobe Illustrator and Photoshop on her dad's laptop. Little did she know that one day Adobe would hire her for creative projects.

The Internet was Swopes's education. Or, as she recounted in a TEDx Talk in 2019, "I basically googled anything and everything I wanted to learn."[76]

Within the first year of Instagram's launch in 2010, Swopes started posting selfies and food photos she took on her iPhone. She discovered an inspiring community of creators who were developing a whole aesthetic with iPhone photography. At the time, Swopes had dropped out of college, had no job, and was staying with friends. Using an iPhone 4 with a cracked screen, she continued to shoot photographs and post them to Instagram.[77] She started editing her photographs with apps on her phone, to create surreal images for which she is now well known. Her works infuse "a fantastic magical realism to urban landscapes as she manipulates the everyday into something from another world."[78] For example, several of her captivating works feature giraffes traversing through a maze of skyscrapers in different cities. She even created a character, the Swopes Giraffe.

Swopes amassed more than 270,000 followers on Instagram.[79] Her artistry on the iPhone earned her collaborations with big brands, including Adobe, Adidas, Apple, Burger King, Coach, Google, Kellogg's, McDonald's, and Uniqlo.[80]

In 2016, Swopes and other influencers faced greater challenges on Instagram, when it switched from a reverse chronological feed to one determined by an algorithm.[81] Despite her massive following, some of her followers said they didn't see her work on Instagram as they did before, apparently due to this algorithm.[82] As she lamented in a *Forbes* interview in 2017, "It can feel like my whole existence is lying on this freaking company."[83]

NFTs brought a new opportunity. Swopes moved to New York City in March 2020, during the first wave of COVID. The pandemic didn't hurt her business as an influencer. In fact, because she had been working virtually as a content creator her entire adult life, her business thrived. Then, in November, Swopes learned about NFTs on Twitter as other artists and friends discussed them. At first, she didn't understand. But as the discussion increased, so did her interest. She told her management team to make it a priority.[84]

In 2021, SuperRare, a curated NFT marketplace, accepted her application. In March, she sold her first NFT. The artwork, titled *Where Focus Goes, Energy Flows*, is a surreal creation based on an iPhone photograph, depicting a cityscape with animated waterfalls flowing from the buildings, with the "Freedom Tower" in the background.[85] The NFT sold for 11ETH ($17,632). Swopes, then thirty-two years old, recounted to CNBC her astonishment: "Oh my god, my life is going to change. And it has ever since then. It's definitely brought me a lot of opportunity."[86]

In less than ten months, Swopes sold NFTs worth more than $200,000.[87] She found the whole NFT experience liberating as an artist, far different from—and, in some ways, better than—her experience as a successful Instagram influencer.

In an interview with the NFT Roundtable Podcast, produced by

Black NFT Art, Swopes noted the difference between her social media collaborations and NFTs. With the social media work, "I feel like I'm always trying to owe things to people or something and I have to . . . do a brief or a marketing scheme of some sort," she stated. "But with [NFTs] it's like I could just be me and that feels freeing and wonderful."[88]

A few years earlier, Swopes had set a personal goal of getting her works shown in galleries. However, because her digital works are created on the iPhone, she felt that she would have trouble finding gallery representation.[89] She even considered painting her artworks to fit within the gallery world. But with NFTs, she didn't have to fit in. She showed her first exhibition of the beautiful, surreal artwork she's known for. In April 2021, SuperRare invited her to be a part of a group virtual exhibition titled *Invisible Cities*.[90] After her NFT experience, Swopes no longer desired to be in traditional art galleries, which take a percentage from each sale as a commission, typically around 40 to 50 percent. NFTs offer artists a far better deal: they don't have to give up half of their earnings to a gallery. And they keep control.[91]

"If I could just be a crypto artist," she stated with emotion on the NFT Roundtable Podcast, "I would be living. I would be so happy."[92]

When I had the chance to speak with Swopes in summer 2022, her views of the NFT market had evolved. Although she still believed in the great potential of NFTs for artists, she also noted challenges that artists face in that market. Artists must spend considerable time in promoting NFTs on social media—which means less time to create art. Working on social media gigs, Swopes has more power to set her fees for collaborations with brands, while the market for NFTs has been more volatile, especially during the crypto winter. Swopes also worried about the need for greater inclusion in the NFT market and for greater collective recognition and effort, especially among the powerful and wealthy in the NFT market, to develop the space for the public good.

Swopes tries to do her part. Given her position as a successful artist, influencer, and business owner, Swopes hasn't hesitated sharing her knowledge with other artists, including other Black artists, through her podcast, *Swopes So Dope*, newsletter, video tutorials, and mentoring. She partnered with BrainTreeMedia to create an app that enables people to do what she does: take photos and edit them with waterfalls and wild animals.[93] A daily practitioner of meditation at 5 a.m., she's also a vocal advocate for mental health. She's been quite open about her own past drug addiction and depression, and has spoken on her podcast about her practice of daily affirmation and her past stay in a psychiatric hospital.[94] During the pandemic, Swopes managed to find time to earn her college degree and was already planning to pursue a master's and then a PhD in behavioral psychology.

Swopes is also a part of the Sunrise Art Club, a creative impact agency whose mission is to help marginalized people of color. In 2022, the club produced one NFT of a new photograph of the sunrise each day for a year. Seventy-five percent of the revenues from the NFT sales are used to fund projects by the club to promote inclusion. For example, the club is developing Night on the Yard, the first NFT marketplace for incarcerated artists. Another project is an accelerator program to promote the work of artists who are women of color and from the LGBTQIA+ community. Swopes said these programs are designed to assist people who don't have a voice. She even used revenue from the sales of her own NFTs to buy the NFTs of up-and-coming artists, especially ones who were being overlooked and could use the support. Sunrise Art Club has instituted a purchase program in which artists from marginalized communities can apply to have the agency buy their NFTs.[95] Swopes is a model for how NFTs can be used to give back—and do good.

GOLDCAT

As a new, disruptive technology, NFTs have sparked great controversy. They've been attacked as scams, Ponzi schemes, you name it.

To avoid the backlash, the next artist we'll consider adopted the art alias "goldcat."

"It has been absolutely the best decision and I am so glad about it," goldcat explained to me in an interview. "I want the art to be focused on not my face or my person. It is a safety issue, too, as women tend to receive way too many unsolicited advances than they should have to deal with." Adopting an alias or a virtual identity has become a broad social phenomenon beyond Web3, including among so-called VTubers (or virtual YouTubers) who create videos using avatars, partly to avoid the toxic environment of social media.

Based in Germany, goldcat was a freelance illustrator before she got into NFTs. She worked with indie game publishers and self-publishing authors, with moderate success. She was leery of working for a major video game company due to the industry's reputation for sexism, as well as for being a grind. But, after five years of freelance work, goldcat started feeling burned out. She lost her passion for the work, which required her to create in a commercial style that didn't interest her.

Then goldcat discovered NFTs. She noticed that two of her illustrator friends had used "#NFT" as a hashtag on social media. They provided her some guidance. goldcat then went down the rabbit hole of researching NFTs. She was captivated. "As a digital painter, the idea of digital originals was mind blowing to me," goldcat elaborated, referring to the problem digital artists faced before NFTs, i.e., that every copy can substitute for the original. "I immediately thought that this was a major opportunity for underpaid artists to create a new stream of income."

goldcat's interest escalated in March 2021, when she read that the conceptual artist Ben Mauro had made $2 million from the sale of his first NFT collection, titled "Evolution." Before the sale, Mauro had great success working in major movie productions and video games, but even then, he "struggled to find the funds and platform to fully pursue his own personal projects as a digital artist," according to an interview with Decrypt.[96] Mauro's life changed with NFTs.

So did goldcat's. She made a life-changing decision: she would become an NFT artist. Starting in March 2021, goldcat launched numerous NFTs for her artworks on Hic et Nunc (meaning "here and now"), a popular marketplace based on the eco-friendly Tezos blockchain. Most of goldcat's NFT drops sold out quickly, even during the crypto winter.

goldcat's artistic style is dark and moody, perhaps fitting for the pandemic. "There is a lot of power in facing darkness and a lot of mystery ready to be experienced by everyone differently," she explained. To me, her works capture the dark romanticism of Edgar Allan Poe, only in images, not words.

Like other digital artists in Web3, goldcat has started exploring AI generative art. For her artwork *The Conjured*, she painted various assets that were randomly stacked by computer code into sixty different works out of thousands of possible combinations. Her artworks feature a dark, mysterious man. For *The Ganjured*, she used a VQGAN program, which interprets text prompts into novel visual imagery drawn from a large database of images. VQGAN, which stands for vector quantized generative adversarial network, has become popular for creating AI-generated art through the use of text.

What's different about the Virtual Renaissance from past renaissances is the rise of AI in contributing to the creation of artworks. Indeed, some generative artworks require little, if any, human input. (The less human input there is in the creation of a work, the less likely the work can qualify for copyright. The U.S. Copyright Office has taken the position that authorship requires creation by a human author, not a machine. Courts will soon have to wrestle with how little is too little.) The first AI-generated artwork sold at auction was the *Portrait of Edmond de Belamy*, which sold for $432,500 in 2018. By establishing a market for digital art, NFTs have ushered in a new era for generative art. Algorithms that translate text into imagery and NFTs provide a new form of creativity. There are now platforms, such as Eponym, that make the process accessible to everyone.[97] In the Virtual Renaissance, we will likely see a breathtaking explosion of creative works by not only digital artists, but also machines.

goldcat was invited to collaborate with Val Kilmer to create an NFT artwork. After he lost his voice due to treatment for throat cancer, which went into remission, Kilmer focused on his art over acting.[98] Art was a healing force, Kilmer said on his website.[99] Kilmer, too, became enamored with NFTs. He launched a platform called Kamp Kilmer, inviting other artists to collaborate with him. The platform provides a virtual space for collaboration, which Kilmer launched as a substitute for his physical art gallery, HelMel Studios in Los Angeles, after it was temporarily shuttered when the pandemic hit.[100] Kamp Kilmer selected goldcat as one of its first collaborators. The work *Shamrock Clock* features goldcat's digital artwork of a man resembling Kilmer, accompanied by a poem written by Kilmer and narrated by the producer Laurence Fuller.[101]

Reflecting on her success with NFTs, goldcat described her experience: "What I am most happy about is that I am finally finding my voice as an artist. People are recognizing my work, and I would have never been able to pursue my own vision if I had been stuck working for someone else."

BETTY, PSYCH, AND DEADFELLAZ

The COVID pandemic wasn't the only calamity that Australia faced in 2020. Bushfires that had started in September 2019 were still raging in many parts of the country. At the time, Betty and her spouse, Psych, ran their own creative agency and worked with big corporate clients on marketing and design projects. (Betty prefers to be known just by her nickname, and Psych prefers his pseudonym.) Betty was the ideas person, an outside-the-box thinker and entrepreneur, and Psych was the artist. The two complemented each other's skills well. But, during the pandemic, they started to lose their corporate contracts as businesses tightened budgets. On top of that, Australia was experiencing a severe housing crisis caused by a spike in the price of homes, a drop in available dwell-ings, and significant increase in rents,[102] especially in Queensland, which forced them to move three times with their family of three young children.

In January 2021, Betty and Psych struggled financially. They felt the need to find a way out of the stressful situation with a more secure, pandemic-proof source of income. Psych reconnected with his friends in Depthcore, an international collective for digital art-ists. Some of the artists told Psych to try out NFTs because they were amazing for digital artists. Psych did, with no hesitation. When he explained it to Betty, she was so excited, she grabbed him and screamed.[103]

"Immediately I was completely taken," she recounted to me. "I thought, *Oh my God, this is amazing!* This is something I've been waiting for—a new technology, a new shift, valuing creatives."

Betty understood right away how NFTs solved long-standing problems that artists faced. "We constantly had to defend the value of creative work. Any creative will say the same thing. That is hon-estly a nightmare," Betty explained. NFTs now offered artists a new market that valued their creations.

Psych started experimenting with NFTs. He collaborated with other Depthcore artists for a few NFT drops and did commissioned work for DAOs and other projects. Meanwhile, Betty followed the vibrant NFT communities on Clubhouse and Twitter for a few months—observing, studying, and learning. The discussion about NFTs on social media provided an invaluable education: NFT 101.

By May 2021, Betty had studied the NFT scene enough. She had come up with her next big idea. She turned to Psych and pro-posed they make an NFT collection. "We can do this," she said to Psych. "This is our wheelhouse."

"Immediately yes," Psych replied. They were all in.

Their NFT collection was called Deadfellaz. Betty, who has a love for horror, zombies, and what she described as "the almost scary," came up with the idea. Deadfellaz are 10,000 green zombie characters, "randomly generated from a combination of over 400 individually drawn traits."[104] Betty felt the horror element filled a gap in the NFT market. The characters had "no traits explicitly gendered to allow all genders to find representation."[105] Betty believed greater representation was important because, at the time, NFT collections had little inclusivity and were heavily male-focused.

Over the next two months, while Queensland was in lockdown, the couple worked around the clock. Deadfellaz launched on Friday, August 13, 2021. Thirteen was Betty's lucky number: Psych and she married on the thirteenth, and thirteen is a divine feminine number for the lunar cycles in a year. Some of the Deadfellaz have thirteen on their jerseys. The Deadfellaz sold out in fifteen minutes. Although it would've been more poetic if it were thirteen minutes, the launch was still impressive.

The collection gained immediate attention in the NFT market. It attracted numerous celebrity buyers, including Reese Witherspoon, Odell Beckham, Jr. (OBJ), Lil Baby, Elijah Wood, and Gary Vaynerchuk. OBJ used his Deadfellaz character, clothed in purple fur, as his avatar or profile pic (pfp) on Twitter. Purple fur was a rare trait, which only 2 percent of the collection had. Owners of the rare trait even formed their own "purple fur gang" on social media.

Betty is beloved by Deadfellaz owners, who all are a part of the "horde." Being a Deadfellaz owner entitles one to be a part of the horde, or community. For collections of NFTs that are meant to serve as avatars—so-called pfp collections—NFTs are being used in far more interactive ways. The intellectual property license that accompanies the Deadfellaz NFT purchase entitles the owner to make full commercial use of the associated Deadfellaz character, including in merchandise and other derivative works.[106] The NFT owner keeps all the profits. I call this type of license a decentralized collaboration or De-Collab license, an innovative approach to cultural production that we'll examine in Part II.

Deadfellaz owners are entitled to other perks, including free invitations to Deadfellaz events, such as a Halloween party in the virtual world Decentraland with the DJ Steve Aoki. On November 1, 2021, Betty and Psych posted an ambitious road map of future Deadfellaz activities and perks, including merchandise, a game in the Sandbox, a music platform, an OnCyber art gallery, and brand partnerships.[107] Betty and Psych signed with United Talent Agency to represent the Deadfellaz collection in future deals with traditional media and sponsorships with brands—a path that many of the top, or "blue-chip," NFT collections are also pursuing. In September 2022, the project announced a collaboration with Wrangler in a tweet depicting a Deadfellaz wearing Wrangler jeans.[108]

NFTs create a new type of ownership that I call *interactive ownership*. I explain my theory in greater depth in Part II. For now, it's important to recognize that NFTs can be used in ways far beyond recording a transaction on blockchain. They can help to establish a person's identity online in a pfp based on an NFT cartoon character, such as a Deadfellaz with purple fur. They can also foster community, collaborations, and ongoing engagement among the project creators and the NFT owners. Any NFT creator can organize their own community. That's why many big brands are already developing or exploring NFTs. They want to engage their own community—or horde. Because NFTs are still developing, we've only scratched the surface of their vast potential.

The incredible success of Deadfellaz, within just a year, enabled Betty and Psych to put their creative agency on hiatus. Reflecting on the freedom NFTs have brought, Betty can't imagine ever going back to work on corporate accounts.

"This is my life," she told me. "I enjoy being on the cutting edge of something. . . . It feels like how I imagine . . . artists would gather together in cafés in Paris and discuss new concepts and new ideas."

CHAPTER 3

HOOPS, HOPS, AND HAUTE COUTURE

I love fashion as much as I love basketball.

—HAKEEM OLAJUWON

NFTs aren't just for artists. NFTs are computer programs that can be adapted for a myriad of uses. Big brands are racing to figure out how to utilize NFTs for their businesses—the so-called use cases—especially in the emerging metaverse, a virtual world promising a more immersive experience than viewing a flat screen, potentially enhanced by augmented or virtual reality. Citi estimated that the metaverse will create a new market worth potentially between $8 trillion and $13 trillion by 2030.[1] That forecast was made before the crypto winter and major economic downturn in 2022, but it reflects the investments that companies are making to build the next phase of the Internet, which will be more immersive and integrated into daily life. The race to build the metaverse is so intense that, in 2021, Facebook changed its name to Meta and reorganized its entire business focus away from its social media platform.[2] The decision was less shocking in 2022, when Meta and other social media companies reported drops in their revenues—leading some tech analysts to predict the demise of traditional social media, with the upstart TikTok in the securest position.[3]

Three of the earliest adopters of NFTs were, surprisingly, not the tech or entertainment industries but the National Basketball

Association (NBA), Anheuser-Busch, and the fashion industry. This chapter examines the ways in which these businesses use NFTs, both to chronicle their development and to provide ideas for other businesses. But it's important to remember: the potential uses of NFTs are infinite. We'll likely see many other creative uses of NFTs. Indeed, they may become so integrated into our daily lives that we won't refer to them as NFTs. They will be subsumed within things we already know, such as property deeds, records, subscriptions, and tickets. The term *NFT* may drop from usage just as *dot com* did. The label is less important than the application or what the technology does.

Consider the NBA's new product line, for example. The NBA uses NFTs as collectibles, consisting of video highlights instead of photographs of players. The NFTs also serve as a means of generating fan engagement and entitling the owners to rewards. It's akin to a customer loyalty program, but think of it now as what might be called an (NFT) *owner* rewards program. Anheuser-Busch uses NFTs in a similar fashion as collectibles and in its owner rewards program, but also in other innovative ways: as a way to promote aspiring musicians, as voting power entitling the NFT owners to help the company make merchandising decisions, and as a way to expand its consumer base with an innovative partnership with the Nouns DAO, a leading project in the NFT space. The fashion industry is using NFTs to develop a new kind of digital fashion, targeting especially the next generation: younger consumers. The fashion comes in two forms: digital-only for use on avatars in virtual worlds, and phygital, meaning it includes both digital and physical clothing for the owner. Because digital-only fashion doesn't require manufacturing of raw materials, it has liberated fashion designers to imagine otherworldly designs. And it has offered the fashion industry a new path for sustainability.

These innovative uses of NFTs offer new digital products for our virtual world, new sources of revenue, and new ways to engage consumers in communities and owner rewards programs—for example, by giving NFT owners the ability to vote on the company's marketing strategy. NFTs also provide a way for businesses to expand their market to the next generation of consumers and to collaborate with and support talented artists.

DAPPER LABS AND THE NBA TOP SHOT MOMENTS

One unexpected effect of the pandemic was a surge in the market for sports trading cards.[4] Prices skyrocketed. In 2021, a T206 Honus Wagner from 1909 sold for $6.6 million. A rare "one of one" Steph Curry rookie card sold for $5.9 million, a 1952 Mickey Mantle rookie card and a 2003 LeBron James autographed rookie patch each sold for $5.2 million, an autographed Luka Doncic rookie card for $4.6 million, and a 2017 Patrick Mahomes rookie card for $4.3 million.[5] Even during the economic downturn, a 1952 Mickey Mantle rookie card sold for $12.6 million, becoming the highest sale ever.[6] In fact, the top ten highest sales of sports cards all occurred during the pandemic. According to eBay, sales of sports cards on the platform increased by 142 percent in 2020 over the prior year, with more than 4 million sports cards sold.[7]

What sparked the craze for trading cards? Theories ranged from people having more time stuck at home during the pandemic and more disposable income, including from stimulus checks, to wanting to diversify their investments.[8]

Whatever the reasons, the NBA couldn't have timed the market for collectibles any better. In October 2020, it launched a new kind of digital trading card called Top Shot Moments, short video highlights of NBA stars. They are the brainchild of Dapper Labs, a Web3 startup that develops applications for blockchain. Dapper Labs' CEO Roham Gharegozlou started out at Axiom Zen, a Vancouver-based venture studio that he founded. It created one of the first popular NFT collections, called the CryptoKitties, back in 2017. Seeing the huge potential for NFTs, Gharegozlou spun off a new company, Dapper Labs, in March 2018, with fifty Axiom employees joining him.[9] "It was a big, big bet," he admitted.[10]

What Dapper Labs did was to reimagine the trading card for the virtual world. This strategy of virtualization is one that all businesses can consider: Do any of our products lend themselves to a new virtual form that can expand our market? By virtualization, I mean making something in virtual form online, such as digital artwork or, here, a video highlight. One benefit of virtualization is that physical materials are unnecessary, thereby saving costs. Given the pervasiveness of smartphones, virtual interactions have become increasingly integrated into daily life. Virtual products—and ownership—are just the next stage in that transformation. A related concept is tokenization: converting something into a unique token on blockchain that can be traded and owned. Dapper Labs did both: it virtualized past video highlights and tokenized them into the Moments NFTs. As we'll see, this same strategy was used by Anheuser-Busch in creating its first collectible NFTs and by the fashion industry in creating digital fashion. Dapper Labs' strategy was astute because the new collectibles didn't substitute for traditional cards—which reduced the possibility that the NFTs would cannibalize the existing market for trading cards. But the concept of Moments is similar to traditional cards for which the value is determined by rarity. Like traditional cards, the rarity differs depending on the Moment.

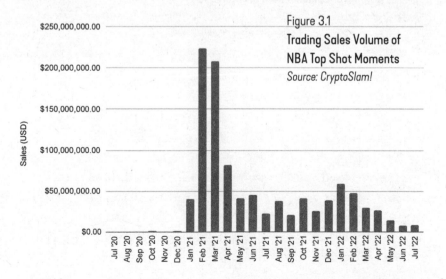

Figure 3.1

Trading Sales Volume of NBA Top Shot Moments

Source: CryptoSlam!

The NBA Top Shot divides Moments into four categories, from the least to the most rare: common, fandom, rare, and legendary.[11] The most rare command the highest prices.

The NBA Top Shot Moments had meteoric success in 2021. Within just a year and a half, Moments surpassed $1 billion in sales volume.[12] Sales dropped after the peak in February 2021, as shown in Figure 3.1. The peak was likely fueled by speculation.

If we compare the NBA Top Shot Moments' sales to CryptoPunks, one of the top all-time NFT collections, during the same period between July 2020 and July 2022, the NBA's digital collectibles performed reasonably well, as shown in Figure 3.2 below. Moments even eclipsed CryptoPunks during a three-month stretch at the beginning of 2021. During this time, NBA Top Shot Moments and CryptoPunks were commonly viewed as the two NFT market leaders.[13] The meteoric success of Top Shot, which attracted considerable media attention in the first quarter of 2021, was likely a catalyst for the NFT market's explosion in sales volume that year. It later became evident that Moments and CryptoPunks are NFTs with different utility (with CryptoPunks used for pfp/

Figure 3.2
Sales of NBA Top Shot Moments v. CryptoPunks
Source: CryptoSlam!

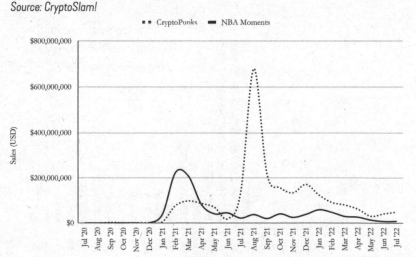

identity and Moments for sports collectibles), making comparisons between them less apt.

Even during the crypto winter and economic downturn, the total transactions for Moments were respectable, with more than half a million transactions in July 2022.[14] Other collectibles (e.g., sports cards, sneakers) were down, too.[15] The market for Moments is likely cyclical, just as it is with traditional cards.

The NBA Top Shot's achievement is undeniable. Moments remained the market leader for sports NFTs with more than $1 billion in sales, opening up an entirely new market for the NBA. The Top Shot platform had 1.1 million registered users.[16] Moments provide a new revenue stream on top of the NBA's licensing of traditional basketball cards. And, unlike traditional cards, for each resale of a digital Moment, the NBA, the Players Association, and Dapper Labs share a 5 percent royalty.[17] (We'll examine resale royalties, one of the features of NFTs most attractive to creators, in Part II.) Under the current partnership, NBA players don't receive a direct cut from Moment sales. But the players Spencer Dinwiddie, Kevin Durant, Klay Thompson, Andre Iguodala, JaVale McGee, Alex Caruso, Aaron Gordon, and Garrett Temple own equity stakes in Dapper Labs, as do the NBA, the Players Association, and Michael Jordan.[18]

How did the NBA Top Shot Moments find immediate success? As mentioned above, great timing was one factor. But the NBA and Dapper Labs made several strategic decisions that led to the immediate success of Moments. First, they decided to make Moments as accessible to the public as possible. The term *NFT* wasn't even used (except buried in the Terms of Use license, which the average consumer is unlikely to read[19]). Not even the NBA Top Shot's first announcement of Moments mentioned NFTs.[20] Given the criticisms of NFTs, such as consuming too much energy or being outright scams (which are discussed in later chapters), the decision to avoid using the term turned out to be a smart one.

Dapper Labs also worked to make the technology for Moments run smoothly for people. Dapper Labs built its own Flow blockchain, where the NFTs are created and recorded. Not only did Flow consume far less energy than the more popular Ethereum blockchain,[21] it also reportedly can handle transactions more quickly. Gharegozlou wanted to avoid a situation similar to what had occurred when the demand to purchase CryptoKitties crashed Ethereum.[22] (We'll put aside the debate over which blockchain is better.) Perhaps even more important to attract a broad audience, Dapper Labs also created a crypto wallet that enables consumers to purchase Moments with a credit card or the more common forms of payment in cryptocurrency.[23] One of the greatest barriers to onboarding consumers to purchase NFTs is the technical hoops one must run through to set up a crypto wallet, such as a MetaMask.

Dapper Labs also studied card collectors and tried to replicate the fun in opening a new pack of cards.[24] Gharegozlou understood that card collectors create short videos of themselves for social media, unveiling the new pack as they flip through the deck of cards, hoping for a rare rookie card. Even though some videos may be staged for the dramatic effect of finding a rare card in the pack, there's still palpable excitement displayed by the collector in the video. Dapper Labs tried to capture the same excitement for the collector by bundling Moments in digital packs. When Moments were booming in February 2021, the digital packs quickly sold out.[25]

There were many well-documented hiccups along the way, especially during the peak of demand in February 2021, when Dapper Labs had to institute a queue system to provide some order to what had been a "chaotic scrambling" to buy Moments when they were released.[26] But Dapper Labs has worked to fix issues as they arise. These technical glitches were not unique to Dapper Labs: other blue-chip NFT projects, including CryptoPunks, CloneX, and Otherdeed, experienced technical problems during launches.

Moments are more than just collectibles. The NFTs establish an owner rewards program. Owners are eligible to win tickets to NBA playoff games and the NBA draft, as well as to receive rewards for interacting with the Top Shot platform during a designated game.[27] Top Shot is also developing new ways for fans to engage with the NBA's superstars. In January 2022, Top Shot offered its first special collection featuring six Moments of Kevin Durant, titled "Game Recognize Game," curated by KD himself. Top Shot is also developing a blockchain-based game called Hardcourt in which Moments can be used to upgrade or develop the players in the game based on the highlights captured in the Moments.[28] The game sounds promising, but, in summer 2022, its rollout was delayed. (To get a sense of the utility of NFTs for rewards programs, Starbucks announced in September 2022 its adoption of NFTs for that very purpose.)

Although some card collectors may still have nostalgia for traditional paper cards, the NBA's digital Moments offer several advantages. First, blockchain reduces the possibility of counterfeits, which have plagued sports card collecting, especially during the pandemic.[29] If you buy a card on eBay or at a card show, you take a certain risk that the card could be counterfeit. However, because blockchain records all transactions related to an NFT, you can trace the provenance back to the original owner and know it's authentic.[30] Plus, if a Moment is sold on the NBA Top Shot marketplace, the chance of a counterfeit is virtually eliminated. In addition, paper cards can get damaged easily or even be printed slightly off center. Any imperfection, such as even the slightest rounded corner, will reduce the value of the card considerably. For that reason, collectors typically put their most valuable cards in plastic casing and store them in a safe or other location under dry, cool conditions. Collectors might not even view their most valuable cards very often,[31] as they want to keep their cards in perfect condition—and there's no better way of doing so than locking them up and never touching them. Grading the quality of trading cards has become a whole cottage industry, with various companies vying to provide grades for trading cards. With a digital file, such as a Moment, there's no need to grade anything. Plus, you don't have to lock away your digital collectible—unlike paper, it won't degrade.

A year after the meteoric rise of Moments in the first quarter of 2021, the volume of sales has come back down to earth. Some collectors wondered if it was still a good investment.[32] Others faulted the NBA for the drop in sales volume and values of Moments after the peak: the NBA Top Shot met the greater demand for Moments by increasing the supply.[33] Dapper Labs also faced legal uncertainty: a class action lawsuit was filed against the company and its CEO, Gharegozlou, on the grounds that Moments are unregistered securities in violation of federal securities law.[34] In August 2022, Dapper Labs moved to dismiss the case on the grounds that Moments are just collectibles like sports trading cards, which do not constitute securities.[35] (The court had yet to rule on the motion as of this book's writing.) In Part III we will examine whether some NFTs are securities. In the case against Dapper Labs, some legal experts expressed a degree of skepticism, agreeing with the company's position.[36]

Regardless of these uncertainties, NBA Top Shot has proved that the concept of sports NFTs works. Indeed, using NFTs as collectibles is a natural fit. Dapper Labs heard the complaints of collectors and began addressing the perceived oversupply issue. It instituted a program by which collectors can trade in their Moments for tickets that can be used to purchase exclusive packs; the Moments traded in are sent to a "locker room," increasing the overall scarcity of Moments.[37] The Top Shot trade-in program is akin to a company's buyback of shares of its stock. The NBA Top Shot said the program would remove half a million Moments from circulation.[38] Probably the greatest strength of Dapper Labs and the NBA is their willingness to learn from their mistakes, listen to the complaints of their community of owners, and make constant adjustments to produce a better product and experience.[39]

Other professional sports leagues recognize the tremendous success of Top Shot Moments and are already developing their own NFTs. Although the NFTs don't displace traditional sports cards, they will likely foster greater understanding and acceptance of digital collectibles among fans. In September 2021, Dapper Labs signed a deal with the NFL and NFL Players Association to produce digital highlight NFTs for football games on the new marketplace NFL All Day.[40] The NFL's NFTs had an impressive start, even during the crypto winter. The startup Sorare has partnered with more than 230 soccer leagues and clubs around the world, including an NFT-based fantasy game for Major League Soccer.[41] Major League Baseball has a deal with Candy Digital to produce collectible NFTs.[42] DraftKings offers a wide array of sports NFTs, including for NFL players in a gamified experience for the 2022–2023 season.[43] The Reignmakers Football Game, touted as "the next generation of fantasy," enables fans to buy NFTs of players and "play" them in fantasy football, with the chance to win a share of $1 million each week.[44] Tom Brady cofounded Autograph to provide a platform for athletes to sell NFTs,[45] and the company secured a deal with ESPN to launch the network's products. The first ESPN collection will be for a docuseries for none other than the GOAT himself: *Man in the Arena: Tom Brady*, coproduced by ESPN Films.[46] Brady also launched a new "Signature Experience" line of NFTs that gives owners "a chance to participate in an exclusive collaboration with Tom Brady, attend in-person and online events, and claim custom goods—both digital and physical—crafted specifically for the community."[47] Not every NFT will be a success. But the ones that are successful will engage fans in innovative ways.

Being a card collector myself, I can foresee the eventual integration of physical trading cards and NFTs, which can be designed for both virtual and physical cards, providing authentication for the cards. That would help to address the problem of counterfeits. Moreover, the NFT could entitle the owner to a replacement physical card, so the value of the investment would not degrade as the physical material did. Nor would the value depend on the subjective judgment of a professional grading service. Of course, taking this path will change the dynamics of sports card collecting, but the NFT would potentially become a better long-term investment than a physical card. And that's just one example of a phygital trading card using NFTs. Instead of a static photo, the digital card can be dynamic and change over time—let's say, different photographs of LeBron James from his rookie year that the NFT owner receives. The NFTs can be programmed to interact with each other: a LeBron James NFT and a Steph Curry NFT can entitle the owners to a video highlight involving both players, such as from the 2016 NBA Finals or the 2022 All-Star Game. The possibilities are vast.

ANHEUSER-BUSCH AND BEER NFTS

Founded in 1852, Anheuser-Busch is the largest brewing company in the United States. It makes some of America's most famous beers, including Budweiser, Bud Light, and Michelob ULTRA. Adolphus Busch, the son-in-law of Eberhard Anheuser, the company's cofounder, helped to make the firm an innovator in brewing. It was the first American brewery to use pasteurization, which, along with the use of refrigerated train cars, opened up a national market for beer and enabled Anheuser-Busch to become a national and then international company.[48] (In 2008, Anheuser-Busch was acquired by InBev and became a wholly owned subsidiary of the parent company, Anheuser-Busch InBev SA/NV. The following discussion relates to the subsidiary, Anheuser-Busch.)

Even today, Anheuser-Busch is an innovator. It is one of the first major brands in the beer industry to adopt NFTs, and it has done so in a variety of innovative ways that show their vast potential. Indeed, few other big brands in any industry can rival Anheuser-Busch's creative uses of NFTs.

The company's first strategy was virtualization of its "archived photos, ads and designs from throughout Budweiser's storied history."[49] Anheuser-Busch took designs from its past and turned them into new collectible NFTs. In November 2021, the company launched its first NFTs, the Budverse Cans Heritage Collection, consisting of 1,936 NFTs depicting unique digital cans (1,900 were priced at $499, 36 at $999, available only to consumers of legal drinking age) to commemorate the first Budweiser can in 1936.[50]

Beyond being collectibles, the NFTs established an owner rewards program: "Each NFT will act as an entry key to the Budverse, unlocking exclusive benefits, rewards and surprises for all 21+ (or legal drinking age) NFT holders."[51] The NFTs sold out in less than an hour.[52]

Buoyed by the success of its Heritage Collection NFTs, Anheuser-Busch launched another NFT collection early the next year to promote its new zero-carb beer, Bud Light NEXT. The Bud Light N3XT Collection included 12,722 NFTs, priced at $399 each.[53] In addition to exclusive perks, NFTs owners were granted "exclusive voting rights" to help Anheuser-Busch decide branding and merchandising decisions for Bud Light NEXT.[54] This use of NFTs to entitle the owners to voting power is popular with decentralized autonomous organizations, or DAOs, examined later in the book. The collection sold out in less than a week, right before the Super Bowl, reportedly generating $4.5 million in revenue.[55]

Anheuser-Busch invited all the NFT owners to Budweiser's first Beerfest, held at the Anheuser-Busch brewery in St. Louis in March 2022. The company provided the NFT owners VIP tours of the brewery and NFT art gallery, merchandise, and, of course, free beer and food. A drone even "airdropped" beer onstage. "As a company, we believe that IRL experiences and events are an important aspect of community building," Julie Garneau, senior director and head of NFTs, Blockchain & Metaverse, explained to me in an interview. "That is why it was important to us to bring our community together and specifically to bring them to St. Louis, at our home brewery."

Anheuser-Busch also partnered with twenty-two emerging musicians to launch their first NFTs as a part of the Budweiser Royalty collection in January 2022. Budweiser has a long history of working with artists, including Big Boi, Nelly, Big Sean, and Halsey. NFTs offered a new way to collaborate with such artists. By purchasing an NFT for $499, fans can support promising musicians, with the revenues generated by the sales going directly to them, except for 2 percent retained by Budweiser for promotion.[56]

The Budweiser Royalty NFTs were described as "rookie cards" of the musicians and were randomly assigned different rarity levels—core, rare, and ultra-rare—that gave the owners different perks and access to the musicians.[57] Two of the Budweiser Royalty artists, Fresco Trey and Millie Go Lightly, performed at the first Beerfest. Based on the breakout success of his song "Need You" on TikTok, Trey later signed a music deal with Warner Records.[58] In Part II, we'll examine startup companies developing new platforms for financing musicians through NFTs.

Anheuser-Busch's uses of NFTs as collectibles, membership in an owner rewards program and community, and support for emerging artists constitute an impressive amount of exploration within a short time. But the company went even further. In its most cutting-edge NFT use, Anheuser-Busch collaborated with one of the leading NFT projects, called Nouns. The Nouns characters are produced not by a company but by a DAO. Each day, a new Nouns NFT is minted, typically selling for upward of $100,000 each. (We'll examine the Nouns DAO's innovative use of Creative Commons licenses in Part II.) The Nouns characters all wear square glasses, their signature trait. During the Super Bowl in 2022, Anheuser-Busch aired a sleek commercial for Bud Light NEXT that included the distinctive Nouns glasses.[59] As a part of the partnership, the Nouns DAO approved the transfer of a Nouns NFT to Anheuser-Busch that included voting privileges in the DAO's future proposals. The company planned to exercise its Nouns vote in the DAO based on the collective votes of owners of Bud Light N3XT NFTs, who even selected a name for the company's Nouns NFT: Brewski.

Why would a beer company partner with a DAO for NFTs to produce a Super Bowl commercial? A big reason is to expand the consumer base to include NFT-savvy individuals, many of whom are Millennials and Gen Zs. The Nouns DAO is on the cutting edge, not only in NFTs, but also in decentralized cultural production.[60] "When we launched Bud Light NEXT and our commemorative N3XT collection, the brand set out to bring more consumers into the brand family," Garneau elaborated. "To affirm our commitment and authenticity in the NFT space, we partnered with one of the industry's leading forces, Nouns DAO."

As Garneau mentioned, another reason is authenticity. Businesses must understand the culture before launching NFTs. Otherwise, they may flop. NFT enthusiasts tend to be skeptical of NFTs from big corporations and celebrities, especially if they perceive the NFT projects as inauthentic or as money grabs. "They don't know anything about Web3 culture" is a recurring criticism I read on my social media feeds. To learn more about the culture, one of the best strategies for big brands is collaborating with NFT projects that have already established a level of authenticity among NFT enthusiasts. That's what the NBA did with Dapper Labs. And that's what Anheuser-Busch did with the Nouns DAO. "In many ways DAOs are at the core of the Web3 philosophy, and it was important for us to get more deeply involved and knowledgeable about the space," Garneau explained.

Anheuser-Busch's collaboration with the Nouns DAO portends a new kind of partnership between big brands and leading NFT projects. The Anheuser-Busch Super Bowl commercial was the first ever to feature artwork from an NFT, not to mention DAO. We're likely to see many other collaborations of this kind in the future as brands try to connect authentically with NFT enthusiasts and the Web3 culture. Anheuser-Busch's early adoption of NFTs, in a variety of different uses, adds a new chapter to its storied history as an innovator.

THE FASHION INDUSTRY

Imagine working remotely from Bali, lured by its five-year digital-nomad visa and absence of taxes on foreign income. Today you have an important presentation to give. You change your virtual background on Zoom to something more appropriate for work, an image of a modern office, instead of the beach, where you are sipping a cappuccino. Conveniently, you don't have to change from your bathing suit into business attire—it's sweltering on the beach. Instead, you select a filter that enables you to wear digital clothing. Sporting a Balenciaga digital suit, which is perfectly tailored, you

TABLE 3.1. FASHION INDUSTRY DIGITAL WEARABLES AND NFTS

Company	Number of drops	Type of content
Auroboros	1	*Digital wearables in Decentraland and AR
Balenciaga	2	*Digital wearables in Fortnite Collectibles
Balmain	1	Digital apparel for Barbie avatar
Burberry	2	Collectibles
Dolce & Gabbana	3	Digital wearables (some phygital) Collectibles
Dress X	market	Digital wearables and AR (some NFTs)
The Fabricant	market	Digital wearables and AR
Gap	3	Digital wearables (some phygital) Collectibles
Givenchy	2	Collectibles
Gucci	4	Digital wearables for 11 NFT collections Collectibles
Jimmy Choo	1	Collectibles
Jonathan Simkhai's	1	Digital wearables in Second Life
Karl Lagerfeld	3	Collectibles
Louis Vuitton	2	*Digital wearable for League of Legends (some phygital) Collectibles
Prada	2	Collectibles
Ralph Lauren	2	*Digital wearables in Zepeto, Roblox
Rebecca Minkoff	4	Digital wearables (some phygital) Collectibles
Roksanda	1	*Digital wearable (with Institute of Digital Fashion)
Wrangler Jeans	1	Digital wearables (some phygital) Collectibles
Zara	3	Digital wearables, some for Zepeto (some phygital)

*digital wearable or skins but not NFTs

deliver a killer presentation. Your coworkers and boss are all impressed. Later that afternoon, you change into your digital Adidas track suit and Nike digital kicks to attend Justin Bieber's virtual concert—while still in your bathing suit but now sipping cocktails.

The scenario above may sound fanciful, but it isn't science fiction. It's not how the dystopian metaverse sounded in 1992, when Neal Stephenson coined the word in his novel *Snow Crash*.[61] At least it sounds more fun. I've made up the scenario, but it sounds real because all of it is possible today. Bali does, in fact, offer a five-year digital-nomad visa to lure remote workers. Anyone can don digital clothes on Zoom or virtual platforms,[62] and wear digital fashion in gaming worlds, such as Decentraland, Roblox, and Sandbox.[63] During the pandemic, Justin Bieber performed a virtual concert; viewers weren't given the ability to select avatars, but that technology exists.[64] (In 2022, MTV even recognized a new award for the best metaverse performance, although Bieber, who was nominated, didn't win.) Digital fashion is not only possible, it's happening as we speak.

No industry has embraced NFTs and the metaverse as quickly as the fashion industry. From haute couture to athletic wear and streetwear, fashion designers are reimagining apparel and accessories for both digital and physical use. An entirely new class of digital-only fashion has been invented, along with a new class of phygital goods—fashion your digital avatar can wear in the metaverse and you can wear IRL. As summarized in Table 3.1, many fashion brands have launched NFTs for digital fashion and for collectibles.

And, as shown in Table 3.2 below, all the top brands in the athletic-wear industry have launched NFTs. Both Adidas and Nike have ambitious plans for the metaverse and are racing to develop NFTs in innovative ways—and to beat each other to become the leader in the space.

Why are the fashion and athletic-wear industries racing to produce NFTs? The short answer: digital fashion opens up a vast new market for the next generation of consumers. This innovation was

TABLE 3.2. ATHLETIC-WEAR INDUSTRY DIGITAL WEARABLES AND NFTS

Company	Number of drops	Type of content
Adidas	4	Digital wearables Collectibles
Asics	2	Digital sneakers
Nike (acquired RTKFT)	5	*Digital sneakers in Roblox CryptoKicks sneakers (phygital) Air Force 1 sneakers (phygital) AR Genesis Hoodie (phygital) SZN 1 apparel, sneakers (phygital)
Puma	1	Collectibles
Reebok	2	Collectibles
RTFKT (before Nike acquisition)	8	Digital sneakers (phygital) Collectibles
Under Armour	2	Digital sneakers Collectibles

*digital wearable or skins but not NFTs

started by visionary startups that disrupted both industries. At first, this concept might be hard to grasp, especially for non-gamers. Looking at digital fashion on a computer might seem like you are looking at an image of physical clothing, like looking at a rendition for a concept car. But that's a mistake. Digital fashion is meant to be worn virtually. It is not merely a collectible—it functions as clothing for avatars in virtual worlds. To stress this feature, I'll use the term *digital wearable*.

This dramatic reimagining of fashion sprouts from gaming, but it now encompasses a much broader application, including for non-gamers. The use of NFTs for digital wearables is a natural evolution from the popularity of "digital skins" in video games and platforms. One of the most popular and lucrative aspects of the online gaming market is the sale of "skins," which change the appearance of a player's avatar, including clothing, accessories, and weapons. The skins can be earned as rewards or purchased, with the rarest skins commanding several thousand dollars. According to a DMarket estimate, the market for skins totals $40 billion annually.[65] In one survey, 85 percent of U.S. gamers between thirteen and forty-five years old are familiar with skins.[66] Plus, 75 percent of gamers say they'd spend more on skins if they could be resold for use across different platforms.[67]

Enter NFTs. Before NFTs, skins were created as files within specific games, such as Path of Exile or Fortnite, stored on the servers of the game publishers.[68] By contrast, NFTs are built on blockchain and are meant to be sold and used across different platforms. The advantage of tying digital wearables to NFTs is that NFTs are assets that can be bought and sold, and the underlying digital wearable can be made interoperable for use on different platforms—potentially increasing its value.[69] A person can buy one NFT digital wearable and use it on any virtual platform with interoperability.

RTFKT X NIKE

In January 2020, at the start of the pandemic, Chris Le, Benoit Pagotto, and Steven Valisev (aka Zaptio), cofounded RTFKT, pronounced "artifact," a name referring to valuable objects obtained in gaming worlds.[70] The three combined their strengths from different work experiences: Le, based in Salt Lake City, was the visual artist and creative director, who produced visual effects, music videos, and video game skins; Pagotto, in Paris, had extensive experience working with big brands in fashion, luxury, and gaming; and Valisev, in Miami, was the serial entrepreneur with experience starting companies.[71] They all were die-hard gamers who saw a big gap: the fashion industry didn't understand the opportunity that the gaming culture presented. And the gaming industry itself hadn't embraced the utility of NFTs to make skins even more valuable assets (in part due to fear of backlash from gamers). "[W]e were the perfect three brains to make this brand of the future and out-innovate everyone," Pagotto remarked.[72] It was, as Le put it, "a match made in heaven."[73]

Seizing the opportunity, RTFKT launched a series of NFTs in 2021 that transformed digital fashion. RTFKT introduced an audacious new aesthetic, what Pagotto described as "an aesthetic for gamers." RTFKT started with sneakers, which, in physical form, already had a huge market with rabid collectors known as "sneakerheads." On March 3, 2021, RTFKT launched NFTs for phygital sneakers in collaboration with FEWOCiOUS, a talented eighteen-year-old artist, then relatively unknown, who would soon catapult to become one of the most successful and noteworthy artists in NFTs. The FEWOCiOUS x RTFKT sneaker NFTs sold out in seven minutes for $3.1 million. Some digital sneakers even resold for $15,000.[74] The sneakers were phygital, with the NFT entitling the owner to collector-edition physical sneakers. RTFKT followed in May 2021 with another successful launch, this time for Metapigeon NFTs in collaboration with Jeff Staple, an acclaimed streetwear designer who helped to spark the sneaker craze in a collaboration with Nike in 2005 when he remixed a physical Nike sneaker with a pigeon logo.[75] RTFKT quickly proved there's a market for digital sneaker NFTs.

In November 2021, RTFKT took things to the next level. It launched the CloneX NFTs, 20,000 futuristic 3D avatars designed in collaboration with Takashi Murakami, the acclaimed artist from Japan. CloneX avatars are humanoids, which have been likened to anime and Pixar characters.[76] CloneX avatars wear next-gen streetwear fashion. They look young, hip, and futuristic. Although the CloneX launch experienced technical glitches, the collection sold out on the first day and quickly attained blue-chip status in the NFT community.[77] By September 2022, the collection had amassed $730 million in sales, placing it ninth in the top ten NFT collections, according to Cryptoslam.[78]

The utility of CloneX is clear—the avatars can be used in virtual worlds, including video conferencing platforms such as Google Meet. Using a free kit provided by Daz 3D, CloneX NFT owners can convert and customize their avatars into full-body 3D characters that can be used in virtual worlds.[79] As the metaverse develops, the utility of avatars will only increase.

Another important component of CloneX is its commercial license. Along with other upstarts in Web3, RTFKT adopted a license that promotes decentralized collaboration. By purchasing CloneX NFTs, the owners receive a license to make commercial uses of their characters (though not on any footwear and without using the brand name RTFKT), including the right to modify their characters.[80] Any CloneX NFT with a trait created by Murakami has a more limited commercial license, which requires registration on the RTFKT website.[81] Put these ingredients together and the utility of the NFTs grows: owners can develop not only their identity for the metaverse, but also their own business and brand based on their CloneX character—and keep the profits derived from their monetization of their CloneX characters. Just as with the Deadfellaz collection discussed in the last chapter, CloneX facilitates decentralized collaboration. I call this type of license a De-Collab license, which is a major—potentially revolutionary—development in the use of intellectual property that we'll examine closely in Part II.

Pagotto explained to me why it was important for RTFKT to grant NFT owners commercial rights: The CloneX characters become a part of owners' identities, so they should be able to use them. It also builds a community, and the best advertising for a company is its community. According to Pagotto, instead of asking how much money they can make, businesses should be asking, What are we building for our community? RTFKT even forbids referring to its NFT owners as "consumers"—that's not what being a co-owner and co-creator in a community is about.[82] RTFKT is reimagining not only digital fashion, but also the relationship between companies and people. It's not based on consumerism. It's based on community and decentralized collaboration. As Valisev put it, "We're trying to identify all the different core groups of the community, from the creators to the artists to the collectors, and trying to support and empower them to be able to achieve and live in this new world that we're building together."[83]

Big brands have already taken notice. Indeed, Nike outright acquired the red-hot RTFKT on December 13, 2021, shortly after the CloneX launch.[84] Nike valued RTFKT so highly that it even included RTFKT's logo in its Mount Rushmore of iconic logos—the Nike swoosh, Air Jordans, and Converse. It was a remarkable achievement for the upstart RTFKT. But, even before launching the company, the cofounders had envisioned their startup "making Nike a road map of 2025 in 2020," even designing the RTFKT logo with inspiration from the Nike swoosh.[85]

RTFKT said it hoped "to make Nike learn from us and understand it's a different game."[86] In less than a year since acquiring RTFKT, Nike quickly launched three innovative NFTs: Air Force 1 sneakers, CryptoKicks sneakers, and AR Genesis Hoodies. The Nike products are all phygital: NFT owners can claim a physical good through a process Nike calls forging. The Air Force 1 "Space Drip" collection involved collaborations with nineteen artists to remix the iconic Nike sneaker.[87] The other two projects were dynamic. The CryptoKicks design can be changed by using different "skin vials" sold as NFTs. Based on Nike's patent for CryptoKicks, Nike envisions the future ability of CryptoKicks owners to "breed" new designs from a combination of the designs in two Nike NFTs, creating an offspring or remixed sneaker design.[88] NFT owners who breed the offspring may be entitled to a new pair of physical Nike sneakers with the remixed design. (The idea is similar to how CryptoKitties "mated" to produce more CryptoKitties.) "Just Do It" could take on a whole new meaning.

If that doesn't sound impressive, consider the AR Genesis Hoodie, a phygital wearable for CloneX avatars and for physical wearing. It "comes with an NFC (near field communication) chip and is trackable using augmented reality, giving the wearer the option to wear, for example, virtual wings."[89] The NFC chip can authenticate that a physical good is genuine—thereby potentially reducing the problem of counterfeit Nike goods.[90] The launch for the AR Genesis Hoodie had technical difficulties (for which RTFKT apologized), but the collection still sold out.[91] RTFKT followed with a forging season entitling each CloneX holder to claim bespoke digital Nike AF1s and phygital CloneX apparel, tailored to the "DNA" of the holder's CloneX avatar.[92] One can foresee how owning a single NFT can be used to entitle the owner to Nike's latest phygital fashion, while guaranteeing its authenticity *and* enabling the owner to breed other designs. The NFT can also be used as a part of one's identity in the metaverse, potentially enhanced by augmented reality. The ability to distinguish genuine from counterfeit Nike products alone is incredibly useful. But combine it with all the other utility of owning an NFT, and it becomes apparent why so many businesses are exploring NFTs for their products.

Nike and RTFKT have emerged as a leader on the cutting edge of digital fashion for sneakers and athletic wear, although Adidas is working on its own ambitious "Into the Metaverse" collaboration, examined in Part II.

AUROBOROS AND THE FUTURE OF HIGH FASHION

Disruption is also occurring in high fashion. Auroboros, DressX, the Fabricant, and UNXD are among a group of innovative start-ups reimagining fashion, creating a new type of digital-only fashion. This approach could make the industry more sustainable by reducing consumption and waste of materials. People can look good virtually, without having to buy physical clothes. Some of the innovators, such as the Fabricant, enable people to cocreate the digital fashion designs, which might become a trend in the future.[93] DressX offers a smartphone app that enables you, as you take a selfie, to wear the digital clothing through augmented reality, similar to using a Snap filter.

Perhaps most disruptive of all is that fashion design is now liberated from physical constraints. Although some digital designs are made into physical clothing, that isn't a requirement. Digital-only

is a distinct class. Neither the cost of the materials nor the man-
ufacturability of the design operates as a limitation to digital-only
fashion. This liberation unleashes creativity. Haute couture looks
more futuristic—even like science fiction.

Auroboros is one of these high-fashion disrupters. Alissa Aulbekova and Paula Sello, the visionary cofounders, first met in
2018 at a techno party held at Corsica Studios, an underground
club in London that hosts music and arts events. The two immediately recognized they were kindred spirits, not only based on
their fashionable attire, far overdressed for Corsica Studios, but
also based on their intellectual and artistic interests, as well as
childhood experiences. Aulbekova said their connection was "instant." Both were artsy and played video games growing up, were
greatly influenced by their grandmothers, and lived in itinerant
families, a lifestyle that exposed them to different countries and
cultures. Both studied fashion at prestigious schools: Aulbekova
at Central Saint Martins in London, and Sello at Goldsmiths,
University of London, and the Fashion Technology Academy.
Both were also captivated and influenced by the futuristic world
in the movie *Avatar*, which they viewed as groundbreaking in its
innovation for cinema and, despite what others criticize as a colo-
nial narrative, inspiring in its vision of a solar-punk world, merg-
ing technology with nature. As it turned out, the two women
were already following each other on Instagram. Fittingly, they
met first digitally.

The chance encounter between Aulbekova and Sello in 2018 led
to the birth of Auroboros. The name refers to the ancient, mythical
serpent eating its own tail in circular fashion, symbolizing eternal
change and regeneration. The symbol was used in different ancient
cultures around the world, including in Kazakhstan, where Aulbekova's family originates. She studied her family's shamanic roots
and the deep respect for nature in her culture. Regeneration and
respect for nature are what she and Sello made the mission of their
company.

The two saw a big gap in the fashion industry. "Fashion is supposed to be a mirror of society," Sello explained. Then why weren't fashion brands reflecting the world Sello and Aulbekova were experiencing, including on digital screens? Sello and Aulbekova decided to change that. "Auroboros was born from a lack of cultural representation [in the fashion industry]," Sello elaborated. They wanted to make sure the future of fashion was inclusive and sustainable.

With initial support from Sarabande: The Lee Alexander McQueen Foundation, which helps "artists and designers who are creatively fearless and unafraid of overturning prevailing orthodoxies,"[94] the two designers set out to reimagine high fashion. Auroboros debuted its first fashion line at the London Fashion Week in 2021, making it the first brand to present a digital-only line at the event.[95] But that wasn't the most impressive part: the fashion was. As the name suggests, the Biomimicry collection was modeled on elements drawn from nature. Auroboros even created a physical Biomimicry gown, "made from salt crystals and recycled plastic that changes colour and shape in real time, mimicking the growth of a flower."[96] To top it off, the physical Auroboros gown was modeled by a robot, Ai-Da, at the Victoria and Albert Museum. It was the first couture gown that grew in real time. "It was . . . the Edison, light-bulb moment," Sello recounted to me. "People were seeing this huge innovation that normally would be behind closed doors." Unlike the exclusive world of haute couture, Auroboros invited the public to see the innovation. People were blown away. Auroboros shared its Venustrap dress as a QR filter that enabled people to wear the digital dress on their smartphones—and 2.5 million people did.[97]

The style of Biomimicry dazzles the mind. It's a colorful blend of futuristic tech and nature whose beauty deserves to be seen, not described.[98] Auroboros didn't sell the Biomimicry collection as NFTs. The company was planning to launch its first NFT collection for its next fashion line, Mesmer, with an expected launch in fall 2022 that will include the option of collaboration or cocreation for owners. Derived from *mesmerizing*, the collection draws inspiration from the Enlightenment, which, the two cofounders believe, has parallels with the pivotal time we now face.

To close the first Metaverse Fashion Week in 2022, Auroboros collaborated with the musician-artist Grimes, who performed a concert in Decentraland using an avatar wearing a futuristic violet bodysuit designed by Auroboros.[99] To the driving beat of techno music, Grimes's avatar danced in the Auroboros bodysuit, with dazzling lights showering her like raindrops. I attended the concert. It was a spectacle to behold.

I'm not a gamer, so attending the Grimes concert—for which I selected and created my own avatar, of course, with blond, Liberty-spiked hair—was a Eureka moment. Attending the concert virtually was like looking into the future—and seeing how the virtual world will become a basic part of daily life, if it's not already. The pandemic accelerated this shift as people were forced to work and study online. Enjoying a concert or cultural event will be as simple as touching a virtual button on your phone.

What's also clear to me is that people who grew up in virtual worlds already recognize this development. Although RTFKT and Auroboros are in much different areas of digital fashion, one common thread that ties the cofounders of both startups is the fact that they all grew up playing in gaming worlds. That virtual experience was crucial to their creative vision for digital fashion. "It was such an unbelievably creative sphere, where really the sky is the limit," Sello explained. Gaming also provided "the first seeds of community," added Aulbekova, emphasizing the importance of community-building for Auroboros. In an interview with *Women's Wear Daily*, Pagotto likewise stressed the importance for big fashion brands to play video games first—"Go deep and actually play, because if you don't, you're going to get even more lost."[100]

In a short time, Auroboros has reimagined high fashion. Sello and Aulbekova create what they call "magic realism," a dazzling intertwining of the possibilities of the digital and physical, as well as the limitless possibilities of technology, fashion, and nature. It's magical, but it's real.

NEXT-GENERATION FASHION

The big fashion brands have taken notice of the disruption in digital fashion. There's growing demand for next-gen digital fashion, especially among the younger generation of consumers. According to one survey, 88 percent of Gen Zs and 70 percent of Millennials frequent virtual worlds.[101] Recognition of this cultural phenomenon is what drives the brands' entry into digital fashion.

Consider the strategy of Ralph Lauren. In 2018, the company, which is more than half a century old, outlined an ambitious five-year plan, titled the Next Great Chapter, "to deliver sustainable, long-term growth and value creation."[102] First among its strategic priorities was to "win over a new generation" of consumers. It did so by going where young consumers were located: virtual worlds. In December 2021, the company launched the Ralph Lauren Winter Escape in Roblox, a gaming world with 47 million users. With bold, cheery colors, the company created a snowy alpine experience for people to visit. They could customize their avatars by buying digital winter gear by Ralph Lauren, priced between $1.25 and $3.[103]

When the CEO, Patrice Louvet, reported third-quarter earnings in February 2022, the company beat expectations, having earned $1.8 billion, up 27 percent from the prior year. Revenue grew by double digits in Asia, Europe, and North America, which included a 40 percent increase in digital sales revenue.[104] Beyond the numbers, Louvet touted the company's successes in winning over a new generation of consumers on Roblox.[105] Alice Delahunt, then the company's chief digital and content officer, explained that the strategy "underlines our belief in the opportunity that virtual spaces and economies present—especially when it comes to the next generation of consumers."[106] The success of Ralph Lauren's Winter Escape in Roblox followed its impressive debut in Zepeto, a virtual world produced by the South Korean company Naver Z. Louvet reported that Ralph Lauren's digital store received more than 2.5 million visits, making it the number one brand on Zepeto.

Although the digital wearables weren't sold as NFTs, Louvet said the company was considering NFTs.[107]

So is the entire fashion industry.

In November 2021, Morgan Stanley issued a report which estimated that NFTs for luxury brands may grow to $56 billion by 2030, as the metaverse develops.[108] Even though this will take time, the firm concluded that "NFTs and social gaming present two nearer-term opportunities for luxury brands."[109]

Morgan Stanley's forecast was made before the major downturn in the financial markets in summer 2022, including in cryptocurrencies and NFTs, but the long-term projection still seems on target. A key insight of the report is that digital fashion NFTs tap into the pervasive practice of wearable skins that exists in the gaming world.

Digital fashion is likely to draw from several markets. In 2020, 2.69 billion people were active gamers, with a projection of the number surpassing 3 billion in 2023.[110] According to the Entertainment Software Association's 2022 survey, 215.5 million Americans, or 66 percent of the population, play video games—with a fairly even split between female gamers (48 percent) and males (52 percent).[111] The greatest percentage of gamers were in the younger generations: 36 percent were ages eighteen to thirty-four years old, and 24 percent were under eighteen.[112] In China, there were 665 million gamers in 2020.[113] Digital fashion is also likely to draw from the markets for cryptocurrencies and NFTs, which tilt toward Millennial and Gen Z investors. Millennials (twenty-five-to-forty-year-olds, who constituted 76.45 percent) and Gen Zs (eighteen- to twenty-four-year-olds at 17.4 percent) comprise the largest number of cryptocurrency buyers per capita in the United States.[114] The two younger generations invested a substantial amount, ranking only slightly behind Gen X (forty-one-to-fifty-six-year-olds), who have greater disposable income. The average Gen X investor spent $9,611 on cryptocurrency in a year, followed by Millennials at $8,596 and Gen Zs at $6,120.[115] Boomers were more conservative at $4,567. Interest in NFTs was also higher among Millennials and Gen Zs, both in the United States and globally.[116]

And there's every reason to believe that Generation Alpha (born after 2010) will be even more attuned to virtual worlds and interactions.[117] Indeed, roughly 55 percent of the 43.2 million daily active users on Roblox are from Gen Alpha.[118] The average daily user spends 2.6 hours per day in the virtual world.[119] Increasingly, the virtual world will be integrated into the real world and daily activities.

Digital fashion offers brands the opportunity not only to create a new market for digital fashion, but also to capture—and potentially cocreate with—new generations of young consumers. Especially for people who already spend lots of time in virtual worlds, digital fashion is a natural development. As the world increasingly shifts to virtual experiences, digital fashion will likely become a necessity. And, paradoxically, NFTs make digital fashion more like physical clothes in one valuable respect: NFTs can be resold.

PART II

TOKENISM AND DE-IP

CHAPTER 4

TOKENISM

Every step, by which they have advanced to the
character of an independent nation,
seems to have been distinguished by some token of
providential agency.

—GEORGE WASHINGTON, INAUGURAL ADDRESS, 1789

Gelett Burgess graduated with an engineering degree from MIT in 1887. He taught at Berkeley, but left and became a creator.[1] In 1895, he founded a humor magazine titled *The Lark*.[2] It was "an odd journal that attracted the attention of the literary world."[3]

So did Burgess's poem "The Purple Cow," published in *The Lark*'s first issue. The poem was short: "I never saw a purple cow / I never hope to see one; / But I can tell you, anyhow, / I'd rather see than be one!"[4] But it became a national sensation. It is touted as the second-most-quoted American poem of the twentieth century, behind only "The Night Before Christmas."[5] Burgess didn't like the fame, however. He penned another poem that threatened to "kill you if you quote it!"[6]

The fame of "The Purple Cow" was hard to top. But Burgess went on to write one of the most important early articles about modern art. In 1910, "The Wild Men of Paris" was the first article introducing the United States to Cubism, a radical new style of art developing in Europe that sparked great controversy. Indeed, *Cubism* originated in France as a pejorative. The art critic Louis Vauxcelles derided the "bizarre cubes" in a painting of a house by

French painter Georges Braque, a close contemporary of Pablo Picasso's and a cofounder of the Cubist style.[7] However, by century's end, to call an artist Cubist was no insult. It was an honor to see *and* be one. Cubism was widely recognized as one of the most influential art movements of the twentieth century. As the art critic Max Kozloff put it, "Most of what came afterward is unthinkable without Cubism."[8]

Burgess's article was a humorous but historically significant examination of modern art and Cubism. Published in the *Architectural Record* in New York, it told the hilarious tales of his tour of the exhibition at the Salon des Indépendants in Paris. The article was lengthy, running fourteen pages and more than five thousand words without ads, and included not only photographs of the artists but also reprints of some of their paintings. Burgess scored interviews with a pantheon of notable artists, including Henri Matisse, Picasso, Braque, and others.[9] *The New York Times* later published a lengthy excerpt from Burgess's article, with a brief introduction expressing befuddlement: "Is this art or madness?"[10]

Burgess's article was a hoot. Walking among "well-dressed Parisians in a paroxysm of merriment, gazing, through weeping eyes," Burgess "gasp[ed]" at beholding the new art.[11] "It was a thing to startle even Paris. I realized for the first time that my views on art needed a radical reconstruction," he wrote. "Suddenly I had entered a new world, a universe of ugliness. And, ever since, I have been mentally standing on my head in the endeavor to get a new point of view on beauty so as to understand and appreciate this new movement in art."[12]

Burgess was beside himself. He found the paintings "dire," "crude," "shocking," and "ugly," with "atrocious" color—or lack thereof.[13] They resembled the doodles of a child with a box of crayons. Put bluntly, Burgess thought "there were no limits to the audacity and the ugliness of the canvasses."[14] Burgess even called Picasso "a devil," but "in the most complimentary sense." Picasso's paintings "outrage nature, tradition, and decency."[15] Of course, Burgess was being a bit tongue-in-cheek. But his shock at and difficulty in understanding Cubism sound sincere. Burgess admitted he "needed a radical reconstruction" of how he viewed the art—"a new point of view on beauty so as to understand and appreciate this new movement in art."

That he did. As did many others.

At the time, people had a hard time understanding Cubist art because it was a radical departure from existing art. Cubism was disruptive. Under the prevailing approach of the Renaissance, objects were portrayed from a linear, single-point perspective to appear three-dimensional, with the aspiration of a realistic rendition from one vantage point. Just think of the famous scene in Leonardo's *The Last Supper*. The painting adopts the perspective of what you might see in a photograph. Cubism shattered these conventions of the Renaissance—and altered human perception and our understanding of it. Cubism didn't abandon the aspiration of depicting the world realistically; instead, it did so in a completely different manner that made one question the nature of reality. Cubism adopted a new technique, often using fragments of multiple viewpoints assembled into overlapping geometric shapes—likened to cubes—to represent reality.[16] It embraced ambiguity and incompleteness of representation,[17] and ultimately offered a new, modern understanding of reality. To his credit, Burgess sensed the "serious revolt" in art that Picasso and other modern artists were waging: "[S]omething so virile, so ecstatic . . . that it justifies Nietzsche's definition of an ascendant or renascent art."[18]

Cubism's shift in perspective was as momentous as the Copernican shift in understanding Earth's place in the galaxy. Once a person made the shift, one's entire outlook on the world changed. Cubism's radical shift was not just in style, but also in conception. It was self-conscious of the role of the artist or viewer in creating reality. As Albert Gleizes and Jean Metzinger explained in their influential book on Cubism in 1912, the style was more faithful to reality: "An object has not one absolute form, it has many: it has as many as there are planes in the region of perception."[19] Gleizes and Metzinger believed that "the visible world can become the real world only by operation of the intellect."[20] Or, as Braque put it, the goal was "not to try and *reconstitute* an anecdotal fact but to *constitute* a pictorial fact."[21]

Cubism turned Renaissance artistic rendition on its head. Just as Copernicus's theory put the Sun, not Earth, at the center of the universe, Cubism made the mind, not the external world, the center of artistic representation. As Kozloff eloquently explained: "The reality that art must approach, and by which art is tested, is located effectively within, rather than outside, the beholder."[22] Cubism let the genie out of the artistic bottle, so to speak. If art wasn't limited to a single-point perspective, but instead was limited only by the artist's imagination, then not even the sky was a limit. Artists were freed to develop their own views of the world through their creations—even beyond a Cubist approach. It marked a liberation from conforming to artistic convention. Free your mind. That's why Cubism is today recognized as one of the most influential approaches in modern art that opened up unlimited possibilities and new understandings of the world even beyond art.[23]

Of course, whenever something's disruptive, there's bound to be controversy. Under what we might call the Tao of innovation, disruption and controversy are yin and yang. The more disruptive an innovation, the more controversy it sparks. Cubism was disruptive and controversial from the start. Incredibly so. Indeed, some people had outright contempt for Cubism, believing it needed to be completely extinguished from society to protect especially the young. It was no laughing matter.

Even in the United States, the reception to Cubism was hostile. Art critics shared Burgess's bewilderment. Park West Gallery, based in Michigan, collected a number of old newspaper clippings from the early 1900s.[24] The newspapers found Picasso's art bizarre and even deranged. In 1911, the *Salt Lake Tribune* ran a subtitle that sounds like a subtweet today: "It Requires an Odd Sort of Taste to Appreciate Their Crazy Drawing, but One Parisian Faction Hails Them as Geniuses Regardless of What Another Set Calls Them."[25] The article had a hard time taking Cubism seriously and even said that a painting by the donkey Lolo, prodded by two students, "was so much better" than other Cubist paintings, including the works of Picasso, "one of the most eccentric cubists."[26] The *Ogden Standard-Examiner* worried that this art was making women less beautiful, "utterly lacking in the appealing charm of other days."[27] The article even questioned "if the human race was evolving or degenerating into a strange, new type."[28] The notion that Cubism was degenerate would unfortunately spread.

Art exhibitions drew protests. In 1913, the Armory Show, featuring modern art for the first time in the United States, met scorn from the art establishment in New York City.[29] But in Chicago the reception was even worse. Students at the Art Institute organized a mass protest, drawing more than a thousand people outside the storied building. The art students "convicted" Henri Matisse, a post-Impressionist (but not Cubist), of "artistic murder" in a mock trial for his degenerate art and even burned three mock Matisse paintings. One local paper reported the spectacle in a headline: "Students Burning Futurist Art and Celebrating Cubists' Departure."[30] Another read: "Students Wreak Vengeance upon Cubist Designs."[31] A student explained that the protest was "a public rebuke to . . . all cubist art and artists."[32] *The New York Times* published a scathing editorial endorsing the view that Cubism was "a part of the general movement . . . to disrupt and degrade, if not to destroy, not only art, but literature and society, too."[33] Cubism was a "false art"—or, in today's vernacular, a fake art. Civilization was viewed in jeopardy with Cubism's rise.

It took nearly a decade before another major exhibition of modern art occurred in the United States. In 1921, the Metropolitan Museum of Art held its first modern exhibition. But the climate for Cubism was still hostile, so the Met's curator decided to exclude Picasso's Cubist art, instead opting for the artist's less controversial paintings.[34] The exhibition still sparked what one newspaper described as "one of the most extraordinary attacks ever leveled against an exhibition."[35] A self-described group of "citizens and supporters of the Metropolitan Museum" published an anonymous four-page pamphlet against the "degenerate 'modernistic' works."[36] In a polemic that might make today's conspiracy theories seem tame, the pamphlet attributed the rise of modern art to a "modernistic degenerate cult" spurred by Bolshevist propaganda, a greedy "coterie of European art dealers" and "egomaniacs in Paris" who were "worshippers of Satan, the God of Ugliness," and the insanity of the artists who suffered from a "peculiar type of visual derangement."[37] The pamphlet took aim at the artworks of Picasso, Cézanne, Degas, and Gauguin. It implored the public "to write to the authorities of the Museum of Art expressing their disapproval of the present exhibition as having a destructive influence in both art and life."[38]

A group of prominent physicians in the United States even provided the imprimatur of medicine to support the polemic against modern art. Why? The doctors thought the art was abnormal—and resulted from mental illness.[39] Dr. William E. Wadsworth, a brain specialist, explained: "My protest is not against these debauched defectives who should be under institutional care; it is against the sane men and women, directors of art museums, who permit this stuff to be placed on exhibit for the eyes of youth to see and call it art."[40] Dr. Charles W. Burr, a prominent professor at the University of Pennsylvania Medical School, called the art "humbug" and "degenerate." Dr. Francis X. Dercum, a top neurologist who was a pioneer in the field,[41] concurred: "I have seen the work of insane persons confined in asylums who lean toward art, and I will say that the drawings of these insane artists are far superior to the alleged works of art I saw at the exhibition."[42]

The Met appeared to end the exhibition abruptly.[43] *The Washington Times* even stated that if the allegation that modern art is degenerate was proved, "[q]uarantine must be put around their studios, and who knows, perhaps another amendment to the Constitution will be necessary."[44] Well, there goes freedom of speech.

In his recent book on Picasso, Hugh Eakin traces this "pseudoscientific" thinking on cultural degeneracy to Max Nordau, a Hungarian physician and conservative social critic, whose 1895 book

Degeneration was influential in the United States and elsewhere.[45] In the United States alone, it sold more than 600,000 copies.[46]

Tragically, the view that modern art was degenerate was shared by Adolf Hitler and the Nazis, who confiscated artworks including Picasso's and other Cubist works, classified and censored them as "degenerate art," and sold them to fund German operations in World War II. Hitler preferred classical and realistic art. In 1937, the Nazis even held a "Degenerate Art" exhibition to show Germans what not to like. They posted signs saying "crazy at any price" and "how sick minds viewed nature" next to the "degenerate" works.[47]

"Cubism, Dadaism, Futurism, Impressionism . . . have nothing to do with our German people," Hitler declared.[48] "Works of art which cannot be understood in themselves but need some pretentious instruction book to justify their existence . . . will never again find their way to the German people."[49] The Nazis confiscated more than 16,000 "degenerate" artworks that were recorded in the Nazi propagandist Joseph Goebbels's records, but, by some estimates, the amount totals more than 650,000 works.[50] Hitler held a far different view of creativity. "It is not men of letters who are the creators of a new era, but the fighters, those who are truly creative, who lead their people and thus make history."[51] Madness.

TARANTINO'S QUESTION

Quentin Tarantino's second film, *Pulp Fiction*, was an absolute sensation in 1994. It won the coveted Palme d'Or at the Cannes Film Festival and became a worldwide box office hit, grossing more than $200 million—a first for an independent film. Film critic Janet Maslin of *The New York Times* raved how Tarantino, "a mostly self-taught, mostly untested talent," created a movie "of such depth, wit and blazing originality that it places him in the front ranks of American film makers."[52]

Pulp Fiction defied convention. The film used nonlinear storytelling, intertwining three crime stories involving different shady but likable characters. It starts chronologically with the diner scene, but then adopts a nonlinear narrative, intertwining the views of different characters, whose paths collide. This approach offers the audience a chance to view a scene from different perspectives. The opening scene shows a couple in a diner discussing robbing restaurants, but the audience does not learn what happened to the couple until the end of the movie, when it returns back to the climactic scene but, ultimately, from the perspective of the hitmen Vincent Vega and Jules Winnfield, played by John Travolta and Samuel L. Jackson.[53] The diner scene bookends the movie and gives the intricate storytelling a dramatic punch.

Pulp Fiction is an example of cinematic Cubism.[54] Instead of a single-point perspective, it uses multiple views of the same events. The movie's nonlinear storytelling conveys a dynamic set of perspectives from different characters whose experiences are intertwined in a complex web involving different plots, which offer the audience simultaneous viewpoints of events. The events or story lines can be viewed as fragments that are composed simultaneously in the movie, offering different perspectives of the overall story. Film provides a medium well-suited to a Cubist approach, given the ability to capture multiple viewpoints of the same scene, as well as to provide a panoramic perspective in the film. As art critic John Berger described in his book on Picasso, "the film is the medium which, by its nature, can accommodate most easily *a simultaneity of viewpoints*, and demonstrate most clearly *the indivisibility of events*."[55] Indeed, some commentators and the documentary *Picasso and Braque Go to the Movies* contend that the advent of films in the early 1900s influenced the development of Cubist thought.[56]

Fast forward to 2021. Tarantino announced he would sell his handwritten screenplay to *Pulp Fiction* as NFTs, which included his audio commentary of different scenes. At a conference organized by the website nft now, Tarantino likened the NFTs for his handwritten *Pulp Fiction* screenplay to an imagined example of an NFT for a napkin on which Bob Dylan handwrote some lyrics.[57] Both were rare.

A few moments later, Tom Bilyeu, the successful entrepreneur who was a fellow panelist, offered a show-stopping suggestion to Tarantino. "I don't know how you get the rights to all this stuff, but if you were to actually NFT-ize every frame of *Pulp Fiction*, let's say, the shot where [Jackson and Travolta] are holding the guns [that] has become . . . that meme image . . . that would sell for millions for sure, tens of millions that one frame—"[58]

Tarantino interrupted. "Okay, okay . . . to not sound like a clueless dork, how is that different from all the stills [of the movie] that already exist?"

"All right, so this is where it gets interesting," Bilyeu explained. "Right-click save, that's the big question in the NFT space. But here's what people aren't thinking about: the image of the NFT isn't the thing. It's the sense of ownership. Now when you own it, now we're down to the blockchain. . . . At the level of the blockchain, think of that image as having matrix code inside of it *literally*. And now I can detect through technology whether you have the real one or a fake one."

"Gotcha," Tarantino acknowledged.

The exchange lasted barely a minute. But it was a pivotal moment. It identified the central question or conceptual challenge that NFTs pose, the question that most people don't understand at first. Let's call it Tarantino's question: How does something that already exists in many copies, whether physical or digital, such as copies of scenes from *Pulp Fiction*, become unique or non-fungible? Is that even possible?

Most people, not just "clueless dorks," probably have the same quizzical, if not skeptical, reaction as Tarantino. The key to understanding NFTs is to recognize there is a difference between the NFT and the image. Granted, this is hard to do. Typically, the only thing people see when buying NFTs involving artwork is a digital image of the artwork, so it's understandable that people might be fooled into believing the image is what they are buying. But it's not. As Bilyeu said, the NFT is *not* the image.

The value of the NFT lies in the ownership of the virtual token plus any additional rights of ownership or use granted by the NFT creator. The NFT isn't really a token at all, but instead a unique identifier—what Bilyeu called "the matrix code"—in a computer program called a smart contract stored on blockchain. We'll walk through the mechanics of NFTs shortly. But, before we do, we need to shift our perspective. To understand why anyone would believe there's any value in an imaginary token, we, like Gelett Burgess when first encountering Cubism, need a "radical reconstruction" of how we view ownership in the twenty-first century. We need to mentally stand on our heads in the endeavor to get a new point of view. And, once we do, a whole new world opens up.

TOKENISM

To explain the paradigm shift caused by NFTs, I offer a new theory called Tokenism. In its ordinary meaning, *tokenism* carries negative connotations—such as in a business's hiring of a person of color merely to avoid criticism, a practice that should be condemned. Some articles about NFTs have already likened the supposed lack of diversity among NFT creators to this conventional sense of tokenism.[59] My use of Tokenism shouldn't be confused with this meaning, however. I have purposely chosen to use *Tokenism*, with the potential baggage *tokenism* brings, to convey how NFTs have upended our conventional understandings of ownership and value. Just as *Cubism* started out as an insult but later signified one of the most influential art movements of the twentieth century, *Tokenism* is used here in a much different way than the negative conventional meaning. What Cubism did to artistic perspective at the start of the twentieth century, Tokenism is doing today to our perspective of ownership.

Tokenism can be defined as an artistic, cultural, and technological movement that creates value and a new kind of ownership in a new type of property—symbolized by a virtual token—through a process of technological abstraction and artificial scarcity effectuated by NFTs. This new type of ownership and property are constructed by a complex arrangement involving primarily two elements: (1) a technological component: unique tokens identified in smart contracts executed on blockchain, a decentralized public ledger; and (2) a legal component: additional rights granted to the buyer in licenses typically (at least for now) executed outside blockchain, or "off chain." Ownership of the NFT gives the owner both elements: the token and any additional rights granted by license.

To understand how this new kind of ownership works, we need to go over some basic components of NFTs. Let's start with what creates NFTs: computer programs called smart contracts, meaning they operate automatically to effectuate transactions on computers. Of course, most people are familiar with computer programs. Well, smart contracts are no different, other than they are stored and executed on blockchain. The smart contracts create, or "mint," the NFTs. All transactions involving the NFTs are automatically recorded on blockchain; each transaction creates a new block in the chain. Each NFT has its own unique number, or "token ID."[60] That's what makes it non-fungible. It's similar to how every passport has a unique number. This approach helps to ensure the uniqueness of the passport or NFT—each number or ID identifies only one passport or NFT.

The smart contract could end there—with the creation of unique tokens on blockchain. But that wouldn't be very practical. It would be hard for anyone to tell what each virtual token represents—or how it has any value. It would be like assigning passport numbers without any corresponding names or photographs. Just imagine the only information in your passport is a number. Hard to tell what the number means! The TSA would have a fit. The same problem would arise if a smart contract had only a token ID. Thankfully, NFT creators don't stop there. They program the smart contracts to identify something else that they own, such as artwork, music, or virtual real estate they created. When people buy NFTs, they typically see a digital image displayed as the NFT. But, as we all now know, the NFT is *not* the image.

What, then, is the NFT? It's a new type of property that involves ownership in a unique token of something else—for example, a token of artwork or Tarantino's script. The NFT buyer owns the token, plus whatever additional rights the NFT creator includes. The NFT can be used to identify an ownership stake in just about anything else, including art, collectibles, music, digital fashion, financial instruments, intellectual property, membership in communities or clubs, real estate (in the real world and the metaverse), tickets and perks to events, rights to services, etc. The uses are as broad as human imagination.

The process of creating a token—or tokenization—can be likened to creating a single share of stock. In 1602, the Dutch East India Company (commonly referred to as VOC in the Dutch acronym) was the first company to sell "shares" in itself to the public.[61] The shares could be freely traded by their owners. But shareholders in VOC didn't receive any physical paper for their share of stock. (Storing thousands of paper slips would be impractical.) Instead, the share was imaginary. VOC had a public ledger or book that kept track of each shareholder's shares and recorded all transfers of shares.[62] For anyone familiar with NFTs, this example should sound eerily similar. NFT owners don't receive any physical tokens. Instead, the token is imaginary. There's a public ledger, blockchain, that keeps track of each owner's NFTs and records all transfers. Just as the share of stock indicates an ownership interest in a company, the NFT indicates an ownership interest in something the NFT creator has designated. NFT owners are like sole shareholders of their particular NFTs. (The analogy suggests that NFTs might be securities that should be subject to regulation, an important topic we'll return to in the last part of the book.)

When the NFT involves an ownership interest in copyrighted artwork, such as a cartoon character or digital art, the final ingredient of the arrangement is a content license. This is where things get tricky. Indeed, some NFTs have been minted without a formal content license, resulting in a lot of confusion for buyers. Even the now legendary CryptoPunks were launched without any written content license in 2017, to the dismay of the NFT owners, many of whom had become millionaires in the NFT value of their CryptoPunks. The problem apparently wasn't addressed until 2019 in a post by Larva Labs' Watkinson on social media announcing the adoption of an NFT license that granted the CryptoPunks owners a limited commercialization right, capped at $100,000 in annual revenues.[63] In 2022, after Larva Labs sold the intellectual property rights to the CryptoPunks to Yuga Labs, the latter company issued the CryptoPunks owners a new, exclusive license with unlimited commercialization rights—a far better deal for the owners.[64] Ironically, after starting out with no written license at all, the CryptoPunks owners received perhaps the most advantageous license possible.

A content license sets forth the permissible uses of the copyrighted artwork the NFT buyers are entitled to make. Some licenses, such as the one for the NBA Top Shot Moments, are restrictive and give only limited rights to the NFT owners for personal, noncommercial uses of the artwork.[65] Other licenses, such as the one for Deadfellaz or CryptoPunks, are more permissive and give buyers unlimited commercialization rights or even full IP rights in what I call De-Collab licenses, a topic we'll discuss in chapter 7.[66]

No doubt, NFTs are complex arrangements. They represent ownership of a virtual token and any additional rights set forth in a license. The owner of the NFT owns the token and can resell it, but does not typically own the artwork or image (unless a content license says so).

Some readers may scratch their heads and wonder, Why would anyone in the world ever buy NFTs? If people don't own the art, isn't this a scam?

The $27 billion in sales of NFTs in 2021, plus the number of big businesses investing in or producing NFTs, suggest not. The list of big businesses grows by the day: Adidas, Budweiser, Burberry, Charmin, Chipotle, Coach, Coca-Cola, Dolce & Gabbana, Gap, Gucci, Lamborghini, Louis Vuitton, Martha Stewart, Mattel,

McDonald's, Robert Mondavi, NBA, Nike, *Rolling Stone*, Taco Bell, Ubisoft, Universal Music, Visa, Walt Disney, Warner Music, and others.

Tokenism explains this phenomenon. It's not a scam. It's a shift in understanding of ownership—a radical shift. That's why it's so puzzling. Like Burgess, the doctors, and American newspapers encountering Cubism for the first time, it's easy to jump to the conclusion that people are odd or even crazy to believe NFTs have value. But, following Burgess's suggestion, what if we undertake a "radical reconstruction" of how we view ownership drawing on the lessons we've learned from Cubism? What if we change our perspective of ownership as Cubism changed our perspective of art?

The parallels between Cubism and Tokenism are striking. I have listed the major points of comparison in Table 4.1.

It's important to recognize first the parallel time periods in which Cubism and Tokenism originated. Cubism started at the turn of the twentieth century, around 1907 with Picasso's *Les Demoiselles d'Avignon*; Tokenism started at the turn of the twenty-first century around 2014.[67] (Because NFTs are executed on blockchain technology first used for Bitcoin, we might consider 2008 as the start of Tokenism, but it's not crucial to pick an exact year.[68]) Both periods were characterized by dramatic advances in science and technology.

Cubism originated during the Second Industrial Revolution. Arthur I. Miller's book *Einstein, Picasso* makes a compelling case that, to understand Picasso's art, one must recognize how it paralleled the major scientific advancements of the period, including Einstein's influential theory of relativity conceived in 1905.[69] Einstein's and Picasso's works occurred amid profound technological innovation—automobiles, airplanes, wireless telegraphy, X-rays, cinematography, and a fascination with the fourth dimension in mathematics.[70] "The truth is that [Cubism] is a technological art," the curator Bernice Rose explained. "It's involved with what we've come to know as the Industrial Revolution."[71]

Tokenism's connection to technology is even easier to spot. Tokenism is embodied in blockchain technology, computer programs, and the Internet. It's no surprise that two early developers of NFTs, Matt Hall and John Watkinson, the "creative technologists" behind CryptoPunks, have engineering backgrounds. Knowing how to code comes in handy. NFTs are part of a much larger technological and social movement to build a more decentralized Internet

TABLE 4.1. COMPARISON BETWEEN CUBISM AND TOKENISM

	Cubism	Tokenism
Inception	Circa 1907	Circa 2014 for NFTs or 2008 for cryptocurrency
Prior conventional view	Single-point, linear perspective of Renaissance art.	Items have inherent value. Ownership of items diminishes in value by greater number of digital copies of item.
Radical shift in view	Perspective of reality is created by human mind.	Value is created by human mind and can exist in virtual tokens. Value of NFT is not diminished by digital copies.
Method of transformation	Fragmentation: artist uses geometric shapes or "cubes" and overlapping planes.	Tokenization: creator uses computer program to create non-fungible "tokens" plus license for associated content.
Effect	Creating and viewing art radically changed from past convention to more complex representation for modern world (visual Cubism).	Owning art or content radically changed from past convention to more complex arrangement for virtual world (virtual Cubism).
Contemporaneous criticism	Bizarre, ugly Degenerate and product of mental illness Harmful to youth, women, and society Ploy for profits for European art dealers	Bizarre, ugly Ponzi scheme, scams, MLM Preying on young and vulnerable Speculative bubble "Crypto bro" culture Harmful to environment
Influence	Influenced other styles of modern art, architecture, design, film, and thinking.	Disrupts art, business, entertainment, fashion, film, music, other industries, and cultural production. Provides new means for online identity, community, governance, decentralized collaboration, De-IP.

commonly called Web3, and a more immersive experience in the metaverse. NFTs exploded in popularity during the COVID pandemic when people became accustomed to interacting and working virtually through Zoom.[72] The more a person's experiences are purely virtual, the less strange the idea of owning a virtual token is.

Amid profound technological changes, Cubism and Tokenism both resulted in revolutionary shifts in understanding. For Cubism, artistic depictions changed from the single-point view of Renaissance art, such as Leonardo's *Last Supper*, to a more complex representation that included overlapping fragments, geometric shapes, and planes, such as in Picasso's *Girl with a Mandolin*. Cubism's shift wasn't just aesthetic. It marked a radical change in the understanding of art. Art *created* a representation of the internal conception and imagination of the artist. The perspective of reality is, in other words, created by the human mind. Today, that shift may no longer sound radical. Indeed, we've seen so much modern art—of infinite variety—that the shift probably sounds trite. But when Cubism was first introduced, many people thought it was bizarre and degenerate. Indeed, top physicians in the United States did.

The most intriguing parallel between Cubism and Tokenism is their method of representation. For Cubism, the artist uses geometric shapes or "cubes" and planes to depict complex, simultaneous representations of things. For Tokenism, the creator uses a computer program to create non-fungible "tokens" that represent an ownership interest in a complex arrangement involving a smart contract and licensed uses of related content. The "tokens" are often symbolized in representations as either circles or hexagons, while the blockchain where the tokens are stored is symbolized as, hold your breath, cubes! Through either coincidence or recurrence, we've come full circle to a radical conceptual shift. Perhaps the use of geometrical shapes for both Cubism and Tokenism shouldn't be surprising. A recent study by cognitive neuroscientists suggests that representing facets of the world by geometrical shapes is unique to humans.[73] What "cubes" did to human perceptions of art, "tokens" are now doing to perceptions of ownership.

Like Cubism, Tokenism marks a radical change in perspective. Tokenism has shifted the perspective of ownership from a perceived single item, such as a painting or sneaker, to a complex arrangement of ownership involving a virtual token of an artwork or other item designated, plus any additional rights granted by license. This new type of property in NFTs radically changes the significance of copying: the existence of digital copies of artwork doesn't diminish the value of the NFT because the copies don't substitute for the unique token. That explains why a new market for digital art has blossomed for Beeple, Krista Kim, Osinachi, and many other digital artists around the world—with billions of dollars in sales.

To underline this important parallel: just as Cubism radically upended how art is created and viewed in "cubes," Tokenism radically upends how art (or other content) is owned in "tokens." Cubism ushered in art for the modern world. Tokenism, ownership for the virtual world.

Indeed, because of these striking parallels, NFTs can be viewed as a kind of a virtual Cubism for ownership, appearing simultaneously to be several things—a unique token, a digital asset, a display of associated art or content, membership in a club, community, or rewards program, and a source of identity and status, such as the use of a cartoon character (e.g., a CryptoPunk) as one's pfp on Twitter. No one can see virtual tokens. They are imaginary. That's why NFTs may appear different depending on one's perspective. Just as Cubism exposed how perspective in art is constructed by the human mind, so, too, Tokenism exposes how both ownership and value in property are constructed by the human mind. In so doing, Tokenism has opened up unlimited possibilities for (re)imagining ownership for the twenty-first century.

SCAM ARTISTS?

Just as the early skeptics of Cubism had a hard time understanding it, skeptics of NFTs today have a hard time figuring them out. I'd like to focus here on two criticisms reminiscent of the attacks on Cubism at the turn of the twentieth century: NFTs are ugly and scams. These attacks aren't surprising. Remember the Tao of innovation. The more disruptive the innovation, the greater the controversy.

Critics have called the art sold in NFTs ugly.[74] One critic called the popular Bored Apes "objectively hideous procedurally generated ape cartoons."[75] Another critic lamented the artwork for many NFTs as "effing hideous."[76] And we've already learned how art critics have widely panned Beeple's works. The hostile reaction to Cubism—the "universe of ugliness," in Burgess's words—in the early twentieth century serves as an important lesson. Don't be too quick to judge. As the saying goes, beauty lies in the eyes of the beholder—or NFT holder. Sure, cartoon apes aren't for everyone. Nor are cartoon mice. Sorry, Mickey. Art critics attacked Picasso's works as ugly and degenerate. But that criticism didn't age well. Picasso loved drawing animals—bulls, dogs, owls, penguins, pigs, roosters, you name it.[77] Apparently, no apes. But he reportedly owned a painting by Congo the chimpanzee and displayed it in his studio.[78] NFTs have existed for only a few years. Who's to say that the next Picasso will not emerge from the ranks of new NFT artists, either now or in the future? Keep your eye on FEWOCiOUS.

Another common attack on NFTs is that they're scams— multilevel marketing (MLM), Ponzi, or pyramid schemes.[79] These attacks go beyond the concern that NFT prices are speculative, to something far more sinister. NFTs are nefarious scams suckering vulnerable people, especially the supposedly gullible, younger generation, to buy NFTs and pump more money into the pockets of the crypto whales. By the sounds of it, NFTs are even worse than the scam perpetuated by the greedy coterie of European art dealers purportedly peddling Cubist art.

Everyone should DYOR, or do your own research. The debate over crypto and NFTs has inflamed heated arguments on both sides—and that's likely to continue. My goal is not to resolve this important debate, much less to persuade people to buy NFTs or cryptocurrency. Instead, it's to provide a theory to explain how NFTs are transforming ownership and important aspects of creative production. However, because my theory depends on the premise that NFTs create a legitimate form of ownership, I believe it's important to respond to attacks that they are scams.

The sweeping accusations that NFTs are scams, Ponzi schemes, or MLMs suffer from several fallacies. The biggest fallacy is that the attacks often conflate two arguments: (1) that all NFTs are scams or the entire NFT market is one giant scam, versus (2) that some NFTs can be used by some bad actors to scam people. Of course, there's a huge difference between the two arguments. But the attacks on NFTs often conflate the distinction. It's important to remember NFTs are just computer programs or technology. People use them in a myriad of ways, including to donate money to nonprofits helping children in developing countries.[80] As I'll discuss later, Ukraine's government sold NFTs to help fund its defense against Russia's invasion, and artists around the world sold NFTs to help Ukraine. Far from scams.

Granted, some scammers have used NFTs to do quick "rug pulls" of their NFT projects after promising ambitious road maps to develop future utility for the collection. Rug pulls are serious problems that the Department of Justice has already started to address with criminal indictments.[81] Scams can also include "pump and dump" schemes using misleading statements to pump up the price of an NFT or cryptocurrency, only to dump (or sell) the asset at a higher price.[82] We'll examine these problems in Part III.

But scams abound in nearly every context—email, telemarketing, financial investments, real estate, and even trademark registrations and patents. No one seriously contends that the scams in these areas warrant shutting them down. That'd be throwing the baby *and* the bathtub out with the bathwater.

Take, for example, email. Every day, email is exploited for spam, malware, and phishing. In 2009, fully 90 percent of all email was spam. Fortunately, this was reduced to about 45 percent in 2021 due to better filters, but spam is still a major problem.[83] Gmail stops 100 million phishing emails each day.[84] Email is the source of 94 percent of all malware.[85] Despite the high percentage of harmful emails that are sent every day, it's a fallacy to conclude that all emails or the entire technology of email is harmful or a big scam or phishing expedition. People use email for work and pleasure every day. Email still provides significant advantages over snail mail: it's cheaper, instantaneous, paperless, and more environmentally friendly.

Detractors of NFTs latched on to an early figure tweeted by OpenSea, the largest NFT marketplace. In January 2022, OpenSea said that bad actors had misused the marketplace's unlimited free minting: "Over 80% of the items created with this tool were plagiarized works, fake collections, and spam."[86] As email has already shown, when something's offered for free, bad actors will exploit it. Every platform from Amazon to YouTube has to deal with fakes or unauthorized copies. OpenSea is no different. Before placing too much weight on the 80 percent figure, we need more information, such as what percentage of copied, fake, or spam NFTs were actually sold on OpenSea. Some buyers can spot fakes based on whether the account of the seller is verified on OpenSea. (For that reason, I propose in Part III that OpenSea should allow everyone to apply for a verified account.) We also need more recent data. In May 2022, OpenSea announced the deployment of a "copymint" filtering technology, supplemented by human review, to stop fakes on OpenSea.[87] This filtering system will likely reduce the amount of fakes on the platform. We'll examine OpenSea's filtering system in Part III—it is a step in the right direction.

Another fallacy is that NFTs are allegedly multilevel marketing schemes or even illegal Ponzi schemes. We'll tackle first MLMs and then discuss Ponzi schemes afterward. Because the MLM trope has been mentioned in prominent sources, such as *The Wall Street Journal* and *The New Yorker*, I'd like to dissect the comparison.[88] (If you already think the MLM attack on NFTs is flimsy, feel free to jump to the next section.)

First, it's important to recognize that MLMs that sell legitimate products, such as Amway and Mary Kay, are not illegal. According to the Federal Trade Commission, MLM businesses "involve selling products to family and friends and recruiting other people to do the same."[89] Members in an MLM business earn income by gaining profits on their direct sale of the products to consumers and by earning commissions from the product sales by any recruits they enlist.[90] This business model is legitimate if the organizers intend to sell real products or services. But it's an illegal Ponzi or pyramid scheme if the organizers have no such intention, but instead are trying to profit from luring workers to pay fees to the organizers, who abscond with the money. When detractors liken NFTs to MLMs, which are not illegal, they are trying to create a moral panic so people stay away from NFTs. But the attack doesn't hold water.

TABLE 4.2. DIFFERENCES BETWEEN MULTILEVEL MARKETING AND NFT COLLECTION

	Multilevel Marketing (MLM)	NFT Collection
Individuals	Workers	Owners or investors
Product	Unlimited, mass-produced goods.	Limited number of NFTs (e.g., 10,000), each unique.
How individuals make money	Workers sell more mass-produced products and recruit more people to sell more products.	Owners sell their NFTs at higher price than purchase price. Short-term flips. Long-term HODLers hold their NFTs, buy more NFTs from same collection, and wait for appreciation before selling.
What happens after selling?	If workers sell their supply of products, company sends more supply to sell.	If owners sell all their NFTs, they are out. Company does not send more NFTs.
Is recruitment of others a direct source of income?	Yes based on commission percentage from sales of recruits.	No
Is recruitment of others expected part of joining?	Yes	No

As Table 4.2 summarizes, the dynamics and business models of NFT collections are vastly different. MLM involves an unlimited supply of mass-produced goods, all fungible. By contrast, NFT collections involve a limited number of NFTs, each unique. MLM workers receive a constant supply of mass-produced goods and must keep on selling them to receive their income. By contrast, people who buy an NFT from an NFT collection are not tasked in an ongoing business to sell products to consumers. Once owners sell their NFTs from a collection, they have nothing left to sell. The investment in an NFT is more like buying stock in a company than selling products in MLM.

Because the business models of MLM and NFT collections are different, the incentives are different. To make money in MLM, people must sell products and recruit other sellers—those are the only sources of income. By contrast, instead of selling, NFT owners often make a better return on investment by *not* selling or even recruiting. In the long term, NFT owners may be best served by not recruiting anyone, so they themselves can buy the rarest NFTs from the limited collection and accumulate a war chest of NFTs. Indeed, the most successful NFT investors typically own many NFTs—potentially hundreds—from the same blue-chip collections. Although some investors try to profit by flipping NFTs, similar to day trading in stocks, NFT owners probably can make the greatest return on investment by keeping—"HODL" (hold on for dear life) or "diamond hands"—blue-chip NFTs and buying more NFTs from the same collection when the price dips, such as by "sweeping the floor," meaning buying multiple NFTs from the same collection when the floor price (for the lowest-priced NFTs) is low. Those who don't HODL, but instead "paper hands" their NFTs, such as CryptoPunks, may lose out by selling too soon. In one survey of NFT enthusiasts in Asia, more than 50 percent said they favored the HODL approach.[91] That's a far cry from the incentives for MLM workers, who never have any incentive to ever HODL the products they must sell. The comparison to MLM is even less tenable for NFTs for individual artwork (so-called one-of-one pieces), where the incentive to HODL for the long term is even greater. The crypto winter is likely to place an even greater premium on long-term investments in blue-chip NFTs instead of "get rich" speculation or day trading.

Of course, things get more suspicious when NFT collections enlist paid influencers to pump up their collections, or when some big NFT investors pump up a collection without full disclosure of their own self-interest. The consumer watchdog group Truth in Advertising warned a number of celebrities about the need to disclose financial interests when promoting NFTs.[92] But we already have a mechanism in place to police lack of disclosure. The Federal Trade Commission (FTC) has started to crack down on influencers who fail to disclose their financial interests in their social media posts.[93] The Securities and Exchange Commission (SEC) has also cracked down on similar violations of failing to disclose financial interests in touting initial coin offerings.[94] But even illegal promotions of investments on social media by failing to disclose paid sponsorship are far different from MLM.

The most serious charge against NFTs is that they are illegal Ponzi or pyramid schemes.[95] That broad allegation would never hold up in a court of law, but it's a powerful narrative advanced by opponents of NFTs and cryptocurrency. The attacks against NFTs often fail to name specific NFT projects or, when they do, point to a few rug pulls by bad actors to insinuate that all NFTs are one giant Ponzi scheme. It's not surprising that accusers don't typically name names of NFT creators engaged in Ponzi schemes, much less offer specific allegations of their wrongdoing. Falsely accusing a business or individual of being engaged in a Ponzi scheme without any basis in fact constitutes defamation and can subject the false accuser to liability for substantial damages. Indeed, one of the largest damages awards for online defamation ($38.3 million) involved false accusations that the CEO of a real estate investment firm was engaged in a Ponzi scheme, scam, or shell game.[96] To the extent any examples are offered, the attacks cherry-pick the bad apples to portray all NFTs as rotten. The attacks ignore all the legitimate

NFT projects that have changed artists' and owners' lives for the better.

Many attacks against NFTs are really attacks against cryptocurrency—and its "tech bro" culture, which some even describe as a "cult." NFTs use the same blockchain technology underlying cryptocurrencies and require cryptocurrency to purchase.[97] The same "scam" attacks made against NFTs have already been made against cryptocurrency.[98] We could spend a whole book debating Bitcoin and cryptocurrency.[99] We don't have the space to do so here. DYOR. Let me offer a couple of points to consider, especially to readers who haven't already formed a view. (Disclaimer: this is not financial advice.)

First, remember the Tao of innovation. Any disruptive technology will spark controversy. Paul Krugman, a Nobel laureate in economics, cagily likened Bitcoin to, what else, a Ponzi scheme.[100] But let's not forget this is the same Paul Krugman who predicted in 1998: "The growth of the Internet will slow drastically. . . . By 2005 or so, it will become clear that the Internet's impact on the economy has been no greater than the fax machine's."[101] Krugman's point was to debunk the idea that technology will lead to dramatic progress.[102] In an interview in 2018, Krugman said he was just being "provocative," but "got it wrong."[103] Ironically, we know that Krugman misunderstood the Internet's vast potential in 1998 because the Internet recorded it. A decade later, Krugman even forgot the source that published his erroneous prediction.[104]

Second, investments by big businesses and successful executives can provide helpful clues to whether something is legitimate or one massive scam. This indicator is not foolproof, of course, as the financial crisis in 2008 when risky investments in mortgage-backed securities toppled Lehman Brothers and Bear Stearns, and required the federal government to bail out the entire industry of big investment firms.[105] But established businesses have their reputations to protect. Knowingly engaging in a massive fraud or Ponzi scheme is illegal. The big banks, investment firms, and payment services allowing crypto-related investments or cryptocurrencies include

Citigroup, JP Morgan Chase, Goldman Sachs, Morgan Stanley, Mastercard, PayPal, Visa, and Venmo. In April 2022, Fidelity announced that it was offering the 23,000 employers that use Fidelity's service for 401(k) retirement accounts the ability to include, for their employees, the option of investing up to 20 percent of an account in Bitcoin.[106]

Even though the Labor Department criticized Fidelity's move as risky, cryptocurrency is one issue that most fund managers will likely have to consider in the near future. As Kevin Roose of *The New York Times* stated: "its power, both economic and cultural, has become too big to overlook."[107] In Q1 2022, $9.2 billion across 461 equity deals poured into crypto startups globally.[108] The crypto winter of 2022 slowed down venture capital investments in Q2, but they were still well above the amount in 2020.[109] During the downturn, the market cap for cryptocurrencies fell to around $1 trillion in September 2022, shedding a staggering $2 trillion from its peak.[110] No doubt cryptocurrencies are highly volatile. But high inflation and the Fed's aggressive efforts to reduce it by raising interest rates rattled the stock market, too, with the average U.S.-stock mutual fund down 17.3 percent for the year.[111]

Tim Cook of Apple said the company wouldn't invest in cryptocurrency "because I don't think people buy Apple stock to get exposure to crypto," but he personally owned cryptocurrency and believed it was a reasonable part of a diversified portfolio (though he wasn't giving financial advice, of course).[112] JP Morgan's CEO, Jamie Dimon, who once said Bitcoin was a fraud, recanted that statement. Without necessarily backing Bitcoin, Dimon said he regretted the comment and acknowledged, "The blockchain is real."[113] In February 2022, JP Morgan issued a white paper, "Opportunities in the Metaverse," that forecast a new market for the metaverse, including NFTs, with a value of more than $1 trillion annually.[114] And JP Morgan recognized that "crypto payments and NFT/digital assets" will play a huge role in commerce.[115]

"We see companies of all shapes and sizes entering the metaverse in different ways, including household names like Walmart, Nike,

Gap, Verizon, Hulu, PWC, Adidas, Atari and others," JP Morgan noted.[116] The list of big businesses developing NFTs or metaverse strategies is extensive and keeps growing.[117] JP Morgan was so bullish on the metaverse that it established the first bank in the virtual world of Decentraland. In a 186-page white paper, Citi estimated that, by 2030, the market related to the metaverse could be valued at $8 trillion to $13 trillion.[118] To put that number into perspective, the global apparel market was $1.5 trillion in 2021, and the automotive market, $2.86 trillion.[119]

Even the Oracle of Omaha, Warren Buffett, the CEO of Berkshire Hathaway and a vocal skeptic of Bitcoin, has included within Berkshire's portfolio a $1 billion investment in Nubank, a fintech bank in Latin America that allows its customers to invest in a Bitcoin exchange-traded fund (ETF).[120] During the same period, Buffett dumped Berkshire's shares of Visa, Mastercard, and Wells Fargo.[121] After once slamming Bitcoin as "probably rat poison squared" with "no unique value at all,"[122] Buffett no longer appears to be reluctant to get at least a taste of it.

In early 2022, President Biden and Treasury Secretary Janet Yellen recognized that cryptocurrency was innovating financial services, and expressed the need for the government to develop policies for "responsible financial innovation" along with safeguards against the financial risks.[123] Yellen acknowledged the importance of studying whether the United States should issue its own central bank digital currency (CBDC). Analysts disagree over whether a U.S. dollar CBDC would ultimately supplement or supplant existing stable coins (i.e., cryptocurrency pegged to another asset), but the government's interest in digital currency indicates some appeal in the concept. The U.S. government's approach was seen as an "acknowledgement that cryptocurrency is here to stay."[124] The crypto winter in 2022 caused some major carnage in the cryptocurrency market.[125] But it's unlikely to signal its demise. Instead, it may lead to greater regulation to protect investors—which is precisely what some believe will lead to mainstream adoption of crypto.[126]

The Russian invasion of Ukraine in 2022 showed how cryptocurrency, which can be transferred instantaneously without the need for a bank or conversion of currency, can be useful. People donated an estimated $100 million worth of Bitcoin and cryptocurrency to Ukraine's government to help the country fight Russia's military.[127] The Ukraine government spent $15 million on bulletproof vests, other military supplies, and medical supplies.[128] The government even sold NFTs to help finance the war against Russia.[129] Artists from Ukraine and countries around the world also sold NFTs to provide financial assistance to Ukraine, including over $1.7 million from thirty-seven NFT artists in the group RELI3F, which provides humanitarian aid to causes around the world.[130]

The Ukraine government's sale of NFTs was reminiscent of the U.S. government's issuance of $450 million worth of paper money or "greenbacks" during the Civil War, a move that sparked great controversy because the paper money was not backed by gold.[131] It was funny money. The greenbacks were the first fiat money used by the United States, meaning they were created by the government without the backing of gold or another commodity.[132] Although greenbacks were retired in 1879, fiat money eventually prevailed as the approach to U.S. currency in 1971, which continues to this day.[133]

Fiat money has its own problems. During the Russian-Ukraine war, the U.S. dollar and other fiat currency around the world experienced great inflation—in the U.S. hitting a forty-year high at 9.1 percent.[134] Inflation makes less valuable an individual savings account with a $5,000 deposit, which, at the average annual percentage of 0.06 percent, yields only 25 cents in interest.[135] Even though Bitcoin and other cryptocurrencies are volatile in price, backers view some cryptocurrency as better stores of value than fiat money, which erodes in value due to inflation. And, when compared with weak currencies in foreign countries, cryptocurrencies seem far more secure. That's why the highest percentages of crypto adoption are in countries with weak currencies: Nigeria 32 percent, Vietnam 21 percent, Philippines 20 percent, Turkey 16 percent, and Peru 16 percent.[136]

The debate over cryptocurrency raises a fundamental difference in philosophy: whether a financial system is better with a central regulator like the Fed, controlling interest rates and the supply of fiat money, or with a decentralized approach in which no one controls the supply of cryptocurrency after it has been set. The two approaches aren't mutually exclusive—the current situation is proof. But, increasingly, businesses and consumers are adopting cryptocurrency around the world.[137] Many big brands and startups are also developing NFTs. Both developments are part of an effort to build a more decentralized Web. Maybe this is one giant, global conspiracy to prey on the young and vulnerable. Or maybe it's an indicator that cryptocurrency and NFTs provide utility to solve needs that were being unmet. You be the judge.

MAKING THE CONCEPTUAL LEAP

Just as Cubism exposed how artistic reality is constructed, so does Tokenism expose how ownership and value are constructed. But that's not a reason for skepticism. We construct ownership and value in most things, including land, luxury goods, stocks, mutual funds, other financial instruments, fiat money, and even diamonds. Contrary to popular belief, diamonds are common gems, whose value is not determined by their rarity compared with other gems.[138]

The token is not a hollow gesture. The token is the prize. NFTs reflect not only a new type of technology, property, and ownership, but also a new type of thinking—a mind-bending one at that. The Larva Labs cofounders Hall and Watkinson, who created CryptoPunks in 2017, admitted the NFT was a crazy idea that required "a conceptual leap" for people to believe they owned something real in buying NFTs. The idea may have been crazy then, but there's no doubt people have taken the leap. And there's no looking back.

Although Picasso, ever the innovator, moved beyond the Cubist style in 1921,[139] Cubism led to a creative diaspora. Indeed, Cubism influenced not just modern art of the twentieth century, but architecture, film, design, and literature. It's too early to tell what To-kenism's influence will be. But the early signs portend something that could be even more far-reaching than Cubism—transforming ownership, art, cultural production, business, governance, the cre-ative industries, intellectual property, the Internet, and beyond.

..

If Gelett Burgess were still living, what would he think of NFTs? Of course, he'd make fun of them. But my guess is that, as an illustrator, he'd understand them. And he'd love creating them and relish in the irreverence shared by many NFT enthusiasts who often go by funny user names such as Pablo Punkasso, Pranksy, and Vincent Van Dough. Burgess wrote and illustrated a children's comic book series, the Goops, to teach kids manners with amus-ing poems. He created a collection of different Goop characters, each with a name and depicted with the same bald head, circular in shape, but each had distinctive traits or arrangements.[140] The Goops could easily be NFTs today.

Indeed, they are. Andrew Friesen, an artist who goes by the handle "Toronto person," created a collection of 8,000 Goopdoods NFTs.[141] The Goopdoods are also bald, but their bodies are adult in stature. Plus, they are far more colorful and cosmic, and set in more outlandish scenes than Burgess's Goops. Some even have differ-ent characters vomiting a colorful stream around the Goopdoods, wrapped in puke like a boa constrictor. Burgess, who admittedly "enjoy[ed] the bizarre, unique, and grotesque,"[142] would have loved them.

CHAPTER 5

INTERACTIVE OWNERSHIP

Keep in mind the following: what you really value in
life is ownership, not money.

—50 CENT, *THE 50TH LAW*

"For a while now, one of the hottest tech trends has been NFTs, or non-fungible tokens," Stephen Colbert explained in a segment on his TV show. "It's hard to believe in just one year, we've gone from having no idea what they are to having no idea *why* they are."[1] Laughter.

Indeed, who needs NFTs?

In his charming but deadpan way, Colbert explained that NFTs were "digital assets that you can buy and your ownership is encoded in a blockchain-encoded proof of purchase." Plus, if you collect enough proofs of purchases, you send them to Kellogg's in exchange for a "cereal bowl shaped like a baseball cap." More laughter.

Not quite. But Colbert was on the right track.

Ownership is the key to NFTs. Ownership is no longer just a title. NFTs entitle the owners to something more. NFT creators decide what that is. It could be cereal bowls, sure. But it's often something more meaningful. That's why today's Creator Economy, teeming with millions of influencers and content creators on TikTok, YouTube, and other platforms,[2] is transforming into the Ownership Economy or a Creator-Ownership Economy, in which economic rewards are distributed more broadly to people through ownership of NFTs.[3] The Ownership Economy is related to the movement to build Web3, discussed below. The latter term focuses on the technological side to make the Internet more decentralized, while the former focuses on the economic side.

The Ownership Economy empowers people to acquire financial stakes in what they consume and create online. It is "an economy built on inter-dependence amongst a decentralized community where users have ownership in the products that they use and are rewarded for the value they create," as Clara Lindh Bergendorff described in *Forbes*.[4] People are no longer treated as "users" of the Internet, subject to ad monetization and the algorithms of Big Tech. Instead, people are treated as co-owners in a community, such as one established by an NFT project that grants owners commercial rights. You can also own an NFT that can be "staked," or committed for use in a virtual world, which entitles you to receive passive income in the form of additional NFTs or cryptocurrency.[5] Plus, you don't surrender your personal data. You own that, too.

Understanding how NFTs have transformed the concept of ownership unlocks the mystery behind NFTs—*why* they are.

In law school, all first-year students learn a fundamental principle of property law: owners have the right to exclude. Exclusion is a defining feature of property. Adults don't even need to go to law school to understand this basic principle. They practice it every day. Homeowners put up fences and NO TRESPASSING signs around their land, and tell trespassers to "get off my property." Car owners lock their doors and have alarms to scare off intruders. People use face ID and passwords to exclude others from accessing their smartphones and laptops. Plus, others aren't supposed to take the clothes off your back—at least not without your consent. If someone violates the property owner's right to exclude, the person is breaking the law. Exclusion is part and parcel of property.

In one famous case, a driver was held liable for trespass on a couple's farmland by driving through their snow-covered field to deliver a mobile home over the couple's "adamant protests."[6] The couple even refused the defendant's offer to pay money for their permission to drive over their land. It was the most direct route, and the only other option was a private road "covered in up to seven feet of snow" with "a sharp curve," which was precarious for the delivery truck.[7] Even though the land suffered no damage, the couple was awarded $100,000 in punitive damages to punish the driver's willful trespass. As property owners, the couple had the right to exclude. The driver violated it. The law punished the driver. As the Supreme Court of Wisconsin explained, "Private landowners should feel confident that wrongdoers who trespass upon their land will be appropriately punished."[8]

The case gives you an idea of how important is the right to exclude. As the U.S. Supreme Court recognized, "The power to exclude has traditionally been considered one of the most treasured strands in an owner's bundle of property rights."[9] Indeed, it may be "the most fundamental of all property interests."[10] As the influential legal commentator Blackstone wrote in the eighteenth century: "There is nothing which so generally strikes the imagination, and engages the affections of mankind, as the right of property; or that sole and despotic dominion which one man claims and exercises over the external things of the world, in total exclusion of the right of any other individual in the universe."[11] Whether Blackstone meant to endorse or only to describe such a strong view of property is debatable,[12] but it greatly influenced property law in the United States.

The right to exclude also plays a central role in intellectual property (IP) for creations of the mind. Inventors and authors are granted the "exclusive right"—a term even mentioned in the U.S. Constitution—to prevent third parties from unauthorized use of items protected by their patents and copyrights. When the World Trade Organization (WTO) passed an international agreement for IP in 1994, the WTO used "exclusive right" to describe trademark owners' rights, too. For every infringement lawsuit, IP owners claim that the defendant has violated at least one of their exclusive rights. For IP, land, or other property, this traditional view of property situates the right to exclude at the center of the bundle of rights held by property owners.

INCLUSION AND INTERACTIVE OWNERSHIP

NFTs upend our understanding of ownership not only by reimagining it for the virtual world as discussed in the prior chapter, but also by making a right to *include* others a more central feature of NFTs than it is for traditional property. NFTs are often used to include people in a community, with ongoing communication, collaboration, events, and rewards for the NFT owners. This utility reflects the fact that NFTs can operate as a decentralized organizing or governance system, by establishing a community and its members based on their ownership of NFTs for the same project.[13] Through these ongoing relationships, NFTs facilitate a new type of *interactive* ownership.

The right to exclude remains important for NFTs, but the right to include has assumed a new level of importance, especially for NFT projects aimed at building communities. NFT projects are granting new rights to include their NFT owners in a variety of ways. The right to include arises from a license or agreement that gives additional benefits to the NFT owners, or, perhaps more often, simply through the road maps, norms, and practices established by the NFT creators. Although these agreements and practices don't recognize a "right to include" by name, I believe the term aptly describes a central feature of many NFT projects. Ownership of NFTs is being used in numerous ways to include people—in a club, community, or DAO; in owner rewards' programs and events; in gaming worlds, immersive experiences, and metaverses; in collaborations, creative production, and business partnerships; and in other dynamic interactions among the community.

Who gets included? Whoever buys and owns the NFT. Ownership is the entitlement to inclusion. Indeed, the right to include may be even more important than the right to exclude because inclusion offers something that the right to exclude does not: utility.

That's why NFTs are. To answer Colbert's question, NFTs are valuable for two important reasons. Not only do they act as digital assets or proofs of purchases in a new type of virtual property, which solves the problem of owning digital art. But NFTs also offer creators and businesses the ability to offer additional utility through rights of inclusion to communities, experiences, entertainment, collaborations, and other interactive activities. Beyond owning the token as property, owners receive utility from being included in activities and experiences organized by the NFT projects. Property ownership becomes interactive. Ultimately, the choice whether to adopt interactive ownership is up to the NFT creator, but it's more common to see interactive ownership used by NFT collections, such as Deadfellaz, than by an NFT for a single visual artwork. Fittingly, NFTs that adopt interactive ownership are commonly referred to as "utility NFTs."[14]

Some lawyers may object that I've mistakenly lumped together property and contract to conjure up a hybrid arrangement for NFTs that isn't really property—the right to include is a fake property right. I haven't conjured up this arrangement, however. NFT creators have. And there's nothing fake about it. Property law has long recognized the use of contracts to create conditions or restrictions on the use of land. In studying property law, every first-year law student learns about equitable servitudes and real covenants. They sound technical—and they are. But, for our purposes, all we need to know is that they are contracts that create conditions on the ownership of land, such as a requirement of the owner to maintain a pond or allow a person to live on the property, or not to build a house or use a mobile home on the land. A key element of both servitudes and covenants is that the conditions "run with the land," binding future owners of the property.[15] The agreements "constitute *property* rights which run with the land," as the Supreme Court of New Mexico explained.[16] Because the agreements bind all future owners of the property, the agreements become a part of owning the property.

NFT ownership operates in a similar fashion. Just as a covenant creates conditions on the ownership of land, NFT licenses, road maps, and practices establish the conditions of NFT ownership. These conditions "run with the NFT," binding future owners. The license typically indicates that the conditions of the license apply to whoever owns the NFT.[17] The arrangement is somewhat analogous to how a homeowner's association membership runs with the land,[18] but HOAs are probably viewed today more as a source of restriction enforcement than as a source of community-building—policing everything from landscaping and pets to smoking and trash. By contrast, for many NFT projects, community-building is what NFTs are all about.

The covenants for NFTs are often less formal than covenants for land, which require a written agreement. For example, NFT projects typically announce "road maps" of their goals, as well as, periodically, the upcoming perks and privileges the NFT owners will get. The road maps might look more like a sketch—in fact, some are just pictures of road maps—so they might not qualify as a written agreement of the kind required for a covenant for land. But I consider project road maps that promise a potpourri of future privileges for NFT owners a covenant of owning the NFTs, similar to a traditional covenant for land. Whoever owns the NFT, including a subsequent buyer in the secondary market, will receive the benefit of the project's implementation of its road map. The future benefits run with the NFT. Granted, some road maps might not constitute legally enforceable contracts, but that aspect becomes a potential issue only if the NFT project fails to deliver on its road map goals.

There is another major difference between covenants to land and NFT content licenses and road maps. Covenants to land often restrict use of the land—e.g., don't park a mobile home on the property. Indeed, for that reason, they are called restrictive covenants. Although NFT content licenses sometimes include restrictions (e.g., no commercial use of the artwork or no uses in hate speech), increasingly they are being used in more expansive ways, along with road maps that are not restrictions at all. Instead, they are rights to commercialize the artwork, including the making of derivative works, as well as rights of inclusion to a broad array of activities and experiences, such as parties, exhibitions, and participation in online gaming and virtual worlds. These NFT agreements are *inclusive* covenants, benefiting a community of co-owners.

NFT covenants are establishing a commons in which owners from the same collection of NFTs can collaborate and cocreate in ventures, including businesses, using the artwork or characters associated with the NFTs. To draw on Elinor Ostrom's influential work, we can characterize a project of 10,000 NFTs as comprising a common pool of artworks (e.g., CryptoPunks) whose uses are governed by individual ownership of each NFT, but, through an inclusive covenant, a shared interest in the commons (e.g., the CryptoPunks ecosystem) established by the entire collection.[19] NFTs provide the governance system for the commons or collection.

By combining virtual tokens with inclusive covenants, NFTs have created a new kind of interactive ownership. Ownership of NFTs entitles the owners to interactions. The interactions can be between people, such as the engagement between NFT creators and the entire community of owners, both online and at meetups in real life. The interactions can also involve interactions between the owners and new types of content, media, experiences, and metaverses.

For example, the creators of Doodles NFTs, known for their joyful pastel colors, hosted an interactive IRL experience for Doodles owners and other invitees at SXSW in 2022. The Doodles installation drew long lines and rave reviews. It was one of the first major installations to show the power of NFTs. The Doodles team collaborated with VTProDesign, whose mission is to "push the limits of the worlds we can create." That's exactly what they did. The enchanting Doodles SXSW installation set a new standard for conferences. Doodles owners received physical passports, which were embedded with RFIDs that enabled the Doodles characters from their NFTs to come to life, virtually, at the installation.[20] Invitees ordered lattes with a Doodles character drawn on the foam. And, as an example of business ventures created by NFTs, Behr partnered with Doodles for a paint display, given Doodles' distinctive use of colors.[21] Entering the Doodles installation was like traveling to a magical world reminiscent of Disney.[22]

Interactive ownership is a big change from traditional ownership. For traditional property, ownership is inert, not interactive. Just think of owning a bike, a coffeemaker, a toaster, or a pair of sneakers. The owner isn't entitled to anything beyond those items. The relationship between the owner and the object is static. By contrast, NFTs are often created with privileges—inclusive covenants—that entitle the NFT owners to additional perks and rights. The relationship between the owner and the object is interactive: it evolves over time and enables the owner to develop the artwork or character as a part of a business or identity. Interactive ownership is one of the main reasons many big businesses are racing to develop NFTs for their products and services. Interactive ownership offers a new way to engage people in a meaningful community.

INTERACTIVE OWNERSHIP IN WEB3

Anyone who remembers the inception of "Web 2.0" in 2004 may be wondering how interactive ownership is any different from what people said about social media, blogs, and other platforms for user-generated content. Web2 was hailed as more interactive, enabling sharing and collaborations online.[23] What's so special about interactive ownership?

The key is understanding the importance of ownership, which enables greater, potentially more meaningful interactions. As shown in Table 5.1 below, the Web's development can be divided into three periods, with each period empowering people to do even more.

From roughly 1989 to 2004, Web1 was a read-only (RO) network, with people as passive viewers of content similar to watching TV.[24] Reading is great, but it involves a one-way transmission of information. Then, from 2004 to the present, Web2 was a read-write (RW) network, with people able to easily create and share user-generated content with friends and followers, such as on Facebook, Twitter, and YouTube. The Web became a two-way street, allowing people not only to receive content, but also to create and share their own content with many others. Social media amplified people's voices by giving them audiences potentially in the millions.

However, there was a dark side to social media. Social media companies became dominant platforms—aka "Big Tech"—with centralized control over millions, if not billions, of users on their platforms. During the pandemic, the companies became embroiled in having to make difficult decisions on removing misinformation of all kinds, but that led to a backlash among some people who decried the "censorship" by the companies. Moreover, people on these platforms are treated as mere "users," who must typically share

TABLE 5.1 COMPARISON OF WEB1, WEB2, AND WEB3

	Web1	Web2	Web3
Functions Enabled	Read Only (RO)	Read Write (RW)	Read Write Own Interact (RWOI)
Major Elements	Birth of Web, e-commerce, static webpages.	Rise of Big Tech platforms, user-generated content, and social media. Content moderation by Big Tech.	Rise of blockchain, NFTs, and interactive ownership.
Centralized v. Decentralized	Decentralized but limited interactivity.	Centralized by Internet platforms and Big Tech.	Decentralized by blockchain technology.
Interactivity	Limited interactivity.	Greater interactivity on platforms and social media.	New interactivity based on NFT ownership. Interactivity along several dimensions, including outside of platforms and in real life.
Privacy	Websites decide.	Internet platforms monetize personal data and decide privacy policy for users.	Self-sovereignty. People control their own identity and data by cryptocurrency wallet and NFTs.

their personal data to participate and who are subjected to powerful algorithms that control what they see. The Internet platforms then monetize people's personal data by selling ads to companies that target users based on their online activities. In 2019, Harvard Business School's Professor Shoshana Zuboff wrote a scathing indictment of this predominant business model, which she aptly described as "surveillance capitalism."[25]

We are now beginning Web3, which features interactive ownership. Web3 is different because it is being built on the decentralized, peer-to-peer technology of blockchain. One goal is to avoid Web2's centralized Internet platforms that can censor people, monetize their personal data, or deplatform them, meaning kick them off Facebook, Twitter, or other social media. Instead of treating people as mere users, Web3 empowers them to become owners, not only of their personal data but also of NFTs, which entitle them to rights of inclusion in communities and experiences.

Web3 is a read-write-own-interact (RWOI) network. Not only can people create and share online, they can also own a stake in and interact in new, creative ecosystems, collaborations, and businesses. To continue the metaphor, in addition to the two-way street of read-write culture from Web2, Web3 now offers people the ability to *own* a part of the land surrounding the street and *interact* with other owners in building a community or even a business. The right to own and interact (OI) comes through buying NFTs—and the owners don't have to give up their personal data. A central tenet of Web3 is self-sovereignty: people are empowered to control their personal data and don't have to disclose it to participate.

TYPES OF INTERACTIVITY THROUGH NFTS

NFTs can be used to include owners in numerous interactions. Table 5.2 summarizes several major examples. This list is not meant to be exhaustive—indeed, we should expect many other innovative uses to develop in the future, especially given that utility-based NFT projects have existed for only a few years. But the list shows the vast potential of using NFTs.

TABLE 5.2. NFT OWNERSHIP FACILITATES INTERACTIONS

NFT Ownership Facilitating Interactions	Description
Content	NFT owners interact with content associated with NFTs, including dynamic content that changes.
Community	NFT owners interact with other owners in the same collection and with NFT creators.
Patrons	NFT owners serve as patrons of NFT creators.
Experiences	NFT owners interact in immersive experiences in metaverses.
Decentralized collaboration	NFT owners collaborate in creative production, including new uses and derivative works of content associated with NFTs owned.
Decentralized business	NFT owners are included in business model to build overall brand.

We'll discuss how NFTs create interactions for owners through content, community, patrons, and experiences in this chapter, focusing on three individual creators. In the next two chapters, we'll consider the last two types: decentralized collaboration and decentralized business.

The simplest example of interactive ownership is a person's interaction with the content of NFTs. When you buy a painting, it's static. Except for the natural deterioration of the materials, the art stays the same. By contrast, NFTs can involve dynamic content that increases, evolves, or morphs over time. NFT projects can airdrop additional content, such as a second generation or derivative version ("V2") of the content in the original NFTs. The NFT owners get, in effect, a bonus NFT. And the generations don't have to end with V2. There can be an unlimited number of generations, akin to a family of NFTs. If the NFT collection is popular, owning more than one generation of NFTs can be quite lucrative.

Take the Bored Ape Yacht Club (BAYC), which involves apes

that look, well, bored. The owners received free "serum" from BAYC for their apes to drink, which created Mutant Apes that still look bored but more bizarre. Very bizarre! BAYC used three different kinds of serum, which progressively increased the bizarreness: 7,500 M1, 2,492 M2, and only 8 M3 or Mega Mutant.[26] Taylor Gerring, the cofounder of Ethereum, paid $3.5 million for a mega-mutant serum that transformed his original Bored Ape into Mega Mutant Ape #30004, which resembled a dystopian Cyclops. The mutation was even live-streamed to more than 10,000 people on Twitch.[27]

BAYC owners also received a free digital dog from the Bored Ape Kennel Club to keep their Apes company. And, if that wasn't enough, BAYC air-dropped the owners a new cryptocurrency called ApeCoin, which was administered by ApeCoin DAO, run by BAYC owners. A person who was a part of the launch of the BAYC in April 2021 and minted just one NFT for around $200 would have received a Bored Ape, a Mutant Ape, a Kennel Club dog, and ApeCoin, with a total value of more than $800,000 in April 2022—and even greater value for the rarer Bored Apes.[28] Just by buying a cartoon ape NFT for $200, a person could have become a millionaire within a year. An appreciation of mind-boggling proportions. A collector who goes by the name Dingaling—great name—had more than three hundred NFTs from BAYC (including Mutant Apes and Bored Ape Kennel Club dogs), which, when coupled with the free ApeCoin, was worth at least tens of millions of dollars in March 2022.[29] The value of ApeCoin dropped during the crypto winter later that year, but the floor price (in ETH) for Bored Apes remained steady (near 80 ETH at the end of September 2022, though ETH values had dropped compared to the dollar).[30]

"Mating" is another cool, interactive feature of NFTs. The idea dates back to 2017 and one of the first popular NFT collections, the CryptoKitties. If you bought a CryptoKitty, you could mate it with another CryptoKitty to produce a new CryptoKitty, which combined the traits of the parents. Sounds fun, right? Within a month since launching, the CryptoKitties had $20 million in sales among 180,000 owners.[31] However, the popularity of the CryptoKitties faded almost as quickly. Analysts hypothesized that the CryptoKitties were victims of their own success: CryptoKitties overproduced from mating, causing an oversupply of Kitties and depreciation of value.[32] Too many Kitties.

The fate of the CryptoKitties serves as an important lesson: producing more NFTs for a collection might seem like a benefit to owners, but it's risky because it can dilute or devalue the original collection. Some collections may have made the same CryptoKitties mistake by allowing a second generation of NFTs to dilute the first.[33]

If CryptoKitties sounds like child's play, remember Nike plans something similar for its sneakers called CryptoKicks. Nike patented the method of "breeding" CryptoKicks.[34] As with mating CryptoKitties, owners can mate Nike CryptoKicks to produce digital "shoe offspring," meaning a second-generation digital shoe with a new design based on the parent sneakers.[35] And here's the kicker: the offspring shoe design could entitle the NFT owners to physical sneakers with the same design.[36]

With dynamic content, artists are reimagining what's possible. An even more mind-bending example of dynamic content is "The Merge" by the elusive artist Pak. The collection of 250,000 NFTs sold for $91.8 million, making it the highest NFT sale.[37] The dynamic NFTs are programmed to merge the so-called mass when in the same wallet. The images appear bigger, with more mass. Another unusual feature is that the NFT images are stored in the smart contract on blockchain, which "allows future visual customizations, with 100 secret classes distributed evenly among all tokens."[38] If the Merge sounds mysterious, it is.

If that doesn't blow your mind, just wait. Programmers are already developing NFTs that include artificial intelligence (AI)—called "intelligent NFT" or iNFT. The iNFT goes one step beyond NFT collections whose artworks were randomly generated by computer programs or AI. For iNFTs, even after creation of the artwork or content for an NFT, the AI is intelligent, with interactive and learning capabilities. The London-based artist Robert Alice and the Open AI company Alethea AI teamed up to create the first set of thirteen iNFTs. Sotheby's sold the collection for nearly half a million dollars in 2021.[39] The iNFT shows the AI in the form of a human avatar named Alice, who is able to interact, respond to your questions, and learn. Talk about wonderland.

Another important way NFTs can produce interactive ownership is by including NFT owners in a community. Indeed, many Web3 proponents strongly believe that building communities is what NFTs are all about. "To succeed," Larry Dvoskin, a strategic projects chief at NFT Oasis, wrote in an article for *Rolling Stone*, "is to become part of an interwoven community."[40]

This practice developed organically, starting out small, but it has become an important feature of NFT collections. CryptoPunks, one of the earliest NFT collections, created a community by offering 9,000 NFTs for free in 2017. The lucky individuals who scooped them up became members of the CryptoPunks or Punks community, which held discussions on the official Discord Chat organized by Larva Labs, the creator of the NFTs. The owners also started using the pixelated CryptoPunks characters as their pfp on Twitter and other social media, further engaging their community in daily discussions. Anyone can join the CryptoPunks Discord, but only owners can comment. The NFT owners enjoy the full benefits of being CryptoPunks owners, especially the incredible return on investment. In September 2022, the floor price for a CryptoPunk was around $82,000, while the most expensive sale so far was $23.7 million for CryptoPunk #5822, one of only nine alien punks.

The CryptoPunks community has turned into one of the most exclusive clubs in the world—OGs of the NFT world, meaning the originators (aka "original gangsters"). As some Punks owners told *Tech Crunch*, owning a CryptoPunk is a "digital flex."[41] It's like wearing a Rolex, only instead of a luxury watch, the owner dons a cartoon character.

Larva Labs set the playbook for establishing a community for NFT owners: creating 10,000 NFTs plus discussion groups on Discord and Twitter spaces. On Twitter, CryptoPunks owners are often known only by their NFT. For example, Punk 6529, one of the more visible and influential owners, is building an Open Metaverse (OM), which will consist of ten virtual cities with a maximum population of 10 million people. Genesis City includes a museum district, which, in just the alpha phase, showcased artworks from two thousand of the most valuable NFTs.[42] 6529 has even become the name of the project, whose "mission is to accelerate the development of an open metaverse."[43] NFTs are considered essential to the OM's foundation because they are open and interoperable, instead of being assets controlled by Internet platforms.[44] 6529 is just one example of how being a CryptoPunk owner has turned it into a stepping stone for bold plans to build the metaverse.

Many credit Larva Labs for starting the NFT craze. But Larva Labs' playbook didn't have many plays. Although Larva Labs signed with United Talent Agency for exploration of possible movie, TV, and game deals involving the CryptoPunks characters, no Hollywood deals were announced before Larva Labs struck a deal of a much different kind. In a shocking move announced in March 2022, Larva Labs sold the IP rights to CryptoPunks, along with its other collection, Meebits, in 2022 to Yuga Labs, creator of the popular Bored Ape NFTs and, at the time, Larva Labs' closest competitor. The move was akin to Microsoft selling its rights to Windows to Apple.

While Larva Labs was a pioneer in the development of NFT collections, Larva left it to Yuga Labs and other NFT creators to develop greater utility for NFTs beyond being collectibles or profile pics. Yuga Labs lured away Noah Davis from Christie's (who had helped set up Beeple's *Everydays* auction) to oversee the CryptoPunks collection. But don't expect ambitious road maps for the CryptoPunks. They've cemented their place as a blue-chip collection, and perhaps the most prestigious one—the Mona Lisa of NFTs.

Luckily, there was no shortage of talented people to take on that task—to produce NFTs to build new collaborations, businesses, and worlds. We will study next three examples of interactive ownership—showing how NFTs can foster interactive art, community, collaboration, patronage, and the metaverse.

THE FLOWER GIRLS: INTERACTIVE ART AND COMMUNITY

Varvara Alay is a visual artist in Tbilisi, Georgia, where she lives with her son, Larick, and their dog, Murzik.[45] Alay describes her style as creating "highly detailed and endlessly fascinating worlds that blend fantasy and realism in an intricate web of elaborate characters and majestic patterns."[46] In August 2021, she created a few NFTs for her Flower Girls, female characters she had been drawing for more than fifteen years. But the Flower Girls NFTs received no sales.[47]

Based on a friend's encouragement, Alay decided to persevere and launch an entire collection of 10,000 Flower Girls. Alay worked around the clock with the help of her son and assistants, not to mention the patience of her dog. Alay created a beautiful collection of 10,000 unique Flower Girls, each with ornate flowers on their heads, along with a bird or butterfly encircling, in a style that looks far more classical than most NFT collections. The project is on a metaphorical journey to Venus, which the project calls the ancestral "planet of all Women."[48]

This time, the Flower Girls sold out in thirty minutes—all 10,000. Alay credited the boost to her sales to the entrepreneur Gary Vaynerchuk (aka Gary Vee) and his brother AJ Vaynerchuk, who bought twenty-one of her other artwork NFTs right before the launch of the Flower Girls. Gary Vee, who creates and sells his VeeFriends NFTs, is an OG in the NFT world. The brothers stopped by the Discord chat for Flower Girls, which attracted others to the Flower Girls online group.[49] On Twitter, after the Midas touch from Gary Vee and AJ, Alay admitted she was on an "emotional rollercoaster," alluding to how she has to support her "family

on an art teacher's salary."[50] Alay thanked the Vaynerchuks, calling them her guardian angels. Reese Witherspoon, Eva Longoria,
Gwyneth Paltrow, and Brie Larson also purchased Flower Girls, in
their support for women-led NFT projects.

From there, Alay's NFT project blossomed. The Flower Girls
art itself is interactive. In the first few months after launch, the
project sent the NFT owners twenty special-edition NFTs with
additional artwork on Christmas, Valentine's Day, International
Women's Day, and other occasions.[51] To celebrate Spring 2022, the
project air-dropped "seeds" to NFT owners that germinated, so to
speak, in a seed purse given to each owner.[52] The seeds were created
through interactions—called "cross-pollination"—by Flower Girls
owners with a Flower Girls NFT: "Each day, your flower girls are
visited by other flower girls' companions," which causes the NFTs
to interact "and develop seeds which are automatically collected in a
Seed Purse."[53] Each seed sprouts into a unique artwork created by
Alay. The new seeds can be used in three ways: to hold as artworks,
to trade as NFTs, or to exchange for items in a Seed Store for the
Flower Girls.[54]

The Flower Girls project has a deep sense of community. Its road
map of future initiatives was developed with close input from NFT
owners on Discord. Some Flower Girls owners are "botanists" and
founding members of the Flower Girls community. The project has
interacted with Flower Girls owners in numerous activities, including giveaways, art contests, and discussions on Discord. Some of
the most active members in the Discord community were rewarded
with special-edition NFTs.

Being a part of the Flower Girls community involves not only
being a patron of Alay's beautiful art, but also supporting children.
Indeed, one of the most important missions of the Flowers Girls is
its charitable work. The project donates 20 percent of sales profits to
children's charities.[55] In less than five months, the project donated
more than half a million dollars to children's charities, including
St. Jude's Children's Research Hospital, Feed the Children, Save
the Children's Ukraine Crisis Fund, and the Malala Fund.[56] An-

other 5 percent of the profits (more than $75,000) went to the project's own Children's Art Fund, which supports child artists whose works are displayed and sold as NFTs.[57] Alay planned a special-edition artwork for the children of winners of the several giveaways the project held for NFT owners.

Flower Girls has announced ambitious plans to develop "television series, books, games, music, events, and merchandise" in partnership with Dolphin Entertainment, an independent marketing agency.[58] Eventually, the project plans on developing a flower garden maze in the metaverse. If Flower Girls' future road map succeeds, the interactive ownership will entail new experiences for the owners in both the traditional world of entertainment and the metaverse. The Flower Girls collection provides an excellent example of the utility of NFTs—how they can be used for interactive art, community, engagement, and charitable support for children.

The Chicago Bulls selected Alay as one of twenty-three artists to contribute to a Bulls NFT collection. Part of the proceeds will go to After School Matters, a nonprofit that provides programs for high school students in Chicago. Alay reimagined the Chicago Bulls logo in the Flower Girls style with colorful birds, butterflies, and flowers surrounding a red bull crowned with a chrysanthemum, the city's official flower, and standing in a magical garden, reflecting Chicago's motto, "city in a Garden."[59]

"NFTs have allowed me to expand my art practice and integrate blockchain technology," Alay explained in an interview with *Creative Bloq*. "[T]hrough my art, I can interact with my audience in different ways—I can build a story that is ever-changing, interactive and immersive."[60] Interactive ownership of NFTs invites creators to think bold.

3LAU: FOSTERING PATRONS FOR ARTISTS

Justin Blau studied finance in college, but dropped out in his senior year before getting his degree. Growing up, Blau, whose dad was a hedge fund manager, dreamed of getting a lucrative Wall Street job.[61] But Blau's decision to drop out wasn't hasty. He was a popular electronic music DJ and producer during college, who was making enough money at gigs and showed enough talent that one of his economics professors even called his parents to support Blau's decision.[62] Blau turned down a coveted internship at BlackRock, the investment company. This decision turned out to be the right one. Blau, or 3LAU as he's known (but still pronounced "Blau"), became successful in the electronic music world, playing at Lollapalooza, Electric Zoo, and EDC Vegas, and producing his music for his own independent label, Blume Records. Only a few years after his dropping out of college, Forbes estimated that 3LAU had grossed more than $2 million.[63]

As successful as 3LAU is as a musician, he's become even more successful as an entrepreneur. Indeed, he is pioneering a major transformation in the business of selling music. It's still early, but the transformation could prove to be even bigger than streaming. Getting a college degree in economics wasn't needed. Instead, NFTs were.

3LAU was first introduced to cryptocurrency in 2014 by, of all people, Cameron and Tyler Winklevoss. The twins were, of course, famous for suing Mark Zuckerberg for allegedly stealing their social network idea while students at Harvard. In what may be the greatest second act in history, the Winklevoss twins took some of their $65 million settlement—Facebook money—from the lawsuit and invested it in Bitcoin back when few people even knew what it was.[64] The Winklevosses became billionaires based on their early Bitcoin investment and started Winklevoss Capital, to invest in crypto-related businesses, and the cryptocurrency exchange Gemini. While in LA for the Grammy Awards in 2015, 3LAU stayed with the Winklevosses. Naturally, they discussed Bitcoin.

3LAU later told *Forbes*, "I was immediately fascinated by it."[65] He soon began studying cryptocurrency, which led him to NFTs.

In 2017, 3LAU experimented with NFTs and explored ways to use NFTs as tickets to concerts or as digital assets the audience could receive.[66] But it wasn't until the pandemic when 3LAU had an epiphany after seeing Beeple sell his first NFT: like visual art, music can be sold as NFTs.

On his own website, he sold thirty-three limited-edition NFTs for his *Ultraviolet* album, which already had more than 1 billion streams since being released three years earlier. 3LAU divided the privileges that came with the NFTs into three tiers based on the amount of their bids. In the lowest, silver tier, twenty-seven bidders received NFTs for three songs from the album, plus a bonus vinyl copy of the album. In the gold tier, five bidders received even more privileges: the right to a custom mix from 3LAU with "creative direction from the winners," a bonus vinyl album, access to 3LAU's unreleased music, and NFTs for seven songs. The top bidder in the platinum tier received the same privileges as the gold tier's, plus NFTs for all eleven songs from the album and the right to collaborate with 3LAU in creating a custom song, which itself would be sold as an NFT.[67]

3LAU's NFTs use interactive ownership for patronage and collaboration. The NFT owners get different rights of inclusion, depending on the tier. They get to interact with 3LAU and his music, to be his patrons, and, for the gold and platinum levels, to collaborate with him in creating mixes and new music. 3LAU's sale was a huge success, earning $11.7 million. At the time, it was the highest sale for NFTs.[68] Even 3LAU was stunned.

Then 3LAU took it to the next level. In August 2021, he secured $16 million in seed funding to launch Royal, a platform "building tools to connect artists and fans all around the world like never before."[69] Musicians can sell NFTs that entitle the buyers to own a share of the copyright royalties from streaming of the musicians' songs, along with other perks. This kind of interactive ownership enables fans to become direct investors in—or patrons of—musicians and receive a cut of the streaming royalties. Fans are included in the business of their favorite musicians. In November, Royal secured another $55 million, with investments by the heavyweights Andreessen Horowitz, Coinbase Ventures, Founders

Fund, Creative Artists Agency, and Paradigm, as well as several musicians.[70] In July 2022, Royal paid its first share of streaming royalties, $36,000 in total, to people who owned NFTs for the songs "Ultra Black" and "Rare" by Nas, "He's Not You" by Vérité, and "Worst Case" by 3LAU.[71] In an interview with *Hypemoon*, 3LAU said he was working full-time on the Royal platform and scaling back his own music to make Royal a success.[72]

It takes no genius to see how music NFTs have the potential to revolutionize the entire music industry, which is dominated by three major record companies (Universal Music Group, Sony Music Group, and Warner Music Group) and three major publishers (Sony Music Publishing, Universal Music Publishing, and Warner Chappell). NFTs offer musicians an alternative financing model that could prove to be fairer than the approach in the music industry today.

For most musicians, it's difficult to make a living. Spotify's distribution of royalties is estimated to be approximately "$4,000 per million streams, or less than a half a cent per stream."[73] For musicians signed to a major label, that distribution gets divided further. According to *Billboard*, for every $1 in streaming royalties, a major music label typically receives 64 cents, while the performer gets only 16 cents (plus 9.4 cents each to the songwriter and the publisher).[74] One doesn't need an accountant to figure out that musicians can't live on today's streaming royalties.[75] For example, Kevin Kadish, who cowrote one of Meghan Trainor's hits, said he received only $5,679 for 178 million streams of the song.[76] Daniel Allan, whose songs had millions of streams, earned only a few hundred dollars a month, which forced him to take on additional jobs working on other people's music.[77] Musicians are in "a business of pennies (and fractions of pennies)," as *The New York Times* put it.[78] Meanwhile, revenues for Sony Music, Universal Music Group, and Warner Music Group were all booming.[79]

The pandemic made things worse because concerts were canceled, temporarily eliminating an important income stream for musicians. Most musicians face daunting challenges. According to one survey in 2020, roughly 80 percent of musicians made only 40 percent or less of their income from work related to music, while 67 percent didn't even make 20 percent of their income from music.[80] The report concluded: "The vast majority of musicians cannot earn a living wage through music-related work."

Royal disrupts the music industry by offering an NFT platform that can eliminate the 64 cents on every dollar of streaming royalties that would go to the music label and give it back to musicians. Musicians are funded directly by fans who own the musicians' NFTs and share a portion of the royalties. Using this new business model, is it possible for musicians to cut out the "middlemen" and thrive as independent artists?

It's too early to tell, but the possibility is real. That's why Universal, Sony, and Warner have all partnered with music NFT platforms, such as OneOf and MakersPlace, or plan on launching their own music NFT platform. The competition is fierce. 3LAU showed how selling music NFTs can generate millions of dollars in revenue—without any percentage going to a label. His platform, Royal, is designed to make that possible for other musicians. And other music NFT platforms, including OneOf, OurSong, and Opulous, are doing the same.

To many musicians, anything would be an improvement over the current situation. The plight that most musicians face is well documented. Signing with a major label typically requires new artists to transfer the copyright to their sound recordings, or "masters," to the label—what some call a devil's bargain.[81] Even Taylor Swift had to do so. She wrote a Tumblr post about her ordeal with a message to young artists: "You deserve to own the art you make."[82] Swift's advice encapsulates what we might call the Creators' Credo: creators deserve to own the art they make.

Enter NFTs. Although NFTs are not necessarily a panacea, they do offer an alternative. Musicians don't have to sign away their copyrights to major labels. They don't have to give 64 percent of the streaming royalties to the labels, either. Instead, they can own the music they make, and keep a higher percentage of streaming royalties while tapping into a new source of income by selling NFTs and turning their fans into patrons.

Steve Aoki, a top DJ and early adopter of NFTs, said he made more money ($888,888.88) from selling one NFT than he earned in ten years from advances for his six albums.[83] Aoki launched his own AOK1VERSE to use NFTs to foster a community of fans. AOK1VERSE offers AOK1 Passport NFTs, which enable the owners to receive access to live performances and to a private Discord chat with Aoki.[84] Participation in AOK1VERSE entitles the owner to additional perks—another example of interactive ownership.

"What is the future of what community looks like? Definitely in the metaverse. It's definitely in Web3, and definitely in NFTs," Aoki explained to *Decrypt*.[85]

Like the music industry, the movie industry is facing a similar disruption caused by NFTs. Independent filmmakers, including Miguel Faus, Mark O'Connor, and Julie Pacino, are using NFTs to finance their movies. The Anthony Hopkins movie *Zero Contact*, directed by Rick Dugdale, was first released as NFTs for viewing on the platform Vuele.[86] (Hopkins, who is a visual artist as well, has become a serious NFT collector who engages with others on NFT Twitter.) The new financing model for films through NFTs has the attractiveness of allowing a filmmaker to own the intellectual property to the film. As Faus explained to *Cointelegraph*: "Filmmakers can decide together with their community how the power of owning the IP, and the ownership of the film, is going to be used both financially and strategically."[87] This new approach may not replace the big-budget Hollywood blockbuster and franchises, but it may lead to a greater diversity of independent films and perhaps the next *Pulp Fiction*.

Historically, art patrons were rulers, or the powerful and wealthy of society. During the Italian Renaissance, Cosimo de' Medici and his grandson Lorenzo de' Medici, from the powerful banking family, two of the most famous art patrons, sponsored Donatello, Fra Angelico, Botticelli, Michelangelo, and Leonardo.[88] Some of this same dynamic of wealthy patrons occurs with high-priced NFTs.

Vignesh Sundaresan and Anand Venkateswaran, who made fortunes in Bitcoin, purchased Beeple's *Everydays* for $69.3 million.[89] But one doesn't need to be a billionaire to be the patron of an artist. The crowd-sourcing sites Patreon and Go Fund Me have already proved that. NFTs offer a different model of patronage, one in which ownership of NFTs provides artists with new sources of funding. Chris Berg, the codirector of the Royal Melbourne Institute of Technology's Blockchain Innovation Hub, contends that NFTs offer a more inclusive approach to patronage: "Rather than relying on a small community of the rich in, say, Venice, digital artists can immediately reach a global supply of patrons."[90]

SNOOP DOGG: BUILDING THE SNOOPVERSE

On their show *2021 and Done*, Snoop Dogg explained to Kevin Hart the metaverse. "So the metaverse is like, it's real, but it ain't real. But then again, it is real, okay?"

With a puzzled face, Hart nodded. "Yeah."

"And it's a place where you live with avatars," Snoop continued. "You got all kinds of things going down. Like, whatever I do in my real life is happening in this world. And then we're selling property, we're selling avatars, we're selling space, and we're selling all of the above with the NFTs in that world to create a whole, another metaverse outside the universe."

The camera panned to Hart, who looked absolutely bewildered.

"And I know you don't understand nothing about what I'm saying, but just listen to me."[91]

No celebrity has embraced NFTs as early and as much as Snoop Dogg. He's an avid collector of blue-chip NFTs. He caused a stir when he tweeted that he was the pseudonymous NFT collector "Cozomo de' Medici" on Twitter, a nod to the wealthy patron in Florence during the Renaissance.[92] The person on Twitter who goes by the handle Cozomo de' Medici owned NFTs valued at $17 million in September 2021. Later, Cozomo launched an entire family of other

Twitter accounts for the Medici family, including one for the singer Sia, who revealed herself as the person behind Bianca Medici.[93] Cordell Broadus, Snoop Dogg's son, assumed the pseudonym Champ Medici.[94] As with a lot of tweets, people weren't quite sure if Snoop's tweet about being Cozomo was tongue-in-cheek. One plausible theory is that Snoop may have a connection to the Twitter account for Cozomo de' Medici, but it's really run by an "asset manager for celebs."[95] That strikes me as more likely. Regardless, there's no doubt about Snoop Dogg's influence in the NFT community.

In 2022, Snoop Dogg acquired Death Row Records, the first label he signed with to produce his debut album, *Doggystyle*, in 1993. "Death Row will be an NFT label," Snoop announced on Clubhouse. "Just like we broke the industry when we was the first independent to be major, we want to be the first major in the metaverse."[96]

In 2022, Snoop Dogg unleashed a tsunami of music NFTs. He released a new album, *B.O.D.R.*, as 25,000 NFTs, which in the first week had $44.3 million in sales on the Gala Music platform. An NFT "box" was sold for $5,000 for each of seventeen songs. Anyone who bought NFTs for all seventeen songs ($85,000) would "receive massive real-life and digital rewards, including an exclusive concert + pre-party with Snoop, limited edition Death Row bling, and more."[97] Snoop sold a collection of "Dogg on it" NFTs with him singing a capella. As a part of the sale, buyers received ownership of rights to the music, including the right to remix it.[98] Snoop also collaborated with his fellow rapper and Bored Ape owner Wiz Khalifa to create an eight-track mixtape NFT, which revolved around the Bored Ape Yacht Club and its release of ApeCoin.[99]

By the looks of it, Snoop aspires to be as powerful and as influential a patron of the arts as Cosimo de' Medici was during the Renaissance. Only this time, it's the Virtual Renaissance. Snoop is building his own metaverse called the Snoopverse in the Sandbox, a blockchain-based metaverse that allows people to buy plots of virtual land and develop it for people to engage in entertainment, gaming, and more.[100] To buy land in the Sandbox, one buys NFTs. Three plots of virtual land next to the Snoopverse sold for

$450,000, $410,000, and $338,000.[101] Pricey, but who wouldn't want to be Snoop's neighbor?

Snoop sold a collection of 10,000 Doggies NFTs, digital avatars of, well, himself, garbed in different threads, with the ability to do hip-hop dance moves. The Doggies use voxel graphics, or a 3D rendering of a pixel that resembles a cube, and can be used as playable avatars in the Sandbox.[102] To join Snoop's community, one could buy a pass entitling the owner to early access to the Snoopverse, exclusive NFT drops, "whitelist" privileges to Doggie NFTs, an invitation to the grand opening of the Cozomo Art gallery, and even the chance to provide input in the development of Snoopverse.[103]

Snoop Dogg's flurry of NFT projects runs the risk of oversaturating the market for his NFTs, potentially depressing their price. As a successful musician, celebrity, and entrepreneur, Snoop stands in a much different position from most NFT creators, however. And that's a good thing. He can focus on developing NFTs, taking more chances, and building the metaverse.

On April 1, 2022, Snoop released the music video for "House I Built." It received more than 2 million views in just twelve hours,[104] and was touted in *Billboard* as the first music video shot in the Sandbox metaverse.[105] The video shows Snoop's avatar entertaining, rapping, dancing, and, of course, smoking weed among friends in his palatial mansion in the Snoopverse. Part promo, part autobiography, "House I Built" is a synopsis of Snoop's career. Ownership of his music turns out to be a big deal in the song. Snoop raps about retrieving the rights to his masters for his bestselling album, *Doggystyle*.[106]

Snoop Dogg has earned wide respect among NFT enthusiasts, despite their skepticism of most celebrity projects. Snoop was an early adopter of NFTs. Plus, his flurry of creative activity—from avatars to music collaborations to virtual real estate—has established his street cred in the NFT world. As one comment to his "House I Built" video put it: "Only Snoop could transition into this new generation so perfectly."[107] And we haven't even discussed his development of a new identity and business around his Bored Ape, which he named Dr. Bombay, a topic covered in the next chapter. Snoop Dogg has shown how creators can use NFTs to promote their own brand, collaborate with others, and build their own virtual space in the emerging metaverse.

The metaverse is just being built, but we've seen a glimpse of what it offers: a more immersive experience online. Instead of scrolling through a social media feed, you can walk through a virtual art gallery or enjoy a music concert, stand-up comedy act, or a dance-off with a Doggies avatar. You can attend a cultural event simply through an app on your phone. For example, using the app called some·place, Reese Witherspoon set up a virtual gallery of her artworks from NFTs she acquired, including from the women-led projects World of Women, Flower Girls, Boss Beauties, and Deadfellaz.[108] Witherspoon's avatar walks through the art gallery with her cute dog and then heads to a virtual building marked BOOK CLUB—it's easy to envision Witherspoon holding her popular book club there for people to attend. And the metaverse isn't just for stars. Everyone will be able to set up a virtual space—and invite friends and family to a social gathering or reunion.

It's still early, though, with businesses racing to develop their visions of the metaverse. McKinsey estimated that businesses had already invested more than $120 billion in this area in the first five months of 2022, and projected that the metaverse may add $5 trillion to the economy by 2030, transforming many different sectors.[109] Today, we're so used to large Internet platforms for social media, it's easy to think the metaverse will simply be a distinct virtual world offered by Decentraland, the Sandbox, or other platforms. But that's a mistake. Think of these virtual worlds as just part of something much bigger: a more immersive virtual experience through your smartphone, AR/VR headset or glasses, or other screen. We have clues that this broader view of the metaverse is where we're headed, if we're not already here. Meta said it isn't building a "Meta-run metaverse" (notwithstanding its Horizon Worlds), but instead it's building tools and applications (e.g., Oculus VR headset) for a "universal, virtual layer that everyone can experience."[110] Meta already makes the Oculus Quest 2 VR headset. Microsoft, the HoloLens 2. Apple, Google, Qualcomm, and Samsung are all reportedly developing AR headsets. These clues suggest that the metaverse will be a major upgrade of what already exists today. The average person views digital screens nearly seven hours each day.[111] The metaverse will make people's viewing more advanced and immersive, more three-dimensional and interactive. Virtual experiences will become more impressive, realistic, and seamlessly woven into daily life—just as the smartphone is today.

The term "metaverse" isn't crucial to understanding how creativity is conveyed through screens, inviting people to partake of entertainment, information, and the fruits of human imagination. From movies to television shows to the multimedia of the Internet (now viewed on smartphones, tablets, and computers), people experience new worlds imagined by creatives. The metaverse is next in this progression. Virtual experiences that became so common during the pandemic will become even more immersive—and seamlessly interwoven into daily life. This shift will be seismic and more profound than the shift from silent to sound, black-and-white to color, and analog to digital.

The metaverse may not sound exciting to everyone. That's okay. Social media isn't for everyone, either. Only a few years ago, most people probably had never participated in a Zoom meeting. In a few years, we're likely to see more immersive experiences for online gatherings, including for classes, work, business, and recreation.

During the pandemic, Seoul, South Korea, did so for elementary and middle school students. The classes in the metaverse included Gather Town, a virtual science exhibition where students could walk around examining the projects.[112] Seoul's metaverse included music classes, AI-based art classes, and astronomy. Seoul is so bullish on building the metaverse, it has committed $186.7 million to "create a world-class metaverse ecosystem," according to Park Yungyu, head of the Ministry of Communication and Policy.[113] Seoul aims to create 1.5 million jobs and to produce 40,000 professionals related to the metaverse.[114] NFTs have exploded in popularity in South Korea, a country often seen as a global tech innovator. The big tech companies Samsung and LG are developing smart TVs optimized for NFTs.[115] Korean retailers, including CJ Olive Networks, Lotte Home Shopping, and SSG.com, are incorporating NFTs into their businesses.[116]

"Koreans are more open and understanding when it comes to NFTs, which is another form of digital asset," Doo Wan Nam, cofounder of the crypto investment firm Stablenode, explained to *Cointelegraph*.[117] BTS, the worldwide K-pop sensation, planned on selling NFTs despite some backlash from fans who raised environmental concerns about the energy used to produce them. BTS plans on using less energy-intensive NFTs; whether that will placate the fans remains to be seen.[118] Why would BTS risk alienating its millions of fans around the world? Like 3LAU, Snoop Dogg, and other musicians, BTS sees the vast potential of interactive ownership—and providing "fans with more varied experiences and opportunities to express themselves," according to John Kim, BTS's agency's project lead.[119]

Interactive ownership is about to transform the Web. It offers the potential for far more meaningful experiences than scrolling through social media, "fed" to you by powerful algorithms that monetize your online habits with targeted ads. Instead of being fed content by Big Tech platforms, you are empowered to interact with people and content online and IRL. You choose. You can be dazzled by interactive content, be a part of vibrant communities and immersive experiences, be patrons to independent artists and charitable causes, and even be part of a decentralized business, a topic we'll turn to next. NFTs are the entrée to a new world of possibilities. And, best of all, you can own a stake in it.

CHAPTER 6

DE-IP

My life didn't please me, so I created my life.

—COCO CHANEL

In 2021 Justin Aversano was a twenty-eight-year-old photographer based in NYC. To honor his fraternal twin sister who died in his mother's womb due to a miscarriage, and his mother, who years later passed away from ovarian cancer, Aversano embarked on an emotional journey of photographing one hundred sets of twins at locations of their choice, in cities around the United States and in other parts of the world.[1] Aversano called the series Twin Flames.

The series of portraits took a year to shoot, starting in May 2017, with three film cameras of different formats: Polaroid, 120 mm, and 4 x 5. The photographs were vivid and emotionally compelling. The different sets of twins—some fraternal, others identical—and the different moods and locations provided a captivating, intimate glimpse into the lives of twins. The photographer's own personal loss heightens the emotion in viewing the portraits. Knowing Aversano's personal tragedy, one can feel the deep connection not only between the twins in each portrait, but also between Aversano and his subjects—a bond that perhaps only twins can fully understand.

Although Aversano showed the Twin Flames series as printed photographs at an exhibition in NYC in 2019, on the second anniversary of starting the project, financial success didn't come his way. In fact, he took on a debt of $100,000 to finance the project himself. Aversano inquired with museums, but wasn't able to find a home for his collection. He believed in the project, but he told me he experienced "highs and lows" during the process. "I couldn't find any support," he candidly revealed. "So I was in a down dump of 'did I mess up?'" But he took the risk. "It was something in me that needed to be done. To heal. And also to create."

In early 2021, Aversano saw that an NFT collector who goes by the handle "gmoney" had just purchased one of the CryptoPunks NFTs for six figures.[2] Aversano messaged gmoney on Instagram with what Aversano thought was a better offer.

"Hey man, if you bought the CryptoPunk for that, would you want to buy 100 [physical] pictures for $100,000? You just spent more on a JPEG," Aversano, speaking to CNBC, later recounted his message, echoing the common knock on NFTs that they are just JPEGs.[3] Perhaps at the time, Aversano's idea wasn't naïve. But by the summer, it would be. Some CryptoPunks would sell for more than a million dollars. In June 2021, the so-called Covid Alien even sold for $11.7 million.[4]

Instead of taking up Aversano on his offer, gmoney counteroffered: keep the printed photographs and instead sell NFTs of the Twin Flames photographs. That free advice turned out to be life-changing for Aversano.

On Valentine's Day 2021, Aversano became one of the first photographers in the NFT market. Gmoney bought a few of the Twin Flames NFTs. Others did, too. The collection sold out in two days.[5] "I was just filled with joy and disbelief," Aversano shared with me. After he hit rock bottom, his "art was finally finding its way into the world, and a new world that was started through this technology—and found people who cared."

Within five months, Aversano earned more than $130,000 by selling his NFTs on the marketplace OpenSea. When he launched his collection in February 2021, he priced each NFT at $1,000. By the end of the year, some of them were being resold for close to $1 million, a thousandfold increase in just ten months—an astonishing multiple that has become common in the NFT market for the blue-chip collections that skyrocket "to the moon." By October 2021, the all-time sales volume for Aversano's collection was $13 million,[6] a mind-blowing figure for a photographer in just a year.

One of Aversano's NFTs even resold for more than $4 million as part of a fundraising campaign to help support one thousand photographers. Twin Flames #49 was especially personal to Aversano. The photograph depicted Alyson Aliano standing in front of a mirror with her eyes closed. Aliano was Aversano's photography instructor at the School of Visual Arts. Knowing the Twin Flames series, one cannot help but wonder, Where's her twin? Only in reading the Sotheby's description for the auction does one realize that Alyson lost her twin sister, Courtney. In the photograph, the paper in front of the mirror is Courtney's death certificate.[7]

In June 2021, Sotheby's chose Aversano's NFT to be a part of its *Natively Digital: A Curated NFT Sale.* The auction sold Aversano's NFT for $35,280. Aversano donated the proceeds to SevensGrant, a nonprofit dedicated to supporting artists with grants and exhibitions. "I was chosen by the community, I gave it back to the community," Aversano explained.[8]

The giving back didn't end there. The anonymous buyer of Twin Flames #49 sold it for 506 ETH ($2.3 million) to Luiz, a cofounder of a decentralized autonomous organization, or DAO, that collects, curates, and produces content—so-called fingerprints—on blockchain. Fingerprints DAO then resold the NFT, for more fundraising, in an online sale using a party-bid approach that allowed many people to donate collectively to the sale to reach the reserved price. Eventually, six hundred people contributed to the cause for a total sale of 871 ETH (then $4 million), one of the highest amounts ever paid for a photograph-related sale.[9] All of the money was donated to the RAW DAO, an organization whose mission is to "create a cultural movement around photography NFTs."[10]

Even with his unparalleled success, Aversano believes it's important to help other photographers. "Those of us who found success in NFT art look to bring in other artists and help them through encouragement and collaborations," he told *Barron's*.[11] Aversano is a cofounder of the nonprofit Save Art Space, which promotes community art in public spaces. As the nonprofit's website explains, "Public art matters because our communities gain cultural, social, and economic value through public art."[12] Like many other artists who have achieved overnight success with NFTs, Aversano has a great sense of community and supporting others.

Aversano has become one of the most recognized photographers in the NFT world, practically overnight. Snoop Dogg and Gary Vaynerchuk, both avid collectors of NFTs, have reportedly invested in Aversano's NFTs. By all appearances, he's achieved a level of financial success that probably was unimaginable before he created NFTs. Indeed, it's hard to think he was living on five dollars a day, eating rice, beans, pita, and hummus in NYC, before creating NFTs.[13]

One reason for Aversano's financial success: his adoption of resale royalties for his NFTs. Before NFTs, Aversano wouldn't have earned any money from resale of his works. Not even a penny. Had Aversano sold a printed photograph for $1,000, that would be all the money he would get, even if a buyer later resold Aversano's print for $1 million. All of the profits from the $1 million resale would go to the reseller—and not Aversano.

NFTs changed that. NFT creators can now choose a right to resale royalties. This isn't a new concept. Since 1920, France has recognized this right (called *droit de suite*) for artists under copyright law. The law was meant to help starving artists and their heirs who otherwise wouldn't benefit from a dramatic increase in the value of artwork after it was sold, especially after the artist's death if the artist achieved fame.

Jean-François Millet, who painted French peasant life, served as the poster artist, so to speak, for this perceived injustice. Millet lived much of his life in poverty, but he experienced financial success later in life. After he died, however, his family was destitute. Millet's widow reportedly had to sell flowers in the street to survive.[14] One of Millet's paintings, *L'Angelus*, originally sold for 1,000 francs, but later resold for 553,000 francs, then the highest auction sale for a painting, with a huge profit to the seller but none to his widow.[15] Had the right to resale royalties been recognized back then, Millet's widow would have been entitled to a royalty from that sale and every resale of Millet's painting until the copyright expired. In 1920, the French parliament officially adopted the right to resale royalties for artists, with the memory of Millet's plight as an impetus.

Today, eighty countries recognize a right to resale royalties,[16] but the United States does not. The United Kingdom recognized the right in 2006 and, within fifteen years, 5,624 artists received a total of £100,286,451 in royalties.[17] According to the Design and Artists Copyright Society (DACS), a collecting rights organization for visual artists, "These payments overwhelmingly benefit artists selling work at the lower end of the scale, with over 50 percent of eligible sales falling under £5000."

The U.S. Copyright Act leaves authors out in the cold, however. What's worse, the omission may disqualify U.S. artists from receiving resale royalties in many other countries. Even if the resale of a U.S. artist's work occurs in a country that recognizes a right to resale royalties, the Berne Convention, an international agreement that now applies to 181 members around the world, allows its members to deny resale royalties to authors who are nationals of other countries, such as the United States, that lack a right to resale royalties for authors.[18] For example, U.S. visual artists do not receive a resale right in France even if the resale of the U.S. artist's work occurs there.

NFTs filled the gap in U.S. copyright law, virtually overnight, albeit outside of the copyright system.

What's remarkable about the right to a resale royalty for NFTs is that it is created by artists through smart contracts on blockchain, not legislation or copyright law. From 1978 to 2015, Congress considered six different bills to amend the Copyright Act to recognize a right to resale royalties for authors. But, each time, Congress rejected the idea.[19] The Copyright Office studied the desirability of resale royalties and issued two reports, cautiously supporting

Congress's consideration of adopting a right to resale royalties for visual artists in its 2013 report, a reversal of the Office's position in 1992.[20] As is typical for an office that must accommodate many competing stakeholders, the Copyright Office issued tentative support for resale royalties.[21] But Congress failed to act.

In 1977, California tried to fill the gap by becoming the first and only state to recognize under law a right to resale royalties for sales of works in the state. But, in 2018, a federal court ruled that the Copyright Act preempted state law (as the exclusive decider of copyright law in the United States), rendering California's law invalid.[22] In short, for more than 230 years, there were no resale royalties for visual artists in the United States—until NFTs changed everything.

For sales of NFTs, every artist can now choose to have a right to resale royalties, which typically can range up to 10 percent of the sales price (the maximum allowed on OpenSea).[23] Artists love it. As Aversano explained, "Artists can take the power back and put their art in a platform that will actually help them be abundant financially."[24] Because the resale royalties go back to the NFT creator, they are commonly referred to as creator royalties on NFT marketplaces. (To highlight the right's origin in copyright law, I use the term resale royalties.)

To understand the difference for artists, let's use one of Aversano's NFTs. He sold Twin Flame #2 for $1,076 (0.55 ETH) in February 2021.[25] Twin Flame #2 is a portrait of Jessica and Joyce Gayo, two Black women sitting on their unmade beds. The image captivates because one twin is in sharp focus, but the other is artistically blurry while smiling and holding what appears to be a squirming cat.

The first buyer resold the NFT for $29,763 (16.66 ETH) in July 2021. The second buyer then resold it for $292,006 (88.88 ETH) in September 2021. That buyer resold the NFT for $958,784 (207 ETH) in November 2021. By my estimate, if Aversano chose a 10 percent royalty (a figure I'll use to simplify the math—remember, I'm a lawyer), he would have earned $128,055 in resale royalties after he originally sold the NFT for just $1,076. Instead of making only a thousand dollars from the original sale, Aversano would have earned more than $125,000 from the resales of his NFT. And, for all future resales, Aversano will continue to receive royalties.

Before his success with NFTs, the major galleries and the art establishment didn't care about Aversano's work or reply to his emails.[26] Now they do. Christie's sold the NFT for Twin Flames #83, titled *Bahareh & Farzaneh*, an image from the cover for his self-published book, for $1.1 million.[27] The sale included prints of the entire Twin Flames collection. Aversano received $900,000 from the sale. He donated half to his nonprofit Save Art Space and then used another $200,000 to pay every twin in the project $1,000.

Similar to what 3LAU did for music NFTs, Aversano has parlayed his incredible NFT success into launching an NFT platform, Quantum Art, for photographers and other artists to experience their own success. Quantum, which curates the art that can be sold on its website, started out with a focus on photography but has expanded to other visual art.[28] Aversano also opened a brick-and-mortar NFT gallery, Quantum Space, in Santa Monica. People can buy Quantum Key NFTs to get exclusive access to an owners' lounge at the gallery.[29] People who visit the gallery can buy the NFTs on display—and have them immediately transferred to their crypto wallet without the need to lug around or ship the art. Virtual has its advantages.

Visual artists believe that royalties from NFTs can provide them with something they never had: a source of income that authors of other types of works—books, music, movies, etc.—already receive from direct sales and public performances. Without resale royalties, visual artists face the same problem that Millet faced: selling an artwork for $1,000 but earning nothing when it later resold for much more. Hard to sustain an artistic career that way. As the Copyright Office concluded in backing the adoption of resale royalties, "Under the current legal system, visual artists are uniquely limited in their ability to fully benefit from the success of their works over time."[30]

Despite the Office's recommendation, Congress did nothing. Faced with over two centuries of disparate treatment, visual artists finally found their own way—through NFTs—to improve their financial plight.

The current system of resale royalties isn't foolproof. Resale royalties for NFTs based on the popular ERC-721 standard for smart contracts are not interoperable but instead marketplace-specific.[31] They require the original marketplace to honor and carry out the payment of resale royalties to artists.[32] OpenSea does. But a seller can evade resale royalties by reselling an NFT on a different marketplace. (Developers have created alternative standards, such as EIP-2981, that address this problem, but it remains to be seen if they are widely adopted.) During the crypto winter, some fledgling marketplaces became royalty-free or made resale royalties purely optional at the buyer's discretion.[33] The move drew sharp criticisms from artists. The approach reminds me of the expression "bad facts make bad law." Well, bear markets make bad policy. The bear market for NFTs shouldn't drive the formulation of a policy that denies artists all resale royalties or enables buyers to choose unilaterally not to pay them. Such a policy is short-sighted. It disempowers creators—and diminishes their ability to survive financially.

"*Sustainability* is the key word—artists seeking sustainability through their artwork and fostering a career," Aversano emphasized to me. "The reason I got into the technology was simply because it provided royalties for artists, which was never the case. That's truly what protects and keeps artists sustainable throughout their career."

FROM DE-FI TO DE-IP

NFTs' adoption of a resale royalty right for artists is just one part of a much larger transformation. NFTs operate as a new form of decentralized intellectual property, or "De-IP" for short.

To understand De-IP, we need to situate it in relation to the larger movement to decentralized finance, or De-Fi, and, even more broadly, to decentralize the Web through blockchain technology. The world is witnessing a profound movement, still ongoing, to adopt De-Fi through blockchain and cryptocurrency. In the last chapter, we discussed the controversy over cryptocurrency—whether it's superior to fiat money or just a scam. We won't rehash that debate here. Instead, let's discuss how blockchain facilitates decentralized governance for whatever purpose it is deployed.

Blockchain is a decentralized, peer-to-peer (p2p) network that operates through the Internet. That may sound mysterious, but you've probably encountered p2p networks before. Starting around 1999, p2p networks—from Napster to Limewire to BitTorrent—were created to share content, including the illegal sharing of copyrighted music and movies.[34] (Perhaps you even used one of these p2p networks during college.) Although "piracy" on p2p networks may have given them a bad name, p2p networks are just technologies that enable decentralized activities, without the need for centralized servers or Big Tech platforms. To set up a p2p network, people download and run open-source software that creates a p2p network online. The advantage of a decentralized network is that no one authority controls the network, the content, or transmissions on the network.

In 2008, blockchain offered a new kind of p2p network—a network used not for sharing music and movies, but instead for money.[35] A new kind of money: Bitcoin. In that year, the enigmatic and perhaps mythical figure Satoshi Nakamoto published online a nine-page white paper, "Bitcoin: A Peer-to-Peer Electronic Cash System."[36] It may go down as the most influential nine-page paper in history.

Bitcoin's network eliminates the need for a central authority, bank, or intermediary to oversee money, to verify transactions, or to avoid the double-spending problem, in which a person spends the same money twice in electronic transactions before it is detected. The Bitcoin network does so through an elaborate consensus protocol that basically ensures that every new transaction is verified (by people on the network who operate as "miners" by using computer programs to satisfy the required "proof of work" in the form of solutions to complex math problems) before it is recorded on blockchain. Then, once a verified transaction is recorded, the information becomes part of a "chain," adding a new block that contains not only the new information for the current transaction, but also a bit of information from the previous block (called a hash) for the prior transaction. It's like two links of a chain interlocking—information from two adjacent blocks are intertwined. The new block of information is then automatically sent to and recorded by all other computers or nodes on the network, which verifies the information by a consensus among all nodes.[37]

This ingenious system makes it very difficult to alter or fabricate any record on blockchain. Consider a simplified analogy. Remember when your grade school teacher told you, "This is going down on your permanent record." Blockchain is like a student's permanent record—only it's far more permanent.

Just imagine all students' permanent records are stored by every grade school in the world, in a manner similar to what's described above. Now imagine some conniving student wanted to alter a demerit or poor grade in his permanent record. The student would have to change his record stored at every grade school in the world. Hard to do. Even if the student changed his record at one or several schools, all the other schools could easily detect the improper change—and reject it. Altering or removing an entry in a student's record would be easily noticed because part of the information is also recorded in the next student's record. Changing one student's record would trigger changes to the other students' records—making them all inconsistent with the records stored elsewhere. Blockchain operates in a similar manner.[38] Using a system of redundancy and consensus, blockchain makes it practically impossible to change a verified record—or for someone to cheat the system.[39] Blockchain is immutable.

Nakamoto's 2008 white paper didn't mention any criticism of fiat money. It wasn't until February 2009 that Nakamoto reportedly posted a blog making the connection: "The central bank must be trusted not to debase the currency, but the history of fiat currencies is full of breaches of that trust."[40] By creating a decentralized network for cryptocurrency based on a consensus protocol, Nakamoto offered an alternative to fiat money controlled by a central bank.

De-Fi proponents believe it offers a financial system that is more transparent, trustworthy, and efficient than our current currency and banking systems, which can be manipulated by centralized financial institutions such as the Federal Reserve.[41] Manipulation can lead, in turn, to meltdowns like the 2008 financial crisis.[42] Critics, however, contend that De-Fi is just as susceptible to its own financial crisis,[43] especially because the top 1 percent of holders—the crypto whales—held about 27 percent of all Bitcoin in 2021.[44] That warning gained traction during the crypto winter, during which the cryptocurrency Terra Luna crashed to zero in value and several De-Fi companies went bankrupt, including crypto lender Celsius Network.[45] Coinbase and Gemini, two of the major crypto exchanges, had sizable layoffs. During this time, Congress ramped up consideration of various bills to provide regulatory oversight for cryptocurrency.

With fears of inflation roiling the Fed and fears of a recession unsettling businesses, the major downturns in both the stock market and cryptocurrencies in 2022 made it difficult to assess the comparative advantages of a centralized or decentralized financial system.[46] In fact, during this volatile period, Bitcoin and cryptocurrencies were moving in tandem with the stock market, largely downward in response to the Fed's raising of interest rates.[47] While still in the downturn, perhaps the best that can be said was that it was "a punishing six months for investors."[48]

How De-Fi plays out—whether it overtakes centralized financial systems, gets regulated by them, or coexists with them—is not crucial for our purposes. What is crucial is seeing how blockchain and cryptocurrency offer an alternative to the current, centralized system. An alternative that is decentralized, running on blockchain.

Other developers saw the vast potential that blockchain offered beyond cryptocurrency. Bitcoin protocol is good for Bitcoin, but it's slow and not very versatile. In 2014, Vitalik Buterin, Mihai Aisle, Amir Chetrit, Gavin Wood, Charles Hoskinson, Anthony Di Iorio, and Joseph Lubin created the Ethereum protocol for blockchain.[49] It was quicker than the Bitcoin protocol and had a different cryptocurrency, called Ether. More important, Ethereum facilitated the use of blockchain for creating and recording smart contracts, which can be programmed for numerous uses, including to create NFTs.[50]

As we learned in the previous chapter, NFTs are a powerful technology that enables creators to adopt a new interactive ownership, with inclusive covenants that (re)arrange the rights for both the creators and the NFT owners. Because NFTs are programmable, they offer tremendous versatility. Indeed, NFTs are "mini-computers," as William Quigley, cofounder of the NFT market Worldwide Asset eXchange, put it.[51] "Anything that you can program, or creatively conceive of, can be an NFT, therefore every industry on earth will ultimately embed NFTs in their business."[52]

De-IP operates in a similar fashion to De-Fi. Instead of relying upon Congress, a centralized institution, to provide the changes needed to modernize copyright law, people can fashion their own changes using blockchain and NFTs. There is nothing sinister about this development. Our copyright system depends on private ordering.[53]

Just as cryptocurrency offers an alternative to the dollar as a store of value, NFTs offer an alternative to copyrights. They don't replace copyrights, but instead, enable people to reconfigure how copyrights are used and, in some respects, to make enforcing copyrights far less important because the NFT itself is a new type of property with independent value. Accordingly, creators of copyrighted content can use NFTs to (re)arrange IP rights to suit their needs better. For example, they adopt resale royalties for themselves and grant far more permissive rights to NFT owners and the public to use and even commercialize the copyrighted content than the default approach of our copyright system. These changes to the copyright system are creating the new system of De-IP.

In short, what De-Fi does to currency, De-IP does to copyright. Table 6.1 outlines the main differences between the U.S. copyright system and De-IP.[54]

TABLE 6.1. COMPARISON OF U.S. COPYRIGHT SYSTEM AND DE-IP APPROACH USING NFTS

Element	U.S. Copyright System	De-IP via NFTs
Core intellectual property	Copyright	NFT
Subject matter	Limited to "original works of authorship fixed in any tangible medium of expression."	No limit.
Exclusive rights	Section 106 rights to copy, distribute, make derivative works, publicly perform, and publicly display.	Rights to create, own, sell, and transfer NFT on blockchain. Right to virtual identity.
Inclusive rights	Copyright owners can choose open-source licenses for computer software and Creative Commons licenses for more flexible public uses of copyrighted works.	NFT creators can choose licenses with inclusive covenants for NFT owners to be in communities, as well as Creative Commons licenses for the public.
Unauthorized copies and Derivative Works	Potential infringement by unauthorized copies or derivative works.	Web3 norms are more permissive in allowing unauthorized copies and derivative works.
Right to resale royalty for creators	None in the United States.	Artists can choose resale royalties for NFTs.
Term	Author's life plus 70 years for individual authors. For corporations, the shorter of 95 years from publication or 120 years from creation.	Unlimited or indefinite.
Intermediaries	Commercial market dominated by major labels, studios, publishers, art galleries and auction houses, collecting societies, Internet service providers.	Decentralized marketplaces.

The starting point for understanding De-IP is recognizing that NFTs are a new form of intellectual property, created not by Congress, but instead by computer code using blockchain. The World Intellectual Property Organization (WIPO) defines *intellectual property* as protection for "creations of the mind."[55] It "enable[s] people to earn recognition or financial benefit from what they invent or create."[56] An "IP system aims to foster an environment in which creativity and innovation can flourish."[57] That is precisely what NFTs do. Like other intellectual property, NFTs are protections for intangible creations of the mind. They are imagined virtual tokens that can be programmed to identify almost any subject matter—even beyond copyrighted content—in a manner described as creating a virtual twin. NFTs create property interests in that intangible creation of the mind, the virtual twin, meaning the combination of tokens and subject matter. They enable artists, especially digital artists, to earn recognition or financial benefit from what they create. And they have instituted a new system— De-IP—that fosters an environment in which creativity and innovation can flourish.

To understand how De-IP is an alternative to copyright, consider that some successful NFT projects, such as the Nouns and Moonbirds, have completely abandoned their copyrights by adopting Creative Commons 0 licenses, meaning anyone can freely copy and monetize the Nouns and Moonbirds artworks. Yet, despite the lack of copyrights for the artworks, the lowest priced NFTs from each project still commanded over $93,000 and $13,000, respectively, in October 2022.[58] How is that possible when the artworks are both free of copyright and free to copy? The NFTs are *independently* valuable as a new form of intellectual property.

Another sign of this independent value is the widespread practice of using NFTs to create online identities for the owners, such as CryptoPunks owners. By empowering owners to adopt unique identities, NFTs operate like the right of publicity, intellectual property that protects a person's identity and likeness from unauthorized, commercial appropriation.[59] NFTs from pfp collections encompass what we might call a right of virtual identity. Web3 norms discourage others from commercially exploiting or appropriating the online identity of an NFT owner, especially if the identity is well known, such as Snoop Dogg's Bored Ape, Dr. Bombay. And, if the owner receives an exclusive license to the artwork (e.g., a CryptoPunk character) related to the NFT, the owner can sue to prevent others from such appropriation.

In addition to the adoption of resale royalties, one of the biggest transformations of De-IP is to recalibrate the bundle of exclusive rights and to add new rights of inclusion or inclusive covenants described in the previous chapter. Owners of NFTs have exclusive rights to exclude, to transfer, and to use or possess the NFTs they own.[60] Once NFTs are created for their owners and recorded on blockchain, no one else has rights to the NFTs, which have a built-in technological protection against appropriation.

Paradoxically, copying itself, which is the foundation of the Copyright Act, has become less significant in online activities related to NFTs. By creating a new type of IP, NFTs have made unauthorized copies and unauthorized derivative works of the associated content far less significant or worrisome. In other words, NFTs may help to solve the Internet dilemma for digital artists. Unauthorized copies don't diminish the value of NFTs.

Of course, NFT creators can still assert copyright infringement claims. Typically, that involves sending a Digital Millennium Copyright Act (DMCA) notice of alleged infringement to the marketplace, such as OpenSea, where the infringing NFT is being offered for sale. Under the notice-and-takedown process Congress set forth in the DMCA, the intermediary then must expeditiously remove the allegedly infringing content. Some DMCA notices have been filed against NFT projects, leading to their removal from OpenSea, at least temporarily.

But, especially for the most popular NFT collections, such a move may invite backlash among some Web3 proponents, who envision a more permissive approach to copyright. For example, Larva Labs faced tremendous backlash for DMCA notices it sent against the CryptoPhunks, which reversed the images of Larva Labs' CryptoPunks as an asserted parody, and the so-called V1 CryptoPunks, which were, in fact, the original CryptoPunks disseminated by Larva Labs, but they had a big error in the smart contract that required a second version of CryptoPunks to be issued by Larva Labs.[61] Both the CryptoPhunks and V1 CryptoPunks projects contested the DMCA notices. Eventually, both were restored to OpenSea. Notably, after the first controversy with CryptoPhunks, Larva Labs apparently didn't file DMCA notices for the many other CryptoPunk clones and derivatives. According to a community-organized list, there were nearly 170 other Punks projects.[62] A more permissive Web3 ethos treats them as creativity, not piracy.

NFTs' diminishment of the significance of copies shouldn't be that surprising. For visual art, "copies play almost no economic role in the art market, and when they do, the role is trivial," as Amy Adler, a legal scholar specializing in art law, explained.[63] "[T]he norm of authenticity, which forms the foundation of the art market, makes copyright superfluous. The market's insistence on authenticity ensures that even if an artist's content is stolen, the thief cannot misappropriate the economic value of the work."[64] Although Adler was speaking about art, not NFTs, her theory fits here as well. Like traditional art, authenticity is one of the most important features of NFTs. Indeed, the creation of a unique token authenticated on blockchain is the raison d'être of NFTs.

In one fell swoop, NFTs have addressed a chronic problem with our current copyright system. Every copy is considered potentially infringing, even if it might be fair use. That approach makes no sense in the twenty-first century and the digital world we live in. Writing at the start of Web2, Lawrence Lessig, an influential legal scholar and a visionary for the "free culture" movement, identified this key insight: "All the ordinary uses of a creative work are now regulated . . . because, again, any use is a copy."[65]

In 2001, Lessig tried to fix this problem. He founded Creative Commons (CC), a nonprofit that offers, for free, different copyright licenses that businesses and individuals can choose and attach to their works. The CC licenses are intended to "allow creators to keep their copyrights while sharing their works on more flexible terms than the default 'all rights reserved.'"[66] Under an "all rights reserved" approach, the authors or copyright holders retain all of their IP rights over their works. Any use of the works by consumers that might infringe on those rights—such as a public performance of a musical work or a remix of a movie—is not permitted unless consumers seek permission from the rights holders. Disney typically follows the "all rights reserved" approach. By contrast, CC licenses offer a more permissive approach by enabling authors to choose a more flexible arrangement, such as allowing consumers "to distribute, remix, adapt, and build upon the material in any medium or format, so long as attribution is given to the creator."[67]

CC licenses are similar to open-source licenses for computer programs, which were founded in 1998 to enable programmers to collaborate in developing programs in a decentralized fashion. Under a standard open-source license, each programmer must donate any improvements she makes for others in the community to enjoy under the same terms of the license. For Creative Commons, an open-source license is just one of several options (the "share alike" option) offered.

Both open-source and CC licenses can be viewed as early forms of De-IP. They both rearranged the default "all rights reserved" arrangement under the Copyright Act with more permissive licenses. The licenses are decentralized. They do not require an amendment by Congress. And, because they are licenses to the public en masse, they eliminate the need for individual licenses, not to mention pricey lawyers to negotiate them.

NFTs take De-IP to the next level. Unlike open-source and Creative Commons licenses, NFTs offer a new form of IP—the virtual token, including the property interest in any accompanying subject matter. The NFT's creation of a new type of intellectual property, with its own independent value, marks a paradigm shift. It has changed the entire dynamics and economics of licensing artistic works and diminished the significance of copying online. NFTs can even be used with CC licenses. Some projects have adopted the CC0 license, abandoning the copyright entirely and donating the work to the public domain. Indeed, the use of CC0 licenses with NFTs underscores how the latter have independent value—even if the copyright has been abandoned. In the next chapter, we'll study one of the most innovative uses of the CC0 license by the Nouns DAO.

The VC firm a16z has built on the concept of CC licenses and devised a new set of six public licenses (including CC0) tailored for NFTs.[68] In a nod to Google's early motto, a16z calls them "Can't Do Evil" licenses. The public licenses provide yet another example of how NFTs are being used to refashion the copyright system. As a16z's Miles Jennings and Chris Dixon explained, "Previous copyright licensing regimes were overly restrictive for many creators, and couldn't keep pace with what the internet and then-new digital technologies made possible."[69] Can't Do Evil licenses are designed to foster a Web3 permissiveness that enables a "shared culture and knowledge production."

De-IP does raise some concerns. A decentralized process doesn't ensure the public's interest is protected, especially if big corporations end up controlling how Web3 develops. Just as Congress can be captured by special interests, Web3 can be, too. It's up to people—meaning us—to not let that happen.

Another complication that De-IP raises is that unlike copyrights, NFTs don't have limited terms. Under the Constitution, however, copyrights can last only for limited times, a requirement that the Framers included to prevent perpetual monopolies such as had been allowed under the British Crown. Selling an NFT after the copyright to any associated artwork expires doesn't present a problem. Just as a Picasso painting can be sold for great value after its copyright has expired, the selling of an NFT even after the copyright to any associated artwork has expired shouldn't raise an issue. Resale royalties for NFTs may create a problem, however. Resale royalties can continue indefinitely for NFT sales, even though the copyright for an artwork associated with the NFT has expired. The Supreme Court has held that a license requiring royalties to use a patented invention even after its patent has expired was preempted by the Constitution's requirement of a limited term for patents.[70] A key question is likely to be whether resale royalties for NFTs conflict with copyright's limited term.[71] (The right to resale royalties is typically limited to the term of copyright, as it is under French law.)

As long as the NFT creator allows the public to freely copy and utilize the artwork once the copyright has expired, there is no conflict, in my view.[72] The NFT isn't the artwork, which the public can freely use, unlike the situation with the license to use an invention whose patent has expired. In the latter case, the licensee can't freely use the invention without paying royalties. However, in the case of an NFT, everyone can freely use the artistic work whose copyright has expired.

A similar issue of preemption may arise with the whole concept of resale royalties, which Congress has rejected. NFTs are different from the California law that recognized resale royalties, however. A federal court ruled that the California law was preempted because it interfered with the first-sale doctrine, which extinguishes a copyright owner's right to control the distribution of a physical copy of a work after the copy is sold.[73] Under the first-sale doctrine, people can sell their lawful copies of copyrighted works, such as used books and music CDs, without having to pay resale royalties. NFTs are different, however, because they aren't copies of works. (And, even if they were, the first-sale doctrine does not apply to digital copies.[74]) More fundamentally, apart from the expired term issue, courts have not typically found a conflict with copyright law created by contracts—which are what create resale royalties for NFTs.[75] Indeed, in recommending that Congress consider enacting a right to resale royalties for artists, the Copyright Office also endorsed an alternative: voluntary initiatives among private parties that recognize *contractual* resale royalties for artists.[76]

Although the transformation to De-IP is just beginning, its

potential is vast. De-IP provides an alternative way to update copyright law for the twenty-first century by using a complex web of private ordering, NFTs, licenses, and blockchain instead of legislation. There's no need for Congress to enact a right to resale royalty or a major update of copyright law with the "next great Copyright Act," as some policymakers have called for.

With NFTs, people can do it themselves. And they already do.

CHAPTER 7

THE DECENTRALIZED DISNEY

You can't wait for inspiration.
You have to go after it with a club.

—JACK LONDON

Interactive ownership of NFTs facilitates hybrid business models. We'll examine two of the most innovative business models involving decentralized collaboration, which enable owners of NFTs to commercialize the artwork associated with their NFTs. Before we do, let's start by examining how traditional media businesses operate and engage in centralized collaboration that maximizes a business's control over its intellectual property.

DISNEY AND A CENTRALIZED BUSINESS MODEL

If there's one company that symbolizes the approach to content production in the twentieth century, it's Disney. At the end of the Roaring Twenties, with Hollywood in its golden age, Walt Disney turned a lovable cartoon character later named Mickey Mouse into a cartoon titled *Steamboat Willie*, the first animated film with synchronized sound.[1] Disney's fledgling studio struggled mightily until 1928, when Walt and his brother Roy came up with the brilliant idea to create an animated film with synchronized sound. The brothers were inspired by *The Jazz Singer*, the first such feature-length film.[2] Disney Studio would be the first to create something new and magical: sound cartoons.

Walt Disney was a visionary and entrepreneur. He saw the incredible opportunity for creating something that hadn't ever been done—and then transforming it into a media empire. The idea of being animation pioneers energized not just Walt, but the entire team at his studio.[3] A private screening of a trial run of the first animated film, with make-do sounds performed in the studio's backyard, electrified family and friends. *Steamboat Willie* was a riff on the silent film *Steamboat Bill, Jr.*, a comedy by Buster Keaton. Keaton's film flopped, but Disney's was a smash hit. And the rest is cinematic history.

The birth of Mickey Mouse turned out be the genesis for one of the most successful business models in history—whose success continues to this day. Disney created 130 films with the Mickey Mouse character, but didn't stop there. Mickey appeared everywhere—in comic books, TV shows, merchandise, apparel, video games, and, of course, as a character at Disney amusement parks. The idea of licensing Mickey Mouse for use by other businesses came in a chance encounter in a hotel lobby in New York City in 1929. A man approached Walt Disney and asked if he could license Mickey Mouse for use on a paper tablet.

As Disney later recounted, "As usual, Roy and I needed the money, so I took the three hundred [dollars]."[4]

The Mickey Mouse tablet was a big hit. Buoyed by the success, Disney then struck other licensing deals for Mickey to appear on toys, watches, "napkins, wallpaper, books, phonographs, all types of clothing, hairbrushes, toys, and much more."[5]

Disney's merchandising success skyrocketed in 1932, when the company enlisted the services of Kay Kamen, a salesman from Kansas City.[6] Kamen was a force of nature. Within a year of his hire, he secured forty licensing deals for Mickey Mouse merchandise with the most reputable companies. Disney merchandise reportedly earned $70 million in sales globally, equivalent to roughly

$1.5 billion today.[7] Newspapers widely reported Disney's economic prowess. Columnist L. H. Robbins wrote a lengthy article titled "Mickey Mouse Emerges as Economist" for *The New York Times Magazine*.[8] Disney had licenses for "thousands of merchandise items" by 1935. Robbins likened Disney's business model to perpetual motion: Disney movies promote sales of the merchandise, which, in turn, promote the popularity of the movies—on end. Everyone loved Mickey. "Why is it that university presidents praise him, the League of Nations recommends him . . . learned academics hang medals on him, art galleries turn from Picasso and Epstein to hold exhibitions of his monkey-shines, and the King of England won't go to the movies unless Mickey is on the bill?"[9]

Disney also cultivated an audience by establishing Mickey Mouse clubs. Neal Gabler, a biographer of Walt Disney, believes that the clubs provided the "biggest boost" to the Mickey brand.[10] The idea came from Harry Woodin, a young, enterprising manager for a theater in a suburb of Los Angeles.[11] Walt visited the club organized by Woodin and saw the vast potential: it "would help . . . in making this series one of the biggest things that has ever come out."[12] The Mickey Mouse clubs held activities at theaters for children, including pie-eating contests, and the clubs sold Mickey merchandise, of course.[13] Mickey Mouse clubs sprouted all over the country, and, by one estimate, had more than a million members, reportedly more than the Boy Scouts and Girl Scouts combined.[14] Walt boasted that the number was 50 million in 1933.[15] *The Mickey Mouse Club* ran on TV from 1955 through 1959, and then again in 1977 and 1989–1994. The last TV series included the likes of Christina Aguilera, Ryan Gosling, Britney Spears, and Justin Timberlake before they became stars.

Why did the world become so obsessed with Mickey Mouse? Robbins summarized the views of some commentators in 1935: "These observers tell us there is in human nature a streak of rebellion, a yearning to cut loose, to be free to overleap the moon if we like."[16] Robbins offered a couple of other reasons: "Mickey is superlatively funny, and . . . he is simple. The world, in all its continents and islands, wants to laugh, and never more than now."[17] The article was alluding to the Great Depression. Perhaps most impressive was that Disney's incredible financial success started during the worst economic depression in modern history.

Profits from the Mickey Mouse merchandising and films enabled Disney to finance a $2 million production in 1938—then a staggering amount—for the film *Snow White and the Seven Dwarfs*.[18] The movie is considered a masterpiece not because of its story, which was borrowed from the old fairy tale by the Brothers Grimm. Instead, *Snow White* was a masterpiece because it was the first feature-length animated movie in color that created a whole new world. As the late film critic Roger Ebert wrote, "At a time when animation was a painstaking frame-by-frame activity and every additional moving detail took an artist days or weeks to draw, Disney imagined a film in which every corner and dimension would contain something that was alive and moving."[19] Disney imagined a metaverse, if you will, before the concept even existed.

The Walt Disney Company developed a media franchise juggernaut. By 1934, Disney made more revenues from merchandising than from its movies.[20] Through a chance encounter in a hotel lobby, Disney had stumbled upon one of the most successful business models for Hollywood: using memorable characters to create franchises that can be monetized ad infinitum—in sequels, merchandise, and other licensed uses, such as video games. Today, through acquisitions, Disney owns the rights to not just Mickey Mouse, but also Winnie the Pooh, *Star Wars*, Disney Princess, *Spider Man*, *Toy Story*, *The Lion King*, *Avengers*, *Frozen*, and *X-Men*. Disney's business model is far more complex today than it was in 1935, but the main revenue-generating components have remained stable. In Q1 2022, Disney's media content was the source of 35 percent of its revenues, while its theme parks, experiences, merchandise, and IP licensing provided 33 percent.[21] Disney still capitalizes on extensive IP licensing of its now many popular characters.

The Disney Company has protected its famous Mickey Mouse character as its crown jewel. Disney has licensed commercial uses of Mickey to other famous brands, including Lacoste, Levi's, Rag & Bone, Forever 21, Marc Jacobs, LEGO, and Oreo. This approach can be characterized as a model of centralized collaboration in which the IP owner maintains tight control over its IP through negotiated licenses between the parties. Unless the IP owner negotiates a license with another business, the IP owner maintains the "all rights reserved" approach. In a famous lawsuit in 1971, Disney successfully sued the creators of *Air Pirates*, a rogue comic book that depicted Mickey Mouse engaged in adult activities, including sex and drugs. Oh, boy.

Disney's centralized collaboration model exhibits a classic hub-and-spoke arrangement, as shown in Figure 7.1.[22] Disney, the IP owner, is the hub, and Disney's licensees are the spokes. With centralized control, this model promotes a more consistent product—

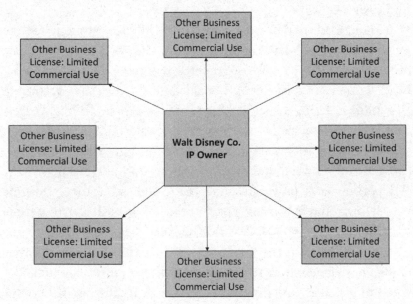

Figure 7.1
Walt Disney Company's Centralized Collaboration

typically subject to approval by the hub—and ensures the quality of the product through centralized coordination. In 1930, when Disney first started licensing Mickey for merchandise, the quality control was lax and the merchandise was "shoddy."[23] But, after Disney brought Kamen in to oversee merchandising, he "quickly canceled contracts with less prestigious and aggressive companies and signed up with bigger and better ones," including Cartier for a Mickey Mouse diamond bracelet.[24] As the IP owner, Disney controls the quality of Mickey Mouse merchandise produced by its licensees.

For Disney, the centralized collaboration model has worked like a charm. Mickey Mouse is the number one licensed character in the world. In 2021, Disney reportedly earned $54 billion just from its sales of licensed products, making it the top company on License Global's list of Top 150 Global Licensors.[25] Disney's licensing revenue nearly doubled its closest competitor's. The merchandising strategy Walt Disney chanced upon in 1929 has worked brilliantly for nearly a century.

Although Disney has dabbled with NFTs, its strategy for the metaverse was still developing in 2022.[26] We got a glimpse of part of it, though: movies with augmented reality (AR). In September 2022, Disney aired its first AR-enabled film, *Remembering*, starring Brie Larson. Using a special Disney app on Apple devices, viewers could watch their screen overflow with a waterfall streaming right into their living room, along with "dolphins, butterflies, trees, foliage, glowing flowers, and other wondrous digital elements."[27] The AR portion lasts only a minute, but a bedazzling one. Imagine your living room becoming a part of the movie with a virtual scene sprouting around you. CEO Bob Chapek has been close to the vest with Disney's plans, but disclosed that the company is developing "next-generation storytelling," with an entire new unit devoted to it.[28] If that doesn't provide enough indication of Disney's investment in the metaverse, Disney's job posting for "Principal Counsel—Corporate Transactions, Emerging Technologies & NFTs" does.[29]

Disney is not alone in the race to the metaverse. New upstart companies are trying to do today what Disney did at the turn of the twentieth century: create a whole new media experience that is magical and enchanting. But what's different from Disney: the upstarts are adopting new ways of doing business.

BORED APE YACHT CLUB AND A HYBRID BUSINESS MODEL OF COLLABORATION

Something is brewing in Web3. A new type of business model is emerging: a hybrid that uses not just centralized collaboration like Disney's approach, but also decentralized collaboration, or "De-Collab," through NFTs. This innovative business model could produce a new type of media-entertainment business—what some analysts call a "decentralized Disney."

Yuga Labs is the creator of the Bored Ape Yacht Club (BAYC), which became the hottest NFT collection in 2021.[30] In just one year, Bored Apes surpassed $2 billion in total sales volume (including secondary sales), becoming the top NFT collection in the world, even eclipsing the CryptoPunks.[31] A "Who's Who" list of celebrities and athletes have "aped in" by acquiring Bored Apes. The list includes Steph Curry, Jimmy Fallon, Snoop Dogg, Paris Hilton, Justin Bieber, Gwyneth Paltrow, Tom Brady, Neymar Jr., Madonna, Eminem, Post Malone, DJ Khaled, Marshmello, Timbaland, Lil Baby, the Chainsmokers, Von Miller, Steve Aoki, Dez Bryant, Logan Paul, Lamelo Ball, Kevin Hart, Shaquille O'Neal, and Mark Cuban. Granted, it may look like an old boys' club, but we'll return to diversity issues in the NFT market later in the book. The Bored Ape Yacht Club has disrupted the entire industry of creative production, garnering media attention from *Fortune* to *GQ* to *The New Yorker* to *Rolling Stone*.

No company has raised as many expectations of becoming the decentralized Disney as Yuga Labs. The company has adopted a hybrid business model that combines a startup company and a club of NFT owners from its collections of NFTs, including Bored Apes, Mutant Apes, Kennel Club dogs, Kodas, and Otherdeed land. Yuga Labs also acquired the IP rights to CryptoPunks and Meebits created by Larva Labs. Remarkably, Yuga Labs owns the top four NFT collections in all-time sales volume: Bored Apes, CryptoPunks, Mutant Apes, and Otherdeeds. (Each has already eclipsed the NBA Top Shot.)

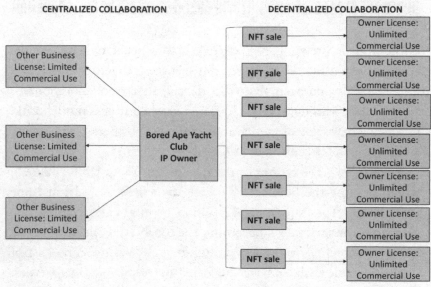

Figure 7.2
Bored Ape Yacht Club's Hybrid Model: Decentralized and Centralized Collaboration

What's distinctive about Yuga Labs' business model is that it embraces De-Collab. Recall the classic hub-and-spoke approach to centralized collaboration by the Walt Disney Company. This places the company in control of every collaboration or partnership involving its IP. By contrast, as depicted in Figure 7.2 above, the Bored Ape hybrid model can be described as having two sides: (i) a centralized collaboration in which Yuga Labs collaborates or partners with other businesses (shown on the left above) and (ii) a decentralized collaboration in which BAYC owners commercialize their own characters, including Bored Ape, Mutant Apes, Kennel Club dogs, and Kodas (shown on the right) as permitted under a De-Collab license that comes with ownership of the NFTs.

If we focused on only the left side, Yuga Labs would resemble a typical startup. The company has engaged in its own deals to build the BAYC ecosystem and brand. In October 2021, Yuga Labs signed a representation deal with Guy Oseary, who managed both Madonna and U2, to develop television, movie, music, and other deals for the Bored Apes.[32] In November 2021, Yuga Labs announced its first major deal: a partnership with Adidas, PUNKS Comics, and gmoney (yes, the same guy who gave the advice to Justin Aversano). Yuga Labs tweeted a teaser: a Bored Ape wearing pink heart-shaped sunglasses and an Adidas sweat suit, with logos of Adidas, gmoney, and PUNKS Comics. The tweet included only emoji, one resembling Adidas's logo: /// 00.[33] A few days later, Adidas launched a splashy video showing Bored Apes, adorned in Adidas sweat suits and sneakers, flying to the metaverse, with Louis Armstrong's "What a Wonderful World" playing in the background.[34]

On December 17, 2021, Adidas sold 29,620 "Into the Metaverse" NFTs.[35] The NFT entitles the owner to exclusive merchandise, including hoodies, tracksuits, and beanies, and participation in "virtual land experiences, cocreated with the community, throughout 2022 and beyond."[36] Time will tell how the Adidas "Into the Metaverse" pans out. The limited sale of NFTs alone brought in $22 million. And that's only the start of Adidas's foray into the metaverse.

Probably nothing, right?

Well, Nike acquired the red-hot startup RTFKT in the same month.[37] As discussed earlier, RTFKT is a trailblazer, innovating with digital sneakers and fashion, along with CloneX avatars, and collaborating with artists such as FEWOCiOUS and Murakami. And, within seven months, Nike and RTFKT launched three NFT collections, including the CryptoKicks and the AR Genesis Hoodie. In August 2022, the CloneX owners were entitled to "forge" two additional NFTs for a new line of CloneX sneakers and phygital apparel whose bespoke designs were tailored to the "DNA" of each CloneX NFT.[38]

That gives you a sense of what companies face in the race to the metaverse. The competition is both ferocious and FEWOCiOUS, so to speak. Big brands are competing not only among themselves, but also with Web3 startups like Yuga Labs and RTFKT, which may have greater "street cred" in the tech-savvy, crypto-savvy community. That's why Adidas partnered with Yuga Labs/BAYC, and Nike outright acquired RTFKT. Game on.

In March 2022, Yuga Labs secured $450 million in seed funding led by a16z, aka Andreessen Horowitz, whose partner Chris Dixon is a leading proponent of Web3.[39] Just a year old, Yuga Labs was valued at $4 billion.[40] The infusion of venture capital may make Yuga Labs seem like any other hot startup, but Yuga Labs is different. The right side of Figure 7.2 shows the difference. Through its thousands of NFTs, Yuga Labs has adopted decentralized collaboration. The Bored Ape license grants buyers of its NFTs "an unlimited, worldwide license to use, copy, and display the purchased [Bored Ape] Art for the purpose of creating derivative works based upon the Art."[41] Plus, the Bored Ape owners keep all the profits they make.

This type of unlimited commercialization license was rare at the time Yuga Labs adopted it in April 2021. It was apparently modeled, almost verbatim, on the license for the Hashmasks NFTs.[42] The more typical NFT license adopted either the "all rights reserved" approach, such as for the NBA Top Shot Moments, or a limited right to commercialize the artwork capped at a certain level of revenue (e.g., $100,000), such as in the original license for the CryptoPunks and the CryptoKitties.

Table 7.1 below summarizes examples of De-Collab by Bored Ape owners, who are commercializing their Bored Apes in new derivative works, merchandising, or other business ventures. This list is not meant to be exhaustive.

Take, for example, the use of Bored Apes in music. Jimmy McNelis, the owner of three Bored Apes and a Mutant Ape, is heavily involved with NFTs. He signed a music deal with Universal Music Group's label 10:22PM, run by Celine Joshua. The plan is to create a music band called Kingship, composed of McNelis's Bored Apes,

TABLE 7.1. DECENTRALIZED COLLABORATION BY OWNERS OF YUGA LABS' NFTS

Area	Business	Owner
Art	Paintings of Bored Apes	Jessica Manning's Painted Ape Club invites Bored Ape owners to have their characters painted.
Art	Mural and Paintings of Bored Apes	Roc Sol invites Bored Ape owners to have their characters painted.
Blogs	The Bored Ape Gazette	Kyle Swenson Bored Ape #8677
Books	Book 1: BAYC owners can buy NFTs entitling them to decide the direction for a collaborative book.	Jenkins the Valet (aka Valet Jones and Safa) Bored Ape #1798
Storytelling	Applied Primate Engineering	Five Mega Mutant Apes
Events	Bored Hospitality Group	Bobby Blaze (aka Robert Murray) Mutant Ape #14
Business partnerships	Bored of Directors	Various
Business investments	Ape Tank	Bored Apes #137, #656, #779, #3613, #4639
Merchandise	Basketball, clothing, notebooks, skateboards, stickers, chess sets, etc.	Various
Music	Collaboration between Eminem and Snoop Dogg, "From the D 2 the LBC"	Eminem and Snoop Dogg Bored Ape #6723 Bored Ape #9055
Music	Music NFTs about ApeCoin	Snoop Dogg and Wiz Khalifa Bored Ape #6723 Bored Ape #1506
Music	Kingship band signed to music deal with Universal Music Group's Web3-focused label 10:22PM.	Jimmy McNelis Bored Apes #1652, #7796, #8824 Mutant Ape #9314
Music	Ape-In Productions (AIP) to produce rap band for metaverse.	Timbaland Bored Ape #590
Music	Ape Rave Club performer	Bored Ape #9814
Podcasts	The Bored Ape Gang Show	Bored Apes #4047, #4545, #6848, #7588

Short film	"The Degen Trilogy" for showing at NFT.NYC	Coinbase invited Bored Ape owners to participate
Sports	Major League Soccer digital player Striker	Bored Ape #6045
Coffee	Bored Coffee	Bored Ape #9006 Mutant Ape #12611 Bored Kennel #3049
Coffee and Merchandise	Bored Breakfast Club	Various
Ice Cream	Dr. Bombay's Sweet Exploration	Snoop Dogg Bored Ape #6723
Sauce	Bored Sauce	Bobby Bellhop Bored Ape #3542
Wine	Bored Wine Co. allows BAYC owners to print their characters on wine	Dionysus, WiV Technology Bored Ape #1839
Beer	Bored Ape IPA	North Pier Brewing Co. Jay Fettig Bored Ape #671
Hard Seltzer	Happy Dad limited edition banana-flavored	Kyle Forgeard Bored Ape #8928
Water	Ape Beverages	Bored Ape #5382
Merchandise for Lifestyle Beverages	Neuro Brands	Sanela Diana Jenkins Bored Ape #8585
Restaurant	Bored & Hungry burger joint, part of Food Fighters Universe	Kevin Seo, Andy Nguyen Bored Ape #6184
Food Truck	Bored Taco	Champ Medici Bored Ape #6368

which will be animated by Jack Lanza.[43] Kingship collaborated with Mars for limited-edition boxes of M&M's, with the Kingship Bored Apes painted on the candy. The famed music producer Timbaland has launched a partnership called Ape-In Productions to produce hip-hop bands for the metaverse with other owners of Bored Ape NFTs. The Zoo, Ape-In's first band, created a music video using Bored Ape characters. Snoop Dogg and Wiz Khalifa have used their Bored Apes to launch their own music NFTs about ApeCoin.

So far, these music collaborations haven't gained mainstream success. But a collaboration between two of the biggest names in rap did. In 2022, Snoop Dogg teamed up with Eminem for a new song "From the D 2 the LBC" and an animated music video in which they use their Bored Ape characters, including Dr. Bombay, the character Snoop Dogg developed from his Bored Ape into the trademark for his new ice cream business. In little over three months, the video received more than 54 million views on YouTube,[44] plus a nomination in the 2022 MTV VMA Awards for Best Hip Hop Video. The animated Bored Ape video could go down as a classic for animated music videos, similar to the Beatles' film *Yellow Submarine*. Snoop Dogg and Eminem's video shows how De-Collab can benefit the cocreators and the overall brand of Bored Ape Yacht Club.

One advantage of De-Collab is that Yuga Labs doesn't have to spend time or resources developing all of its collaborations—or even come up with all the business ideas. Instead, Yuga Labs can unleash its community of thousands of NFT owners to develop the creative ideas. In just one year, Bored Ape owners have created an impressive range of derivative works. They include paintings and murals of Bored Apes, Kyle Swenson's Bored Apes news website, the podcast *Bored Ape Gang Show*, a Bored Ape documentary produced by Coinbase, an assortment of Bored Ape merchandise, plus Bored Ape beer, wines, coffee, sauce, ice cream, tacos, and burgers.[45] The proliferation of Bored Apes is beginning to sound a lot like Mickey Mouse's explosion in the 1930s. But this time the IP commercialization arises from De-Collab.

Some Bored Ape owners are themselves innovating creative production. Valet Jones and Safa, two childhood friends, own a Bored Ape they've named Jenkins the Valet, inspired by the Bored Ape's garb. Through the company they founded, Tally Labs, the two friends have launched an innovative, collaborative book project called the Writer's Room.[46] To participate in the project, Bored Ape owners can buy NFTs sold by Jenkins the Valet. Members then license their Bored Ape and Mutant Ape characters for use in collaborative book projects whose plots are determined by vote of the members.[47] In exchange for the licensed Bored Ape characters, the owners receive royalties (50 percent of net profits) and other perks from Jenkins the Valet. The project reported that 3,000 people joined the Writer's Room, with 4,075 Bored Apes and Mutant Apes licensed for the project.[48]

The first book in the series, written by Neil Strauss with direction from the members, is titled *Bored and Dangerous*,[49] and generated a lot of buzz—and $12 million in seed funding for Tally Labs and the Jenkins the Valet project.[50] Tally Labs also launched Azurbala, an upcoming metaverse under development.[51]

Jenkins the Valet's Writer's Room is a hybrid within BAYC's hybrid business model. The owners of Jenkins and the other Bored Ape owners are using their De-Collab licenses from BAYC to organize their own hybrid business that combines decentralized involvement through purchase of the Writer's Room NFTs, but with a centralized team behind the character Jenkins the Valet, who is represented by Creative Artists Agency (CAA). The Writer's Room is a perfect example of how a De-Collab license can benefit both the IP owner (Yuga Labs) and its licensee (the owners of Jenkins the Valet). Jenkins the Valet's owners are building their own business, but, in doing so, are building the Bored Ape brand.

As BAYC has gained fame, so has its license. Other NFT projects have started to adopt De-Collab licenses as well. These may become the standard, especially for NFT startups willing to take the risk of relinquishing control over their IP in favor of a decentralized approach.

Yuga Labs is willing to take risks. The startup was cofounded by two guys who go by the aliases Gordon Goner and Gargamel. As Goner said in an interview with *Rolling Stone*, "I always go balls to the wall."[52]

The two cofounders aren't the typical "tech bros" you might expect from the hottest NFT startup. They are literary bros. The two met in Miami, where they grew up and discussed their love of literature. They became familiar with NFTs when they noticed the successes of Larva Labs' CryptoPunks and Hashmasks, a project involving a group of seventy artists.[53] Searching for an idea for an NFT collection of their own, they eventually settled on building a virtual world imagined around the cryptocurrency boom. As they recounted to *The New Yorker*, the Bored Ape Yacht Club would be a dive bar where crypto-billionaires hang out with others who "aped in" to cryptocurrency, meaning investing without much research, while throwing caution to the wind. Of course, with the billions they had made, the apes would be kind of bored.[54]

"The idea was that it was this place for degenerates to go, right?" Goner explained in an interview. "Because that's who we were."[55]

The duo enlisted two other friends, who go by the pseudonyms No Sass and Emperor Tomato Ketchup, computer programmers who became quick studies in Solidity, the language for smart contracts. The fact that Goner and Gargamel are storytellers with literary backgrounds, not visual artists, may be one of the reasons for the Bored Apes' enormous success. The story of Bored Apes resonated with the fast-growing crypto culture.

BAYC's popularity skyrocketed in 2021. So did the media attention—and scrutiny. In a controversial article, *BuzzFeed News* exposed—critics say doxxed—the real identities of Gargamel and Goner as Greg Solano and Wylie Aronow, respectively, both in their early thirties.[56] Katie Notopoulos, who wrote the exposé, justified revealing their identities, obtained from public business records, in this way: "*How do you hold them accountable if you don't know who they are?*"[57] The *BuzzFeed News* article sparked a heated discussion over whether founders of big projects in the crypto/NFT world, where there's a lot of money at stake, should disclose their identities.[58] After the article, the other two cofounders revealed their first names, which eventually led to their identification from a company filing with the SEC: Kerem Atalay (Emperor Tomato Ketchup) and Zeshan Ali (No Sass).[59] As it turned out, knowing their real identities proved to be important in evaluating an explosive allegation leveled against the cofounders that year, as we'll discuss below.

So, who are the Bored Ape artists? Well, the original designs for the Bored Apes were created by independent contractors reportedly for $40,000.[60] A bargain. Perhaps too much of a bargain, at least in hindsight. *Rolling Stone* ran an article about the lead artist, All Seeing Seneca (or Seneca), a twenty-seven-year-old Asian American woman who created the bodies and several traits for the Bored Apes.[61] While grateful for the opportunity to work with BAYC, Seneca admitted to *Rolling Stone* that the compensation "was definitely not ideal."[62] But she wasn't at liberty to disclose specifics. The cofounder Solano revealed that the artists Thomas Dagley and Migwashere were also involved, but two others preferred anonymity.

Before launching BAYC, no one could have predicted how successful it would become. But $40,000 split among five artists sounds quite low. It's unclear whether the artists had a right to receive any royalties, either. However, a week following the *Rolling Stone* article about Seneca, Yuga Labs CEO Nicole Muniz told *BuzzFeed News*: "Every single artist of the original five were compensated over a million dollars each."[63] The amount was a bonus given to the artists after BAYC's success.[64]

Seneca, who first discovered NFTs by working on Bored Apes, has moved on from BAYC and started selling NFTs for her own artwork. But her role in creating the Bored Ape characters remains a lasting part of their success—just as the success of Mickey Mouse and *Steamboat Willie* owes considerably to Ub Iwerks, the lead illustrator for Disney, who left in 1930 to start his own studio.[65] In Seneca's first launch, *Little One* sold for 39.69 ETH (then $107,632).[66] "I think NFTs are powerful because they give power back to artists," Seneca told *HypeBeast* in an interview. "We're going to see more platforms that support independent creators and thinkers."[67]

Yuga Labs' use of De-IP is significant. Yuga has granted unlimited De-Collab licenses to its NFT owners. It has elected to receive resale royalties at 2.5 percent for secondary sales of its NFTs. And it has taken one of the most permissive approaches

to unauthorized clones and derivatives of the Bored Ape characters. Yuga Labs, which owns the copyrights to the Bored Apes and
the CryptoPunks (which it acquired from Larva Labs), hasn't at-
tempted to stop the numerous unauthorized clones and derivatives
of either Bored Apes or CryptoPunks.

Both collections have spawned numerous collections that copy
or mimic the underlying cartoon characters of the CryptoPunks
and Bored Apes—to varying degrees of similarity.[68] Indeed, there
is no shortage of cheaper alternative NFTs that resemble or even
"clone" the characters from the CryptoPunks or Bored Apes.
Some clones even explicitly tout their goal as "expansion" NFTs,
which expand access to the underlying artwork by offering vari-
ants of them at much cheaper prices.[69] These collections have been
described in different ways, including as clones, copycats, "copy
pasta," alternatives or alt-versions, expansion versions, flipped or
mirrored versions, and derivatives. Under our traditional doctrines
of copyright law, some of these versions would likely be considered
infringing, while others might not because they are fair uses or copy
unprotected ideas. But Yuga Labs has not discouraged any of these
unauthorized derivative Apes or Punks. In fact, after Yuga Labs
acquired the rights to the CryptoPunks, it announced that it had
no intention of pursuing the copyright claim that Larva Labs had
asserted against the so-called V1 CryptoPunks.[70] To Yuga Labs,
the unauthorized copies of its artwork appear to be no worry at all.

By contrast, in June 2022, Yuga Labs filed its first trademark
lawsuit, suing Ryder Ripps, an artist who used all 10,000 of Yuga
Labs' Bored Ape characters and sold them as "RR/BAYC" NFTs
at the domain rrbayc.om. Ripps's website also used a logo of a
skull, similar to Yuga Labs' BAYC logo, but with the words "This
logo is based on the SS Totenkopf."[71] Ripps's NFTs reportedly
earned $1.8 million in profit.[72] Ripps even used a gold Bored Ape
character as his Twitter avatar.[73] Yuga Labs didn't file a copyright
claim against Ripps. Some legal analysts expressed surprise at the
strategy, given the unauthorized use of all the Bored Ape characters, but Yuga Labs' strategy was consistent with its permissive

approach to copyright and unauthorized copies.[74] A new ethos for Web3.

The trademark lawsuit is a different story. Unlike copyright law, trademark law *requires* a trademark owner "to take reasonable efforts to police infringements of [the] mark," and failing to do so can result in loss or abandonment of the trademark.[75] In August 2021, Yuga Labs objected to Arizona Iced Tea's use of the Bored Ape Yacht Club logo in the latter company's announcement that it had purchased a Bored Ape.[76] Given a trademark owner's duty to police its trademark, Yuga Labs' policing of its trademark isn't surprising.

But the trademark lawsuit seemed insignificant compared with the larger feud between Ripps and the BAYC cofounders. Ripps has waged an online campaign to show two claims: first, that the four BAYC cofounders were allegedly intentionally using coded Nazi symbols—what Ripps calls "Nazi dog whistles" throughout the BAYC project; and, second, that the ape characters are allegedly racist depictions based on "simianization" and the use of other imagery.[77] Ripps published his theory under the domain name GordonGoner.com, referring to the pseudonym of Wylie Aronow, the BAYC cofounder.[78] Before this controversy, Ripps, a conceptual artist, had developed a reputation as an adept "artist of the Internet," including in "imaginative cyberpranks."[79] An *Artsy* interview described Ripps as an "[a]rtist, entrepreneur, programmer, provocateur."[80] Back in July 2021, Ripps sold an NFT titled "CryptoPunk #3100," which he described as the "same CryptoPunk image" but reminted to show how the original machine-generated one was "devoid of humanity."[81] On his websites GordonGoner .com and RRBAYC.com, Ripps touted his knowledge of "the history of alt-right/4chan types in crypto" and asserted that his reminting of BAYC NFTs using Bored Apes was "illuminating truths about their origins and meanings as well as the nature of Web3."[82]

On behalf of the cofounders, Aronow (aka Gordon Goner) issued a denial and refutation of Ripps's allegation, which Aronow described as a "crazy disinformation campaign accusing us—a group of Jewish, Turkish, Pakistani, and Cuban friends—of being super-secret Nazis."[83] The refutation included their explanations of how they chose the company name and their pseudonyms, and how the BAYC logo was designed from ideas in an email Aronow said he had sent to the designer.[84] Later, the media-shy Aronow and Solano sat down for a rare interview with *Input*.[85] The two cofounders again flatly denied Ripps's accusation. Aronow said that it has made them the targets of online hate "all day, every day."[86]

In October 2022, Ripps moved to dismiss Yuga Labs' lawsuit on the grounds that his use of BAYC content was protected free speech as forms of satire, protest, and criticism of the allegedly neo-Nazi and racist material.[87] He sought dismissal under California's Anti-Strategic Lawsuit Against Public Participation (anti-SLAPP) law, which enables defendants to seek early dismissal of lawsuits that chill speech on public issues.[88] Even when there is speech on a public issue, dismissal will not occur if the plaintiff (here, Yuga Labs) shows "a 'reasonable probability' of prevailing in its claims."[89] (I completed this book before Yuga Labs filed its response or a decision was made by the court.)

However the trademark lawsuit is resolved, it's possible the feud will not end.[90] There is no shortage of people who have provided their own analysis of the allegation and support for one side or the other. Of course, to the average person, evaluating the alleged existence of a "dog whistle" isn't easy, given that its meaning is supposedly coded, understandable to some people but not others. No major newspaper has reported Ripps's allegation yet, not even ones such as *The Washington Post* that have covered the trademark lawsuit.[91] As the high-profile lawsuit moves forward (with top law firms on both sides), that may change. Because BAYC is the most successful NFT collection, whose rise has garnered significant media attention, the lawsuit could draw journalists to investigate the allegation, which relates to Ripps's defense.[92] But the lawsuit itself will not likely decide the merits of Ripps's allegation against the

BAYC cofounders, since the case doesn't hinge on determining the truth or falsity of the allegation.

Putting aside Ripps's allegation, Yuga Labs' permissive approach to copyright is unusual for a U.S. media company. More typical is the IP enforcement strategy of Disney, known for its policing of its IP.[93] The *Air Pirates* case is just one example. In 1989, Disney threatened to sue three day-care centers in Florida that had Mickey and Minnie, Donald Duck, and Goofy painted prominently on the centers' exterior walls.[94] Even though Disney's threat drew bad PR, the company stuck to its hard-line position. (A lawsuit was averted when Hanna-Barbera Productions and Universal Studios allowed the Florida day-care centers to use their characters, including Scooby-Doo and Yogi Bear, instead of Disney characters.[95]) Yuga Labs, by contrast, has allowed Bored Ape murals in Austin, New York, Miami, San Francisco, Los Angeles, Florence, Milan, Lagos, and other cities. The more Bored Ape murals, the better.

The BAYC business model involves collaborations and interactions across the entire BAYC ecosystem. The two sides in Figure 7.2 are representations, not actual divisions. Nowhere is that more apparent than in the creation of ApeCoin, an ERC token or cryptocurrency for the BAYC ecosystem and beyond. Owners of Bored Apes and Mutant Apes were air-dropped free ApeCoin, and a separate Ape Foundation was established to steward it, with the ultimate governance entrusted to a newly formed ApeCoin DAO, composed of all ApeCoin owners, who decide on proposals by majority vote.[96] The owners approved two staking proposals in which owners can commit, or "stake," their ApeCoin for a designated time period (e.g., twelve months) with the reward of additional ApeCoin in return.[97] All participants involved—Yuga Labs, its collaborative partners, and its BAYC/MAYC owners—have interests in making ApeCoin and the entire Bored Ape ecosystem succeed. ApeCoin was the currency used for the successful virtual land sale for Yuga Labs' collaborative metaverse project, the Otherside.

THE OTHERSIDE

Yuga Labs' most ambitious attempt at De-Collab involves the Otherside,[98] "a gamified, interoperable metaverse" in which "players own the world, your NFTs can become playable characters, and thousands can play in real time."[99] The project is a hybrid combining both centralized and decentralized collaboration. Yuga Labs invites people to not only buy the virtual land called Otherdeeds, but also to build the metaverse with Yuga Labs and its partners Improbable, the London-based metaverse technology company, and the Hong Kong–based company Animoca Brands.

On April 30, 2022, Yuga Labs launched its much-anticipated virtual land sale with the first 55,000 of 200,000 NFT parcels of Otherdeeds. It was the largest NFT launch in history, raising $320 million.[100] Within twenty-four hours, buyers spent another $242 million on secondary sales.[101] Within a week, 34,000 unique wallets held Otherdeeds property.[102] Within ten days, the most coveted Otherdeeds, based on rarity or prime location, sold for between $750,000 and $1.5 million.[103] (Even during the crypto winter, the prime Otherdeeds were selling for high prices. By September 2022, they surpassed $1 billion in sales volume, ranking as the fourth-highest amount for NFT collections.)

But the launch didn't go off without a hitch. The huge demand caused a "gas war." There was a huge surge in gas fees (paid to the people who are miners to authenticate transactions on blockchain) to mint the NFTs. People were paying between $6,500 and $14,000 in gas fees, instead of the more typical price range, from $50 to $200.[104] The gas fee for two NFTs nearly matched the price of one Otherdeed NFT, roughly $5,800.[105] The gas war even clogged up the entire Ethereum network, causing a delay or failure in many transactions.[106] Afterward, Yuga Labs and the BAYC cofounder Solano apologized,[107] but some Bored Ape owners were vocal in their criticisms of Yuga Labs, including the "tone deaf" apology.[108]

The gas war didn't mar the Otherside's progress. Although still in development, the Otherside promises to be enchanting. In March 2022, Yuga Labs dropped a teaser video showing an animated Bored Ape drinking a liquid and then witnessing an explosion of a new world forming. Yuga Labs' new, alien-like character named Koda transports the Bored Ape through the air to the Otherside, with the Doors' iconic song "Break on Through (to the Other Side)" blaring in the background.[109]

The Otherside plans on being interoperable: people can import other NFT characters beyond ones produced by Yuga Labs.[110] The Otherside will also be "game-changing tech" that can "handle more than half a billion operations per second."[111] In July 2022, I had the chance to preview the Otherside, along with roughly 4,500 other individuals, in a live demo.[112] I'm no gaming expert, but I found the experience fantastic. Powered by Improbable's M^2 technology, the Otherside was magical, immersive, and responsive—with full physics for avatars in the online world, as well as 3D audio that enables people to speak to one another.[113] Afterward, the project issued a "litepaper" setting forth the vision for its future development—a "collaborative ecosystem."[114] A world where people can "bring their visions to life."

The Otherside relies on several types of interactive ownership. First, the content is interactive: "Rather than a static representation of a piece of land, your Otherdeed for Otherside is designed to evolve along with what you choose to do in the game."[115] Second, NFT owners are both community members and patrons supporting the construction and development of the Otherside. Owners can become collaborators and business partners in building the Otherside. A software development kit (SDK) "will allow creators to make things for the Otherside as well as sell them in the game's marketplace—not just characters, but also outfits, tools, structures, and even games."[116] A De-Collab license comes with ownership of any Koda character (10,000 were randomly assigned to Otherdeeds): the Koda owners received unlimited commercialization rights to use the Koda characters on merchandise and derivative works just like the Bored Ape license.[117] However, the license for Otherdeeds land was limited to personal, noncommercial use.[118]

Yuga Labs' strategy to build a gamefied metaverse might capitalize on the popularity of online gaming. In 2021, there were 3.24 billion gamers worldwide, including 1.48 billion in Asia, 715 million in Europe, and 284 million in North America.[119] The United States alone has 244 million gamers.[120] Because gamers are more tech savvy, a gaming metaverse might have great demand.

Yet the strategy comes with risks. According to a March 2022 survey of gamers worldwide, 69 percent "hated" NFTs, although only 12 percent said they fully understood them.[121] Two reasons for the dislike of NFTs: they were changing the gaming space and adding an uncertain financial element to video games. Some gamers reportedly believe that adding a financial element will ruin the fun of game playing.[122] The backlash even caused some game developers, including EA and Team17, to back away from announced plans to integrate NFTs into their games.[123] Ubisoft tried offering NFTs for its game Ghost Recon, but they flopped.[124]

And even when a game succeeds, things can change in a blink of an eye. In 2021, Axie Infinity by the Vietnam-based startup Sky Mavis provided a cautionary tale. Axie Infinity was once hailed as the most successful blockchain-based game that uses the play-to-earn model: gamers buy NFTs for their players known as Axies, or "cute monsters."[125] Players can earn rewards in the form of Smooth Love Potion (SLP) tokens, which they can sell for money.[126] But, starting in February 2022, the game's popularity plummeted from a peak of 2.7 million daily active users to under 300,000 users by September.[127] Sky Mavis's attempt to control the inflation of SLP tokens by scaling back the game's generous grant of rewards to players may have dampened its popularity. Axie Infinity's Ronin Network was also hacked in March 2022, with $625 million in crypto stolen.[128] Sky Mavis said it would reimburse the funds stolen from players.[129] Axie Infinity's game raised more fundamental concerns. An estimated 40 to 50 percent of its gamers were based in the Philippines,[130] a developing country where people faced severe economic hardships during the pandemic.[131] Some played Axie Infinity as their jobs.[132] This model raised criticisms. As Tim Morten, Frost Giant Studios CEO, told *Wired*, "That sounds kind of dystopian to me, to have an economy where people who are struggling to make a living are playing a game just to get by."[133]

The Otherside isn't likely to raise the same concern. The target audience for the Otherside is different, and the litepaper doesn't tout a "play to earn" game. Yet, in another respect, the challenge for any major Web3 platform is the same: how to go mainstream and gain widespread adoption. Walt Disney had a potent combination of movies and merchandise centered on Mickey Mouse, promoted by a club and centralized collaboration, to drive mainstream success. Yuga Labs is banking on something different: a metaverse whose development and enjoyment will be based on a hybrid business model involving both centralized and decentralized collaboration, with the goal of building a virtual world that is interoperable with other NFT projects.

THE NOUNS DAO AND CREATIVE COMMONS 0 LICENSES

Bored Apes' hybrid model isn't the only Web3 business model. An even more radical approach is the use of decentralized autonomous organizations, or DAOs, instead of companies. The DAO runs the business, and the DAO is run by the majority vote of its members, who are holders of NFTs from the DAO. The DAO owns the IP rights to the content for NFTs it creates and decides what types of licenses to adopt—centralized collaboration, decentralized collaboration, or a hybrid of the two.

No DAO has captured the imagination of what's possible more than the Nouns DAO, which hopes to "improve the formation of on-chain avatar communities."[134] One of the cofounders of the Nouns DAO is Punk 4156, one of the most influential NFT collectors and theorists, best known by the number 4156 (from the CryptoPunks he used to own, but sold—more on that later). The

DAO mints one new Nouns avatar NFT a day and sells it by auction—a distinctive strategy that departs from the common minting of 10,000 NFTs in a collection. Nouns is pioneering a new path for media production—and doing so successfully.

By November 2021, only three months after its launch, Nouns DAO had raised a mind-boggling $64 million from its NFT sales.[135] Revenues from the NFT sales go back to the DAO, which can be used to finance other projects approved by the members, including a contribution to finance Miguel Faus's indie film *Calladita*, which is funded by NFT sales.[136] In addition to the Nouns avatars, one of the most successful creations of Nouns is its signature square glasses. The DAO purchased a Nouns avatar for $394,000, gifted it to Anheuser-Busch, and, with the DAO's approval, the brewing company featured the Nouns glasses in a splashy Super Bowl commercial for Bud Light NEXT.[137]

Nouns is a startup company minus the company. If that's not mind-blowing, the Nouns DAO's approach to IP is. The Nouns DAO has adopted the Creative Commons 0 or "CC0" license for its content—meaning it has donated its copyrighted creations to the public domain, free for everyone in the world to use.[138] This decentralized approach is far more permissive than even the Bored Ape license. Indeed, it's the most permissible approach of all— copyright is abandoned and the work is donated to the public domain for the public's unrestricted use. Everyone, not just NFT owners, can copy and commercialize the Nouns name and characters, plus remix them for free and even mint in derivative NFTs. The Nouns characters form a cultural commons that everyone can enjoy, exploit, and monetize. Proponents believe that CC0 licenses are the best for Web3 because they foster an open, decentralized, and collaborative Internet.[139]

"You don't need copyright anymore," Punk 4156 explained to *Decrypt*.[140] "In the same way that academic citations make the original paper more important, citation of Nouns in whatever form they come in . . . will make the originals more important and more valuable." Punk 4156, a true believer in CC0, wanted Larva Labs to adopt the CC0 license for CryptoPunks. When Larva Labs didn't, Punk 4156 sold his CryptoPunk—for more than $10 million—to protest the limited commercial rights granted to owners under Larva Labs' license.

In 2008, writing about Web2, Lessig predicted the rise of hybrid economies in which commercial entities would give away cultural resources to the public not out of altruism, but instead so the business can monetize an economy in which people share things, such as user-generated content, not for money.[141] Think of YouTube videos. People share videos; YouTube makes money from ad revenue, whose value derives in part from how many users YouTube has.

The Nouns DAO is an example—and experiment—of Lessig's theory of a hybrid economy, but for Web3, not Web2. The Nouns DAO is a commercial entity that generates millions in revenues from the sales of NFTs, but it does so while donating the copyrighted characters for its NFTs to the public domain for everyone to share for free. Fittingly, Nouns DAO has created a sharing economy of Nouns content using the CC0 license, which comes from Creative Commons, the nonprofit Lessig founded. The CC0 license has spawned more than 150 projects involving new uses and derivative works of Nouns characters by different creators, including in derivative NFTs, 3D Nouns avatars, a Nouns almanac, clothing, caps, coffee, coloring books, eyeglasses, mugs, prints, and video games.[142] One of the derivative projects is Lil Nouns, a new DAO that creates little Nouns avatars, selling one every fifteen minutes.[143] The Nouns Museum, where anyone in the Nouns community can exhibit their art, is another example of how decentralized collaboration can help to build a new cultural ecosystem.[144] There's even an iPhone app for Nouns that allows you to create your own Nouns avatar—I did so, and it's quite easy and fun. And I've shared my Nouns avatars in the public domain on Twitter.

The Nouns DAO finances new derivative projects that Nouns owners propose and the community votes on. To fund projects more quickly, Nouns DAO adopted an auction system in which proposals are treated as bids and a new structure called "independent houses" for people outside of the Nouns community (who don't own a Nouns NFT) to hold their own auctions to vote on proposals for uses of Nouns.[145] The proposals that independent houses adopt will be funded by Nouns DAO. In September 2022, it held more than 29,000 ETH ($37 million) in its treasury.[146]

One of the projects the DAO approved was the creation of a feature film starring Nouns characters. Screenwriters Van Robichaux and Garfield L. Miller from the BlockbusterDAO were overseeing the production. Their proposal envisioned "the potential for Nouns literally everywhere—from legacy media TV, to IRL breakfast cereals, to AR adventure games."[147]

Similar to Yuga Labs' centralized collaboration with other companies, Nouns DAO is also pursuing traditional partnerships with other media companies. The DAO enlisted David Horvath, an author, illustrator, and cocreator of the popular UglyDolls, to form Nouns Studio1 to "proliferat[e] Nouns in the traditional IP business, with the goal of furthering the brand, the project, and the idea of 'open source' content in Hollywood and beyond."[148]

The Nouns' business model is radically different. Even without any copyright, the Nouns NFTs operate as a more permissive kind of De-IP, entitling the owners to a new kind of intellectual property but also donating the underlying artworks to the public domain. The Nouns use what we might call De-IP-NO©. The NFTs for Nouns are De-IP. But Nouns' copyrights have been abandoned, and the characters have been donated to the public domain— meaning no copyright (NO©). This hybrid approach maximizes the number of people who can engage in De-Collab with a project to include everyone, potentially expediting the spread of the brand. Because the Nouns artworks are in the public domain, they are free for everyone to exploit. Meanwhile, the Nouns DAO can engage in centralized collaboration with Anheuser-Busch in a Super Bowl commercial and other partnerships. But are the Nouns owners disadvantaged by not having exclusive rights to their Nouns characters, which are in the public domain? The typical sales price for a Nouns NFT—over $100,000—suggests not. The owners still own the rights to something no one else has: the NFT. And other people's uses of the same Nouns artwork may ultimately enhance its popularity and value.

How this grand experiment plays out is perhaps the most intriguing question for Web3 cultural production. The Nouns have already sparked a growing movement among Web3 proponents, including one of the most successful crypto artists, XCOPY, to adopt CC0 licenses.[149]

BUILDING A DECENTRALIZED DISNEY

The two hybrid business models adopted by Yuga Labs and the Nouns DAO won't be the only innovative types of arrangements Web3 brings. In a year, Yuga Labs and Nouns have provided tantalizing glimpses of the vast potential Web3 offers for creative production. So far, Yuga Labs' BAYC has captured the most attention—and buzz. BAYC's real competition right now isn't other NFT projects. Instead, BAYC's competition is the traditional business model of successful entertainment companies. Whether BAYC can become the decentralized Disney is the right question to ask. We won't know the answer for some time, but we can compare the two businesses to evaluate the potential, as summarized in Table 7.2.

What's most intriguing is that BAYC has adopted elements reminiscent of Disney's successful business model. Both Disney and BAYC rely on developing memorable cartoon characters, who become central to a franchise to monetize in various media and merchandise. Both Disney and BAYC rely on humor as a major feature of their storytelling. As Neal Gabler described Disney's formula for success: "All cartoons were predicated on a gag—a visual joke or brief comic situation."[150] Walt believed the gag was fundamental to the success of the story. The Bored Apes, likewise, convey the irreverent attitude of being so filthy crypto-rich that you're bored, stuck at a dive bar located on a swamp.[151] Of course, Disney

TABLE 7.2. COMPARISON OF DISNEY AND BORED APE YACHT CLUB

Element	Disney	Bored Ape Yacht Club
Business model	(1) Develop memorable cartoon characters for films for ongoing stories (franchise), (2) monetize in merchandise, other content (video games) and theme parks, and (3) for some time, engage children in Mickey Mouse clubs around the world.	(1) Develop memorable cartoon characters for NFTs for ongoing stories (franchise), (2) monetize in derivative NFTs, art, merchandise, food, beverage, restaurants, and metaverse the Otherside, and (3) engage NFT owners in Bored Ape Yacht Club.
Central character for brand	Mickey Mouse, known as funny, simple, carefree, with a streak of rebellion.	Bored Apes, known as bored, irreverent, crypto wealthy apes.
Origin	1923. Roaring Twenties and during Great Depression.	2021. During COVID pandemic, economic uncertainty, and rise of cryptocurrency.
Licensing approach	Centralized collaboration.	Hybrid model with both centralized collaboration through deals and decentralized collaboration through NFTs and De-IP.
Value	$214.37 billion (Aug. 12, 2022).	Valued at $4 billion in seed funding round of $450 million (Mar. 23, 2022).
Founded	1923 by Walt and Roy Disney.	2021 by Wylie Aronow, Greg Solano, Kerem Atalay, and Zeshan Ali.

humor is usually suitable for people of all ages, including children, while the Bored Apes' humor is at least PG-13.

Yuga Labs' approach has one major difference: BAYC has adopted a hybrid business model that uses both centralized collaboration between Yuga Labs and other companies, including Animoca Brands and Improbable for the Otherside, and Adidas and PUNKS Comic for the "Into the Metaverse" project; and decentralized collaboration between BAYC and all NFT owners of Bored Apes, Mutant Apes, Bored Ape Kennel Club dogs, and

Kodas. De-Collab licenses grant the owners unlimited commercialization rights to monetize and develop derivative works for their characters, including in businesses of their own.

A major advantage of De-Collab licenses is that they enable a business to launch a new creative ecosystem that has the potential to sprout collaborations organically from the bottom up, without the transaction costs of lawyers and conducting negotiations for content licenses. Instead of hiring employees to build the ecosystem, the NFT producer enlists creative, passionate buyers of the NFTs to do so, on top of the producer's own creations. The dual arrangement achieves a decentralized collaboration in which any increase in value or recognition of one Bored Ape increases the value of the entire Bored Ape brand and NFT collection. As Kyle Chayka wrote in a *New Yorker* article: "N.F.T. clubs aim for scalable culture; like open-source software, their cultural creations can expand organically through the efforts of many users while remaining recognizable, resulting in a kind of user-generated mythology."[152] And, as BAYC's cofounder Aronow explained: "Anything that people create with their apes only grows the brand."[153]

Yuga Labs' De-Collab license unleashes potentially 49,600 NFT owners in the BAYC ecosystem to monetize the BAYC characters without limit. Because of the high prices for Bored Ape NFTs—the lowest was selling for more than $105,000 in October 2022—we can expect that some owners have the wherewithal to commercialize their NFTs, even putting aside the celebrity owners of Bored Apes. According to economic theory, using a decentralized process to decide new product development may result in "more bad projects" because there is no central control, but, at the same time, may lead to a greater number of "new and innovative ideas."[154] Indeed, the original premise of the end-to-end principle for the Internet was to allow people to innovate by developing new applications at its so-called end points.[155] As Lessig explained: "[B]ecause the design [of the Internet] is not optimized for any particular existing application, the network is open to innovation not originally imagined."[156] A similar dynamic occurs with De-Collab licenses—they foster decentralized innovation.

The De-Collab licenses may also make their NFTs more coveted and valuable. Buyers may find more attractive NFTs that allow them to make commercial uses of artwork sold with the NFTs. Some NFT buyers may be willing to spend more because of the commercial rights, and others might choose not to buy NFTs that do not grant commercialization rights to owners. If buyers know they can monetize the NFT content, they can factor the expected future income into the price they are willing to pay.

On the flip side, De-Collab licenses come with risks. The IP owner must relinquish creative control over commercialization of its IP. It's unnerving for a business to do so. Remember the depictions of Mickey doing drugs and having sex in adult comic books. The goodwill toward a brand can be tarnished instantly if the brand is depicted in salacious or offensive content, inconsistent with the brand. Perhaps due to that fear, traditional media companies have shied away from decentralized collaboration. But not Yuga Labs.[157]

To return to the $64,000 question: Will the Bored Ape Yacht Club become the decentralized Disney? Given that BAYC is a year old and Disney's been around for a century and is an iconic, global brand, the question sounds almost laughable. Disney has a proven track record since its founding in 1923 and is a global media conglomerate ranked in the Top 20 Most Valuable Brands in the world.[158]

But laugh all you want. It's fitting for the irreverent, self-effacing attitude of today's Web3 creators. As Walt Disney once said, "It's kind of fun to do the impossible."

PART III

MEGA CHALLENGES FOR THE METAVERSE

CHAPTER 8

FOMO AND NFT BUBBLES

For a charm of powerful trouble,
Like a hell-broth boil and bubble.

—SHAKESPEARE, *MACBETH*

Just when you think you've seen it all in the wild world of NFTs, something even more unbelievable happens. On April 16, 2022, Proof, a startup, launched a new NFT collection called Moonbirds.[1] The artistic style of Moonbirds is reminiscent of the CryptoPunks—only instead of punks, the characters are pixelated owls. Each member of Proof Collective, an elite, exclusive club of one thousand NFT holders, was entitled to two free Moonbirds. Another 7,875 Moonbirds were offered, for 2.5 ETH each, to lucky members of the public who secured a spot on the whitelist. The final 125 Moonbirds were saved for future strategic uses and promotions.

None of these details are surprising. Other than the members-only club for Proof, the mechanics for the Moonbirds' minting was standard fare. But what happened next made Moonbirds' launch historic. Moonbirds went to the moon.

On the first day, the floor price tripled from the initial price of 2.5 ETH to nearly 8 ETH in the secondary market.[2] Two days later, the floor price doubled to nearly 20 ETH. A week after the launch, it skyrocketed to 39.9 ETH, a sixteenfold increase in the floor price in less than a week.

To put Moonbirds' first-week, parabolic increase into perspective, the cheapest NFT from its collection went from roughly $7,600 on April 16 to about $114,000, an increase of 1,400 percent in value. In one week, a Moonbirds owner would have accumulated at least $7,000 more wealth (in the value of an NFT) than the median retirement savings ($107,000) of people in their fifties.[3] That's why when NFT enthusiasts talk on social media about getting lucky in minting a blue-chip NFT, they often speak of life-changing, generational wealth, although few collections so far have achieved that status.

The Bored Ape Yacht Club (BAYC) floor price didn't reach 39 ETH until August 26, 2021, four months after its launch, which, of course, was impressive then.[4] But what Bored Apes did in four months, Moonbirds did in a week. Just as impressive, Moonbirds set the record for sales volume for a pfp collection in the first week, beating BAYC's first-week sales volume thirty-five fold.[5]

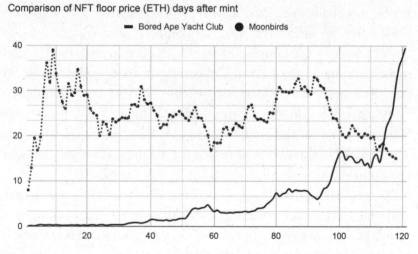

Comparison of NFT floor price (ETH) days after mint

Figure 8.1
Comparison of Floor Prices, Days After Launch of Moonbirds v. Bored Ape Yacht Club
Source: Punk9059 (NFTstatistics.eth)

If we compare NFTs to initial public offerings (IPO) in companies, the increase in Moonbirds' value is even more mind-boggling. According to data collected by Jay Ritter, the average increase in share price on the opening day—the so-called IPO pop—for IPOs from 1980 to 2020 was 18.4 percent.[6] For tech companies, the IPO pop was even better: 31.2 percent.[7] The average IPO pop during the dot-com bubble was 60 percent.[8] In 1999, Akamai Technologies had a dazzling pop of 458.4 percent.[9] But, after the dot-com bubble burst, an opening-day pop of 400 percent is unheard of. The biggest pops for tech IPOs typically are below 200 percent.[10] In 2020, nCino, a fintech company for cloud banking, had an impressive pop of 195 percent, the largest first-day pop for a U.S. IPO since the dot-com bubble.[11]

Of course, the comparison is apples to oranges. NFT collections have a far more limited supply, typically 10,000 non-fungible tokens; shares of stock, by contrast, are fungible, with potentially millions of shares in an IPO. Shares are investments in publicly traded companies; NFTs are investments in something new and more nebulous. Still, whether investing in a company's IPO or a project's NFT, buyers must decide what they are willing to pay for the financial asset. For NFTs, the floor price provides an indicator of the lowest price for an NFT from the project—which, for utility collections, increasingly includes considerations about the project's business similar to investing in a startup. But a buyer of an NFT won't have much information about the business to go on. For an IPO, investors typically have five years' worth of a company's actual performance and revenues to evaluate before it goes public.[12] For an NFT, the only "business" of a new project investors can evaluate is typically how nice the website looks and how many followers the project has on social media, plus some vague ideas floated in a road map. There are no revenues to speak of. Moreover, the relative lack of liquidity of an NFT for digital art—there's no guarantee one will find a buyer for an NFT on the secondary market—compared to a company share sold on the stock market makes the exponential increase in Moonbirds' floor price even harder to fathom.

So why did buyers see so much value in Moonbirds from day one? The exclusive Proof club undoubtedly helped. But another factor may have been that buyers were banking on the cofounder

Kevin Rose, now an Internet entrepreneur, podcaster, and venture capitalist who rose to fame by starting the news aggregator Digg in 2004, when user-generated content and Web2 were popular.[13] As Will Gottsegen of *CoinDesk* wrote in an article, Moonbirds' rise is "one of the clearest examples to date of the way in which crypto can assign a monetary value to reputation and social clout."[14]

Rose became a celebrity when he made the cover of *Businessweek* in 2006, while wearing a baseball cap backwards and awkwardly flashing two thumbs up. While noted for his brilliance, Rose's tenure at Digg was rocky. According to Business Insider, Rose's enthusiasm waned in 2006 after Digg's board of directors rejected a $60 million acquisition offer from News Corp.[15] Even while employed at Digg, Rose reportedly began working on other tech startups as side projects and later focused on angel investing in new companies, including quite successfully in Twitter, Zynga, and Square.[16] After internal turmoil and a disastrous redesign of the Digg platform, Rose left the company in 2011.[17] The next year, Digg was sold, but by then its popularity had waned.[18] Rose's skills in design and investing and overall reputation in Silicon Valley may have helped to spark the Moonbirds' opening pop. In other words, people were expecting big things from Rose.

On the day of Moonbirds' launch, Rose posted an emotional video on YouTube thanking all those who bought Moonbirds, which he said brought in $58 million to the project. "Thank you for being with us on this journey. We couldn't obviously have done this without you and we just look at this as the very, very beginning."[19] He later told *Tech Crunch* the startup's goal: "We're in this to build a big, massive, brand new kind of media company from the ground up."[20]

Moonbirds had the benefit of tailwinds provided by the exclusive club Proof Collective, founded by Rose, Ryan Carson, and Justin Mezzell, the artist. At the time, one Proof Collective membership NFT was trading for 98 ETH, or $285,000.[21] The Collective reportedly gave free membership to Beeple and Gary Vee, two of the biggest names in the NFT world.[22] Before the launch, a lot of money already supported Moonbirds—something that most NFT launches lack. The Moonbirds' road map promised future utility to NFT owners, including access to a private Discord, meetups, and events, as well as future Moonbirds' drops and Proof projects, including its upcoming Highrise metaverse. Owners also can "nest," or stake their NFTs for a certain time, to receive additional rewards as Moonbirds holders.

The Moonbirds' launch wasn't without controversy. A week later, Ryan Carson, the chief operating officer, announced he was leaving the project to start his own NFT venture fund.[23] Critics pointed out that Carson apparently swept up Moonbirds worth $1.2 million before exiting the company.[24] And not everyone would like to see wealthy Web2 entrepreneurs, backed by venture capital, paving the way to build Web3. Some fear that would just lead to Web2 déjà vu. Of course, it's hard to build something big without a lot of capital. Other than the Nouns DAO, no other NFT project appears to have substantial capital without receiving traditional VC backing. The crypto winter made VC funding even more critical. In August 2022, Moonbirds announced it had raised $50 million from a Series A funding round led by a16z, the firm that also led the funding rounds for Yuga Labs and Vaynerchuk's NFT Project VeeFriends.[25] The eventual concentration of market power in Web3 would be consistent with the legal scholar Tim Wu's theory that information industries show a recurring pattern of "brief periods of openness created by new inventions" followed by high concentration or monopoly by "dominant firms."[26] Web3 proponents aspire to end that cycle.

In May 2022, the Moonbirds' floor price dropped as low as 19 ETH, shedding nearly 50 percent from its highest value, during a major downturn not only for many NFT collections, but also for the stock market and cryptocurrencies. The downturn in each sector—NFTs, stock market, and cryptocurrencies—elicited news analysis describing each as a bubble.[27] A trifecta of bubbles. The Moonbirds' floor price held up well, though, during the downturn. Part of the reason was that nearly 95 percent of the Moonbirds owners had nested their NFTs, meaning they had agreed not to sell them for a period of time in exchange for future rewards from Proof.[28]

By early indications, Moonbirds became a blue-chip collection within the first week of its launch. Moonbirds had the sixth-largest market cap for a pfp collection, at more than $492 million, in May 2022.[29] The only collections with larger market caps were four from Yuga Labs (BAYC, CryptoPunks, MAYC, Otherdeeds)—no surprise—and the CloneX-Murakami collection, whose IP rights are now owned by Nike.

The bigger cloud that Moonbirds faced wasn't the crypto winter, but a controversy of its own making. As shown in Figure 8.1, the floor price of Moonbirds dropped significantly, causing it to fall, for the first time, below the Bored Apes' floor price, measured from comparable days after the mint. Why the sudden drop? On August 4, 2022, Kevin Rose shockingly announced on Twitter that the project was changing the license for its NFTs from a commercial license to owners to a Creative Commons 0 (CC0) to the entire public, meaning everyone would now be free to use the Moonbirds artworks.[30] In other words, the Moonbirds project was switching from a commercial license,[31] like the Bored Ape one, to a CC0 license, like the Nouns DAO approach, abandoning copyright altogether. (In fact, Proof later announced that it was committing $2.6 million to establish a DAO to govern the Moonbirds project, similar to how the Nouns DAO operates through decisions made by a majority vote of owners.[32])

The license change was surprising because it came out of the blue—after the website had indicated back in April that owners receive "full commercial art rights to the Moonbird they own."[33] Some Moonbirds owners roundly criticized the decision on Twitter, saying they were duped by a bait-and-switch. The unilateral way in which the change was made, without community involvement, also sparked great backlash.[34] Some believed the change in license diminished the value of the Moonbirds NFTs and potentially hurt owners' ability to commercialize their Moonbirds.[35] Why would a business pay a Moonbirds owner for a collaboration if the business could just monetize the Moonbirds artwork in the public domain? (That same question could be asked of the Nouns, which have retained high value in their NFTs.) Some even questioned whether such a unilateral change was legally valid.

The Moonbirds project used a standard legal clause entitling it to make unilateral changes to the terms and conditions, with the proviso that a person's continued use of the Moonbirds website constitutes the person's acceptance of the change.[36] Without more facts on how the terms were disclosed to buyers during the sale of Moonbirds NFTs and the interaction of Moonbirds owners with the website (if any) after the announced change, I'm loath to speak further on the controversy. Suffice it to say that some U.S. courts in the United States view these so-called browserwrap changes to terms and conditions with scrutiny to see if people had reasonable notice of the change and accepted it.[37]

Putting the license controversy aside, Moonbirds still can turn out to be one of the great success stories for NFTs. On the other hand, there's no guarantee it will. The historic opening week of Moonbirds raises basic questions for NFTs, but ones that are difficult to answer: How does one determine the monetary value of NFTs? Why does one collection go to the moon, while many others do not? Is it all speculation?

INTERNET BUBBLE REDUX

During the height of the NFT boom in 2021, Gary Vaynerchuk, the serial entrepreneur and avid NFT collector who has his own successful line of VeeFriends NFTs, tweeted words of caution: "99% of NFTs won't be good investments and there will be some massive crashes in the next 12 to 24 months . . . many will get confused and think it was a fad . . . that's when it gets really good . . . oh and that 1% will be all-time returns."[38]

Like a modern-day Cassandra, Gary Vee repeated his prophecy

over and over again as NFTs boomed. "I genuinely believe that 98 percent of what's out there right now [in NFTs] will not be a good investment," he told *CoinDesk* in May 2021. "On the flip side, I think the macro concept of NFTs over the next three decades is one of the most significant consumer-behavior technologies we've seen . . . since social media."[39]

In February 2022, a couple of months before a major downturn in NFT prices, Gary Vee likened the NFT boom to the dot-com bubble: "In March 2000 when all those internet stocks which were grossly overrated . . . collapsed, Amazon was sitting there at seven or eight dollars per share, the same thing will play out in the NFT space."[40]

Gary Vee speaks with experience. He saw the potential of dot-com businesses and transformed his family's wine business from $3 million in annual revenues to $70 million by selling online.[41] He promoted the business and grew his own social media brand by creating daily wine-tasting videos on his YouTube channel, Wine-LibraryTV. From there, Gary Vee catapulted to become a successful entrepreneur and investor, bestselling author, motivational speaker, and founder of several media businesses, including VaynerNFT, later renamed Vayner3. Indeed, Gary Vee reportedly made more than $50 million from the sale of VeeFriends NFTs, which also received $50 million in seed funding.[42]

The notion that 98 percent of dot coms failed is a common one. But that figure might not be accurate. The most comprehensive study on dot-com companies' survival rates was conducted by Brent Goldfarb, David Kirsch, and David Miller, who found that 48 percent of dot coms were still in existence at the time of their study in 2004, a survival rate comparable to other emerging industries.[43] The Internet historian Brian McCullough notes a comparable survival rate of dot coms.[44] By comparison, after the 1896 British bicycle bubble burst, 70 percent of British bicycle companies failed.[45]

The survival rate of NFT projects is still being played out. But let's assume that a high percentage of them will go to zero in value as Gary Vee predicted, a reasonable assumption during the crypto winter when NFT sales plummeted. From its record high of $405.75 million in sales on May 1, 2022 (the Otherdeed launch), OpenSea had only $5 million in sales on August 28—a drop of 99 percent.[46] With such low secondary sales, resale royalties drop, thereby making it difficult for NFT projects to sustain themselves or build the business. But the question remains: Are NFTs a transformative technology that will usher in a new era for the Internet as the dot coms did?[47]

I share Gary Vee's view. Online businesses didn't go extinct after the dot-com bubble burst. They only got better—with stronger business models and management. In place of Pets.com, we have Chewy, PetSmart, Petco, and, of course, Amazon.

This book explains my reasons for believing that NFTs are a part of the most important development in the Web since its inception. But it's also important to recognize the risks and uncertainties presented by a new, disruptive technology. NFTs have produced a market for a new kind of property and interactive ownership, new business models for decentralized collaboration, generational wealth for some lucky NFT owners, and great speculation in value, all in a year. There's so much speculation, in part, because collections like BAYC, CloneX, and Moonbirds are still developing the projects in their road maps and building their metaverses. Investing in a hot NFT collection based on its development of a future metaverse is like buying a stake in an invention that not even the inventor has figured out how to build.

NAVIGATING SPECULATION

Financial bubbles have fascinated commentators since the nineteenth century and Charles Mackay's book *Extraordinary Popular Delusions and the Madness of Crowds*.[48] Even with the proliferation of modern finance scholarship, there's still no consensus on the underlying cause(s) of financial bubbles—or even if they exist.

One influential school is Eugene Fama's theory of efficient

markets, which is skeptical that bubbles exist or provide a meaningful financial term.[49] Fama contends that people see bubbles in markets, but they have no way of testing a "predictable ending" for a bubble because the market is random.[50] Fama's theory of "efficient markets" underlies popular index funds that include the stocks of the S&P index or other indexes; typically, index funds have better returns than mutual funds whose stocks are chosen by managers.[51] By contrast, another influential school, based on the behavioral economics theory of Robert Shiller, contends that speculative bubbles can be explained by psychology—and people's susceptibility to cognitive biases.[52] Both Fama and Shiller were awarded Nobel prizes for economics, ironically in the same year.

The finance scholars William Quinn and John Turner find the focus on rational versus irrational unhelpful and "too reductive" of the complexity of factors at play.[53] They propose examining what they call a "bubble triangle," focusing on three factors: marketability of an asset, availability of money/credit, and speculation.[54] Digital assets are especially marketable, and, when money's flowing, there may be "large numbers of novices [who] become speculators, many of whom trade purely on momentum, buying when prices are rising and selling when prices are falling."[55] Quinn and Turner acknowledge, though, that we can't identify a bubble for sure until it bursts.[56]

It's not crucial that we take a side in this ongoing debate over bubbles. If Nobel laureates can't resolve it, we won't, either. What's important for us is awareness. For artists, businesses, and potential NFT investors, it's important to understand how the dynamics of NFT purchases might lead to highly speculative prices, as the NFT boom and bust showed. Here are five key insights to help recognize major risks associated with NFTs.

1. As New Technologies, NFTs Invite Great Speculation

From the great railway and bicycle bubbles in Britain during the nineteenth century, to the dot-com bubble at the start of the twenty-first century, new technologies have been the subject of wild speculation.[57] It's not difficult to see why. Investors recognize the potential of a new technology that may dramatically transform society—for example, by offering an entirely new mode of transportation or a new way to do business online for e-commerce—and want to invest early to reap financial rewards, despite the uncertainties of how the new technology will develop or how successful it will be.

NFTs are confounding because they involve not only new technologies, but also a new type of ownership, often in visual art, which itself is prone to price speculation. On top of that, future uses of NFTs in the metaverse are still being developed. With so much uncertainty and rapid development of a new technology, rampant speculation is to be expected.

In spring 2022, mainstream media seemed convinced that NFTs were in a big bubble, with signs of bursting.[58] Some finance theory supports this view. To draw upon Quinn and Turner's bubble-triangle theory, NFTs have all three ingredients to fuel a bubble. First, NFTs are marketable: they are sold on the producers' websites and then, in secondary sales, on marketplaces such as OpenSea. Indeed, NFTs make art much easier to sell online (no need even for shipping), although the need for a crypto wallet and ETH cryptocurrency require modest tech knowledge that present a modest speed bump for some consumers, especially those lacking cryptocurrency. Second, money and credit were in great supply in 2021: crypto markets and the stock market boomed, while interest rates were low. During the pandemic, the U.S. government's stimulus checks also pumped more money—perhaps too much—into the financial system. Third, the market for NFTs lends itself to great speculation. Not only is the technology new and rapidly evolving, but there's also a recognized culture of being an NFT "degen" (degenerate) on social media and throwing caution to the wind and "apeing" in and making risky investments in NFTs. FOMO, the fear of missing out, has itself become a meme among NFT enthusiasts. Being a degen, apeing in, and FOMO all fit Shiller's theory of herd behavior and contagion among investors, the ingredients for a bubble.[59]

The crypto winter all but confirmed that the NFT bubble had burst. But we should tread carefully before giving too much credence to the "bursting of the NFT bubble" narrative. As we'll examine in the next section, Shiller doesn't think "bubble" is the best way to understand cryptocurrency and NFTs, which, he believes, might continue to survive indefinitely. He proposes to focus on narrative economics, which appeals to investors' psychology and plays into cognitive biases. Moreover, even if *bubble* is a helpful term, it's hard to disentangle the downturn in NFT values and sales volumes in summer 2022 from comparable downturns in the stock market and cryptocurrency.[60] All markets were plummeting. On September 13, 2022, the Dow Jones Industrial Average fell 1,276 points, close to 4 percent, for example. The downturn was a response to the rise of inflation, the Fed's decision to raise interest rates, and fears of a recession. Singling out the NFT downturn amid a general economic downturn—that many analysts characterize as involving "highly unusual" macro-economic factors stemming from the pandemic—would be to miss the forest for the trees.[61]

Moreover, some tech bubbles may be beneficial to society. In their book, Quinn and Turner show how, historically, major tech bubbles have been less pernicious in economic fallout and how, at a macro level, they have yielded net benefits for society in the way of transformative technologies, innovation, and future economic growth.[62] The dot-com bubble may be one such example, Quinn and Turner suggest, with the infusion on investments in the tech sector, including dot coms such as Amazon and eBay and preexisting companies, including Apple and Microsoft.[63] The scholars find similar benefits in the development of bicycles and railways in the nineteenth-century British bubbles.[64] A plentiful supply of bikes promoted exercise, was better for the environment and safer than cars and horses, and was instrumental to the women's equality movement, both in terms of mobility and precipitating changes in clothing.[65] Britain's development of a national railway system facilitated travel, in shorter times, although the national system suffered from redundancies and poorly planned lines.[66] Of course, the macro benefits of tech bubbles provide no solace to all the businesses that failed or people who lost money, possibly life savings, when the bubbles burst. But history has shown that tech bubbles can yield positive societal benefits. Quinn saw little chance that a bubble burst among NFTs would cause a financial crisis for the economy.[67] (In a research paper published in February 2022, Quinn and his coauthors gave a mixed review of the business potential of NFTs for creators.[68])

Because NFTs, the metaverse, and Web3 are still developing rapidly, it's too early to analyze the social benefits of NFTs with any certainty. But we can try to understand what these technologies are, so we are in a better position to evaluate their potential value to artists, businesses, and society, as well as the potential for highly speculative values. In this book, I've identified the potential value I see in NFTs—in establishing a new type of property and interactive ownership effectuated on blockchain; in empowering independent artists, especially digital artists, to create and sell their works in decentralized markets without the need to have the backing of major industry intermediaries and gatekeepers; in enabling consumers to become owners of their online identities and data free of the shackles of surveillance capitalism; in offering businesses a new way to engage and reward people, especially the next generation of consumers; in facilitating the development of new, purely virtual products and more immersive experiences; and in facilitating innovative, hybrid business models involving both centralized and decentralized collaboration. And this is just the beginning. I expect many other future uses of NFTs, with the amount of investments businesses are making. Yet, at the same time, we are so early in the development of NFTs and the future metaverse that we can only speculate on how much of this vast potential will be realized.

Amid this uncertainty, the valuation of NFTs will inevitably involve speculation. And it plays out differently depending on whether the NFT is sold as a "one of one" NFT for a single artwork or as a part of a collection of 10,000 NFTs. A "one of one" NFT presents a simpler valuation. It's similar to deciding how to value a painting. But that, in itself, is notoriously fraught with speculation, especially when the artist isn't well-established with a body of work (or brand) that has already commanded certain sales prices in the market or past auctions.[69] The value of art, like its beauty, is subjective. Plus, a new class of art buyers who are younger may have much different tastes.[70]

So what do buyers say they consider in buying art online? In a 2019 survey by the website Artsy, art collectors identified the following motivations for their online purchases of art: aesthetics was the most commonly cited factor (78 percent of collectors), followed by decoration (71 percent), inspiration (67 percent), subject matter and story behind work (58 percent), support for the artists (51 percent), and the artist's story (43 percent).[71] Interestingly, only 35 percent of the collectors surveyed said they bought the art as an investment, and even fewer (26 percent) said they evaluate artworks based on the likelihood to appreciate in value.[72]

The dynamics of NFT purchases may be different. According to a 2021 survey of 595 art buyers by the Hiscox Online Art Trade Report, 82 percent of NFT buyers surveyed said that investment was the most important factor; and of NFT buyers who spent more than $25,000 on NFTs in the past year, the number increased to 95 percent.[73] But the people surveyed also cited the passion for art (67 percent), social impact and patronage (39 percent), and community (38 percent) as important factors in buying NFTs.[74] Interestingly, gender divided the answers: female buyers more often identified their passion for art as their motivation for NFT purchases, while male buyers overwhelmingly cited the investment potential.[75] Even with these potential differences in the NFT market, deciding how much to spend on a "one of one" NFT is not that different from making the same decision for an original painting. In either case, a host of factors may influence what buyers are willing to spend for an item.

By contrast, a collection of 10,000 NFTs, such as CryptoPunks, BAYC, Doodles, or Deadfellaz, is far more complex in its economics—or what people call "tokenomics." Tokenomics describes all the elements of a type of token or NFT collection, including the total supply; the utility; the rarity of traits in the artwork for the NFTs; the launch mechanics, including the random distribution of NFTs in the collection to buyers and mint price; the staking possibility; and future air drops, all of which may affect its value in the minds of buyers.[76] The NFT creators decide all of these elements. The NFTs with the rarest traits in a collection typically command the highest prices, but, because they are a part of the same collection, they also help to increase the value of the NFTs at the floor.

The top NFT collections are operating as startups—with ambitious road maps of future developments and divisions of labor to perform as media businesses. Relatedly, for collections, NFT buyers are likely including considerations beyond the art collector of "one of one" NFTs. What's the business plan of this NFT project? Do the founders have any experience running a successful business? Does the NFT art have an aesthetic from which the business can build a brand? These are the kinds of questions that, increasingly, buyers will ask before making substantial investments in new NFT collections, especially after the crypto winter made it harder for NFT projects to succeed.

Another factor that fuels NFT speculation is the so-called whales, wealthy investors who have a lot of crypto to buy high volumes of NFTs. According to a Moonstream study of 727,012 accounts on Ethereum between April and September 2021, "the top 16.71% of the NFT owners control 80.98% of the NFTs."[77] A staggering amount. The spending sprees of whales, such as in "sweeping the floor" of a collection, can generate speculation of other buyers.[78] The phenomenon is not new. In the stock market, Nancy Pelosi is considered a whale whose investments (which are often quite successful) are closely followed by other investors, including a website called Unusual Whales that has created an exchange-traded fund (ETF) tracker based on Pelosi's stock picks.[79] There's a similar website that tracks NFT whale purchases.[80]

Not everyone is a fan of NFT whales, whose transactions can

have an outsized effect on the market for an NFT collection. But everyone should be aware of how whales roam the NFT market and can effect huge swings in NFT prices. A related problem often involving whales—the possibility of insider trading, or people buying NFTs based on tips from insiders who have nonpublic information—will be discussed in a later chapter.

2. Beware of FOMO, Hype, and Scams on Social Media

In his 2011 book, *The Thank You Economy*, Gary Vee described the difficulty he experienced, for six years, in trying to convince businesses to use social media.[81] He rebutted eleven excuses businesses offered for not using social media. Perhaps the funniest: "Social media is just another trend that will pass."[82] Nearly two decades of social media use have proved Gary Vee right. In 2022, average daily hours spent on social media among people worldwide increased to 2 hours and 27 minutes.[83] Americans spent, on average, 2 hours and 3 minutes.[84] According to a 2021 National Retail Federation article, Gen Z and Millennials spent, respectively, a whopping 4.5 hours and 3.8 hours a day on social media.[85] Various surveys show that a significant percentage of consumers use social media for purchases, recommendations from influencers or others, and searching. A 2022 report by Accenture predicted that social commerce—in which shopping is integrated into social media—will expand into a $1.2 trillion market by 2025.[86]

Social media also plays a huge part for NFTs. Most collections have their own Discord chat. NFT enthusiasts also discuss NFTs every day on Twitter, LinkedIn, TikTok, and other social media. These discussions can be very informative—providing essential knowledge. Indeed, we've already discussed several successful artists in Part I who learned about and studied NFTs from social media. I did, too. I find Twitter Spaces a great forum to learn various viewpoints about NFTs. I confess that a great deal of my knowledge of NFTs comes from being a regular participant in what's called "NFT Twitter" and "NFT LinkedIn."

On the flip side, social media is a cesspool, flooded with misinformation, hate speech, spam, bots, and fake accounts. For NFTs, probably the biggest concern is FOMO, the fear of missing out. First described in 2004, FOMO has elicited a whole body of psychological research into its causes and effects.[87] A lot more research needs to be done, especially about its role in cryptocurrency and NFT investing, not to mention the role of media narratives in potentially making FOMO worse.[88] But we already have a sense of how FOMO operates.

Imagine reading, in June 2017, a *Mashable* article titled "This Ethereum-Based Project Could Change How We Think About Digital Art." It described 10,000 pieces of a new kind of digital art/technology.[89] The pieces were being given away for free. The article included an image of a pixelated woman with wild blond hair, amber sunglasses, and red lipstick. An image that looked like it was from an old Atari game, but also maybe from the future. The article suggested that the digital art could become valuable. But, because you were busy at work, you didn't have time to investigate further. Four years later, you toiled away working at home during the worst pandemic in a century and stumbled on a *Wired* article titled "The 10,000 Faces That Launched an NFT Revolution."[90] Wait . . . You check, and, yes, the article is about the same art discussed in the *Mashable* article from 2017. Oh no, you see the art pieces you thought of buying, but didn't, are now selling for millions of dollars—one even sold for $11.75 million. But there's more. Other people read the same *Mashable* article and were smarter than you: they scooped up some of the cool art pieces and are now multimillionaires, with a level of generational wealth unimaginable for most people. To make you feel worse, you see some of the owners using the cool, pixelated characters as their pfp on Twitter, including Jay-Z.

Most of this scenario occurred. I have taken poetic license by creating a person who read the *Mashable* article, but didn't follow through in buying a CryptoPunk. No one has come forward and admitted that. But, according to John Watkinson, the cocreator of the CryptoPunks, the *Mashable* article caused a huge spike in demand. The CryptoPunks were all taken a day after the article: "one man who saw the post amassed 758 of them."[91]

If you were in the shoes of the person who missed out on the CryptoPunks—and the generational wealth that it later brought—how would you feel? Most people would probably be kicking themselves for not following through and grabbing a CryptoPunk when they had a chance. They knew about the CryptoPunks, but missed out. That's a worse feeling than not knowing at all. In 2005, Warren Buffett told students that he considered his biggest mistakes the investments that he knew about, but didn't make or allocate enough money in.[92] Buffett said he doesn't dwell on the mistakes, but not many people have the financial acumen, years of investing success, or wealth of Warren Buffett. Once stung by missing out on CryptoPunks, probably many people would resolve not to miss out on the next CryptoPunks—and the lure of getting rich quick by buying an NFT. It only takes missing out once to make you fear missing out again.

For anyone who's followed discussion of NFTs on Twitter or Discord, FOMO was palpable in 2021 during the NFT boom. Of course, sometimes FOMO can turn out to be right. Kyle Swenson, the creator of the *Bored Ape Gazette*, told *The New Yorker* that FOMO is what caused him to buy two Bored Apes when they came out and others on Twitter had aped in.[93] A problem with FOMO, though, is that it's constant. Until lucking into generational wealth, hitting the NFT jackpot, one can FOMO into dozens of NFT collections with great losses. With every new collection that experiences an even modest increase in value—it doesn't have to be a Moonbirds' parabolic increase—the narrative that people can become rich buying NFTs seems more enticing. As *Bloomberg Businessweek* encapsulated in a headline on its June 14, 2021, cover: "Why Is Everyone Making Money but You?"[94]

In his Nobel Prize lecture in 2013, Shiller defined a financial bubble in a way that captures how narratives and psychology play a huge role in financial speculation:

*A situation in which news of price increases spurs investor en-
thusiasm which spreads by psychological contagion from person
to person, in the process amplifying stories that might justify the
price increase and bringing in a larger and larger class of investors, who, despite doubts about the real value of the investment,
are drawn to it partly through envy of others' successes and partly
through a gambler's excitement.[95]*

More recently, Shiller said the concept of a financial bubble—
that bursts and ends—is not helpful to describe the market for
cryptocurrency and NFTs.[96] He pointed out that Bitcoin has plummeted in price several times, but hasn't burst and could last indefinitely, as gold eventually did.[97] Shiller believed "epidemic" or
"contagion" is a better way to describe the spread of a narrative to
invest in a hyped asset, such as cryptocurrency and NFTs, which
may mutate over time like a virus.[98]

In his latest book, Shiller described the role of stories in sparking
financial contagion and investment decisions as narrative economics.[99] He contended that understanding how a narrative can go viral
and affect people's investment decisions will help economists make
better economic forecasts of major events or calamities, such as a
financial crisis.[100] The preface and first chapter of Shiller's book begin, respectively, with two examples: one from the Roaring Twenties and one from today. Shiller wrote his book before the COVID
pandemic, so his discussion of the Roaring Twenties (after the 1918
pandemic) at the start of his book seems clairvoyant.

Quoting a passage from Frederick Lewis Allen's book *Only
Yesterday: An Informal History of the 1920s*, Shiller captures the eu-
phoric atmosphere of investors before the 1929 stock market crash:
Americans at dinner tables heard "fantastic stories of sudden fortunes" of people, young and old, getting rich quick and being "fixed
for life."[101] In Allen's words, "Thousands speculated—and won
too—without the slightest knowledge of the nature of the company
upon whose fortunes they were relying, like the people who bought

Seaboard Air Line under the impression that it was an aviation stock."[102] Seaboard was a railroad; "air line" meant the shortest distance, a straight line, between two points. Today, Allen's description of the "fantastic stories" of people getting rich quick and being set for life by buying stocks during the Roaring Twenties sounds eerily similar to the success stories of early investors in crypto or NFTs. Though Shiller didn't speak about NFTs, his analysis of one narrative for Bitcoin "as a membership token in the world economy" can apply equally to NFTs.[103]

Of course, identifying a powerful narrative is often easy. Social media helps us to spot them—just follow the trending hashtags, such as #FOMO or #degen. But evaluating whether it's good or bad, valid or flawed, accurate or false, helpful or harmful to human behavior is far more difficult, especially when the underlying conditions you're attempting to evaluate are changing by the day. An added problem is that humans are prone to understanding complex situations or concepts more easily through narratives. Shiller's book, for example, can be described as a narrative about narrative economics—how in the past, traditional macroeconomics literature ignored narratives as motivating factors for people's decisions, but here are a bunch of historical examples, including the stock market speculation during the Roaring Twenties and Bitcoin today, that show how contagious stories underlie major economic changes.

But reliance on some narrative to explain a theory isn't a fault of Shiller's. In a way, a theory is a story. Theorists want their stories or big ideas to go viral, especially among their peers. Indeed, this book includes its own narratives—for example, creators taking control through NFTs—while critiquing other narratives. It's perhaps impossible to avoid narrative if you want other people to understand your theory. The best example of this paradox is Nassim Nicholas Taleb's theory of the black swan, a metaphor that he uses to describe unpredicted, unforeseen occurrences that defy our expectations.[104] As Taleb ironically put it: "I prefer to use stories and vignettes to illustrate our gullibility about stories and our preference for the dangerous compression of narratives."[105]

Even if we can't escape narratives, we can be more aware of them. The narrative of "getting rich quick" isn't new. But it's important to recognize how it can foment FOMO, especially on social media. Once we do, we will be in a better position to evaluate our own financial decisions and expectations to see if they are realistic or just fantasy.

Another risk of social media involves outright scams and phishing to steal NFTs. As NFTs have exploded in value so have the number and sophistication of scams. One of the most common scams occurs when a bad actor hacks the Discord, Twitter, or other account for a legitimate NFT project and then posts a fake minting link that can gain access to buyers' private keys to their crypto wallets—and then abscond with the buyers' money or illegally transfer other NFTs from the wallets.[106] Justin Kan's platform Fractal fell prey to this hack, resulting in people's loss of $150,000, which Fractal reimbursed.[107] Bad actors are getting very clever: they use fake accounts posing as legitimate NFT collections that have "verified" status, such as the blue check on Twitter, or outright hack the legitimate, verified accounts of NFT collections. Some fake Moonbirds' accounts on Twitter even reportedly had verified blue-check marks.[108] Someone hacked the official Instagram account of Bored Ape Yacht Club and pulled off the same phishing technique, resulting in more than $1 million worth of Bored Apes stolen from owners.[109] Phishing to steal NFTs has become so easy that a common piece of advice in the NFT community is to never click a link on social media. We'll return to the growing problem of stolen NFTs in a later chapter. How to address stolen NFTs has become one of the most controversial issues for Web3.

A related problem involves spam bots that have overtaken the discussion of NFTs and cryptocurrency on Twitter. Tweeting terms related to NFTs and cryptocurrency may trigger bot replies asking you to register your wallet, click a link, or sign up for some project.[110] Because I tweet about NFTs, I've been bombarded by spam on Twitter. When Elon Musk made an offer to acquire Twitter in 2022, he recognized the bot problem there. "A top priority I would have is eliminating the spam and scam bots and the bot armies that are on Twitter," Musk said in an interview at a TED conference in Vancouver. "They make the product much worse."[111]

3. It's Okay to Take Risks, but Remember to DYOR

Being a degen and throwing caution to the wind is a badge of honor among NFT enthusiasts, many of whom self-identify as such on Twitter. Who doesn't like the sound of throwing all worry aside and just making risky but potentially life-changing investments? Indeed, there's something glamorous and alluring in being an NFT degen—it's reminiscent of the riverboat gamblers on the American frontier. During a pandemic resulting in the loss of millions of lives, why shouldn't we take risks and pursue our passions—while we can? The researchers Muhammad Shadab Iqbal and Lin Li conducted a study of two hundred Americans and found a correlation between COVID proximity and risk-taking: people were more willing to take risks in investments, the greater the number of COVID cases in the neighborhood.[112]

But being a degen doesn't mean being stupid. One can be a degen and DYOR, starting with taking stock of one's own budget and figuring out how much money, if any, one can realistically spend—and lose—on an NFT purchase. The amount of research one would devote before buying an expensive car, painting, or diamond ring should be similar to the amount of research one conducts before buying an expensive NFT. For launches, buyers can examine the websites of various NFT collections and compare their road maps and IP licenses, plus the teams behind each project, including their business experience. The Twitter and Discord accounts can give more information about a project, including the number of followers it already has and a better sense of the community for the project as well as its popularity. But take those numbers with a grain of salt: they might be inflated by followers who were bought. For secondary sales, numerous websites provide analytics of sales volumes, floor prices, the number and rarity of NFTs in the collection, and the number of owners. And always be on the lookout for fake accounts and suspicious links. Buyer beware.

4. NFT Marketplaces Should Inform Buyers of NFT Prices in Dollars with Equal or Greater Prominence

Marketplaces can also help curb speculation. NFTs are often listed in ETH prices. A few marketplaces, such as Nifty Gateway and NBA Top Shot, denominate prices in U.S. dollars for sales, but it's more common to see prices listed in ETH (or other cryptocurrency). OpenSea, the largest marketplace, doesn't include both ETH and USD prices on the collection's landing page. Instead, the USD price is included only once a consumer selects a particular NFT and is taken to the individual NFT webpage. But the ETH price is in much larger type size and in bold, while the USD price is in smaller font and in a very light typeface. LooksRare and Coinbase use a similar approach, but LooksRare includes USD prices in even smaller font than OpenSea.

The visual prominence of ETH prices over USD prices in NFT marketplaces might encourage overspending by consumers. Conducting a behavioral experiment with foreign currencies, the business scholars Priya Raghubir and Joydeep Srivastava found that consumers who were unfamiliar with a currency were biased by the face value of the currency and overspent when its value was a fraction of a dollar or the person's home currency.[113] Drawing on Amos Tversky and Daniel Kahneman's influential theory of anchoring and adjustment, the researchers contended that consumers anchor on the face value of foreign currency—which, in the fraction scenario, would be a smaller value than the real amount in dollars— and then inadequately adjust for the conversion to dollars.[114] Put in simpler terms, consumers see a smaller number in the foreign currency and end up overspending because the smaller number makes it seem as though they aren't spending as much as they are.

Although further study is needed to test whether this face-value effect occurs in the NFT context, we can make an educated guess that it does. ETH typically is a small fraction of a dollar. For example, on August 12, 2022, 0.0005311855 ETH equaled 1 USD—precisely the kind of scenario involving a currency with an exchange rate by a fraction of a dollar. If the bias that Raghubir and Srivastava identify also applies to cryptocurrency, buyers shopping for NFTs on OpenSea or other large marketplaces using prices in ETH are likely to anchor on the price listed on the collection's landing page, which is typically denominated only in ETH. After buyers select a particular NFT and go to its individual webpage, the ETH price is so much more prominent than the USD price that it's hard to expect the USD price will undo the anchoring bias for the ETH price. That anchoring bias may be compounded by the buyer's cryptocurrency wallet, such as a Metamask, which also may use much larger type for ETH versus USD.

I didn't have the time to perform a behavioral experiment to test my hypothesis before this book's publication, but let me suggest why I think it's a reasonable hypothesis, based on Raghubir and Srivastava's study. If I asked if you'd be willing to spend 4 ETH on a young, new artist's NFT, you might at least consider it. But if I asked if you'd be willing to spend $5,000 on the same NFT, you might be far less willing to do so. Indeed, you might immediately reject the offer. You instantly understand the value of spending $5,000—for example, how many months' rent or mortgage payments you could make. Even when the USD price is designated in smaller type, the anchoring bias might cloud a consumer's perspective, causing the consumer to latch on to the more prominent ETH price and then overspend.

Until there's testing of this hypothesis, prudence counsels caution. Unfortunately, it's hard for people to avoid anchoring bias based simply on recognition of the cognitive bias. My recommendation is that NFT marketplaces and NFT creators should list NFT prices in USD (or relevant foreign currency for consumers abroad) with equal or even greater prominence than ETH prices. Below I compare the actual size of prices of an NFT on OpenSea (as viewed on my desktop) and how they can be revised in the same format on every webpage in which prices are listed for the NFT, including the collection's landing page:

Example of prices for an NFT on OpenSea[115]:

66 ($132,244.86)

Example of prices for an NFT in same format:

66 ($132,244.86)

To counteract the potential anchoring bias and face value effect, marketplaces should list prices in USD (or relevant foreign currency) in the same size and format as the ETH price. And prices should never be listed in ETH alone.

5. Most NFTs Won't Become the Next Bored Apes—and That's a Good Thing
The most successful NFT collection so far is the Bored Ape Yacht Club, valued at $4 billion in its seed funding round in 2022. But BAYC isn't mainstream yet even though it aspires to be. The prior chapter examined the innovative, hybrid business model that BAYC utilizes—and its potential for becoming a decentralized Disney. The path for reaching that level is by no means guaranteed.

The meteoric rise in value of NFTs from CryptoPunks, BAYC, Moonbirds, CloneX, and other blue-chip collections may lead to unrealistic expectations. First, others who aspire to create the next hot NFT collection like BAYC may think it's easy. It's not. It takes a lot more than just creating cartoon characters through randomly generated art. To do what BAYC or any other blue-chip utility NFT project is doing, you need to establish a business, hire the right people, have a plan for marketing and cultivating demand for a new NFT collection, and identify something that distinguishes your project from the many others. And that's only the starting point. Even after a successful launch of the collection, you need to execute your road map of future projects, including building new uses of your NFTs for the metaverse. And you need to know how to manage your NFT owners' expectations, especially when other projects are going to the moon and yours is not. All of that takes money, talent, and business skill. Even those ingredients don't guarantee success. You also need some luck—to be at the right place at the right time.

One founder of an NFT project who goes by the name King-pickle on Twitter shared the many challenges of starting a new NFT business. It's a full-time job, requiring lots of money to pay for the smart contract development, marketing, moderators, legal work, plus creation and tweaking of the generative art, which requires a lot more time than one thinks.[116] There's also the challenge of screening out the many wannabe NFT advisors who have no clue about NFTs. Every project must also consider whether to buy followers on social media, because without followers it's hard for a new project to be successful, such as in landing collabs.[117] Even if you do everything right, that may not be enough. You have to "pray that someone notices the hard work and vibes with the mission or art."[118]

The crypto winter provided warning to all aspiring NFT project creators. The boom was over. Building a successful business required far more than minting NFTs.

Another unrealistic expectation occurs on the other end, with buyers. The success of BAYC and other blue-chip collections has raised some buyers' expectations to perhaps unattainable levels. If buyers expect to become millionaires overnight by buying an NFT, that's unlikely to happen. New projects will be judged against the utility and perks provided by BAYC and other blue chips to their communities. The competition is fierce. If the launch of the CryptoPunks had occurred today instead of in 2017, buyers would likely expect greater utility than just being a pfp collection without a road map of future perks, which is all that Larva Labs offered.

Most NFT collections won't become the next Bored Apes. The promise of Web3 is decentralization, enabling a myriad of creative communities, big and small, to flourish. BAYC represents one of the most interesting hybrid business models, combining centralized and decentralized collaboration, plus funding from venture capital, wealthy investors, and individual NFT sales. But, if Web3 becomes dominated by a few businesses like BAYC, Web3 would be a failure. There's so much more potential that Web3 offers.

Vitalik Buterin, the twenty-eight-year-old visionary cocreator of Ethereum blockchain, spoke of this potential in an interview with *Time*. Buterin noted the promise that decentralization holds in curbing the control Internet platforms have accumulated over people's online lives.[119] But Buterin also worried about the crypto culture's obsession with becoming rich. "The peril is you have these $3 million monkeys and it becomes a different kind of gambling."[120] In a tweet, Buterin clarified: "I don't hate apes, I just want them to fund public goods!"[121] For the record, Yuga Labs does donate to charities, including reportedly 10 million ApeCoin to the Jane Goodall Legacy Foundation.[122] Yuga Labs also donated $1 million to aid Ukraine. But Buterin probably expresses the views of many Web3 proponents who are uneasy about the prospect of BAYC turning into another big company backed by Silicon Valley.

The first step in achieving the true promise of Web3 is for everyone to realize that most NFT collections won't be the next Bored Apes—and that's a good thing.

CHAPTER 9

REGULATING WEB3?

We cannot be mere consumers of good governance.
We must be participants; we must be cocreators.

—ROHINI NILEKANI

In 1996 John Perry Barlow, a cofounder of the Electronic Frontier Foundation and former lyricist for the Grateful Dead, wrote his 844-word "Declaration of the Independence of Cyberspace."[1] No essay captured the cyberlibertarian ethos at the Web's beginning better than Barlow's manifesto. Writing from the World Economic Forum in Davos, he addressed the "Governments of the Industrial World," including, directly by name, those of China, Germany, France, Russia, Singapore, Italy, and the United States.

"I declare the global social space we are building to be naturally independent of the tyrannies you seek to impose on us," Barlow boldly declared. "You have no moral right to rule us nor do you possess any methods of enforcement we have true reason to fear."[2]

Barlow's declaration of independence was different from the one Thomas Jefferson wrote in 1776. In speaking about government, Jefferson recognized "the Right of the People to alter or to abolish it, and to institute new Government, laying its foundation on such principles and organizing its powers in such form." Eventually, the Framers formed a new government for the United States in the Constitution. By contrast, what Barlow imagined sounded less formal, less institutional: "We believe that from ethics, enlightened self-interest, and the commonweal, our governance will emerge."

Indeed, the only law cyberspace "would generally recognize is the Golden Rule."[3] Do unto others, you get the rest.

Barlow's vision sounded idyllic, reminiscent of Locke's state of nature. Indeed, in a nod to Locke, Barlow declared: "We are forming our own Social Contract." With the passage of twenty-five years, Barlow's declaration has received its share of criticisms as being wrong, utopian, and naïve. Of course, governments around the world passed laws that regulated the Internet, which wasn't "naturally independent" of the rest of the world as Barlow claimed.[4] In 2016, however, Barlow stuck by his original view, telling *Wired*, "It's very simple. They don't have jurisdiction."[5]

Whether Barlow was right about the inability of national governments to regulate the Internet is not crucial for us to revisit (plenty has been written on that topic). Instead, it's far more important for us to focus on what Barlow didn't anticipate in 1996 and what even the *Wired* article in 2016 ignored: the rise of large Internet companies and platforms, such as Facebook, Twitter, and YouTube, which have profoundly shaped online governance in the past two decades. Barlow imagined people would develop governance of the Internet through "ethics, enlightened self-interest, and the commonweal." Not once did he mention Internet companies.

Barlow's omission was understandable. In 1996, there was no social media to speak of: the biggest Internet companies (AOL, Webcrawler, Netscape, Yahoo!, and Infoseek) didn't have the kind of sharing platforms requiring the vast amount of oversight that social media now require.[6] The rise of large sharing platforms— Facebook, Twitter, YouTube, etc.—threw a monkey wrench into the cyberlibertarian vision of the Internet. These platforms, spurred by powerful network effects (a network becomes more useful and attractive as more people join it) and market consolidation, emerged in the first decade of the twenty-first century. These Internet platforms became the de facto regulators of billions of people online. The platforms didn't want to become regulators of online content—as Mark Zuckerberg repeatedly said, including in testimony before Congress, Facebook wasn't the arbiter of truth.[7] Plus, patrolling social media for harmful comments requires a lot of money and resources. It's a lot easier to do nothing.

So what changed? In 2016, the Russian Internet Research Agency launched a massive disinformation campaign on every major social media platform in the United States to interfere with the U.S. presidential election. A bipartisan report, issued by the U.S. Senate Select Committee on Intelligence, documented the Russian interference in great detail, including many examples of fake posts and deception.[8] The Russian interference was a wake-up call. People using fake accounts were able to weaponize the Internet platforms for malicious purposes. Afterward, the Internet platforms invested more staff and resources to stop that from happening again, especially the spread of harmful misinformation during the pandemic and the 2020 election.[9]

The backlash against Big Tech companies today is, in part, a reflection of (and perhaps overreaction to) some people's disagreement with how Internet platforms moderate the content posted by their users for violations of the platforms' community standards. These community standards, devised by the companies as the policies their users must abide by, have become a hot-button political issue in the United States because some prohibited misinformation related to topics that became politically polarizing: misinformation about the 2020 U.S. election, and COVID and vaccine misinformation. But the community standards typically regulate plenty of other harmful content that probably many people can agree is worthy of moderation, including child sexual exploitation materials; harassment targeted at a person; hate speech attacking people on the basis of race, sexual orientation, gender, religious affiliation, and disability; spam; promotion of terrorism, violence, or suicide; and inauthentic manipulation, such as using bots to disseminate fake posts and disinformation. Some platforms prohibit pornography and adult content showing nudity and sex. Needless to say, Internet platforms find themselves in the unenviable position of having to decide the outer bounds of what's okay to share on their sites, which any teenager can access.

We need not digress long on the current political debate over how much content moderation Facebook, Twitter, YouTube, and other social media should exercise, or whether Congress should enact new laws restricting their content moderation to rein in Big Tech. (Texas did so, passing a controversial law titled HB20 that forbids large Internet platforms with more than 50 million monthly active users from moderating a user's post because of its viewpoint, and that gives people the right to sue Internet platforms for violations.[10] In September 2022, a federal court of appeals ruled, in a 2–1 decision, that HB20 does not violate the Internet platforms' First Amendment rights.[11] Given the decision's import, the Supreme Court might decide to review it.) It's worth noting, though, that in April 2022 Elon Musk sought to acquire Twitter as a company because of his public disagreement with Twitter's current content moderation.[12] Musk envisioned far less moderation of content on Twitter and would reverse its ban on former president Donald Trump, a decision Twitter made following Trump's controversial video posted during the January 6 insurrection.[13]

"Twitter is the digital town square where matters vital to the future of humanity are debated," Musk proclaimed in his agreement to buy Twitter in April 2022.[14]

Musk's intended acquisition of Twitter drew both praise and scorn. However, by July 2022, Musk had said he intended to pull out, prompting a lawsuit by Twitter to enforce the deal.[15] Musk questioned Twitter's estimate of fake accounts (under 5 percent) as too low.[16] Musk's planned withdrawal also came amid a huge downturn in the stock market, which only worsened in the summer. Then, in early October 2022, Musk reportedly revived his offer to buy Twitter.[17] Regardless of the outcome of the lawsuit or the deal, Musk's original plan to acquire Twitter throws into sharp relief how Internet platforms engage in online governance. Musk wanted to buy Twitter because he wanted to change how it *governed* people's content under its policy. What Barlow imagined people would develop "from ethics, enlightened self-interest, and the commonweal," Internet companies have developed on their own. That's why

Adrienne LaFrance, executive editor for *The Atlantic*, wasn't too far off when she described Facebook as "The Largest Autocracy on Earth," ruled by Mark Zuckerberg.[18] Some worried the same thing would happen to Twitter if Musk acquired it—to become, in effect, Twitter's ruler.[19]

The key lesson to draw from the years since Barlow's declaration is that the choice of online governance is not simply one between governments and people. Instead, the choice is among governments, Internet companies, and people. And, at least for Web2, the choice has been decided by the two dominant players: national governments and large Internet platforms. The ascendance of Internet platforms as authorities of online governance can no longer be ignored.

Drawing upon a term that the constitutional law scholar Laurence Tribe used back in 1991, I have elaborated a new theory that explains why we should view large Internet platforms as *virtual governments*.[20] They are virtual in two senses: they govern large sectors of the online world, and they operate as governments "in essence or effect though not formally recognized" as such.[21] While Barlow distrusted the rules national governments sought to impose on the Internet, we should have a similar concern about the rules virtual governments seek to impose. That is especially so if, as is common, the virtual governments don't solicit public comment or input in the rules they formulate, whether for content moderation, privacy, surveillance capitalism, the deployment of artificial intelligence, or other areas that affect users, if not violate their individual rights.

These Internet companies also govern the online world by the way they design their platforms. To take a simple example: Why does Twitter limit who is eligible to receive a verified account to "prominently recognized individual[s]"?[22] If Twitter has a problem with too many fake accounts as Musk suggested, allowing everyone to apply for a verified account might help to address the problem. Or, why do secret algorithms determine what people see on social media—even to the point of allegedly limiting a post's audience on Instagram to only a fraction of one's followers, a claim that the company denies?[23] Of course, the answer is: ad money. Algorithms enhance a platform's control over what users see based on the algorithm's assessment of their online activity and enable the platform to charge marketers more for targeted ads to users. (Facebook said ad revenues dropped by $10 billion after Apple enabled iPhone users to stop being tracked by apps, thereby diminishing the effectiveness of targeted ads on Facebook.[24]) Or, why don't "Help Centers" of social media companies provide more direct channels of communication, such as the call or chat centers that are commonly available from other businesses, including food delivery apps? The so-called Help Centers are designed to avoid direct human contact. These platforms establish their own regulations, procedures, and rules of governance—with practically no input from the public. In 1999, when Barlow's declaration of independence was still fresh, Lessig encapsulated how the architecture of the Internet itself establishes rules governing people online in the now famous phrase: "code is law."[25]

The development of Web3 forces us to ask the same governance questions that Barlow asked at the Web's beginning. Who should govern Web3? How should it be governed—under what rules and means of enforcement? Even if successful—and that's a big if—the aspirations of building a more decentralized Web, freed from the rule of the virtual governments of Big Tech, don't resolve these fundamental questions. Even the choice of a DAO—widely viewed as the darling of Web3—as the governing institution doesn't provide any guidance on the rules or their enforcement. Just as we saw in the development of Web1 and Web2, we are likely to see an intense competition among governments, Internet companies, and people to decide how to govern Web3.

My inclination is that we need to see much more involvement of people in online governance—and much less by national governments and virtual governments. The current fervor in Congress to regulate Facebook and other Internet platforms is understandable, but imposing restrictive national regulations on Internet platforms could end up being a cure worse than the disease. In a democracy, dispersion of power is a healthy antidote to centralized control over the Internet by either national or virtual governments. National governments controlling virtual governments is no better than virtual governments controlling people online. We should be equally skeptical of both.[26]

Even if we agree that Web3 should have greater involvement of people to decide issues of online governance, the challenge we face now is reminiscent of the one courts faced at the Web's beginning. "The history of the Internet is a chronicle of innovation by improvisation, from its genesis as a national defense research network, to a medium of academic exchange, to a hacker cyber-subculture, to the commercial engine for the so-called New Economy," a federal court of appeals cautioned in a decision in 2000.[27] "Like Heraclitus at the river, we address the Internet aware that courts are ill-suited to fix its flow."

Web3 is developing rapidly. Huge downturns in the financial markets and world events, such as Russia's invasion of Ukraine, made 2022 far more volatile than 2021, when the enthusiasm for NFTs and Web3 skyrocketed. The NFT market downturn in the summer of 2022 probably corrected the financial speculation from 2021's bull market, but it may have also affected the NFT market in many other ways that I wasn't able to diagnose while writing this book. It would be foolish to devise any regulation without gathering more information—and perhaps just waiting to see how things in Web3 unfold. Yet, at the same time, the past two decades of the Web should make us all the wiser. Not reaching final decisions on Web3 regulation now doesn't suggest we ought to sit on our laurels. We can and should start deliberating on what to do—even formulating plans on how regulation might work and debating who is best to carry it out. This chapter outlines three principles that I believe we should adopt for Web3, while the next chapter discusses legal controversies that NFTs have already raised.

THREE PRINCIPLES FOR WEB3

The starting point is identifying and agreeing on the goals of Web3. This debate might not lead to a uniform set of goals for all entities, companies, people, and contexts. The whole point of decentralization is to avoid a straitjacket approach to online governance and to encourage more governance by various groups at the local level. But recognizing at least some common ideals of Web3 can help to provide overarching principles that are important to operationalize or, alternatively, to consider whether other public values justify departures from them. I discuss three principles for Web3 below.

First Principle: Favor Decentralization

The foundation of Web3 is a return to decentralization. This ideal is a direct response to the centralized Internet platforms, especially for social media, including Facebook/Instagram, YouTube, Tik-Tok, and Twitter. Web3 proponents offer various reasons in favor of decentralization. Perhaps the biggest reason is to provide an alternative to the Internet platforms' business model—or surveillance capitalism—which monetizes users' data by selling ads to businesses targeting users based on their surfing habits.[28] Relatedly, Web3 is viewed as a way to empower people and enable them to escape Big Tech's imposition of rules and enforcement decisions, including censorship and deplatforming (or ostracizing from the platform)—policies that people had no say at all in creating.[29] As I stated in prior scholarship, "community standards" that were formed without any input from the community are Orwellian.[30] Decentralized payment systems through blockchain are also touted as eliminating the need for financial services intermediaries, who can charge service fees, collect personal data, and even block payments for content they disapprove.[31]

As these examples show, when Web3 proponents speak of decentralization, they may be referring to different things. In Figure 9.1 below, I have identified six different types or levels of

decentralization. Other theorists have proposed different categories.[32] But the ones I adopt provide an approach that is both comprehensive and understandable.

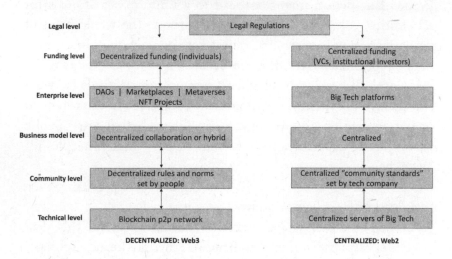

Figure 9.1

Decentralized v. Centralized Governance in Web3 and Web2

First is the technical level, where code is law. Blockchain operates at this technical level. The code of blockchain, the way it's
designed, achieves decentralization in the way that transactions involving cryptocurrency and NFTs are recorded on a p2p network
among many computers around the world. The design of blockchain also enables people to participate in Web3 websites through
anonymous crypto wallets. The discussion of Web3 often focuses
on this technical level of decentralization through blockchain, at
least as a starting point.[33]

No one should be so naïve as to believe that blockchain ensures
decentralization, however. Researchers have found that in the first
two years of Bitcoin, between 2009 and 2011, it was concentrated
among sixty-four miners.[34] That high concentration for Bitcoin
mining has persisted. In 2021, researchers from the National Bureau of Economic Research "found that the top 10% of miners control 90% of the Bitcoin mining capacity, and just 0.1% (about 50

miners) control 50% of mining capacity."[35] Ethereum apparently had greater decentralization with several mining pools that individual miners could join, the top three of which had a hundred thousand different miners or more.[36] The top five mining pools controlled only 65.4 percent of ETH mined.[37] An estimated one million people served as Ethereum miners.[38] In September 2022, the "merge" changed Ethereum to the far more energy-efficient proof-of-stake approach. The merge eliminated the need for miners; instead of miners, people can become validators of transactions on blockchain by staking or committing the requisite ETH for the chance of being randomly assigned to validate a transaction.[39] At the time of the merge, four staking pools were responsible for 60 percent of the existing staked Ethereum.[40] Some analysts worried that the merge will lead to greater centralization of validators, which could, in turn, make Ethereum more susceptible to hacking (what's referred to as a "51 percent attack").

Even if staking for Ethereum maintains a level of decentralization, that doesn't guarantee Web3 will be decentralized. Decentralization—or centralization—can occur at five other levels. If any of these other levels is highly centralized, then the decentralization achieved at the technical level of blockchain may be diminished. To understand why, take a simple example. Facebook, now called Meta, is building its own metaverse, including potentially with NFTs.[41] Yet, if past is prologue, we can expect that Meta's metaverse will be run in a similar way to Facebook—with centralized community standards devised by Meta, centralized servers owned by Meta, and a high concentration of Meta stock held by institutional investors. For example, Meta has implemented a centralized user policy for its metaverse, Horizon Worlds, allowing some mature content with proper tags.[42] Horizon Worlds doesn't use blockchain or decentralized technology, at least not yet, although both Facebook and Instagram have begun to accept crypto wallet connections and NFTs. Even if Meta eventually uses NFTs and blockchain for its metaverse, we'd be hard pressed to call it decentralized if most aspects of Meta are centralized. (In 2022, Meta sought the input of some Facebook users regarding misinformation about the environment. The experiment was encouraging, and Meta planned on soliciting greater input in the future—a process that Casey Newton called "platform democracy."[43] Greater public participation in developing community standards is a positive step.)

The other types of decentralization are just as important to examine as the technical level. First, the community level involves the rules and norms that govern people. These can be devised in a decentralized manner by people (e.g., by majority vote in a DAO), or in a centralized manner by a central authority, such as the government or an Internet company imposing regulations from the top down. Web3 proponents who decry "censorship" by Big Tech platforms seek greater decentralization at the community level—in deciding the rules and norms, the so-called community standards, governing people online.

Second, the enterprise level describes the entities in the market that provide services and platforms to people online. The entities can be in a decentralized, competitive market with many players, or they can be in a highly concentrated market with a few dominant players. A major challenge to decentralization online is that network effects operate like a gravitational force that favors increasingly large, concentrated networks. Although still early, OpenSea had an estimated 80 percent of the market share of NFT trading in February 2022.[44] OpenSea, the biggest decentralized NFT marketplace, operates more like a Web2 Internet platform, with centralized funding and centralized creation and enforcement of its terms of service for its users. Although some Web3 proponents don't like OpenSea's increasing power, centralization of some sort is not necessarily a bad thing. As we'll discuss in the next chapter, we may want centralization at the community level, at least in limited instances, especially when recurring problems, such as copyright infringement or theft of NFTs, arise. A centralized response to recurring problems isn't a panacea. But it is likely more efficient.

Third, the business-model level relates to our prior discussion.

A business can choose a highly centralized approach like Disney, maintaining tight control over all aspects of its business, especially its intellectual property. Or it can choose a decentralized collaboration model or a hybrid business model incorporating both decentralized and centralized collaboration, as Yuga Labs does. The most innovative Web3 proponents favor decentralized collaboration through NFTs.

Fourth, the funding level can take a decentralized approach, with funding by many individual investors, or a centralized approach with funding by a few venture capital firms and large institutional investors. Centralized funding doesn't necessarily turn a Web3 entity into a centralized business. For example, we could imagine that institutional investors contribute to a DAO, but the DAO still operates in a decentralized manner on blockchain, with a decentralized business and governance. But, as more VCs back a project, the greater the expectations for the business to generate revenues and deliver financial gains for the investors. If a startup is successful, the typical path leads to an IPO. Because NFT owners retain the profits derived from De-Collab, the startup may have greater incentive to develop its business through centralized collaboration, hoping to produce revenues attractive for an IPO. In other words, VC funding favors centralized collaboration to yield revenues leading to an IPO.

Finally, the legal level can adopt a decentralized approach by preferring a more deregulatory or market-based approach, or it can adopt a centralized approach by imposing legal regulations requiring the involvement of administrative agencies and courts for enforcement. It's important to note that the enactment of a national law doesn't automatically indicate a centralized approach from the government. Two of the most important laws for the Internet—the safe harbors for Internet companies under the Digital Millennium Copyright Act and under Section 230 of the Communications Decency Act—are immunities from liability for service providers; the laws favor a deregulatory approach designed to keep the courts from having to resolve every online dispute involving alleged copyright infringement or content moderation.[45] These safe harbors shifted the responsibility to Internet service providers, which, over time, became consolidated in large platforms (e.g., Facebook, Instagram, TikTok, Twitter, and YouTube) that adopted centralized business models and community standards. This centralization in Big Tech is one of the main reasons Web3 proponents are advancing an alternative approach.

DAOs probably have the greatest potential of maximizing decentralization at all levels (excluding the legal level, which is decided by government). That's not surprising given that DAOs were created for blockchain and Web3.[46] DAOs typically have decentralized funding through the sale of NFTs. To the extent DAOs involve media businesses such as the Nouns DAO and Gutter Cat Gang DAO, they often adopt decentralized collaboration in their licenses.[47] And the community runs the DAO: NFT owners get one vote per NFT on resolutions passed by the DAO and determine the agenda of the DAO. As its name indicates, the DAO is designed for decentralization.

A word of caution. Just because a Web3 entity starts out decentralized on all levels doesn't guarantee it will stay that way. As NFT marketplaces and the emerging metaverses become more popular and successful, network effects may propel those entities to resemble the Big Tech platforms of Web2. That's why Tim O'Reilly, who defined the term *Web 2.0* for the period that gave rise to social media, was skeptical in February 2022 that Web3 could avoid the pattern of consolidation we've seen.[48] That's happening already with the dominance of OpenSea among NFT marketplaces. It's still early, and other NFT marketplaces may serve different markets, but there's an obvious advantage of selling in the marketplace that commands the most volume of sales.

Consider also the Bored Ape Yacht Club, which has quickly become the industry leader among NFT projects, with even greater aspirations of becoming the premier Web3 media/entertainment business. There's no guarantee that BAYC will stay decentralized beyond the technical level on blockchain. Yuga Labs, BAYC's creator, has already received $450 million in seed funding from the venture capital firm a16z, Google Ventures, Animoca Brands, Tiger Global, Thrive Capital, FTX, and other institutional and individual investors.[49] And Yuga Labs acquired the IP rights to the CryptoPunks and Meebits NFTs from Larva Labs in a blockbuster deal. In 2022, Yuga Labs controlled the top three collections in terms of all-time sales volume: BAYC, CryptoPunks, and MAYC. Greater centralized funding and acquisition of CryptoPunks and Meebits do not necessarily make Yuga Labs a centralized company. It still utilizes a hybrid business model with a significant portion devoted to De-Collab, plus reliance on blockchain for decentralization at the technical level. But the centralized side of Yuga Labs' business model is growing fast, in its various partnerships with Adidas, Animoca Brands, and Improbable, as well as in its seed funding from institutional investors. Yuga Labs also must confront whether to adopt centralized community standards for its metaverse. The company appears to be planning a modified approach, no doubt aware of the controversies that Web2 companies faced with content moderation. In its litepaper for the Otherside, Yuga Labs recognized the need for input from the public: "We are committed to creating governance systems that are built from the bottom up and truly representative of the evolving community needs."[50] This approach to community standards would be a marked improvement from the standard approach of Web2 Internet platforms.

Second Principle: Protect Self-Sovereignty, Identity, and Privacy Against Surveillance Capitalism

Another principle of Web3 is the ideal of protecting an individual's right to self-sovereignty, identity, and privacy, including data privacy. This right is intended to end the surveillance capitalism of Big Tech platforms, which collect and monetize people's online data with advertisers.[51] Theorists have described this right as self-sovereign identity (SSI);[52] in popular discourse it's often referred to as "self-sovereignty." The basic idea is that people should have total control or ownership over their identities and personal data online.

Giving up their identities or personal data shouldn't be the price people must pay to enjoy the Internet.

Blockchain is viewed as a technological facilitator of self-sovereignty.[53] Privacy is protected as a part of the code or architecture of blockchain. Blockchain enables a person to make transactions and participate on different platforms using a crypto wallet, which doesn't contain a person's identity or email. Instead of creating a user account with one's name and email, one interfaces a website simply by connecting one's crypto wallet. (There is a trade-off: phishing ploys can make crypto wallets vulnerable to theft, a problem discussed in the next chapter.)

An additional aspect of self-sovereignty is that people can choose their online identities, whether to remain anonymous or pseudonymous. NFTs are often used by people as their avatars—and can become a part of their public-facing identities. Just spend a little time on NFT Twitter, and you will soon find that many owners of NFTs identify as their NFT characters—and other people recognize them only by their NFTs. It's hard to say who is the most famous person in Web3 recognized only by an NFT character. But it may be Punk 6529, who is engaged in an ambitious Web3 project building the Open Metaverse, which, fittingly, is being developed at the website 6529.io.[54]

But, as with the first principle, protecting self-sovereignty at the technical level using blockchain doesn't guarantee it will be protected on every level. A Web3 enterprise can impose on the community a requirement of KYC ("know your customer"), asking for personal information to participate in some events or transactions.

For the Otherside land sale, Yuga Labs, in partnership with Animoca Brands, imposed a KYC requirement for anyone who wanted a chance to buy an NFT during the launch. The KYC requirement was handled by Blockpass, a company specializing in KYC and compliance service. Yat Siu, the cofounder of Animoca Brands, said none of the personal information would be sent to Yuga Labs or Animoca, and that the information would be destroyed after Blockpass verified a person's information.[55] BAYC didn't reveal a specific reason for requiring KYC at the time, but left people in suspense while tweeting that it "didn't like KYCs either."[56] In a tweet following the controversial mint for Otherdeeds, Yuga Labs later indicated that KYC was used as a "rigorous gating mechanism" to help assuage the expected high demand for Otherdeeds, which did, in fact, materialize.[57] Whatever its reason, the KYC requirement sparked backlash against Yuga Labs.[58]

This example shows that blockchain helps to operationalize self-sovereignty at the technical level, but it can't guarantee that self-sovereignty is preserved on other levels. Companies or legal regulations may require true identities. We already discussed how the cofounders of Yuga Labs/BAYC, Gordon Goner and Gargamel, were identified by *BuzzFeed News* from public corporate filings they made. And any NFT creator who sues or is sued for copyright infringement will be named in the legal filings, which are a matter of public record. For example, the creators of the Caked Apes NFTs had to reveal their identities in lawsuits against each other over disputed authorship of the designs.[59] Real identities may be required.

Third Principle: Empower Creators and Owners in a Creator-Ownership Economy

A third principle of Web3 is empowering people to be creators and owners.[60] NFTs are the primary vehicle to achieve this goal, as detailed in prior chapters. For artists, NFTs provide a new way to earn a livelihood, in potentially life-changing ways, without having to sign the devil's bargain of transferring one's copyright to an industry intermediary. The Web3 ecosystem should attempt to empower artists by, for example, respecting their right to resale royalties, a vital component for building a livelihood through their art. For the public, NFTs provide a new type of interactive ownership, offering exciting opportunities for online identity, community, patronage, and collaboration. People aren't treated as users; instead, they are owners who control their online identity and can interact with others, on equal footing, in a community and business ventures.

These three principles of Web3 aren't meant to be exhaustive. Other important principles may be worth recognizing. But these three provide some bearings—a North Star—for our examination of the desirability of regulating Web3 to address several key areas: securities, fraud and rug pulls, infringement of intellectual property, and phishing and stolen NFTs. In these areas, we are likely to face difficult questions about whether NFTs or Web3 should be regulated, and, if so, by whom—national governments, virtual governments, or people.

My recommended approach is to consider how the three principles above can be operationalized and promoted, and, if a centralized approach is being entertained, to examine how many of the six levels of decentralization it affects and whether it undermines the three principles.

CHAPTER 10

LEGAL CONTROVERSIES

Change is the law of life. And those who look only to
the past or the present are certain to miss the future.
—JOHN F. KENNEDY

Whenever a new technology is disruptive, the law lags behind. It takes time for the law to develop, in court cases, agencies, or legislatures. The wheels of justice turn slowly, especially when confronting a new, disruptive technology. Judges, bureaucrats, and lawmakers typically aren't the most tech savvy—and some may be the least so. A healthy dose of humility—acknowledging "when we know too little to risk the finality of precision," as Justice David Souter recognized in an early Internet case in 1996—is an important starting point when considering possible legal regulations for NFTs.[1]

This chapter discusses four controversial areas related to NFTs that decision makers are likely to confront in the near future: securities regulation, rug pulls and fraud, IP infringement, and phishing and theft of NFTs. My discussion is not meant to be a final resolution of the debate over how best to address these controversial areas, but it is meant to highlight key points that help to understand the controversies—and put us in a better position to address them.

SECURITIES, ORANGE TREES, AND NFTS

In the 1920s, the real estate developer William J. Howey purchased 60,000 acres of land outside Orlando, Florida. He started a lucrative orange-growing business and formed two related companies for his business: the Howey Company sold plots of the land and the Howey-in-the-Service Company offered ten-year service contracts to the purchasers to lease the land to the Service Company and to allow it to cultivate oranges on their land and sell them with a percentage of the profits going to the landowners.

Land purchasers weren't required to use Howey's service, but most did, understandably. Most were people from outside Florida who had visited the area and stayed at a nearby Howey-owned hotel. During their stay, the patrons were pitched with buying not a time-share, but a plot of land for orange trees. Howey's representatives boasted about the 20 percent profits during one season, while noting that a 10 percent return was expected over the ten-year period. Apparently, the pitch worked. Those who signed up for the service contract were "attracted by the expectation of substantial profits."[2] That expectation was driven by Americans' increasing consumption of orange juice beginning in the 1920s, when ads touted the health benefits of vitamin C.[3] Land ownership under the Howey deal was in name only: the purchasers really had "no desire to occupy the land or to develop it themselves."[4] They were investors in a booming orange-producing business, spurred by Americans consuming more orange juice.

The SEC sued both Howey companies for selling what the SEC considered to be unregistered securities sold to the public in violation of the Securities Act. The Supreme Court agreed. In defining an investment contract, which falls within securities subject to SEC regulation, the Supreme Court set forth what is now called the *Howey* test: an investment contract involves (1) an investment of money, (2) in a common enterprise, (3) with a reasonable expectation of profits solely derived from the efforts of others.[5] The court easily found that Howey's arrangement in selling land with related services to grow orange trees met all three requirements.

How do NFTs fare under the *Howey* test? There's no legal issue whose resolution can roil the NFT market as much as this one. If NFTs are classified as securities, the NFT projects would be subject to a whole panoply of SEC regulations. First, securities must be registered in a statement with the SEC *before* their sale to the public, including financial disclosures in a prospectus given to investors before the initial offering. The project must adhere to a quiet period before the initial offering, refraining from public comments that could alter the company's statement. Instead of just a website, a vague road map, and social media posts, an NFT project that falls within the *Howey* test "must clearly describe important information about its business operations, financial condition, results of operations, risk factors, and management," including audited financial statements.[6] The statement filed with the SEC, which includes the prospectus, is a lengthy document prepared by a securities lawyer hired by the company filing the registration. (If you're curious to see what one looks like, a link in the note provides an example.[7]) After the initial offering, the project would be subject to ongoing disclosure requirements and regulation by the SEC, including, importantly, a prohibition on insider trading.

In 2022, the SEC was expected to issue guidance on whether some NFTs constitute securities. It was reportedly investigating whether some NFTs sold as fractional interests in an asset are securities.[8] But it's likely the SEC investigation encompasses more common uses of NFTs, such as in the collections involving cartoon characters, avatars, virtual land, and other content. That issue is squarely presented in an ongoing class action lawsuit filed against Dapper Labs, the maker of the NBA's Top Shot NFTs, pending in a federal court.[9]

While writing this book in 2022, I didn't have the benefit of a ruling from the SEC or the courts on whether NFTs are securities. I expect the SEC will likely find that (1) NFTs that are sold simply as collectibles (similar to baseball cards or paintings) are not securities, but that (2) NFT projects that include road maps of future business development or future perks that add value are securities, which must be registered before being sold to the public.

We already have hints that the SEC is leaning toward this view. Before stepping down as the SEC's director of the Division of Corporation Finance, William Hinman gave a speech at a Yahoo! Finance Summit in 2018 comparing the oranges in *Howey* to how some tokens and coins were being marketed: "Just as in the *Howey* case, tokens and coins are often touted as assets that have a use in their own right, coupled with a promise that the assets will be cultivated in a way that will cause them to grow in value, to be sold later at a profit."[10] Although Hinman was speaking about digital assets, such as initial coin offerings (ICOs), before the rise of NFTs, his analysis seems on point for NFT collections that go beyond mere collectibles or "one of one" art into the realm of developing an ongoing business venture. As Hinman elaborated, "Funds are raised with the expectation that the promoters will build their system and investors can earn a return on the instrument—usually by selling their tokens in the secondary market once the promoters create something of value with the proceeds and the value of the digital enterprise increases."[11]

The SEC's Strategic Hub for Innovation and Financial Technology's analysis of ICOs in 2019, although nonbinding, suggests a similar conclusion if we apply it to NFT collections that have ambitions for future business development (usually identifiable by a road map).[12] The analysis identifies scenarios that may fall within the *Howey* test, including at least one relevant here: a company "[m]aking or contributing to managerial level business decisions, such as how to deploy funds raised from sales of the digital asset." Drawing upon the SEC's analysis of ICOs, Commissioner Hester Peirce, who is affectionately known as "crypto mom," cautioned NFT creators: "If you're doing something where you are saying, 'I'm selling you this thing and I'm gonna build this . . . so that this thing that you are buying has a lot of value,' that's gonna raise the same kinds of questions that these ICOs have raised and so you've got to be very careful when you do something like that."[13]

If Peirce's comments don't raise alarm bells, they should. NFT projects that include ambitious road maps of future business development, as well as staking of NFTs to receive future rewards, sound exactly like what both Peirce and Hinman cautioned against. NFT projects might contend their vague road maps aren't binding contracts like the service contract in *Howey* because they never explicitly promised or touted a return on investment. That defense elevates form over substance—which the Supreme Court in *Howey* rejected in favor of examining "economic reality."[14]

Do people who buy NFTs from projects that plan future business development have a reasonable expectation of profits derived from the efforts of the NFT project team? That question is likely the key issue under *Howey* and will ultimately depend on the facts. Expecting an NFT to appreciate in value like a painting is different from expecting an NFT to appreciate in value due to the entrepreneurial or managerial efforts of the project team, such as in building a metaverse where the NFT can be utilized. The latter is more likely to fall within *Howey*'s test.

A lurking issue is one that the Supreme Court has avoided: Does the *Howey* test require that the buyer "expect[s] profits *solely* from the efforts of the promoter or a third party"?[15] The lower federal courts, adopting a pragmatic approach, have interpreted "solely" to mean "significantly."[16] Thus, if a buyer's expectation of profits derived significantly from the efforts of others in a common enterprise, the final part of the *Howey* test is satisfied, even if the buyer expected profits also from the buyer's own efforts.

In a case after *Howey*, the Supreme Court avoided reviewing this approach and even acknowledged that situations involving a dual scenario in which a buyer is "offered both a commodity or real estate for use [i.e., things that are not securities] and an expectation of profits . . . may raise difficult questions" for securities law.[17] Some utility NFTs raise a comparable dual situation: buyers are (1) offered to own the NFTs like artworks and use them as their identities and in their own commercialization efforts through De-Collab licenses, but (2) may expect profits (in appreciated NFT value) derived from the NFT project team's efforts to build the business. To highlight this difference: unlike the land purchase in *Howey*, where the landowners had no interest in ever using the land themselves, owners of NFTs typically *do* want to use and publicly display the artwork, and some owners want to develop, commercialize, and make profits from their own efforts as authorized under De-Collab licenses. And if the NFT involves virtual land, perhaps many owners expect to use and develop the virtual land for their own business and entertainment. The prevailing approach to securities law would likely treat this dual scenario as still falling within *Howey*'s test, thereby constituting a security, if a significant part of the NFT owner's profit expectation derived from the efforts of the NFT project team. It's possible, though, the Supreme Court would revisit the issue.

Some companies have already embraced securities registration for their NFTs. In October 2021, the music NFT platform Opulous, along with the investment firm Republic, offered the first music security NFTs, originally called S-NFTs but later renamed MFTs (music fungible tokens).[18] Lil Pump and Ard Adz were the first musicians to offer MFTs on Opulous. Lip Pump's MFTs for his song "Mona Lisa" (feat. Soulja Boy) sold out in two hours and raised $500,000 among 927 investors.[19] Owners receive a share of the streaming royalties each time Lil Pump's song is streamed.[20] Ard Adz's 50,000 S-MFTs sold out in an hour, using a different, lower pricing model: each MFT cost $1 with a minimum purchase requirement of $100.[21] Opulous established an elaborate music platform, using its own token called OPUL that people can buy and then stake for interest like a bank account. The company also provides musicians with De-Fi loans, backed by their future royalties as collateral.

Opulous is an exception. Most NFTs aren't registered as securities. We'll see what the SEC says. But one ominous sign in May 2022: the SEC chair, Gary Gensler, announced the SEC was doubling the size of its Crypto Assets and Cyber Unit by twenty additional staff to investigate crypto offerings and NFTs.[22] In testimony before the Senate Banking Committee in September 2022, Gensler suggested that the staking of coins could make them securities—a comment that rattled the Ethereum community given the recent switch to a proof-of-stake mechanism.[23] Although Gensler wasn't speaking about a particular cryptocurrency (much less NFTs), his comment appeared to apply to any staking of coins or tokens.

The broader question is whether NFT projects that aspire to be businesses, with road maps and future business development, should be subject to securities regulation. Regardless of what the courts and the SEC say, Congress can always amend the Securities Act to add NFTs to the list of exemptions from securities registration or classify them under a different category. In 2022, two bipartisan bills were proposed by lawmakers in Congress to classify cryptocurrency as commodities subject to regulation by the Commodity Futures Trading Commission (CFTC) instead of the SEC.[24] Gensler wasn't thrilled by the proposal but later was more receptive to the CFTC overseeing "nonsecurity tokens," including Bitcoin.[25] None of the bills expressly address NFTs, however.

Assuming the SEC treats some NFT projects as constituting securities, Congress should study the issue to see if a different approach would be better. U.S. securities law is designed, first, to provide investors with financial disclosures (in a prospectus) about the securities before deciding whether to invest in them.[26] Second, the law prohibits material misrepresentations and deceitful practices, including insider trading, and requires companies that sell public securities to register them with the SEC and be subject to the SEC's ongoing reporting requirements.[27]

Securities registration may be a poor fit for NFTs. First, I doubt a prospectus will have much, if any, impact on NFT buyers, especially degens. Would a prospectus provide investors with helpful financial information? In theory, yes. Besides basic information about the management (founders can't remain anonymous) and the financial condition of the NFT project, the prospectus will include a statement on the financial risks. Under the "bespeaks caution" doctrine, a securities registrant has an incentive to include cautionary statements—"Warning signals"—about any future projections in the prospectus because sufficient cautionary language can make any misstatement or omission in the prospectus immaterial and, therefore, immune from a securities lawsuit.[28] For example, an NFT project might include the cautionary language:

> *FINANCIAL RISKS: This NFT project has not launched, has no operating history, and has no revenues. Accordingly, this NFT project will face all the risks inherent in the establishment of a new business enterprise. No assurance can be given that this NFT project will be profitable or will generate any revenues. No assurance can be given with respect to the future growth of the NFT market or its value, including for this NFT project.*

However, a statement on financial risk stuck in a prospectus, which can run forty pages or more, is not likely to be read. Investors are under no obligation to read a prospectus; many probably don't.[29] And, even though a prospectus must be written in "plain English," it's debatable whether the average retail investor will understand it.[30] A 2012 report by SEC staff found that quantitative studies of investor behavior indicated that "investors do not understand the most elementary financial concepts."[31] Even if they understand portions of it, behavioral economics (such as Shiller's theories discussed in the prior chapter) suggests that people suffer from all sorts of biases, such as overconfidence and susceptibility to viral narratives (e.g., being a degen), that might undermine the effectiveness of a warning on financial risks.[32] As the legal scholar Stephen Choi questioned in 2005, "If investors are unable to handle information disclosure, why would these investors have the ability to comprehend and benefit from mandatory disclosures contained in the registration statement and prospectus?"[33]

A warning might be more effective if displayed not in a forty-page prospectus, but prominently on an NFT project's home page and then again right at the time of sale—as a final reminder of the significant risks of buying NFTs. Such dual warnings could maximize the impact on the buyer based on the primacy and recency effects.[34]

In my review of OpenSea and websites for NFT projects, I don't recall ever seeing a prominent statement about financial risks. The Doodles' project comes the closest with a statement stuck in its terms of service, indicating that Doodles NFTs shouldn't be treated as investments and may have no value.[35] Perhaps all NFTs are risky—and people, even degens, should know that, especially after the crypto winter—but having NFT projects state the financial risks prominently at the point of sale could be helpful in promoting greater awareness among investors. But this type of warning is not required by securities regulation.

Securities regulation would likely have a negative impact on the number of NFT projects that are started. Many NFT creators may be deterred from creating collections that aspire to be media businesses, given the legal costs and hurdles of securities registration and reporting, plus the potential for violating securities law by an offhand tweet from a company officer. NFT creators often don't have much capital before launch—that's what the sale of NFTs provides. Hiring a securities lawyer and filing a securities registration might be cost-prohibitive for many aspiring NFT projects. Plus, if foreign jurisdictions, such as China, the European Union, South Korea, and other areas where NFTs are popular, have their own requirements, the legal fees could escalate quickly. In summer 2022, the EU approved the Markets in Crypto Assets (MiCA) law, which will reportedly require NFT collections (treated as asset-referenced tokens) to submit a white paper, similar to a prospectus, although Stefan Berger, one of the lead negotiators, appeared to take a more limited view of MiCA's application to NFTs.[36] Single NFTs, such as for "one of one" art, apparently may qualify for an exemption from the requirement.[37] South Korea was considering enacting its own regulation. As the legal costs of compliance mount, the chilling effect on creators may fall disproportionately on those from underrepresented communities, who might have diminished access to legal assistance or the resources necessary to navigate a web of securities regulations. Burdensome regulations, if imposed, would likely deter creators from trying to develop NFT collections. Granted, securities regulation might serve a helpful role in winnowing out the pie-in-the-sky projects that stand little chance of becoming successful businesses. But the major downturn in the NFT market in summer 2022 may have already done so.

Securities regulation could have a positive impact by prohibiting insider trading of NFTs. SEC Rule 10b5–1 prohibits the purchase or sale of securities on the basis of material nonpublic information from an insider.[38] This illegal practice was highlighted in the Hollywood movie *Wall Street*, starring Michael Douglas as the villain Gordon Gekko, who proclaimed, "Greed is good." Studies suggest that insider trading of securities is a common practice.[39] Although no study has examined practices among NFTs, there's a widespread perception among NFT enthusiasts that insider trading of NFTs is common.[40] But there's probably an equally widespread perception among NFT enthusiasts that insider trading is legal because the SEC hasn't classified them (yet) as securities.

However, in June 2022, federal prosecutors sent shock waves through the NFT market by announcing the indictment of Nate Chastain, a former OpenSea employee who allegedly traded at least forty-five NFTs while working at OpenSea, based on confidential business information that OpenSea would feature the NFTs on its website. Chastain allegedly profited by selling the NFTs at two to five times the original purchase price. The indictment charged a violation of the wire fraud statute, not securities law, based on the allegation that Chastain engaged in fraud by using OpenSea's confidential business information without authorization in a scheme to flip his NFTs based on that confidential information. Supreme Court precedent supports the indictment's use of the wire fraud statute where an employee allegedly misuses confidential business information against the company's policy.[41] Chastain's lawyers disagreed with that interpretation, however, and moved to dismiss the indictment, a motion the court denied in October 2022.

It's unclear whether the wire fraud statute applies beyond the self-dealing scenario alleged in Chastain's indictment, to the more common type of insider trading of NFTs involving an "insider" tip that the creators of a project give to friends. The creators have access to a wealth of nonpublic information and can identify, for example, which NFTs are the rarest before they are revealed. If the creators told their friends which ones were the rarest, the friends could buy the rarest NFTs from the collection at discounted prices.[42] Thus, one potential advantage of regulating NFTs as securities would be to prohibit insider trading of NFTs more directly than the general wire fraud statute. Classifying some NFT collections as securities would also have the benefit of clearly prohibiting the common practice of wash trading NFTs (a sham transaction in which buyer and seller collude to manipulate the sales price),[43] and it would also require paid influencers who pump an NFT project to disclose their financial interests—and subject them to SEC enforcement.

All told, the case for using securities law to regulate NFT projects seems modest. The benefit of disclosures in a prospectus is doubtful. And there's a risk that securities registration could impose much greater legal costs on NFT projects and discourage many creators from even attempting to develop a media business, which could, in turn, stifle innovation and growth in various industries that would have benefited from an influx of ambitious NFT projects. Granted, securities regulation could help deter some of the perceived unethical practices in the NFT market—insider trading, wash trades, and touting by influencers and whales who pump NFTs without disclosing their financial interests.

Congress should hold hearings to study the emerging NFT market to figure out what's the best course to take. According to Chainalysis's survey of unique wallet addresses trading NFTs, the number of NFT owners was probably under 1 million in 2022, and presumably a smaller segment involved Americans.[44] As the number of NFT owners grows, along with the different types of uses of NFTs, Congress would be in a better position to understand how regulation would affect the nascent market. The three principles for Web3—favoring decentralization, self-sovereignty, and the Creator-Ownership economy—militate in favor of a cautious approach. Securities regulation is highly centralized, requires public disclosures, and might impose substantial legal costs to creators that stunt innovation. If insider trading and the other perceived problems warrant legislation, Congress could consider a new law specifically for NFT collections, instead of subjecting them to the burdensome filing requirements of securities law, the value of which seems doubtful here.

RUG PULLS AND FRAUDULENT NFTS

Imagine seeing a dazzling new NFT project about to be launched. The flashy website touts an impressive road map promising extravagant perks: the ability to stake the NFTs in exchange for rewards, the use of the NFTs in an upcoming metaverse, 3D models of the NFT characters, and the ability to breed them with other NFTs to create your own second-generation NFTs. Plus, the cartoon characters for the NFTs look so lovable! So you plunk down a thousand dollars to grab a few of the NFTs at minting. But, within a couple of hours, you learn that the NFT project's website, Discord chat, and Twitter profile have all been taken down. And the NFT creators have vanished.

What you just experienced is a rug pull. It's an illegal fraud involving a scenario in which an NFT producer lures people to buy NFTs from the collection, often by puffing up an ambitious road map and perks for buyers, but then, once the NFTs are minted, abandons the project and takes all the money and runs. The United States already has a law that makes rug pulls illegal—you guessed it, the general wire fraud statute, discussed above for the charge against Chastain. In March 2022, U.S. Attorney Damian Williams announced a criminal indictment of Ethan Nguyen and Andre Llacuna, the twenty-year-old creators behind the Frosties NFTs. The alleged rug pull they committed was similar to the above scenario. According to the indictment, Nguyen and Llacuna abandoned the Frosties project right after selling out the entire collection on the day of the launch and taking $1.1 million from the sale.[45] Nguyen and Llacuna were allegedly about to pull off a second rug pull of another NFT project called Embers before they were arrested.[46] A few months later, the Department of Justice announced a criminal indictment of Le Anh Tuan for an alleged rug pull involving the Baller Ape Club NFTs—indicating the clear interest of federal law enforcement in curbing rug pulls.[47]

Even though the wire fraud statute makes rug pulls illegal and the federal indictments of two alleged rug pulls should deter such activity, securities regulation probably would be even more effective in stopping rug pulls. Few people would engage in a rug pull if they had to disclose their identities in an elaborate public statement filed with the SEC and sit through a waiting period before even offering to sell the NFTs to the public. The whole process of registering an initial offering of NFTs would stop rug pullers from even trying.

Would deterring rug pulls justify securities regulation of NFTs? Based on the scant information available, probably not. It would be helpful to gather better statistics on how significant a problem NFT rug pulls constitute. Chainalysis provided a general analysis of all rug pulls involving cryptocurrency and tokens (but not distinguishing NFTs) and concluded that crypto rug pulls amounted to $2.8 billion and 37 percent of all crypto-related scams in 2021.[48] A London-based group called Rug Pull Finder patrols NFT collections for rug pulls and by May 2022 had compiled a list of nearly 125 projects that it considered to be rug pulls.[49] Such a small number doesn't cry out for securities regulation, especially if the wire fraud statute already applies. The crypto winter made market conditions so bad that it probably curbed rug pulls.

We also need to be careful in defining what qualifies as a rug pull. On social media, people often use *rug pull* far more broadly to encompass any NFT project that has been abandoned for whatever reason, including simply the failure of the business, despite the good-faith efforts of the project's team. But that broad use of *rug pull* is unhelpful. The Rug Pull Finder provides a valuable service, but even its definition of *rug pull* may be too broad.[50] When people are acting in good faith to build a business but fail, that shouldn't be considered a rug pull even if they fail fast or miserably. When the dot coms failed during the bursting of the Internet bubble, we didn't consider their failure sinister, much less illegal. According to recent estimates of businesses generally, 20 percent fail in their first year.[51] To consider any failed NFT project a rug pull is a fallacy. We should limit the term *rug pull* to situations involving illegal fraud such as what's alleged in the Frosties indictment—meaning a situation in which the NFT creators "willfully and knowingly, having devised and intending to devise a scheme . . . to defraud" through the sale of NFTs.

Without evidence of an NFT creator's intent, probably the most prudent course is to reserve judgment. For example, Zagabond, one of the creators behind the highly successful Azuki NFTs, sparked a controversy by revealing, in a curious blog post, that he was involved in the creation of three prior NFT projects in two months: CryptoPhunks and CryptoZunks, two derivatives of CryptoPunks, and Tendies.[52] Only the CryptoPhunks project survived. Zagabond portrayed the prior projects as learning experiences. After sitting down for an interview on Twitter Spaces, Zagabond later apologized to the buyers of NFTs from the failed projects and admitted making mistakes in how the projects were handled.[53] Some critics claimed that the projects were "rug pulls," however.[54] After Zagabond's disclosure, the Azuki floor price plummeted from 23 ETH to 8 ETH.[55] Yet Azukis survived the backlash. Four months after the Zagabond controversy, Azuki remained a blue-chip collection, with Zagabond still on board and a floor price around 10 ETH. In fact, Azuki was in the top five for pfp collections in total sales volume, even besting CloneX, Moonbirds, and Doodles.

Rug pulls are one problem for which a centralized legal response—through criminal law or, possibly, securities regulation—

makes sense. Once a rug pull happens, there's little, if anything, the victims can do on their own. Some Frosties owners organized a community effort to revive the Frosties NFTs (with a new smart contract), although the so-called Wrapped Frosties had few sales after the indictment and struggled to recover their opening-day value. Unfortunately, by August 2022, trading of Wrapped Frosties and activity on its Twitter account had stopped for several months.

Developers proposed a technical solution to rug pulls: creating a refundable smart contract, ERC-20R and ERC721R, which could combat rug pulls by locking funds for a defined period after the launch.[56] It remains to be seen if the approach gains traction. For now at least, a legal response to rug pulls is the best option. NFT enthusiasts understand that. When I posted news of the indictment of the Frosties creators on my website and social media channels, the announcement received uniformly positive reactions. It's rare to get that kind of response to a centralized approach among Web3 circles. People see criminal law's intervention as necessary, not only to help the victims of financial fraud, but also to maintain the legitimacy of the NFT market. The NFT market will never go mainstream if rug pulls run rampant.

IP INFRINGEMENT AND THE WILD WEB

In 2000, the Internet was a relatively new, revolutionary technology that made it easy to share content around the world in ways previously unimaginable, fostering free speech but also copyright infringement. *Time*'s cover showed a photograph of nineteen-year-old Shawn Fanning, grinning while wearing a Boston Red Sox cap and headphones, accompanied by an article describing his development of a new p2p software called Napster, which enabled people to share music files over the Internet—all for free and without permission from the copyright owners.[57] Fanning understood the significance of the p2p program: Napster "unleashes the potential of the Web, the viral growth possibilities of the community, the transgressive power of the Internet to leap over barriers and trans-form our assumptions about business, content and culture."[58] We all know the fate of Napster. It didn't end well.

But the Internet continued to grow exponentially, and it con-tinued to disrupt copyright law. At one point, the Recording In-dustry Association of America filed more than 30,000 copyright lawsuits against people, many college students, for illegal music file-sharing.[59] During this period, it was common to describe these lawsuits as part of a "copyright war."[60] Jack Valenti, the president of the Motion Picture Association of America, even called it a "ter-rorist war."[61]

If it was a war, it's not clear who won—or even if it's over. As we enter Web3 and hear a lot of bluster about rampant "piracy" with NFTs, it's important to remember how we got here. Illegal file sharing still occurs through a different p2p software, BitTorrent, which is even more decentralized than Napster.[62] And the rise of streaming music and movies has created other ways for copyright infringement.[63] Indeed, the popularity of streaming has dimin-ished BitTorrent's usage, which reportedly dropped from 35 per-cent to just 3 percent of global Internet traffic.[64]

At least the RIAA stopped suing college kids. But Malibu Me-dia, a studio that creates porn, assumed the mantle of most litigious copyright owner and, starting in 2012, filed thousands of lawsuits against anonymous "John Does" who allegedly shared Malibu's content using BitTorrent.[65] Regardless of whether a John Doe engaged in the alleged infringement, the typical response was to settle for $2,000 or so, to avoid the public embarrassment, hassle, attorney fees, and potential liability of $150,000 in statutory dam-ages.[66] According to a study by Matthew Sag and Jake Haskell, Malibu Media filed 2,646 copyright lawsuits in 2015 and 2016, a staggering 61.7 percent of the "John Doe" lawsuits (against people to be later identified from their computers' Internet addresses), and roughly 30 percent of *all* 8,760 copyright lawsuits filed in the United States.[67] Of course, copyright owners have a right to file lawsuits against infringers. But a concern is that this litigation turns into a business of extracting settlements from people—some of whom may be innocent. Federal courts expressed great concern about this type of litigation, or "copyright trolling," and viewed Malibu Media's tactics as raising "serious questions about misuse of court procedure."[68] By 2019, the John Doe lawsuits started to decrease. In 2021, Malibu was even ordered to pay more than $100,000 to a John Doe it wrongly accused of infringement.[69]

These lawsuits belie the way that the vast majority of alleged infringement on the Internet is now handled—outside of court, through automated systems involving various Internet platforms. Yes, the same Internet platforms that are attacked as engaging in censorship for moderating user content are also expected to moderate copyright infringement.

One predominant approach involves a process called notice-and-takedown, which is outlined under the DMCA safe harbor added to the Copyright Act in 1998: a copyright owner sends a notice of alleged infringement to an Internet platform, which must expeditiously take down the material to qualify for the safe harbor and immunity from monetary liability.[70] In Web1, notice-and-takedown worked relatively well. In fact, through free-trade agreements, the U.S. government convinced many other countries to follow the same notice-and-takedown approach.[71]

But when broadband and social media developed, the amount of online infringement became a bigger problem. Copyright owners started enlisting automated services to send out increasing numbers of DMCA notices—so-called robo-notices—to Google and other Internet platforms. In 2016, Google received 75 million notices of copyright infringement a month, or more than 2 million a day.[72] One doesn't need to be a statistician to figure out that a company's employees cannot possibly review, expeditiously or otherwise, 2 million notices a day. The sheer volume of robo-notices prompted Internet platforms to resort to automated takedowns for most notices.[73] No humans ever reviewed the vast majority of infringement claims. How could they, with millions of notices a day? Given that the DMCA safe harbor requires expeditious removal of allegedly infringing content, regardless of whether it is in fact infringing, the automated systems removed content at high rates. Google and Microsoft Bing removed links to alleged infringement at a rate of 98 percent and 99.77 percent of the notices they received in 2015 and 2018, respectively.[74]

Under the DMCA safe harbor, users are given the chance to contest a copyright claim by filing a counternotice, but few do. That's not necessarily an admission of guilt, however. People might not understand the technicalities of filing a counternotice or might find the legal terminology intimidating. The automation of notice-and-takedown seems to favor copyright holders by giving them a simple way to remove third-party content from the Internet without human review, much less a court decision. However, some within the copyright industries still complain that the process is like a game of Whac-a-Mole: take down one infringement, another pops up.

In 2019, in response to lobbying by copyright industries, the EU enacted a different approach in the Directive on Copyright in the Digital Single Market (DSM). The DSM Directive requires large Internet platforms that allow sharing of content, such as Facebook and YouTube, to do more than notice-and-takedown. First, Internet content-sharing platforms must make their best efforts to negotiate licenses for copyrighted content posted on their platforms by their users.[75] Second, the platforms are required to deploy filtering of infringement and ensure the infringing content stays down for good. Instead of notice-and-takedown, the platforms must follow "notice-and-staydown." The directive also requires Internet platforms not to impair the rights of people to share legitimate uses of copyrighted content, such as parodies, that fall within a copyright exception.

Of course, what the DSM Directive requires is easier said than done. Artificial intelligence may be getting more sophisticated, but a machine isn't likely able to discern permissible uses of copyrighted content, especially given the different exceptions among EU countries. The Court of Justice of the European Union recognized the possibility of overbroad filtering of legitimate content (meaning erroneous takedowns by the automated system), but nonetheless upheld the law as not violating freedom of expression if users of Internet platforms are given the ability to appeal a filter's removal of content "without undue delay and . . . subject to human review."[76]

None of these systems is perfect. And no one involved—copyright owners, Internet platforms, and users—is completely satisfied with any system. The sheer scale of alleged infringement online defies easy fixes, and it explains why both copyright owners and Internet platforms resort to automated systems, essentially turning over the ultimate decisions to machines. However, because some alleged infringement might be permitted as fair use or under another copyright exception, automated systems are bound to mistakenly remove legitimate content. In empirical studies of DMCA notices, researchers have found errors in the notices. For example, Daniel Seng conducted a study examining more than 3 million takedown notices sent to Google between 2011 and 2015 and found that 3.7 percent of them failed to include even a description of the copyrighted work as required.[77]

The lessons we've learned from addressing online infringement over the past two decades should put us in a more informed position to tackle the issue in Web3. In 1999, the Web was likened to the Wild West, an exciting new frontier, but lawless.[78] The same "Wild West" narrative has resurfaced with NFTs.[79]

Several high-profile lawsuits involving alleged infringement of intellectual property have fueled the narrative of Web3 as a lawless state. Nike sued a sneaker reseller, StockX, for creating NFTs of eight different Nike shoes to act as digital receipts for the shoes purchased from StockX. These NFTs included photos of the Nike shoes being resold.[80] Hermès, the luxury brand, sued Mason Rothschild for selling MetaBirkins NFTs for over $1.1 million. The MetaBirkins NFTs included digital images of faux-fur-covered bags similar to the iconic Birkin bag, which the Hermès CEO Jean-Louis Dumas had created for the actress Jane Birkin in 1984. Rothschild said his creations were protected free speech and artistic expression, with the faux fur on the Birkin-shaped bags in his NFTs calling attention to the need for the fashion industry to use cruelty-free materials.[81] Yuga Labs' trademark lawsuit against Ryder Ripps raises a similar issue of balancing trademark enforcement with the defendant's asserted free speech interests. When Miramax sued Quentin Tarantino for selling NFTs for the original, handwritten manuscript of *Pulp Fiction*,[82] the two sides initially disagreed over whether the movie contract allowed Tarantino to retain any rights to the handwritten manuscript, but ultimately reached a settlement.

Far from signaling a Wild West, these high-profile cases show that existing laws are equipped to address many of the IP controversies related to NFTs. Unless the cases settle, the courts will resolve these controversies, just as they did with Napster, and establish precedent and greater clarity for future disputes involving NFTs. This process of applying IP laws to new technologies isn't new. Starting with the printing press and continuing with copiers, computers, the Internet, and the smartphone, disruptive technologies have enabled new and often more powerful ways to copy and disseminate content, often in tension with copyright law. Each time, the law has had to strike a balance between protection of IP and free expression.

As the federal judge Lewis Kaplan in New York insightfully explained in a keynote address at the beginning of the Web, just as with other revolutionary inventions for mass communication, the Internet "exponentially broadened the reach of the human word" and "offered enormous potential for the betterment of the human condition."[83] But it "carried also the potential for abuse or, at any rate, the potential for perceived abuse." When a new speech technology arises, there's a constant "push and pull . . . over the breadth or narrowness of the limitations" of intellectual property.[84]

We're in the midst of another push and pull with NFTs and blockchain technology. The cases involving Nike, Hermès, and Yuga Labs will help to define the scope of trademarks used in or with images for NFTs. Courts are well-equipped to resolve these disputes, although the outcomes may be controversial. Some may

involve difficult questions requiring courts to balance the competing interests, such as in Hermès' lawsuit against Rothschild, but
the balancing of interests under a legal test is the bread and butter
of federal courts.

The greatest challenges to IP laws will occur outside of the courts.
The past two decades since Napster have taught us that most IP
disputes will be resolved not by courts but by Internet intermediaries. For NFTs, that means OpenSea and other marketplaces. What
responsibilities do NFT marketplaces have in stopping the sale of
NFTs that consist of allegedly infringing material? In the United
States, does the DMCA's notice-and-takedown process define the
responsibilities—and, if so, should any changes be made to the law,
which was enacted in 1998? In the EU, we can ask similar questions
about the applicability of the filtering requirement and notice-and-
staydown approach of Article 17 of the DSM Directive. Are the
responsibilities for NFT marketplaces different in other countries?
They might be: the first case in China held that a marketplace for
NFTs was liable for copyright infringement—violating the "right
to disseminate works through information networks"—when it allowed a user to sell an NFT for a cartoon character by the artist Ma
Qianli, thereby facilitating a violation of the artist's "right to disseminate works through information networks."[85] Given the possibility of conflicting requirements for NFT marketplaces, should
the World Intellectual Property Organization develop a harmo-
nized, international approach for NFT marketplaces?

These important legal questions will likely be answered in the
next several years. For now, the NFT marketplaces are on the front
lines fashioning the policies—and filtering technologies—to address alleged infringement. This approach results in centralization
of copyright moderation at the community level enforced by NFT
marketplaces. But it still enables the users of the marketplaces to
maintain self-sovereignty (other than those who file copyright infringement notices) and fosters the Creator-Ownership Economy
by providing a decentralized marketplace for artists. On balance, a
centralized response by marketplaces is justified.

OpenSea, for example, uses both the DMCA's notice-and-takedown approach and automated filtering of so-called copymints, or unauthorized copies of other NFT collections.[86] The latter approach of filtering is similar to what's required under the EU DSM Directive, so, in some respect, OpenSea's approach combines elements of both U.S. and EU law. In addition to filtering, OpenSea dedicates humans to review the images flagged by the technology, to improve its accuracy in removing copies.[87] Dedicated human review can help ensure that "additive remixes" of existing NFTs are permitted on OpenSea. OpenSea also has a process to verify legitimate accounts, so people know—with a blue check mark—that the NFT comes from a verified creator.

These measures of OpenSea are all sensible approaches. They provide a centralized approach, at the community level, to combat a recurring problem of copyright infringement, but one that preserves a layer of human review to help ensure the filtering doesn't remove legitimate content, what OpenSea calls additive remixes. Some ardent Web3 proponents might not like any centralized copyright enforcement by OpenSea at all. Indeed, on social media, I've heard OpenSea's copyright enforcement attacked as censorship. But doing nothing isn't tenable for OpenSea because it would be sued right out of existence like Napster.

We should expect both the law and OpenSea's policy to evolve as the NFT market grows. For the latter, I think two proposals are worth considering. Both would add elements of decentralization at the community level. OpenSea should invite public comments from its users on the policies it adopts, especially for aspects that are not dictated by the DMCA, the EU Directive, or other law. Web3 is teeming with bright, creative people, who'd like to build a better Web. OpenSea could benefit from their opinions on how to improve the policies and procedures. For example, an open discussion about copymints and clones—which should or shouldn't be allowed—would provide valuable information about the emerging Web3 culture. Even if there's no consensus on what should be permitted as remixes or fair use, just hearing the various viewpoints of different people would make OpenSea better informed in its attempt to draw the line.

OpenSea should also consider including the NFT creators whose works have been copyminted by third parties in the decision-making process if the company isn't doing so already. Before OpenSea removes an unauthorized copymint through its automated system, OpenSea should give the copyright owner the option to allow it. For example, the automated copymint filter could flag a suspicious NFT project, but then send a notice to the relevant copyright owner giving it the option to allow the copymint. Web3 attitudes shared by the most successful NFT projects, such as the Bored Ape Yacht Club, have widely permitted clones and derivatives. My suggested approach is similar to how YouTube's Content ID system ultimately gives the decision to copyright owners to allow unauthorized content that may infringe their copyrights to remain on YouTube (while enabling the owners to monetize the video on YouTube).

IP owners can also use NFTs to combat counterfeits and knock-offs. For example, Nike can sell CryptoKicks NFTs that authenticate both digital and physical Nike sneakers. Consumers can feel more confident they are buying authentic Nikes that are being resold if the physical shoes come with the corresponding Nike NFTs. The NFTs verify provenance. NFTs can also be used as a part of IP owners' digital rights management. For example, RAIR is a digital rights management platform that enables IP owners to stream their content only to consumers who've purchased their NFTs.[88] These examples only scratch the surface of the possibilities that NFTs might offer. Indeed, one day many consumer goods may have accompanying NFTs to establish provenance.

PHISHING AND THEFT OF NFTS

Seth Green owned Bored Ape #8398, but the actor fell prey to a phishing scam that resulted in the theft of his prized Bored Ape, which he named Fred, along with two Mutant Apes and one Doo-dle.[89] The thief reportedly sold the stolen Bored Ape to a person who goes by the username DarkWing84 on OpenSea, an un-identified Australian surgeon who said he bought it in good faith, according to *BuzzFeed News*.[90] The price DarkWing84 paid was 106.5 ETH ($268,282), which was a little above the Bored Ape floor price on that day.[91] The added wrinkle was that, under Bored Ape's De-Collab license, Green was producing a new series titled *White Horse Tavern*, featuring Fred the Bored Ape as a character. Apart from creating a new show whose main character had been "kidnapped," Green's predicament was one, unfortunately, many others have faced. One poor soul had twenty-nine Moonbirds, val-ued at $1.5 million, stolen.[92] Todd Kramer, an art dealer, suffered a similar plight, with a heist of fifteen of his NFTs, including Bored Apes and Mutant Apes, worth $2.2 million.[93] Desperate, Kramer tweeted: "I been hacked. all my apes gone. . . . please help me."[94]

What transpired next with Green's stolen Bored Ape provides a good example of how stolen NFTs are often handled. OpenSea, applying its policy at the time for suspected stolen NFTs, froze any further transactions involving the stolen NFT on its marketplace and labeled it with a "Reported for suspicious activity" warning at the top of the page.[95] OpenSea, however, has limited power: it con-trols only what happens on its marketplace. It can't stop transac-tions involving stolen NFTs that occur outside of its marketplace.

But OpenSea's policy was still controversial. Even though the freezing of the NFT applies only to OpenSea, the warning label might depress the value of the NFT on other marketplaces if po-tential buyers are aware of it. OpenSea's warning label may damage an innocent buyer's financial interest even beyond OpenSea.

So how can owners like Green and Kramer recover their stolen NFTs? The short answer: it's not easy. Even though a phishing ploy (using a bait-and-switch on a person to sign an NFT trans-action that appears legitimate, but isn't[96]) likely violates the Com-puter Fraud and Abuse Act, it's very difficult to track down the thief from a crypto wallet address, especially if the person resides overseas.[97] For example, the FBI reported that two hacker groups in North Korea were responsible for the theft of $620 million in ETH from Axie Infinity users.[98] The U.S. Treasury Department placed one of the crypto wallets involved in the theft on a sanctions list, barring U.S. financial institutions from interacting with the wallet.[99] But even those measures didn't identify the owner of the wallet, much less subject the unknown person to criminal prosecution. By September 2022, U.S. authorities had recovered only $30 million of the stolen funds. The problem is similar for stolen NFTs. After selling the stolen NFT, a thief can just abandon the wallet and start using a new wallet with a different address—and disappear.

So, are people whose NFTs are stolen out of luck? Not necessarily. The most common response is self-help. People try to connect with the person who bought the stolen NFT and convince them to sell or return it. Seth Green reportedly paid DarkWing84 approximately $297,000, or nearly $30,000 more than DarkWing84 had paid for it.[100] Green said that DarkWing84 and he were also "working together to prosecute the original thieves," although he didn't say how.[101] Some people on NFT Twitter have even become Good Samaritans and try to help others who have had their NFTs stolen to recover them, sometimes with success.[102] Kramer, luckily, recovered several of his Bored Apes this way.[103] Green recovered his Bored Ape, clearing the way for his planned series for Fred, *White Horse Tavern*.

Blockchain facilitates self-help because you can identify the wallet address where the NFT is held. It's easier to trace the location of a stolen NFT than a stolen bike. Through Internet sleuthing, sometimes it's possible to track down a sale of an NFT to a social media account, such as when a user announces making a purchase on Twitter. Fitting for Web3, some NFT owners, such as Seth Green, prefer to use self-help instead of seeking a return of the stolen property in court, even if it requires negotiating a deal to buy back one's own property at a premium.[104]

Self-help might be more advantageous than trying to seek

recovery of a stolen NFT in the legal system. Even if one can identify the person who holds the stolen NFT, the original owner might not be able to recover it. Why? Because the law might recognize an innocent buyer (called a bona fide purchaser under the law) as the valid owner of the NFT, even though it was stolen by someone else, provided the innocent buyer had no knowledge it was stolen and bought it in good faith. The law in this area is notoriously complex and varied among countries.[105] Indeed, cases involving art theft have produced conflicting results. So, ultimately, whether innocent buyers of stolen NFTs obtain valid ownership of them will depend on which country's law applies. That countries have disagreed over how to treat stolen property for so long should provide an indication of how difficult the issue is to resolve.

Because NFTs are new, the law also must catch up. In the United States, a committee established by the American Law Institute and the Uniform Law Commission adopted the 2022 Amendments to the Uniform Commercial Code (UCC): Digital Assets.[106] The UCC, which was designed to provide uniformity regarding the law of sales and commercial transactions, has been adopted by all states. The new Article 12 would recognize valid ownership of a stolen NFT under the "take-free" rule, meaning an innocent buyer ("qualifying purchaser") obtained the NFT "for value, in good faith, and without notice of a property claim to" the NFT by someone else.[107] This approach for digital assets is similar in result to the current approach the UCC takes with respect to transfer of tangible property obtained through fraud.[108] If fraud was involved in the original owner's loss of tangible property (e.g., a sale involving a bad check), a subsequent innocent buyer of the property obtains valid ownership of it.[109] The American Law Institute approved Article 12 in July 2022, so it's now up to each state to decide whether to adopt it.

This "take free" approach may sound unfair. In fact, it goes against the general approach that an innocent buyer does not obtain valid title to stolen property. This rule is commonly referred to as "nemo dat," short for a Latin phrase that means "no one can give what they do not have." Buying a stolen car doesn't mean you're the rightful owner. But countries were reluctant to apply this rule in categorical fashion, given the competing interest of respecting commercial transactions involving innocent buyers, who were not at fault.

Which approach is best for stolen NFTs? This issue is debatable, as the historical divergence on stolen property among countries shows. We should have further study and debate on three important issues, including in state legislatures as they consider adopting UCC Article 12.

First, who should bear the loss of a stolen NFT? The new Article 12 of the UCC would put the loss on the theft victim if an innocent buyer purchased the stolen NFT. This approach can be defended on the ground that the victim could have taken greater precautions to avoid phishing, hacking, and scams, such as using a hardware wallet (that stores private keys offline) and never using the same wallet that stores valuable NFTs to sign new transactions. The victim also could have considered buying insurance, although the market for insurance is nascent. By contrast, the traditional rule puts the loss on an innocent buyer (if there is one), who would have no valid property interest in stolen property. This traditional approach can be justified as a way to protect the integrity of the market and to deter theft by making it harder for a thief to sell and profit from it. But the approach produces a harsh result for innocent buyers. Could they have known that the NFT was stolen? Perhaps if it was sold at a lowball price. Otherwise, likely not. And there's probably no insurance yet to cover buyers in this situation, so shifting the entire loss from a stolen NFT to an innocent buyer may seem just as unfair.

OpenSea's policy of freezing reportedly stolen NFTs favors the victim over innocent buyers. This is a difficult trade-off. The ideal situation is, of course, that such a freeze occurs *before* the thief resells it. But if it is resold to an innocent buyer, a freeze is far more controversial. The freeze could force the affected parties, if identifiable, to try to work things out, as Seth Green did. But, if no deal can be struck, both the victim and the innocent buyer may be harmed financially, compounding the harm caused by the theft. On the other hand, if OpenSea favors innocent buyers adopting the "take free" approach of the new Article 12 of the UCC, Open-Sea would have to institute some procedure by which individuals can prove they are innocent purchasers of stolen NFTs. Even then, adopting this approach would give thieves the biggest online marketplace to sell stolen NFTs—a prospect that may be hard for policymakers and legislators to swallow because it provides no deterrence to theft.

Second, what do other online marketplaces do with respect to stolen goods—and are their approaches working? Amazon, eBay, and Facebook all prohibit the sale of stolen goods on their platforms, but the interventions each company takes with respect to stolen items differ in some respects.[110] With the recent surge in thefts at retail stores during the pandemic, some U.S. lawmakers think these online marketplaces should do more to deter the increasing trade in stolen items online and are considering enacting a federal law requiring the marketplaces to verify sellers before allowing them to sell there.[111] Granted, Amazon, Facebook, and eBay are different from NFT marketplaces in that the latter may involve the resale of a stolen item by an innocent buyer. Buyers of products on Amazon, eBay, and Facebook aren't typically reselling them right away. But the experience of these large online marketplaces can provide valuable insight into how stolen NFTs might be better addressed. For example, the idea of verifying sellers more is one that may also help in the NFT market. One alternative measure that OpenSea should consider: allowing everyone to apply for a verified account instead of the current limit to accounts with at least 75 ETH of volume sold.[112] For a verified account, a person must apply to OpenSea and provide a username, profile picture, email address, and a Twitter account. That process should be made universal and open to everyone. That way, every buyer can know that a seller has been verified—or not.

Third, what procedures should marketplaces use to help victims of theft and innocent buyers? Internet platforms too often overlook the issue of procedures, but I think it's one of the most important. Internet platforms must be transparent and set forth, in detail, the procedures they use to enforce their policies. It's a matter of due process. And, especially for controversial issues whose resolution significantly affects people, Internet platforms should invite public comment.

OpenSea didn't outline the process that the company used to clear frozen NFTs until August 2022. OpenSea's announcement came a few days after a lawsuit was filed in Michigan small-claims court against OpenSea for its allegedly "broken" stolen NFT policy.[113] I've read horror stories on Twitter of people who allegedly had their NFTs stuck in limbo on OpenSea, some with what they claimed were mistaken warnings.[114] On August 10, 2022, OpenSea finally admitted on Twitter shortcomings in its policy and announced changes that would enable affected parties to contest a warning and to have a "suspicious activity" warning automatically removed if the alleged victim of theft doesn't submit a police report within seven days.[115] The prior policy had no timeline at all and didn't require a police report to substantiate a claim of a theft.[116] OpenSea's changes to its policy are a step in the right direction, but it is still lacking sufficient details. For example, OpenSea should provide clear guidance on the procedures and standards that it will use to resolve appeals for allegedly incorrect warnings, as well as what happens *after* a police report is filed and submitted to OpenSea.[117] Presumably, victims will file police reports. So the key question remains: How will OpenSea handle a case after receiving a police report? Apparently, in the updated policy, OpenSea plans on leaving the freeze in place indefinitely unless "the original reporter retracts their original report."[118]

What's still unclear is why OpenSea believes this approach is best. Has it considered the "take free" approach of the new Article 12 for innocent purchasers, for example? OpenSea should invite public comment, including from legal experts, to address these questions. Public involvement in shaping the marketplace policy is more consistent with Web3. Any policy adopted should consider how to treat innocent purchasers. If states adopt the new Article 12 of the UCC for digital assets, then innocent purchasers would have valid title to the stolen NFTs they acquired in good faith. In that case, marketplaces such as OpenSea should consider whether the "take free" approach should enable innocent purchasers to resell stolen NFTs in their marketplaces. If so, the marketplaces should institute a procedure by which purchasers of stolen NFTs can prove they, in fact, are innocent—in which case, presumably, they should be able to sell their NFTs free and clear of any warning label. Remember: anyone can create multiple crypto wallets, including thieves who might appear to be innocent purchasers by changing wallets.

An alternative approach that OpenSea should also consider: instead of using a warning label and freezing an NFT, OpenSea might simply delist a reportedly stolen NFT if supported by the victim's filing of a police report. Such an approach would avoid knowingly allowing the sale of stolen NFTs on OpenSea and also be fairer to innocent purchasers of stolen NFTs.

Some Web3 proponents dislike OpenSea getting involved at all. They have criticized OpenSea's policy of freezing stolen NFTs on its platform because it supposedly goes against the Web3 ideal of decentralization. In my view, this criticism of OpenSea is misplaced. Having a centralized policy to combat the trading of stolen NFTs on a marketplace is a sensible approach to address what appears to be an escalating problem of theft of NFTs. According to Comparitech, $86 million worth of NFTs have been stolen.[119]

Do we need greater legal regulation to stop NFT thefts? Perhaps. But theft of NFTs through phishing is probably already illegal under the CFAA. Sure, Congress can enact a law clearly prohibiting phishing and NFT theft, but the challenge would still be tracking down the thief with just a crypto wallet address.

What would be more effective is trying to reduce phishing scams on social media by developing greater filtering or technological solutions to stop phishing, the primary way in which NFTs are stolen. Another technological change that OpenSea and other marketplaces can easily implement is an automated labeling system that posts a warning label next to an NFT price offered well below the current floor price for the same collection. This automated label indicating "for sale X percentage below the floor price" could arise at two points. First, the label can appear *before* the seller posts the NFT for sale at a lowball price, thereby alerting the seller and giving the seller a chance to correct the price if the seller mistyped the price as, say, 0.75 ETH instead of 75 ETH, a so-called fat-finger error.[120] Second, the label can appear *after* the NFT is posted for sale and put buyers on notice that it might involve suspicious activity, potentially diminishing the strength of any defense of being innocent buyers. Of course, the label might also attract bargain hunters. But, if my other recommendation of allowing everyone to apply for a verified account is implemented, bargain hunters might not have a credible claim of good faith in purchasing an NFT at a lowball price from an unverified seller.

My proposed labeling system could mitigate two problems: (1) incorrect prices through mistyping, and (2) lowball sales of stolen NFTs. Of course, in some situations, a lowball price merely indicates a lawful owner's need for liquidity. A separate process— perhaps involving KYC—can be designed to enable lawful owners to engage in quick sales of their NFTs at lowball prices.

..

Our prior discussion provides only a start of the debate over whether new regulations are needed to address problems in Web3. As metaverses are launched, developing community standards for those environments—with much greater involvement of the public, I hope—will become paramount. Given human nature, there's no reason to believe the metaverse and virtual worlds will be immune from the cesspool aspects of social media. (At least two women have already alleged that their avatars were subject to sexual assaults in virtual worlds.[121]) As people and policymakers engage in these debates, it's essential that they realize not only that decentralization has its virtues in dispersing power over the Internet, but also that decentralization and centralization can coexist. A centralized approach is often helpful to address recurring problems, such as rug pulls and NFT theft, which produce harms to people without an easy way for them to remedy their injuries or engage in self-help. But, as illustrated above, the ideal of returning to a more decentralized Web doesn't mean that all forms of centralized regulation, at any level, run counter to that ideal.

CHAPTER 11

DIVERSITY AND SUSTAINABILITY

Courage, my friends;

'tis not too late to build a better world.

—TOMMY DOUGLAS

To build a better world, we must identify the major problems we face today. Otherwise, we risk replicating the same societal problems in Web3. The plan of Web3 visionaries, including Ethereum's cofounder Gavin Wood and a16z's Chris Dixon, was to build a more decentralized Web built on blockchain to respond to the centralized Internet platforms, which have grown to dominate social media and rule the online world.[1] Trying to return to a more decentralized Web is a worthy goal, but focusing on centralization by Big Tech as the chief problem to be fixed runs the risk of transferring other societal problems. It would be a tragedy to spend so much time, money, and resources in building Web3 if it simply migrates our societal problems—or even makes them worse.

In calling for Web3 in 2018, Wood recognized this very dynamic as a failure of the Internet. "Technology often mirrors its past," Wood wrote. "It acts in line with the previous paradigm, only faster, harder, better, or stronger than before. As the global economy went online, we replicated the same social structures that we had before."[2] He criticized how "[m]arkets, institutions, and trust relationships have been transposed to this new platform, with the density, power and incumbents changed, but with the same old dynamics."

Already there are signs of history repeating itself in Web3. After witnessing some of these concerns materialize, the reform strategists Scott Smith and Lina Srivastava warned: "The problems that plague the real world, the original Internet and Web 2.0 also inhabit Web3."[3] Crypto whales wield outsized market power, Bitcoin mining lacks sustainability, and blockchain doesn't ensure accountability or trust.[4] Other critics raise concern about the exploitation of the global South to serve a "crypto-colonialism," by which blockchain depletes resources from that area to serve the interests of the North.[5]

The greatest fear I have for Web3 is that we will make the same mistake again, especially in two areas of vital importance to the world's future: diversity and sustainability. Both issues have become so politicized that it's even hard to discuss them without provoking knee-jerk reactions, denialism, and attacks of "cancel culture" and "wokeism." But, if we listen to the people whose lives will be affected the most by the future Web—the younger generations—these two issues are vital.

In 2022, Deloitte surveyed 14,808 Gen Zs (born between 1995 and 2003) and 8,412 Millennials (born between 1983 and 1994) in forty-six countries.[6] Next to the cost of living, both Gen Zs and Millennials ranked climate change as their top concern.[7] Approximately 75 percent said they "believe the world is at a tipping point in responding to climate change."[8] Only 15 percent said they strongly agreed with the statement that "large companies are taking substantive actions to combat climate change."[9] An employer's commitment to addressing climate change affected people's desire to stay—or leave. Among the respondents who planned on leaving their jobs within two years, 56 percent of Gen Zs and 48 percent of Millennials said they were "not satisfied at all" with their organization's commitment to sustainability. Likewise, 52 percent of Gen Zs and Millennials from that same group said they were "not satisfied at all" with their organization's "progress in creating a diverse and inclusive environment."[10] A 2021 survey of Gen Zs in thirteen countries conducted by Lewis Research found similar results: Gen Zs ranked diversity and inclusion among the most important issues to their generation, with LGBTQ+ rights, gender equality, and racial equality all making the top five societal issues respondents believed Gen Zs care about the most.[11] If a company lacked gender or racial diversity, 46 percent of Gen Zs said they wouldn't work for the company unless it had a strong diversity, equity, and inclusion program in place.

Americans from these generations expressed similar, if not greater, concerns. In 2021, the Pew Research Center found that the majority of American Gen Zs (67 percent) and Millennials (71 percent) believed that addressing climate change should be a "top priority to ensure [a] sustainable planet for future generations."[12] (A majority of older Americans did so as well, but to a lesser degree.) The level of one's personal action to combat climate change decreases with age. The report concluded: "Younger Americans—Millennials and adults in Generation Z—stand out . . . particularly for their high levels of engagement with the issue of climate change."[13] Likewise, Gen Zs and Millennials also showed much higher percentages (62 and 61, respectively) in endorsing the view that increasing racial and ethnic diversity is good for society.[14] Distressingly, only 48 percent of Boomers agreed. High percentages of Millennials and Gen Zs also considered a prospective employer's diversity and inclusion an important factor in seeking jobs, according to other surveys.[15] U.S. employers know that they'll face difficulties in recruiting Millennials and Gen Zs if the company is not committed to diversity and inclusion. These numbers reflect, in part, the greater diversity of America: Gen Zs and Millennials are the most racially and ethnically diverse generations in U.S. history.[16] These numbers suggest that younger generations are both more socially aware and smarter.

Web3's development is still early, but the initial signs are worrisome. To borrow Wood's metaphor, Web3 is mirroring the societal problems we face in many contexts, with the lack of diversity and the lack of sustainability, although the latter is improving. These problems aren't easy to address. But the first step is to look ourselves in the mirror. If we don't, we risk allowing the same failings of society to become "hardwired" into Web3, making them even harder to fix.[17]

DIVERSITY

NFTs intersect with three sectors that have faced problems with a lack of diversity: the tech industry, the art establishment, and, more recently, the cryptocurrency market. Decentralization at the technical level of blockchain won't automatically improve the lack of diversity as Web3 is built. Instead, we need greater collective recognition and action at the other levels—funding, enterprise, business model, and community—to make Web3 more inclusive.

Women face significant underrepresentation in all three sectors, comprising only 26 percent of U.S. professional tech jobs, 28 percent of U.S. crypto holders, 5 percent of the founders of crypto-related startups globally, and 35 percent of artists represented by galleries around the world.[18] Gender disparity in the art establishment is especially disturbing. In a 2019 study of eighteen major art museums in the United States by Chad Topaz and other researchers from the Institute for the Quantitative Study of Inclusion, Diversity, and Equity, an estimated 85 percent of the artists whose works were held in permanent collections were white men; only 12.6 percent were women artists.[19] Historical bias for the male "old masters" may explain the origin of the gender disparity,[20] but it doesn't explain its persistence. From 2008 to 2018, works by female artists represented only 11 percent of acquisitions by twenty-six major art museums in the United States, according to a study by *artnet News* and In Other Words.[21] Auction houses fared even worse on gender diversity. In a study of 2.6 million artworks sold by 1,800 auction houses from 2000 to 2017, fully 96.1 percent of artworks sold were by male artists.[22] Not surprisingly, the composition of artists per capita was similar: 95.2 percent of the artists were men.[23] Even among auctions for contemporary art, women artists were only 9.3 percent of the artists included. Women artists, who comprise at least 47 percent of U.S. artists since 2010,[24] are grossly underrepresented in the art establishment.

People of color faced a similar disparity in the art world. That 2019 study of eighteen major U.S. art museums also found the art-works of white artists dominated, comprising 85.4 percent of the artists whose works were owned by the museums. Figure 11.1 in-dicates the percentages of artists by race whose works were owned by the major museums.[25] Black and Latinx artists faced a lack of representation in the museums.

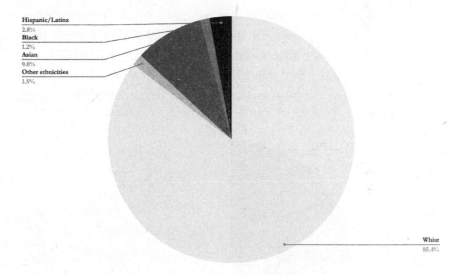

Hispanic/Latinx
2.8%
Black
1.2%
Asian
9.0%
Other ethnicities
1.5%

White
85.4%

Figure 11.1
Race of Artists for Works Held by Eighteen Major U.S. Museums
Source: C. M. Topaz, B. Klingenberg, D. Turek, B. Heggeseth, P. E. Harris, J. C. Blackwood, et al. (2019).

A 2017 class project by CUNY Guttman College students found similar disparities in the works of 1,300 artists represented by the top forty-five art galleries in New York City: more than 78.4 per-cent of artists were white, followed by 8 percent Asian, 6.3 percent Black, 4.7 percent Latinx, and 2 percent Middle Eastern.[26] The representation of works by Black, Latinx, and Middle Eastern artists, while slightly higher than the amount for the major museums, was still very low.

The dynamic in the tech industry is somewhat different. Asian workers fared better in employment by Silicon Valley tech companies, but Black and Latinx workers were underrepresented. In 2018, Reveal from the Center for Investigative Reporting and the Center for Employment Equity at the University of Massachusetts Amherst collected data from the 2016 EEO-1 filings from 177 large tech companies in Silicon Valley.[27] The researchers issued a report compiling the main findings.[28] Figure 11.2 shows the employees in tech companies identified by race or ethnicity. While the percentage of Asian employees has increased to 28.1 percent, there wasn't significant progress in the hiring of Black and Latinx tech workers since a prior EEOC study of 2014 data.[29] Since 2014, the Big Tech companies that publish their diversity reports have shown relatively modest progress in the hiring of Blacks and Latinx tech workers.[30]

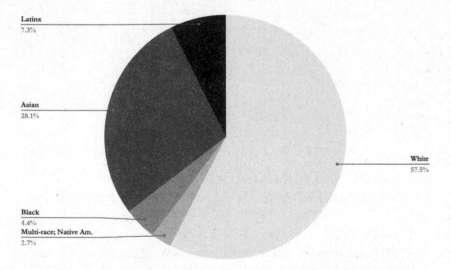

Figure 11.2

Employees by Silicon Valley Tech Companies by Race or Ethnicity in 2016

Source: 2016 EEO-1 filings collected by Reveal from the Center for Investigative Reporting and the Center for Employment Equity.

There is greater racial and ethnic diversity among owners of cryptocurrency—showing at least an opportunity for greater inclusion in Web3. According to a survey of 4,400 Americans by Morning Consult, 37 percent of Hispanics and 35 percent of Blacks said they were likely to invest, compared with 31 percent of whites.[31] Likewise, according to a Pew Research Center survey, the respective percentages of crypto owners within a racial or ethnic group was higher for people of color: 23 percent of Asians in the survey owned cryptocurrency; 21 percent of Hispanics; 18 percent of Blacks; and 13 percent of whites.[32] A Harris poll found 25 percent of LGBTQ Americans owned cryptocurrency, nearly double the percentage for the general population.[33] One explanation offered for the higher interest in crypto among people of color and the LGBTQ community is that underrepresented groups that have been marginalized by financial institutions see the decentralized system of cryptocurrencies as more equitable, even if more risky.[34]

On the whole, these figures are sobering. Although a more decentralized Web offers the potential for greater diversity and inclusion—artists of all backgrounds, gender, nationalities, races, and sexual orientation can sell their art through NFTs—those aspirations are, by no means, guaranteed to come to fruition in Web3. The statistics indicating significant gender and race disparities in the tech industry and the art establishment cast doubt on Web3 realizing its full potential for greater inclusivity—at least not without greater recognition among Web3 proponents of these existing problems. Achieving that goal won't happen by magic. Yet there is an opportunity, as suggested by the greater diversity among cryptocurrency owners and crypto-interested parties.

But initial numbers from the NFT market already provide reason for concern. According to a 2021 Art Tactic study of NFT sales on Nifty Gateway, 77 percent of all sales were for NFTs by male artists and just 5 percent by female artists.[35] Grimes was the only female artist among the ten bestselling artists on Nifty Gateway.[36] The gender disparity in artist sales isn't unique to Nifty Gateway. None of the top twenty highest all-time single NFT sales is by a woman artist (XCOPY and Pak have not disclosed their identity or gender, although they are commonly referred to as men).[37] Putting aside the pseudonymous XCOPY and Pak, all of the NFT artists in the top twenty highest sales are white men. Monica Rizzolli was the only woman artist in the top ten all-time cumulative NFT sales volume; Rizzolli ranked tenth in September 2022.[38] At the 2021 NFT.NYC conference, the largest NFT event in the world, only 18 percent of the speakers were reportedly women, and only 30 percent of the sponsored exhibits were by women.[39] The conference organizers prioritized improving diversity for the 2022 conference, making "Diversity of NFTs" the theme for the event.[40]

These initial statistics of the NFT market are concerning. They suggest women artists face similar challenges in the NFT market as they do in the art establishment. We need to gather additional data, including statistics of artists based on gender and race from other popular NFT marketplaces, including OpenSea, which held 80 percent of the marketplace in 2022, and curated marketplaces, such as SuperRare. Curated marketplaces can provide greater diversity in the way they select artists whose works are sold, instead of leaving everything to the market. OpenSea also has that ability in what NFTs it features on its homepage. Because the NFT market is rapidly developing and changing, having more recent and comprehensive data is important.

The challenges that women artists face in the NFT market probably relate, in part, to the much higher percentage of male buyers of NFTs. Surveys of NFT buyers in 2021 indicate that two thirds of the most frequent NFT buyers were men.[41] Moreover, one dynamic that likely compounds the gender disparity is the use of NFTs from pfp collections as a representation of one's identity. Using the NFT artwork as one's pfp or avatar on social media is a common practice. Indeed, for pfp collections, the practice is the most obvious use for NFTs, such as the CryptoPunks. People who identify as male or of a certain race might tend to buy an NFT character that embodies those traits if people use the characters as their online identity.[42] Of course, some people might feel liberated to choose an avatar or identity that is different. But, because men represent the substantial majority of NFT buyers, the pfp dynamic likely favors characters that appear male. This favoritism for male characters in NFT artwork departs from the predominance of women featured in traditional art: nearly half of the highest auction sales involve paintings depicting women, including artworks taking the perspective of the male gaze, in which a woman is objectified for heterosexual male viewers.[43] A similar pfp favoritism might occur also based on race, given that the majority of NFT buyers in the United States are white.[44] There's some evidence of this pfp favoritism occurring. According to a *Bloomberg* article, the weekly average minimum price for darker-skinned male CryptoPunks was consistently lower than the lightest-skinned male CryptoPunks.[45] Female CryptoPunks were also lower in price, despite their greater rarity. In the collection of 10,000 NFTs, male CryptoPunk characters outnumber female characters by 2,199. These differences in prices based on gender and skin color of CryptoPunk characters likely reflect a pfp favoritism among a white-male majority of buyers in the NFT market. Some successful projects, such as Deadfellaz, addressed the problem by making their characters gender-neutral and in colors that don't rely on a dark-light distinction.

There is still an opportunity for greater diversity in the NFT market. According to a *Variety* and Getwizer survey of 1,700 Americans, Blacks and Hispanics had higher percentages (49 and 47 percent, respectively) of people within their communities with an interest in NFTs compared with whites (30 percent), as well as a higher proportion (21 and 20 percent, respectively) of NFT ownership compared with whites (13 percent).[46] The survey did not report Asians or other racial and ethnic groups as a category. People of color have shown a greater interest in NFTs, similar to their response to cryptocurrency. As Web3 develops, we need more statistics on demographics of NFT artists, as well as a greater commitment to make diversity a goal of Web3.

SUSTAINABILITY

In 1907, Leo Baekeland, a Belgian inventor who emigrated to New York, invented the first entirely synthetic polymer, a plastic, or what he called Bakelite.[47] Because plastic could be molded into any form and then provide a hard, durable—virtually indestructible—material, it was seen as revolutionary.[48] *Time* even put Baekeland on its cover in 1924, with the quote: "It will not burn. It will not melt." In 1907, Baekeland apparently didn't recognize the environmental harms of plastic. Most plastics are not biodegradable.[49] Even worse, they are derived from nonrenewable petrochemicals, including fossil oil, natural gas, and coal.[50]

Starting in the 1970s, the view of plastics as a revolutionary invention had soured. Scientists and societies realized plastics had harmful effects on the environment.

Most plastics today aren't recycled. Researchers estimate that only 18 percent are recycled, 24 percent are incinerated, and 58 percent end up in landfill or the environment, especially the oceans, which were polluted with an estimated 150 million metric tons of plastics in 2015.[51]

This brief history of plastic provides a cautionary tale. Blockchain might become the plastic of the twenty-first century. Like Leo Baekeland at the turn of the twentieth century, Satoshi Nakamoto focused on solving one problem: how to avoid the double-spending problem through a cryptocurrency validated on blockchain. But the system Nakamoto devised created another problem: exceedingly high energy consumption. For Bitcoin's consensus system to work, every transaction requires a competition among miners who use powerful, energy-intensive computers (cooled with an arsenal of fans) to solve a "proof of work" problem.[52] Bitcoin is estimated to consume more energy annually than Argentina, a country of 45 million people.[53]

Figure 11.3 compares the estimated CO_2 equivalent of Bitcoin and Ethereum per transaction, including estimates for an Ethereum transaction before and after the merge.[54] Ethereum is more energy efficient than Bitcoin, but, until September 2022, Ethereum was still energy intensive, as shown in the figure. For reference, the estimated CO_2 equivalents of 1,000-kilometer trips by airplane per passenger, ICE car, and electric vehicle (EV) are also provided. One shouldn't place too much weight on the exact numbers in these estimates. Estimating CO_2 footprint is not an exact science.[55]

A single Ethereum transaction had the lowest estimated CO_2 footprint at 113.15 kilograms, even before Ethereum was changed to be more energy efficient. Recognizing the lack of sustainability, Ethereum developers worked for seven years to switch the validation of Ethereum transactions to a far more efficient proof-of-stake mechanism (replacing the competition among miners under proof-of-work with a random assignment among people who stake their ETH and act as validators to verify a transaction).[56] The switch, called the "merge," took place on September 15, 2022.[57] By all accounts, the merge was a success. The CO_2 footprint of Ethereum

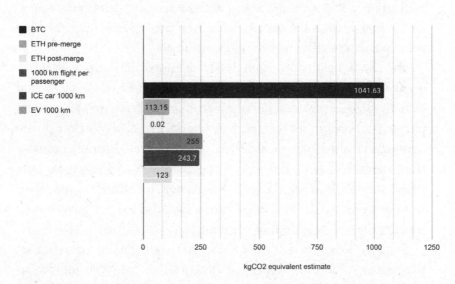

Figure 11.3

Comparison of Estimated Carbon Dioxide (CO_2) Footprint

Source: Digiconomist for BTC|ETH, Our World in Data for airplane, M. Roy, H. Ghoddusi, J. E. Trancik for ICE|EV.

decreased dramatically to 0.02 kg, which is equivalent to the footprint of 44 Visa transactions, according to Digiconomist.[58] Developers claimed that, after the merge, Ethereum's energy use was reduced by 99.99 percent.[59]

The merge was a big step for making Ethereum sustainable. However, some people, including Tron's founder Justin Sun, opposed the merge and planned on launching a spinoff (or "hard fork") version, which would retain the existing proof-of-work protocol but apparently not address the sustainability concern.[60]

Other blockchains using proof of stake or a variant, such as Flow, Polygon, Solana, and Tezos, already offer better energy efficiency.[61] In September 2022, Ethereum blockchain was the most popular for NFTs, followed by Solana and Flow. The merge was a pivotal step to building a more sustainable Web3.

Decentralization Is the Beginning, Not the End

The previous chapter outlined three principles for Web3: decentralization, self-sovereignty, and empowering creators and owners. Even though decentralization is the first principle, it's not the only principle. It's just the beginning, not the end.

The U.S. Constitution intended to do more than simply establish a government. In the opening line, the Framers made clear that "We the People" created a new government to serve greater societal purposes: "to form a more perfect Union, establish Justice, insure domestic Tranquility, provide for the common defense, promote the general Welfare, and secure the Blessings of Liberty to ourselves and our Posterity." This ideal of the Constitution probably is second nature to us—no American views the federal government itself as the ultimate goal of the country.

So, too, Web3 is a form of decentralized governance. But its purpose is to do more than just decentralize the Web for decentralization's sake. With all the focus on decentralization, it's easy to forget that decentralization is only a means to an end. Web3 is meant to serve other, more important goals, such as to protect self-sovereignty and privacy, and to empower creators to share their creative expression without the need for intermediaries. But the list of goals for Web3 shouldn't stop there. People interested in Web3—in imagining a better world—can set the goals and priorities. As John Perry Barlow stated in "A Declaration of the Independence of Cyberspace" at the Web's beginning, "We are creating a world that all may enter without privilege or prejudice accorded by race, economic power, military force, or station of birth."[62] Part of the beauty of Barlow's declaration was its incompleteness. The dream of building a "more humane and fair" world "must now be born anew in us."[63] It's ours to build—or destroy.

Make Diversity and Sustainability Top Priorities

One promise of decentralization is that we can all participate in debating our future within various communities. This book is meant to encourage debate about the future of the Web—in DAOs, Twitter spaces, social media, blog posts, and IRL. Indeed, we should strive to make Web3 a diaspora of discussion groups for people to converse and to confront the world's daunting challenges. To borrow the legal scholar Mary Anne Franks's phrase, we should build "spaces designed for democracy."[64]

In my view, two of our highest priorities should be addressing the lack of diversity and sustainability in society. I've taken my cue from Millennials and Gen Z, the generations whose views about the future should probably matter the most (along with Gen Alpha). Many are "not satisfied at all" with the level of commitment to diversity and sustainability among the institutions they encounter. We shouldn't be, either.

On the diversity front, plenty of people are already leading the way with various initiatives to make Web3 more inclusive. Paris Hilton, an early adopter of NFTs and the first female celebrity in the NFT space, established a fund at the Los Angeles County Museum of Art (LACMA) to purchase the works of women digital artists. The donation furthers LACMA's recent commitment to acquire works by women artists, which has yielded some improvement on that front compared to peer institutions.[65] LACMA's first two acquisitions were the Canadian-Korean artist Krista Kim's *Continuum: Los Angeles* and the British artist Shantell Martin's *The Question*. "As an activist and entrepreneur who likes to push the boundaries in many male-dominated fields, I immediately identified the need to support women in Web3," Hilton stated upon the announcement of the fund.[66] Given the lack of representation of women artists' works in permanent collections of major museums, Hilton's philanthropy is a step in the right direction. Other museums should follow suit.

Other prominent figures have promoted women artists in the NFT market. For example, in fall 2021, Reese Witherspoon and Eva Longoria Baston began championing the work of women NFT artists on social media. Witherspoon, whose media company Hello Sunshine supports the works of women creators, later announced a major partnership with the World of Women NFT project created by Yam Karkai, to develop films, TV shows, and other content based on some of the World of Women characters. Because the World of Women project has transferred the IP rights in the characters to the owners of the World of Women NFTs, the NFT owners can participate in decentralized collaboration. For example, Witherspoon can use her own World of Women character for the Hello Sunshine productions, along with other World of Women characters that the NFT owners license for the productions.

Lisa Mayer, the founder and CEO of My Social Canvas, an organization that provides mentorship and scholarships to young women in high school and college, launched a collection of 10,000 NFTs for Boss Beauties, depicting strong women in an assortment of role models, including astronauts, business executives, chefs, doctors, police officers, and scientists. As Mayer explained to *Cointelegraph*, "The promise here is that all these traits mixed together show that a woman can be anything she wants."[67] Boss Beauties sold out in ninety minutes. In March 2022, to celebrate International Women's Day, Mayer launched a limited collection of thirty-three Boss Beauties Role Models NFTs, which included portraits of women leaders, past and present, including Mother

Teresa and Ruth Bader Ginsburg.[68] Mayer's NFT company raised $4.4 million in seed funding from a group of prominent women-led funds, Serena Williams, Anu Duggal, Brit Morin, and Randi Zuckerberg.[69] Morin is the cofounder of My BFF, a decentralized community for women and nonbinary people to learn more about Web3.

One of the challenges for NFT collections is the inherent tension between rarity of NFTs and the goal of inclusivity. Although people invest in NFTs for various reasons, the potential appreciation of value is probably a major reason for many buyers. Within a collection of 10,000 NFTs, the ones with the rarer traits command the greatest value. Moreover, NFT creators run the risk of diluting the value of their genesis collections if they create second-generation collections that are too similar or even more impressive than the first. Of course, an NFT project could choose to maximize inclusivity by mass producing a great supply of NFTs. However, that may diminish popularity, as the CryptoKitties' oversupply of NFTs showed.

Alexandra Cavoulacos, Allyson Downey, and Max Siegman, the founders of the Meta Angels NFT collection, came up with an innovative—and inclusive—solution to this dilemma. The beautiful artwork for Meta Angels was created by Sarana Haeata, a Māori-Australian artist, who "is passionate about socioeconomic equality, gender and racial representation, and diversity,"[70] including for Indigenous people. The Meta Angels smart contract enables an owner of an NFT to loan it to someone else. The lending program is designed to foster greater access and inclusivity, especially for people who might not have the disposable income to spend on an NFT.[71] The Meta Angels' stated mission is to foster generosity, transparency, and accessibility.

Other NFT creators and organizations are also working to provide greater inclusivity in Web3 to underrepresented communities, including the Black, Indigenous, and People of Color (BIPOC) communities and the LGBTQ+ communities. Iris Nevins and Omar Desire founded Umba Daima, a company that promotes artists and provides Web3 education to the BIPOC community. One of Umba Daima's projects is Black NFT Art, whose mission is to promote and create opportunities for Black artists.[72]

To celebrate Pride month in 2022, Regev Gur, Eliad Cohen, and Amir Lazarovich, along with artist Max Bahman, launched what they tout as the largest LGBTQ+ NFT collection, called Pride Icons, which depict leaders, stars, and advocates for the LGBTQ+ community.[73] Their NFT project has pledged $1 million of the proceeds to various LGBTQ+ organizations. Cohen explained to *Robb Report* the significance of the Pride Icons: "The LGBTQ+ community has been featured in NFT collections but Pride Icons is the first time we are able to fully claim ownership and empower the community to become more involved in NFTs and web3 initiatives."[74]

FEWOCiOUS, a nineteen-year-old transgender male and one of the most successful NFT artists in the world, has broken down barriers and is an inspiration for all creators. FEWOCiOUS, whose real name is Victor Langlois, pursued art to escape his grandparents' strict household.[75]

"I genuinely think [art] saved my life," he said in an interview with *Esquire*.

FEWOCiOUS's first NFT was a Picasso-style digital artwork, "i Always Think of You," that sold on SuperRare for $1,000 in 2020. Then, in April 2021, the phenom artist teamed up with RTFKT to design digital sneakers NFTs, which sold out in seven minutes, earning $3.1 million.[76] That established FEWOCiOUS as a force in the NFT world. A couple of months later, Christie's auctioned FEWOCiOUS's NFT collection titled "Hello, I'm Victor (FEWOCiOUS) and This Is My Life" for $2.16 million. Sotheby's then sold a one-of-one NFT titled "Nice to meet you, I'm Mr. MiSUNDERSTOOD" for $2.8 million. FEWOCiOUS's first generative art NFT collection sold close to $20 million, ranking as the third highest on Nifty Gateway.[77]

David Bowie's estate invited FEWOCiOUS to create an NFT for "Bowie on the Blockchain." FEWOCiOUS's NFT sold for

$127,000, the highest in the collection. In the NFT's description, FEWOCiOUS acknowledged Bowie's influence: "I thought it was so cool that he always was what he wanted to be. And created a world that he wanted to live in. That's really the feeling I try to capture in my art. To my community & me, Bowie felt like hope."[78] FEWOCiOUS also collaborated with *Billboard* with a digital issue of the magazine sold as NFTs. The collection sold out in just twenty minutes, raising more than $10,000 for the Trevor Project, an organization devoted to suicide prevention and crisis support for young LGBTQ individuals.[79] In total, his NFTs have earned $50 million.[80] One already gets the sense that FEWOCiOUS may become one of the twenty-first century's most significant artists—if he is not already.

Artists are also using NFTs to promote greater awareness and inclusion of people with disabilities, who face significant hurdles to finding representation in the art establishment. Lachi, the award-winning recording artist and disability advocate who is blind, collaborated in creating NFTs with several visual artists with disabilities to celebrate the International Day of Persons with Disabilities.[81] Ava, a computer science student in London, founded ARTXV, a collective representing neurodiverse artists, including those with autism, ADHD, and synesthesia. Ava's inspiration was her sister, Tara, who is autistic and nonverbal. During the pandemic, Ava discovered that Tara had an extraordinary talent for art after finding, for the first time, one of Tara's beautiful abstract paintings.[82] Ava approached the art establishment to seek opportunities for her sister's artwork but was reportedly "met with dismissive responses as soon as they realized that Tara was autistic."[83] That's when Ava turned to NFTs. ARTXV launched a collection of one-of-one NFTs created by fifteen neurodivergent artists, including Tara.[84] The 2022 NFT.NYC conference selected some of the ARTXV artists' impressive works for display in Times Square.

These examples are just a handful of the inspirational efforts to build a more inclusive Web3. A more decentralized Web can help break down barriers, but it requires a conscious effort by everyone to support the goal of inclusion.

The same holds true with sustainability. The successful Ethereum merge was a positive step. However, it shouldn't be the last. Blockchain, NFTs, and Web3 can be used in ways to promote sustainability among people. For example, KlimaDAO is an organization that provides five different ways for other NFT projects to adopt sustainable approaches to offset the carbon footprint of the NFT projects. The projects buy tokenized carbon credits from KlimaDAO, which uses the credits to fund projects working to address climate change. The carbon custody NFT (cNFT) enables an NFT project to include in its smart contract a Klima token representing at least one ton of carbon offset credit the DAO has purchased.[85] As the Klima token increases in value, so does the amount of carbon offset it represents.

Klima's larger strategy is to make carbon offset credits more expensive to buy, based on the theory that it will stimulate a greater supply of more companies and projects (who sell the credits) to combat climate change.[86] A carbon offset credit represents the reduction of one metric ton of CO_2.[87] Businesses or individuals can effectively reduce their carbon footprint—from, say, air travel or blockchain transactions—by purchasing carbon offset credits, although some environmentalists criticize the approach as ineffective, akin to the medieval Catholic practice of buying indulgences to absolve sins.[88] By November 2021, Klima reportedly amassed more than 9 million metric tons of offsets, valued at $100 million.[89] Sven Eberwein, an artist who creates "works of the Internet, by the Internet, for the Internet," adopted Klima's cNFT for his artwork *CO$_2$ Compound*. In September 2022, the website indicated that it held 17.885 $Klima token, equaling 37.177 metric tons of carbon offset.[90] This example shows how blockchain and NFTs can be used to promote and fund sustainability efforts.

Web3 Leaders Need to Lead

Despite the incredible work of many people who have promoted diversity and sustainability in Web3, a lot more needs to be done, starting at the top. The visionaries who led the movement to build Web3, along with the creators and blue-chip projects that have already experienced enormous popularity and financial success, occupy positions in the NFT community that command great respect and attention. What they say matters. And it can greatly influence their communities and beyond.

What if the Web3 visionaries all issued public statements on how they plan to make Web3 more diverse and sustainable? What if the most successful blue-chip projects did so, too, including the ways they are working on improving diversity and sustainability in their ambitious road maps? What if the venture capital firms funding Web3 projects with many millions of dollars did the same? If leaders spent even a fraction of their time on diversity and sustainability for Web3, they're bound to come up with brilliant ideas— not to mention influence other people.

Corporate America and big brands have already adopted this practice of publishing their efforts to promote diversity and sustainability. Why? Corporate America knows consumers, especially Millennials and Gen Zs, want to buy products and services from companies that embody the values of diversity and sustainability the consumers share.[91] For sustainability, the SEC was considering a proposal to adopt a mandatory disclosure for publicly traded companies that states "a company's governance, risk management, and strategy with respect to climate-related risks."[92] The proposed SEC rule was based on what many public companies already do: "[N]early two-thirds of companies in the Russell 1000 Index, and 90 percent of the 500 largest companies in that index, published sustainability reports."[93]

I reviewed the websites of the top twenty-five pfp collections in all-time sales volume on OpenSea in June 2022. None had a formal statement on sustainability except a short one by the VeeFriends project.[94] Only three projects, World of Women, Azuki, and Pudgy Penguins, had a statement on diversity and inclusion.[95] This isn't to suggest that the top NFT projects do not care about these important issues. For example, Larva Labs and CrypToadz have reportedly donated to environmental causes. The platforms Art Blocks, Decentraland, and the Sandbox have also posted statements on sustainability.

But the top NFT projects can and should do better. For example, if the Bored Ape Yacht Club published a statement on the project's support for diversity and sustainability on its website, including the concrete steps it plans to take, that would likely influence other NFT projects (as its De-Collab license already has). Given its market share, OpenSea can also become a leader in these areas for Web3. If one of the most common attacks made against NFTs is that they are bad for the environment (a criticism less tenable post-merge), the leaders in the NFT industry should do more to address these concerns in both their words and deeds.

The websites of major Web3 companies and VC firms investing in Web3 were also spotty. Most didn't have pages of their website dedicated to outlining their positions on diversity or sustainability.

But a few provide models for what's possible. FTX, the cryptocurrency exchange started by Sam Bankman, had the clearest, most ambitious statement on sustainability, outlining four goals FTX was committed to, including funding research and organizations to achieve sustainability as a part of its FTX Climate Program.[96] Likewise, SoftGroup, the large Japanese investment company, had a detailed statement on both diversity and sustainability.[97] Following the Minneapolis police officer Derek Chauvin's murder of George Floyd, SoftBank established the Opportunity Growth Fund of $100 million "to invest in visionary Black, Latinx and Native American entrepreneurs and give them access to SoftBank Group's network."[98] The fund apparently was the largest to support BIPOC entrepreneurs.[99] Within two years, the fund reportedly invested $100 million in more than seventy startups founded by Black and Latinx founders.[100] Afterward, SoftBank announced it would make the fund an evergreen that would continue to fund BIPOC entrepreneurs, although it was unclear whether SoftBank's reported loss of $23.4 billion from its main Vision Fund, reported later that year, would affect its other funds and overall investing.[101]

After Floyd's murder, a16z started a similar fund for Black entrepreneurs called the Talent x Opportunity Fund. In two years, the fund invested in seventeen startups launched by Black founders.[102]

Similar investment funds can be devoted to NFT creators and Web3, and be expanded to include underrepresented groups of all kinds, including people with disabilities. Although the economic downturn in 2022 caused a decrease in VC investments in start-ups, some VC firms, such as a16z and Northzone, doubled down on Web3 investments.[103] A newly formed CreatorDAO, backed by $20 million in seed money, aimed to be an incubator for creators.[104]

This isn't to suggest that every Web3 leader is in a financial position to start an investment fund. Leaders can lead in a variety of ways, including simply by using their social media platforms to make diversity and sustainability priorities in the NFT community. Of course, issuing a public statement on diversity and sustainability could be just paying lip service. But it can also be a pledge that commits the organization to action. It's a start.

Everyone Can Help

But we can't expect Web3 leaders to solve these pressing problems on their own. Web3's great promise is that it provides a decentralized system—a global organizing platform—that facilitates people getting involved in ways big and small.

There are many ways people can contribute. The direct way is through one's wallet, either traditional or crypto. Everyone can learn from Millennials and Gen Zs, who are much more likely to avoid brands that don't embody the values important to these generations and to support the brands that do. If enough people adopt this principle and apply it to Web3 businesses, including NFT projects, it would make a lasting impact. One can also directly support women artists, as well as artists from the BIPOC, LGBTQ+, disability, and other underrepresented communities. The support can range from buying their NFTs—becoming an art patron—to simply promoting them on social media or even just liking a post of their work. Their art matters.

It's also crucial to recognize that people can contribute simply by discussion. One can join the online community for an NFT collection and promote greater awareness of diversity and sustainability in the community Discord or chats. One's contribution can be as simple as asking the cofounders what their positions on diversity and sustainability are. There are plenty of corrosive aspects of social media. But, at their best, social media can help to galvanize people's attention on societal problems of profound consequence. Recognizing a problem doesn't solve it. But it can spark action.

CHAPTER 12

THE FLIGHT FOR THE FUTURE

Give a loose rein to your fancy,
indulge your imagination in every possible flight. . . .

—JANE AUSTEN, *PRIDE AND PREJUDICE*

It may seem odd to begin a chapter about the future by discussing the past. In this chapter, we do so, briefly recounting the human quest to fly. Flight is the perfect metaphor for human creativity. And the history of the herculean efforts at the turn of the twentieth century to build a successful flying machine—that could enable humans to fly, what some thought impossible—provides an important lesson for understanding the ongoing efforts to build a better Web, where human creativity can flourish.

THE FLYING MACHINE

The human quest to fly dates back to time immemorial. But it wasn't until the turn of the twentieth century when that quest approached feasibility. Would-be inventors in various parts of the world were trying to a build a flying machine—something heavier than air that could transport humans in flight. Reading U.S. newspapers from this period, one gets a palpable sense of the excitement and optimism of journalists in describing these attempts, despite many failures and deaths.

"This is the age of the airship," *The St. Paul Globe* pronounced on May 9, 1897. "The revolution of the balloon to the flying machine is nearly complete, and it is not improbable that within a few years great aerial vessels for passenger service and monster engines of war and commerce will be seen sailing through space."[1] Of course, at the time, no one knew whether humans would succeed in their quest to fly. Also unclear was whether anything separated credible experimenters from so-called cranks. Optimism for a successful flying machine appeared to be based, in part, on the sheer amount of activity, and number of people, all trying to build a successful one.[2]

But failure was the fate suffered by most inventors. The news reporting of human tragedy was what inspired the most important figures of the period to turn their attention to the quest to fly. In 1896, Wilbur Wright, who co-owned a bicycle store with his brother, Orville, had been caring for Orville, who was bedridden with typhoid fever and, at times, near death.[3] Wilbur informed Orville of the tragic death of Otto Lilienthal, the German pioneer known as the "Flying Man," who had been experimenting with gliders modeled on bird wings and had successfully flown them many times—documented by his own aerial photography.[4] On August 9, 1896, Lilienthal fell from the sky and died.

Lilienthal's death was a harsh reminder of the danger people faced in trying to develop a flying machine. But, for Wilbur Wright, it rekindled a childhood interest in wanting to fly.[5] Fortunately, Orville survived the bout of typhoid fever. The two brothers then joined the quest to fly.

What business did two owners of a bicycle store have in trying to build the first successful flying machine? They were adept mechanics and made their own bicycles, but they had yet to invent anything. In a letter written in 1899 to the Smithsonian asking for any papers on aeronautics, Wilbur admitted he was an "enthusiast."[6] But he wasn't "a crank." Wilbur said that he wanted to learn the state of the art on aeronautics and "then if possible add my mite to help on the future workers who will attain final success."[7]

Wilbur's letter exuded a level of confidence that is nothing short of remarkable. "[T]he experiments and investigations of a large number of independent workers will result in the accumulation of information and knowledge and skill which will finally lead to accomplished flight," he declared to the Smithsonian.[8] A bicycle store owner not only predicting in 1899 that humans will fly, but also believing that he (and his brother) could help to accomplish it? Had this letter been written today, it would sound preposterous. Repairing bicycles was so far removed from flying—or so it seemed.

Richard Rathbun, assistant secretary of the Smithsonian, responded to Wilbur's letter by sending four pamphlets, as well as a bibliography of other relevant literature.[9] Rathbun's response might be the most consequential one ever sent by the Smithsonian. The knowledge shared with the Wrights was instrumental in their successful development of the first airplane.[10]

After four years of experimentation, as well as major setbacks, the Wright brothers made their big breakthrough. On December 17, 1903, at Kitty Hawk, the brothers settled the question.[11] Humans can fly.

As it turned out, the Wright brothers' knowledge of bicycle mechanics—and the need for equilibrium—was critical to the breakthrough they made.[12] Studying Lilienthal's research, they concluded that he failed because he wasn't able to maintain equilibrium.[13] As Wilbur put it, "the problem of equilibrium constituted the problem of flight itself."[14] The Wright brothers succeeded by developing a sophisticated three-axis control system, which gives a pilot full control of the airplane in three dimensions (the pitch, roll, and yaw axes) to maintain equilibrium.[15] The National Air and Space Museum described it as "their single most important design breakthrough."[16] The Wright brothers' control system underlies modern aviation to this day.

THE METAVERSE

To create something revolutionary entails flying from the captivity of the conventional. Daring to imagine something once deemed impossible. Experimenting, and drawing insights and connections across different disciplines—like the Wright brothers did—in the quest to contribute something lasting to society for the benefit of humankind.

This book has discussed innovative creators—Matt Hall and John Watkinson of Larva Labs, Beeple, Krista Kim, Osinachi, and others around the world—who are a part of a Virtual Renaissance that has already produced a breathtaking amount of human creativity within a few years. As a part of this Renaissance, there's a movement to build a better Web. The task of building isn't over. It's just begun.

Much in the same way as the Wright brothers and others did in the quest for human flight at the turn of the twentieth century, people from around the world are racing to build a better Internet—one that is more decentralized, more respectful of privacy and self-sovereignty, more supportive of artists and their creative works, more collaborative, and more conducive to empowering people by treating them as co-owners in a community, not users to be monetized. One that is more immersive, potentially enhanced by augmented and virtual reality. One that fosters wellness and serves humanity.

The builders in this movement come from many different sectors—art, music, tech, computer programming, business, consulting, design, fashion, gaming, luxury brands, law, and even nursing. Indeed, anyone can join. Many of the early developers quit their jobs to build Web3.[17] The brain drain from Big Tech is noticeable.[18] Big brands want in on the action: Balenciaga, Disney, Gucci, Nike, Meta, and many other companies posted new metaverse positions.[19] In India alone, there were an estimated 55,000 metaverse-related jobs.[20] The one qualification that binds the early entrants to Web3 jobs is that, like the Wright brothers, they are enthusiasts.

And we can expect more jobs in the future. Dubai and South Korea, two places with great ambitions to become leaders in the metaverse's development, are making sizable investments and planning for tens of thousands of new metaverse jobs.[21]

This flurry of creative activity to build a better Web is reminiscent of the early attempts to build a flying machine. People from different parts of the world taking a leap—a flight of imagination and a leap of faith—to build something they see as beneficial for civilization and humankind. Success is by no means guaranteed. Many failures are to be expected. The major economic downturn in 2022 presented its own challenge. And the narrative of a dystopian metaverse is a powerful one that probably frightens many people or gives them great skepticism toward the endeavor.

Yet, despite the so-called FUD (fear, uncertainty, and doubt), I'm optimistic about the Web's future. Why? I've had the chance to speak with some of the brightest minds who are working unflaggingly to build a better Web, and I've learned online about many others around the world doing the same. The amount of brainpower being devoted to Web3 is impressive. Marc Andreessen, cofounder of the VC firm a16z, a big investor in Web3, told McKinsey that his firm tracks job shifts involving engineers, the so-called nerds. The nerds are flocking to jobs related to AI, biotech, and crypto/Web3.[22] "Whatever the smart engineers work on is going to get better," Andreessen explained.[23] Similar to what American newspapers saw in the failed attempts to build a flying machine, I see progress in all the creative activity that is occurring. It provides reason for optimism that the artists, developers, and enthusiasts will succeed in building a better Web. Collectively, they are too smart and creative to fail.

I'm also hopeful because we already have some proof of how we can build a better Web. Like the Wright brothers' revolutionary three-axis control system, NFTs provide a technology that empowers people to take control. First, NFTs empower artists to control their artistic endeavors in a way never imagined before, giving them hope of being able to thrive as artists and the ability to control their artistic works through De-IP, including resale royalties and inclusive covenants. Society will ultimately benefit if artists thrive. Because NFTs are independently valuable, they even provide a new way to address unauthorized copies (aka piracy): NFTs diminish the concern over unauthorized copies, which don't substitute for the NFTs. That's why digital artists are beginning to thrive.

Second, NFTs empower people to control their online identity—their self-sovereignty. If Web3 succeeds, people no longer will have to cede control of their personal data to Big Tech simply to use the Internet. Third, NFTs provide businesses and organizations of all kinds a new way to engage people, to include them in a community or a DAO through interactive ownership, and to treat them as cocreators in partnerships and decentralized collaboration. If more businesses adopt De-Collab licenses, innovation is likely to increase. Businesses and developers are building new virtual worlds and more immersive experiences in which we can control our own identities (and privacy) through NFTs, using avatars and digital fashion. Instead of surveillance capitalism, the Web can facilitate humanistic capitalism, which, as Willis Harman described, involves businesses taking "an active responsibility for creating a healthy society and a habitable planet."[24] It shouldn't take a whistleblower for Internet companies to address the *known* psychological harms social media are rendering on our kids.[25]

These three examples of the utility of NFTs in empowering humans to take control of their lives only scratch the surface of the technology's potential. As a governance system, NFTs can facilitate an equilibrium for the Internet—yielding more empowering and humane relationships.

But turning this knowledge into lasting change won't happen by magic. It requires, first, a willingness and desire to reimagine what's possible. That's why the artists, creatives, and developers—the outside-the-box thinkers—have been at the forefront of the Virtual Renaissance and the quest to build a better Web. There's no single vision of what that looks like. But that's a feature, not a bug, of the decentralization envisioned for Web3. With a more decentralized Internet, people have more options and greater freedom to create and interact in more meaningful ways than being fed content by secret algorithms deployed by a handful of social media companies. Web3 should look more diverse and pluralistic than one ruled by Big Tech.

Ultimately, though, the success of this Virtual Renaissance depends on us all. If the Wright brothers built a flying machine that no one else wanted to fly, modern aviation wouldn't have developed. Humans would have remained grounded. One major difference between then and now is far more skepticism today with the ultimate goal. Perhaps that's reflective of the splintered world we live in. Whether for want of courage or want of cooperation, we lack the clarity of purpose that defined the generation that lived at the turn of the twentieth century during which people, including the Wright brothers, risked their lives trying to build a flying machine—for the benefit of civilization. Some even perished in that noble pursuit.

Picasso has loomed large in my discussion for two reasons. First, Tokenism's radical shift in perspective in owning art and other subject matter virtually by "tokens" is analogous to Cubism's shift in perspective in creating and viewing art in fragments simultaneously by "cubes." Both rely on human imagination to construct what is real. To understand the upheaval to our understanding of ownership that NFTs have precipitated, we must understand this key insight, first and foremost.

Second, society's astonishingly hostile reaction to Cubism initially—leading to public protests, a ban by Hitler in Nazi Germany as degenerate art, and even charges by distinguished American physicians that the artworks shouldn't be exhibited because they were the product of mental illness—should give us all pause. In a free society, criticisms are to be encouraged. It's right to scrutinize all the issues discussed in this book, especially my theories. But it's also right to scrutinize all the attacks on Web3, NFTs, the metaverse, and the Virtual Renaissance. When you read such FUD, DYOR. Remember the Tao of innovation—the more disruptive a new technology, the more controversy it will spark—a truism proved many times over, including at the beginning of the Internet. And remember Gelett Burgess, who first thought Picasso's paintings were an "outrage [to] nature, tradition, and decency," so shocking and unconventional they were, but then realized the importance "to get a new point of view on beauty so as to understand and appreciate this new movement in art."[26] History proved Burgess right. (By a twist of fate, Burgess also interviewed Wilbur Wright, who loved *The Goop Tales*.[27] Burgess had an eye for genius.) That Picasso today is widely recognized as perhaps the most influential artist of the twentieth century, the paragon of modern art—after his works were initially rejected as degenerate, ugly, and inferior in various countries, including the United States—gives us ample reason to study the Virtual Renaissance more closely and avoid making knee-jerk judgments on the quality and significance of digital and generative art—or the technology of NFTs that underlies its dramatic growth.

We have a golden opportunity, a chance to fix flaws in the Web and dehumanizing business models—and to create an Internet that is more decentralized, inclusive, and humane. We are at a pivotal moment, one that future generations may look back to and identify as the catalyst of an historic period of unrivaled creativity, empowerment, and enlightenment. A renaissance worthy of humans' loftiest ideals, leading to progress even beyond our wildest imagination. But, like the Wright brothers upon learning of the tragedy of the Flying Man, Otto Lilienthal, we have a choice: Do we do nothing or something?

Borrowing Wright's words: Do we add our mite to help attain final success?

ACKNOWLEDGMENTS

Writing this book was one of the most trying—and terrifying—intellectual endeavors I have ever undertaken. Luckily, I received generous help from many. Hollis Heimbouch, the publisher at Harper Business, was a joy to work with. She provided incisive comments that sharpened my writing throughout the book. I was wise to follow her every suggestion. Plus, her belief in the book's importance was a constant source of reassurance that the many hours I toiled away each day writing was not for naught. Kirby Sandmeyer, the assistant editor, was invaluable in helping to shepherd the book through the entire production process. She answered all of my technical questions, no matter how silly. The entire team at Harper Business did an amazing job, from the copyedit to the cover design, legal review, production, and publicity. To them my gratitude.

My agent, Joseph Perry, immediately saw the book's promise. Being a fellow lawyer specializing in intellectual property, he was indispensable in helping me refine my ideas and writing, starting with the proposal. He reviewed every chapter. But the best part: he provided instant feedback on individual paragraphs I was testing with the note, "Hi Joe, what do you think about this?" I thank his family for allowing him to reply on weekends.

I am forever indebted to the artists and businesses who shared with me their journeys to NFTs. Your creativity is truly inspirational. I can only hope my words are adequate to convey how inspirational. Many other artists and businesses around the world that I didn't get the chance to interview—too many—are doing amazing work in Web3. I hope one day I do.

Chicago-Kent College of Law provided generous financial support through the grant of a summer research stipend. Dean Anita Krug was incredibly supportive of this project, plus generous with her time in reviewing parts of the draft. Other amazing colleagues, Graeme Dinwoodie, Stephanie Stern, and Adrian Walters, reviewed sections of the book and provided invaluable feedback, especially in areas of law beyond my expertise. (All errors are mine.) Harold Krent had the (mis)fortune of experiencing my plunge down the rabbit hole of NFTs dating back to 2021. He reviewed my first blog posts and YouTube videos about NFTs, my law review article, the book proposal, and chapters of the book. Some of my ideas probably sounded outlandish (or, put charitably, "outside the box"), but he was always enthusiastic with the right dose of criticism.

The reference librarians at Chicago-Kent are the best in the world. The director, Jean Wenger; Mandy Lee; and Shannon Conder were outstanding in tracking down sources, even the most obscure, on a wide range of topics from art and business to finance, history, and the law. Wenger's help in locating old newspaper articles was a turning point in my research. My research assistant, Neekita Bhatia, did an amazing job in compiling and verifying the data for the fashion industry's use of NFTs, CO_2 footprints, and the diversity and sustainability statements (or lack thereof) of the top NFT projects. She and another student, Joshua Gablin, provided helpful feedback on parts of the book.

No legal scholar can write about the Internet, copyright, and regulation without coming to grips with Lawrence Lessig's theories on these topics during the Web's earlier days, and his founding of Creative Commons. That I had the chance to work with him at the beginning of my academic career was an opportunity of a lifetime. Indeed, *Code and Other Laws of Cyberspace* was a major catalyst for my decision in 1999 to quit my firm job and become an academic so I could write about these topics. I guess I was a "degen" before that term became popular. Since that time, many other scholars' and theorists' works from different disciplines, including ones I discuss in this book, have shaped my thinking. I am indebted to them as well.

I thank the student editors of three excellent law reviews in which I published my scholarship related to topics in this book: the

American University Law Review, the *UCLA Journal of Law and Technology*, and the *University of Illinois Law Review*. My article "NFTs as Decentralized Intellectual Property" will be published by the *University of Illinois Law Review* around the time this book is published. I am grateful to its editors, especially the editor in chief, Clare Donohue, for accommodating my book's publication, not to mention publishing my article even though its theory is controversial.

I thank the NFT.NYC organizers for inviting me to speak at the 2022 Diversity of NFTs conference. It was the first conference at which I shared my theory of De-IP and announced this book. Seeing the thousands of people from around the world attend NFT.NYC during the crypto winter confirmed to me that what I was writing was not off-base.

I leaned on family and friends for advice and support. Katrina Lee, Amanda Lee, and Ming Shao provided astute feedback on chapters of the book. Brianne Buishas and Stephani Ramirez gave crucial advice on the book proposal and selection of the book cover, and were constant sources of encouragement. I am forever indebted to my wonderful parents, siblings, and extended family for their unending support. My parents sacrificed dearly to give me opportunities they never had.

To all the "degens" in Web3: THANK YOU! I learned volumes about NFTs from the vibrant "NFT Twitter" and "NFT LinkedIn" communities whose daily discussions of NFTs were instrumental to my understanding. Your discussions were filled with insight, good humor, entertainment, and community. You gave me hope—and still do.

No one suffered more during the months I was furiously working on this book—ignoring all else—than my dog, Noodles. He forced me to take breaks and exercise—and constantly reminded me that there's more to life than Web3.

NOTES

Introduction

1. "Fact of the Day: Picasso Produced an Estimated 50,000 Artworks," *IndiaToday* (Oct. 20, 2016), https://www.indiatoday.in/education-today/gk-current-affairs/story/picasso-artworks-347466–2016–10–20.
2. "Most prolific painter," Guinness World Records, https://www.guinnessworld records.com/world-records/most-prolific-painter/?fb_comment_id=77010333974 2041_877734955645545.
3. Larva Labs, "Autoglyphs," Larvalabs, https://larvalabs.com/autoglyphs.
4. Art Blocks, "Learn About Art Blocks," https://www.artblocks.io/learn; Shrimpy Team, "What Is Art Blocks? The Generative Art NFT Platform Explained," Academy.Shrimpy (Dec. 31, 2021), https://academy.shrimpy.io/post/what-is-art -blocks-the-generative-art-nft-platform-explained.
5. Ola, "The 10 Best-Selling NFT Artists of All Time," NFT Evening (Apr. 12, 2022), https://nftevening.com/the-10-best-selling-nft-artists-of-all-time/.
6. "NFT Collection Rankings by Sales Volume (All-time)," Cryptoslam, https://cryptoslam.io/ (viewed Sep. 25, 2022).
7. Elizabeth Palermo and Callum McKelvie, "Who Invented the Lightbulb?," Live-science (Nov. 23, 2021), https://www.livescience.com/43424-who-invented-the -light-bulb.html.
8. "NFT Timeline," NFTtimeline, https://nfttimeline.com/; Branyce Wong, "NFTs, CryptoArt & CryptoCollectibles," Portion, https://blog.portion.io/the-history-of -nfts-how-they-got-started.
9. Sandra Upson, "The 10,000 Faces That Launched an NFT Revolution," *Wired* (Nov. 11, 2021), https://www.wired.com/story/the-10000-faces-that-launched-an -nft-revolution/.
10. "10 Things to Know About CryptoPunks, the Original NFTs," Christie's (Apr. 8, 2021), https://www.christies.com/features/10-things-to-know-about-cryptopunks -11569–1.aspx.
11. Chloe Cornish, "CryptoPunks and the Birth of a Cottage Industry," *Financial Times* (June 5, 2018), https://www.ft.com/content/f9c1422a-47c9–11e8–8c77-ff 51caedcde6.
12. Ibid.
13. "10 Things to Know."
14. "CryptoPunks / Types and Attributes," CryptoPunks, https://cryptopunks.app /cryptopunks/attributes.
15. Jason Abbruzzese, "This Ethereum-Based Project Could Change How We Think About Digital Art," Mashable (June 16, 2017), https://mashable.com/article /cryptopunks-ethereum-art-collectibles.
16. Langston Thomas, "Why Larva Lab's Decision to Dump V1 CryptoPunks Is a Problem," NFTnow (Feb. 5, 2022), https://nftnow.com/news/why-larva-labs -decision-to-dump-v1-cryptopunks-is-a-problem/.
17. Natasha Dailey, "The Massively Popular CryptoPunks NFT Collection Was Buggy and Unnoticed at Launch—Until All 10,000 Suddenly Sold in 24 Hours," Business Insider (Nov. 14, 2021), https://markets.businessinsider.com/news/currencies

/cryptopunks-nft-collection-buggy-unnoticed-launch wired-ethereum-block chain-2021-11.

18. Edward Lee, "The Cryptic Case of the CryptoPunks Licenses: The Mystery Over the Licenses for CryptoPunks NFTs," SSRN (Dec. 6, 2021), 2–3, https://papers .ssrn.com/sol3/papers.cfm?abstract_id=3978963.

19. Ibid., 5–7; Edward Lee, "The Two CryptoPunks, V1 and V2: Can V1 and V2 CryptoPunks Coexist or Will Copyright Tear Them Apart?," SSRN (Mar. 29, 2022), 3–6, https://papers.ssrn.com/sol3/papers.cfm?abstract_id=4032777; Andrew Hayward, "CryptoPunk Owner Explains Why IP Dispute Led to $10M Ethereum NFT Sale," Decrypt (Dec. 10, 2021), https://decrypt.co/88041/crypto punks-ip-complaints-punk4156–10m-ethereum-nft-sale.

20. "CryptoPunks / Top Sales by Ether Value," CryptoPunks, https://cryptopunks .app/cryptopunks/topsales?sortByUSD=true (last visited Oct. 3, 2022).

21. Alex Turner-Cohen, "Queensland Servo Worker Turns $4k into $100m Cryptocurrency, NFT Empire," News.com.au (Jan. 22, 2022), https://www.news.com.au/ finance/business/other-industries/queensland-servo-worker-turns-4k-into-100m -cryptocurrency-nft-empire/news-story/4d2c1a600831111789ddb0ccf2567b32.

22. "Top Sales," CryptoPunks.

23. "10 Things to Know About CryptoPunks," Christie's.

24. "CryptoPunks—Interview with Co-Founder Matt Hall," Artmarketguru (Jan. 6, 2019), https://www.artmarket.guru/le-journal/interviews/cryptopunks-matt-hall/.

25. David Pierce, "How a Pipe-Smoking Alien Became the 'Digital Mona Lisa,'" Protocol (Mar. 17, 2021), https://www.protocol.com/figma-ceo-cryptopunk-nft.

26. Kim Parker, Juliana Menasce Horowitz, and Rachel Minkin, "COVID-19 Pandemic Continues to Reshape Work in America," Pew Research (Feb. 16, 2022), https://www.pewresearch.org/social-trends/2022/02/16/covid-19-pandemic-con tinues-to-reshape-work-in-america/.

27. David Hollerith, "NFTs Explode into $27B Phenomenon as Investors with 'Bigger Bags' Put Them to Work," Yahoo! Finance (Dec. 7, 2021), https://finance .yahoo.com/news/nft-market-explodes-into-27-b-phenomenon-as-investors -with-bigger-bags-put-them-to-work-133112238.html.

28. Shira Ovide, "Our Virtual Pandemic Year," *New York Times* (Nov. 5, 2021), https:// www.nytimes.com/2021/03/12/technology/our-virtual-pandemic-year.html.

29. Edward Lee, "Disclosures," NouNFT, https://nounft.com/disclosures/.

Chapter 1: Moments

1. William H. Sewell, Jr., "Historical Events as Transformations of Structures: Inventing Revolution at the Bastille," *Theory and Society* 24, no. 6 (Dec. 1996): 842.

2. John Schroter, "Steve Jobs Introduces iPhone in 2007," YouTube (Oct. 8, 2011), https://www.youtube.com/watch?v=MnrJzXM7a6o.

3. David Pogue, "The iPhone Matches Most of Its Hype," *New York Times* (Jun. 27, 2007), https://www.nytimes.com/2007/06/27/technology/circuits/27pogue.html.

4. Tim Hardwick, "Former Microsoft CEO Steve Ballmer Admits He Was Wrong About the iPhone," MacRumors (Nov. 7, 2016), https://www.macrumors.com /2016/11/07/former-microsoft-ceo-steve-ballmer-wrong-iphone/.

5. Walter S. Mossberg and Katherine Boehret, "Testing Out the iPhone," *Wall Street Journal* (June 27, 2007), https://www.wsj.com/articles/SB118289311361649057.

6. Connie Guglielmo, "Untold Stories About Steve Jobs: Friends and Colleagues Share Their Memories," *Forbes* (Oct. 3, 2012), https://www.forbes.com/sites/con nieguglielmo/2012/10/03/untold-stories-about-steve-jobs-friends-and-col leagues-share-their-memories/?sh=247dc6366c58.

7. "I Predict the Internet Will Soon Go Spectacularly Supernova and in 1996 Cat-

astrophically Collapse," Quote Investigator, https://quoteinvestigator.com/2020
/03/09/collapse/#f+437530+1+1.

8.   Clifford Stoll, "Why the Web Won't Be Nirvana," *Newsweek* (Feb. 26, 1995),
https://www.newsweek.com/clifford-stoll-why-web-wont-be-nirvana-185306.

9.   Clifford Stoll, *Silicon Snake Oil: Second Thoughts on the Information Highway* (New
York: Anchor Books, 1995), 15.

10.   "End-to-End Connectivity," ICANNWiki, https://icannwiki.org/End-to-end
_connectivity.

11.   Janus Kopstein, "The Mission to Decentralize the Internet," *New Yorker* (Dec. 12,
2013), https://www.newyorker.com/tech/annals-of-technology/the-mission-to-de
centralize-the-internet.

12.   "Free VJ Loops," Beeple-crap, https://www.beeple-crap.com/vjloops.

13.   "Beeple Is Mike Winkelmann," Beeple-crap, https://www.beeple-crap.com/about.

14.   Kalyn Oyer Koyer, "Charleston Artist Beeple Changing Digital Landscape, Made
$3.5M in 1 Weekend," *Post and Courier* (Dec. 21, 2021), https://www.postand
courier.com/charleston_scene/charleston-artist-beeple-changing-digital-land
scape-made-3–5m-in-1-weekend/article_394dcd16–7533–11eb-83e5–33d121b
a910b.html; Tom Judd, Twitter (Mar. 13, 2021), https://twitter.com/tomjudd1
/status/1370816386482716673.

15.   "Beeple's Opus," Christie's, https://www.christies.com/features/monumental-col
lage-by-beeple-is-first-purely-digital-artwork-nft-to-come-to-auction-11510
–7.aspx.

16.   "Everydays," Beeple-crap, https://www.beeple-crap.com/everydays.

17.   Beeple_crap, "Birth of a Nation," Instagram (Sep. 30, 2020), https://www.insta
gram.com/p/CFyQxpeASRC/?hl=en.

18.   "BEEPLE | THE FIRST 5000 DAYS," Christie's (Mar. 11, 2021), https://online
only.christies.com/s/beeple-first-5000-days/beeple-b-1981–1/112924.

19.   "Beeple's Opus."

20.   Mickey Rapkin, "'Beeple Mania': How Mike Winkelmann Makes Millions Selling Pixels," *Esquire* (Feb. 17, 2021), https://www.esquire.com/entertainment/a35
500985/who-is-beeple-mike-winkelmann-nft-interview/.

21.   Katya Kazakina, "'I've Never Even Been to a Gallery Opening': NFT Star Beeple
on Trading Pixels for Paintings in His First-Ever Gallery Show," Artnet (Mar. 3,
2022), https://news.artnet.com/art-world/beeple-jack-hanley-new-york-2080308.

22.   Beeple_crap, Instagram, https://www.instagram.com/beeple_crap/ ("15+ years of
everydays* / free Creative Commons visuals.").

23.   Kyle Chayka, "How Beeple Crashed the Art World," *New Yorker* (Mar. 22, 2021),
https://www.newyorker.com/tech/annals-of-technology/how-beeple-crashed
-the-art-world.

24.   Ibid.

25.   Ibid.

26.   James Tarmy and Olga Kharif, "An NFT Sold for $69 Million, Blasting Crypto
Art Records," Bloomberg (Mar. 11, 2021), https://www.bloomberg.com/news
/articles/2021–03–11/beeple-everydays-nft-sells-at-art-auction-for-60-million
-paid-in-ether.

27.   Ivelina, "Beeple $69m Auction Smashes Records Again—What Really Happened
at Christie's," NFTPlazas (Mar. 12, 2021), https://nftplazas.com/christies-beeple
-auction-69-million/.

28.   Christie's, "Watch Beeple React to the Historic $69.3m Sale of His Digital Work at
Christie's," YouTube (Mar. 11, 2021), https://www.youtube.com/watch?v=S8p1B
8NHLFQ.

29.   Samuel Haig, "Digital Artist Beeple Auctions NFT Art Collection for $3.5M,"

Cointelegraph (Dec. 15, 2020), https://cointelegraph.com/news/digital-artist -beeple-auctions-nft-art-collection-for-3–5m.

30. Shanti Escalante-De Mattei, "NFT Expert Noah Davis Leaves Christie's to Work for CryptoPunks," *ARTnews* (Jun. 21, 2022), https://www.artnews.com/art-news /news/noah-davis-leaves-christies-cryptopunks-1234632488/.

31. Joyce Li, "Christie's Has Sold $150 Million USD Worth of NFTs in 2021," Hype- beast (Dec. 20, 2021), https://hypebeast.com/2021/12/christies-150-million-usd -worth-nfts-2021-announcement.

32. Crystal Kim, "Sotheby's Makes $100 Million in NFT Sales with Younger Au- dience," Bloomberg (Dec. 15, 2021), https://www.bloomberg.com/news/articles /2021–12–15/sotheby-s-makes-100-million-in-nft-sales-with-younger-audience.

33. Jacqui Palumbo, "First NFT Artwork at Auction Sells for Staggering $69 Mil- lion," CNN (Mar. 12, 2021), https://www.cnn.com/style/article/beeple-first-nft -artwork-at-auction-sale-result/index.html.

34. Ivelina, "If Beeple Had Kept His $69M in ETH . . . How Much Would It Be Worth Now?," NFTplazas (Oct. 24, 2021), https://nftplazas.com/if-beeple -had-kept-his-69m-in-eth/; Angus Berwick and Elizabeth Howcroft, "From Crypto to Christie's: How an Indian Metaverse King Made His Fortune," Reuters (Nov. 17, 2021), https://www.reuters.com/investigates/special-report /finance-crypto-sundaresan/.

35. Liam Frost, "Beeple Immediately Converted His $53 Million NFT Earnings from ETH to USD," Decrypt (Mar. 23, 2021), https://decrypt.co/62547/beeple -immediately-changed-his-53-million-nft-takings-from-eth-to-usd.

36. Ibid.

37. Robert Frank, "Beeple NFT Becomes Most Expensive Ever Sold at Auction After Fetching over $60 Million," CNBC (Mar. 11, 2021), https://www.cnbc .com/2021/03/11/most-expensive-nft-ever-sold-auctions-for-over-60-million .html.

38. Kelly Crow and Caitlin Ostroff, "Beeple NFT Fetches Record-Breaking $69 Mil- lion in Christie's Sale," *Wall Street Journal* (Mar. 11, 2021), https://www.wsj .com/articles/beeple-nft-fetches-record-breaking-69-million-in-christies-sale -11615477732.

39. Jason Farago, "Beeple Has Won. Here's What We've Lost.," *New York Times* (Mar. 14, 2021), https://www.nytimes.com/2021/03/12/arts/design/beeple-non fungible-nft-review.html.

40. Blake Gopnik, "One Year After Beeple, the NFT Has Changed Artists. Has It Changed Art? Hardly at All," *New York Times* (Mar. 3, 2022), https://www.ny times.com/2022/03/03/arts/design/nft-art-beeple.html.

41. Ben Davis, "I Looked Through All 5,000 Images in Beeple's $69 Million Magnum Opus. What I Found Isn't So Pretty," Artnet (Mar. 17, 2021), https://news.artnet .com/opinion/beeple-everydays-review-1951656.

42. Ibid.

43. Alastair Sooke, "Silly, Cartoonish, Offensive . . . and Selling for Millions. Is It Time to Take Digital Art Seriously?," *Telegraph* (May 7, 2022), https://www.tele graph.co.uk/art/artists/beeple-interview-has-arts-nft-bubble-burst.

44. Chayka, "How Beeple."

45. Hannah Marriott, "Beeple: How I Changed the Art World For Ever," *Times* (Mar. 12, 2022), https://www.thetimes.co.uk/article/beeple-how-i-changed-the -art-world-for-ever-tggbx99vm.

46. NVIDIA Studio, "Beeple: An Inside Look into His Art, Career and Life | NVIDIA Studio Spotlight," YouTube (Dec. 17, 2021), https://youtu.be/XKBt Ue1E_I8?t=559.

47. Lori McNee, "10 Famous Artists Who Had to Deal with Rejection During Their Lifetime," Lori McNee (Oct. 21, 2011), https://lorimcnee.com/10-famous-artists -who-died-before-their-art-was-recognized/.

48. Kelly Crow, "The Latest Sign That Beeple Has Truly Arrived: An Exhibit at an Italian Art Museum," *Wall Street Journal* (Apr. 11, 2022), https://www.wsj.com /articles/the-latest-sign-that-beeple-has-truly-arrived-an-exhibit-at-an-italian -art-museum-11649682005.

49. Sooke, "Silly, cartoonish."

50. Will Gompertz, "Everydays: The First 5000 Days—Will Gompertz Reviews Beeple's Digital Work ★ ★ ★ ☆☆," BBC (Mar. 13, 2021), https://www.bbc.com /news/entertainment-arts-56368868.

51. Jesse Damiani, "From Crypto to Christie's: How Beeple Put Digital Art on the Map—and Then Catalyzed Its Market," *Forbes* (Feb. 16, 2021), https://www .forbes.com/sites/jessedamiani/2021/02/16/from-crypto-to-christies-how -beeple-put-digital-art-on-the-map-and-then-catalyzed-its-market/.

52. Ibid.

53. KK Ottesen, "The Digital Artist Known as Beeple: 'I'm Just Trying to Expand People's Idea of What Art Is,'" *Washington Post* (Mar. 22, 2022), https://www .washingtonpost.com/magazine/2022/03/22/digital-artist-known-beeple-im -just-trying-expand-peoples-idea-what-art-is/.

54. Ibid.

55. Hannah Marriott, "Beeple: How I Changed the Art World for Ever," *Times* (Mar. 12, 2022), https://www.thetimes.co.uk/article/beeple-how-i-changed-the -art-world-for-ever-tggbx99vm.

56. 60 Minutes, "Beeple and NFTs: 60 Minutes+ Reports on a New Digital Era for Fine Art," YouTube (June 7, 2021), https://youtu.be/bLzcvY8X2RA?t=248.

57. Krista Kim, "We Are Creating a New Decentralized Civilization," Krista Kim studio (Feb. 14, 2021, updated in 2021), https://www.kristakimstudio.com/tech ism-manifesto.

58. Shoshana Zuboff, *The Age of Surveillance Capitalism* (New York: PublicAffairs, 2019), 8–12.

59. Marshall McLuhan, *Understanding Media: The Extensions of Man* (New York: Signet Books, 1964), 23.

60. Kim, "We Are Creating."

61. "Krista Kim Is the Creator of the Mars House, the Continuum Tour, and Founder of the Techism Movement," Krista Kim Studio, https://www.kristakimstudio.com/.

62. "The WorldBuilders of Web3," Rightclicksave (Apr. 4, 2022), https://www.right clicksave.com/article/the-worldbuilders-of-web3.

63. Krista Kim, "Krista Kim Nuit Blanche 2018 Paris," Vimeo (2020), https://vimeo .com/479089239.

64. Bruce Cole, *The Renaissance Artist at Work: From Pisano to Titian* (New York: Routledge, 1983), 18.

65. "Mars House by Krista Kim," Sotheby's (Nov. 2, 2021), https://www.sothebys .com/en/articles/mars-house-by-krista-kim-on-view-in-new-york.

66. "Mars House," SuperRare, https://superrare.com/artwork-v2/mars-house-21383.

67. "Chicago Ranks on List of Top 10 Metro Areas Where Home Prices Are Down the Most," NBC Chicago (Apr. 28, 2022), https://www.nbcchicago.com/news /local/chicago-ranks-on-list-of-top-10-metro-areas-where-home-prices-are -down-the-most/2819155/.

68. Steven Kurutz, "The Curious World of NFT Real Estate and Design," *New York Times* (May 27, 2021), https://www.nytimes.com/2021/05/25/fashion/selling-virt ual-real-estate.html.

69. Coral Murphy Marcos, "NFT: Digital Mars House by Artist Krista Kim Sells for $500k," *USA Today* (Mar. 24, 2021), https://www.usatoday.com /story/tech/2021/03/24/nft-digital-mars-house-artist-krista-kim-sells-500 –000/6979077002/.

70. Marriott, "Beeple."

71. Rosie Perper, "Beeple's 'HUMAN ONE' Generative NFT Sculpture Sells for $29 Million USD," Hypebeast (Nov. 11, 2021), https://hypebeast.com/2021/11 /beeple-human-one-nft-29-million-christies-auction.

72. *NFTs: Enter the Metaverse*, Hulu (2022) (44:21).

73. Deborah Vankin, "Paris Hilton Is LACMA's Newest Patron for Digital Acquisitions by Women Artists," *L.A. Times* (Jun. 9, 2022), https://www.latimes.com /entertainment-arts/story/2022–06–09/paris-hilton-lacma-digital-acquisitions -by-women-artists.

74. Krista Kim, "In the Metaverse, Life Imitates Art," *New York Times* (Jun. 16, 2022), https://www.nytimes.com/2022/06/16/special-series/krista-kim-metaverse-nft -art-reality.html.

75. Musadio Bidar and Dan Patterson, "Virtual Land Rush Is Driving Up the Cost of Space in the Metaverse," CBS News (May 6, 2022), https://www.cbsnews.com /news/metaverse-real-estate-companies-land-rush/.

76. Katie Rees, "These 8 Tech Giants Have Invested Big in the Metaverse," Makeuseof (Feb. 16, 2022), https://www.makeuseof.com/companies-investing-in-metaverse/.

77. Edward Lee, "List of Businesses Adopting or Developing NFTs," NouNFT (Feb. 1, 2022), https://nounft.com/2022/02/01/list-of-businesses-adopting-or-de veloping-nfts/.

Chapter 2: Life-Changing

1. "La Bohème in a Nutshell," Opera North (Aug. 19, 2019), https://www.operan orth.co.uk/news/la-boheme-in-a-nutshell/.

2. Gordon Gerrard, "When It Came to His Wealth, Puccini Knew How to Live a Lavish Life," Leaderpost (Jul. 29, 2017), https://leaderpost.com/entertain ment/local-arts/when-it-came-to-his-wealth-puccini-knew-how-to-live-a-lavish -life.

3. Neda Ulaby, "In Pricey Cities, Being a Bohemian Starving Artist Gets Old Fast," NPR (May 15, 2014), https://www.npr.org/2014/05/15/312779821/in-pricey -cities-being-a-bohemian-starving-artist-gets-old-fast.

4. *The Artfinder Independent Art Market Report: 2017*, Artfinder, 4, https://drive .google.com/file/d/1fozZCEKWffTzUmLz_kxnu8yApehOyYMf/view.

5. Ibid., 6, 14.

6. Ibid.

7. Ibid., 15–16.

8. Ibid., 6.

9. "A Study on the Financial State of Visual Artists Today," The Creative Independent (2018), 9, https://tci-assets.s3.amazonaws.com/pdfs/artist-survey-report/art ist-survey-report.pdf.

10. Ibid., 4.

11. Ibid., 17.

12. Peggy McGlone, "Survey Reveals a Dire Situation for Independent Artists, with Almost Two-thirds Now Unemployed," *Washington Post* (Apr. 24, 2020), https://www.washingtonpost.com/entertainment/survey-reveals-a-dire-situation -for-independent-artists-with-almost-two-thirds-now-unemployed/2020 /04/23/3b87de7c-8598–11ea-878a-86477a724bdb_story.html.

13. Erin Lowry, "Can You Make a Living in the Creator Economy?," Bloomberg

(June 2, 2022), https://staging.bloomberg.com/opinion/articles/2022–06–02/per sonal-finance-can-you-make-a-living-in-the-creator-economy.

14. Jane C. Ginsburg and Francis Gurry, "Copyright in the Digital Environment: Restoring the Balance. 24th Annual Horace S. Manges Lecture, April 6, 2011," *Columbia Journal of Law and the Arts* 35 (Fall 2011): 3.

15. Ibid., 7.

16. Mark Cartwright, "Patrons & Artists in Renaissance Italy," World History (Sep. 30, 2020), https://www.worldhistory.org/article/1624/patrons—artists-in -renaissance-italy/.

17. Cole, *The Renaissance Artist*, 20.

18. Ibid., 13.

19. Bram Kempers, *Painting, Power and Patronage* (London: Penguin Books, 1987), 142, 167–68.

20. Frank Bruni, "Florence Journal; The Warts on Michelangelo: The Man Was a Miser," *New York Times* (Jan. 21, 2003), https://www.nytimes.com/2003/01/21 /world/florence-journal-the-warts-on-michelangelo-the-man-was-a-miser.html.

21. Ibid., 18.

22. U.S. Const. art. I, § 8, cl. 8.

23. *Mazer v. Stein*, 347 U.S. 201, 219 (1953).

24. Clark D. Asay, "Copyright's Technological Interdependencies," *Stanford Technology Law Review* 178 (Winter 2015): 198–99.

25. Jessica Litman, "The Copyright Revision Act of 2026," *Marquette Intellectual Property Law Review* 13 (Summer 2009): 252.

26. Ibid., 253.

27. Jane Ginsburg, "The Author's Place in the Future of Copyright," *Willamette Law Review* 45 (Spring 2009): 382.

28. Litman, "The Copyright Revision," 253.

29. Ginsburg, "The Author's," 387–88.

30. *Mazer v. Stein*, 347 U.S. 201, 219 (1954).

31. *Twentieth Century Music Corp. v. Aiken*, 422 U.S. 151, 156 (1975).

32. *Harper & Row Publishers, Inc. v. Nation Enters.*, 471 U.S. 539, 558 (1985).

33. Litman, "The Copyright Revision," 253.

34. Kelly LeRoux and Anna Bernadska, "Impact of the Arts on Individual Contributions to US Civil Society," *Journal of Civil Society* 10 (2014): 160.

35. Brian Kisida and Daniel H. Brown, "New Evidence of the Benefits of Arts Education," Brookings Institution (Feb. 12, 2019), https://www.brookings.edu/blog /brown-center-chalkboard/2019/02/12/new-evidence-of-the-benefits-of-arts -education/.

36. Ibid.

37. Heather L. Stuckey and Jeremy Nobel, "The Connection Between Art, Healing, and Public Health: A Review of Current Literature," *American Journal of Public Health* 100, no. 2 (Feb. 2010): 254, 10.2105/AJPH.2008.156497.

38. Chris Jackson, "Americans Believe the Arts Are an Important Part of Society and Education," Ipsos (Apr. 9, 2019), https://www.ipsos.com/en-us/news-polls /Americans-Believe-the-Arts-Are-an-Important-Part-of-Society-and-Edu cation.

39. Ibid.

40. Ibid.

41. Ibid.

42. James Tarmy, "Why Do So Many Art Galleries Lose Money?," Bloomberg (July 30, 2015), https://www.bloomberg.com/news/articles/2015–07–30/why-do-so-many -art-galleries-lose-money-.

43. Magnus Resch, *Management of Art Galleries* (New York: Phaidon, 2nd ed., 2016), 24–26.
44. Ibid., 23.
45. Ibid., 33–35.
46. Jan Hoffman, "Gatekeepers to the Art World," *New York Times* (Mar. 30, 2008), https://www.nytimes.com/2008/03/30/fashion/30gallerinas.html.
47. Resch, *Management*, 34–35.
48. National Population Commission, "Nigeria Demographic and Health Survey 1999," DHS Program (Dec. 2000), 2, https://dhsprogram.com/pubs/pdf/FR115/FR115.pdf.
49. SuperRare Labs Team, "Artist Spotlight: Osinachi," Medium (Feb. 19, 2020), https://medium.com/superrare/artist-spotlight-osinachi-4606db461a0b.
50. Michael Stephen Haley, "'Digital Art' Framed and Collected on Blockchain," *Forbes* (Jan. 30, 2020), https://www.forbes.com/sites/michaelhaley/2020/01/30/digital-art-framed-and-collected-on-blockchain/.
51. Ann Marie Alanes, "Osinachi: Higher State of Being," Medium (Feb. 19, 2020), https://medium.com/makersplace/osinachi-higher-state-of-being-29516164a551.
52. Sue Baxter, "Visit These Virtual Museums During the Pandemic," Panoramanow, https://panoramanow.com/visit-these-virtual-museums-during-the-pandemic/.
53. "How Virtual Do We Want Our Future to Be?," Zoom, https://explore.zoom.us/docs/en-us/future-of-video-conferencing.html.
54. International Council of Museums, "Museums, Museum Professionals and Covid-19: Third Survey," ICOM (2021), 17, https://icom.museum/wp-content/uploads/2021/07/Museums-and-Covid-19_third-ICOM-report.pdf.
55. Tula Giannini and Jonathan Bowen, "Museums and Digital Culture: From Reality to Digitality in the Age of COVID-19," *Heritage*, no. 5 (Jan. 2022): 192, https://doi.org/10.3390/heritage5010011.
56. Kelly Crow, "$70 Million in Art at MoMA to Be Sold to Extend Museum's Digital Reach," *Wall Street Journal* (Sept. 13, 2022), https://www.wsj.com/articles/70-million-in-art-at-moma-to-be-sold-to-extend-museums-digital-reach-11663117201.
57. "Artist Talk: Osinachi—Existence as Protest—the Journey Through the Mind of the Artist," Katevassgalerie (May 11, 2020), https://www.katevassgalerie.com/blog/existence-as-protest-osinachi-artist-talk.
58. "Nigeria," Human Dignity Trust, https://www.humandignitytrust.org/country-profile/nigeria/.
59. SuperRare Labs Team, "Osinachi."
60. "Osinachi: Different Shades of Water Offered in First Open: Post-War and Contemporary Art Online," Christie's, https://www.christies.com/features/Osinachi-Different-Shades-of-Water-11897–7.aspx.
61. "David Hockney's Portrait of an Artist (Pool with Two Figures)," Christie's, https://www.christies.com/features/David-Hockney-Portrait-of-an-Artist-Pool-with-Two-Figures-9372–3.aspx.
62. "Osinachi: Different Shades."
63. Ibid.
64. Alex Yates, "Osinachi's Journey from Nigeria to NFTs," NFTnow (Aug. 30, 2021), https://nftnow.com/art/osinachi-interview-nigeria-nfts/.
65. "The Redemption of Major Tom by Osinachi," OpenSea, https://opensea.io/assets/ethereum/0x2438a0eeffa36cb738727953d35047fb89c81417/8.
66. SuperRare Labs Team, "Artist Spotlight: Osinachi."
67. Ibid.
68. The original post on Instagram was removed in 2022. The same post was made on

her Facebook account. Iamlaurael, Facebook (Mar. 17, 2020), https://m.facebook.com/iamlaurael/photos/a.120356412715511/195169378567547/?type=3&_rdr.

69. Ibid.

70. Iamlaurael, Instagram (Mar. 19, 2020), https://www.instagram.com/p/B96-cNnBl-K/.

71. "The Lurkers," Exchange.art, https://exchange.art/series/The%20Lurkers/nfts.

72. TEDx Talks, "Child of the Internet | Elise Swopes | TEDxUIUC," YouTube (May 22, 2019), https://youtu.be/joWNKJlf8N0?t=50.

73. Jsinkovich, "Exploring the World of NFTs with Elise Swopes," Columbia College Chicago (Nov. 23, 2021), https://blogs.colum.edu/business/2021/11/23/exploring-the-world-of-nfts-with-elise-swopes/.

74. That Creative Life, "Elise Swopes Full Interview—iPhone ONLY Graphic Designer w/ an UNBELIEVABLE Portfolio of Work," YouTube (Nov. 16, 2021), https://youtu.be/9IzKAh5_JWA?t=95.

75. Ibid., https://youtu.be/9IzKAh5_JWA?t=185.

76. TEDx Talks, "Child of the Internet," https://youtu.be/joWNKJlf8N0?t=89.

77. That Creative Life, "Elise Swopes," https://youtu.be/9IzKAh5_JWA?t=292.

78. "About," Swopes, https://www.swopes.info/about.html.

79. Jane Claire Hervey, "How This Artist-Influencer Is Preparing for the Instagram Bubble to Burst," *Forbes* (Nov. 19, 2017), https://www.forbes.com/sites/janeclairehervey/2017/11/19/how-this-artist-influencer-is-preparing-for-the-instagram-bubble-to-burst/?sh=296ea285747d.

80. "Paid Partnerships," Swopes, https://www.swopes.info/creative.html.

81. Mike Isaac, "Instagram May Change Your Feed Personalizing It with an Algorithm," *New York Times* (Mar. 15, 2016), https://www.nytimes.com/2016/03/16/technology/instagram-feed.html.

82. Hervey, "How This Artist-Influencer."

83. Ibid.

84. Umba Daima, "Lizzy Idowu & Elise Swopes on Being Black Woman Artists in the NFT Space," YouTube (Feb. 22, 2022), https://youtu.be/6gETgYmNm64?t=686.

85. Elise Swopes (@swopes), "Where Focus Goes, Energy Flows," SuperRare, https://superrare.com/artwork-v2/where-focus-goes,-energy-flows-20021.

86. Taylor Locke, "This 32-Year-Old Artist Brought in Over $200,000 Selling NFTs. Here's How She's Supporting Women of Color in the Space," CNBC (Dec. 19, 2021), https://www.cnbc.com/2021/12/19/this-31-year-old-artist-brought-in-over-200000-selling-nfts-how-shes-supporting-women-of-color.html.

87. Ibid.

88. Umba Daima, "Lizzy," https://youtu.be/6gETgYmNm64?t=184.

89. Ibid., https://youtu.be/6gETgYmNm64?t=2932.

90. Mark Westall, "SuperRare Present Invisible Cities, a Groundbreaking Exhibition of NFT Art Curated by An Rong and Elisabeth Jones," FAD Magazine (Apr. 1, 2021), https://fadmagazine.com/2021/04/01/superrare-present-invisible-cities-a-groundbreaking-exhibition-of-nft-art-curated-by-an-rong-and-elisabeth-johs/.

91. Jsinkovich, "Exploring the World."

92. Umba Daima, "Lizzy," https://youtu.be/6gETgYmNm64?t=2908.

93. "About," Swopes.info.

94. Elise Swopes (@swopes), Twitter (Nov. 25, 2021), https://twitter.com/Swopes/status/1463907721531514883; Swopes So Dope, "Affirmations, Motivation, and Psych Wards," Apple (Jan. 9, 2019), https://podcasts.apple.com/us/podcast/affirmations-motivation-and-psych-wards/id1447015263?i=1000427360555.

95. "Purchase Program," Sunriseart, https://sunriseart.notion.site/Purchase-Program-2ff8b936c77f4c8088de661a12bcf06e.

96. Andrew Hayward, "How a $2 Million NFT Drop Changed Artist Ben Mauro's Life," Decrypt (Mar. 17, 2021), https://decrypt.co/61647/ben-mauro-nft-drop-evolution-interview.
97. Justin Perri, "Eponym NFTs by Art AI: Turning Words into NFTs with AI," Collective (Oct. 14, 2021), https://collective.xyz/blog/eponym-nfts-by-art-ai-turning-words-into-nfts-with-ai.
98. Jex Exmundo, "From Top Gun to NFTs: How Val Kilmer Reclaimed His Voice," NFTnow (Aug. 18, 2022), https://nftnow.com/art/how-nfts-helped-val-kilmer-reclaim-his-voice/.
99. "Vision," Kamp Kilmer, https://www.kampkilmer.io/vision.
100. Ibid.
101. "Shamrock Clock," objkt, https://objkt.com/asset/KT1DC6JiHo69iMtBKYuZqs64356Z9Zk6grdB/4.
102. Joanna Woodburn, "Pandemic, 'Missed Opportunities,' Need for Space Fuelling Australia's Housing Crisis, Report Says," ABC (Mar. 22, 2022), https://www.abc.net.au/news/2022-03-22/report-finds-need-for-space-reason-behind-rental-housing-crisis/100926884.
103. Bankless, "1—Betty NFT & Deadfellaz | Overpriced JPEGs," YouTube (Nov. 13, 2021), https://youtu.be/RPQMCkkaB1s?t=718.
104. "Deadfellaz," Coinbase NFT, https://nft.coinbase.com/collection/ethereum/0x2acab3dea77832c09420663b0e1cb386031ba17b.
105. Ibid.
106. "Terms and Conditions," DeadFellaz, https://www.deadfellaz.io/terms.
107. "Deadfellaz Roadmap 2.0," Medium (Nov. 1, 2021), https://deadfellaz.medium.com/deadfellaz-roadmap-2-0-b5bcaab6ff8.
108. Deadfellaz, Twitter (Sept. 8, 2022), https://twitter.com/Deadfellaz/status/1567846447403651073.

Chapter 3: Hoops, Hops, and Haute Couture

1. Chris Morris, "Citi Says Metaverse Economy Could Be Worth $13 Trillion by 2030," Fortune (Apr. 1, 2022), https://fortune.com/2022/04/01/citi-metaverse-economy-13-trillion-2030/.
2. Mark Zuckerberg, "Founder's Letter, 2021," Facebook (Oct. 28, 2021), https://about.fb.com/news/2021/10/founders-letter/.
3. Mark Sullivan, "Social Networking as We Know It Is Likely on Its Way Out," Fast Company (July 26, 2022), https://www.fastcompany.com/90772561/is-social-networking-dead.
4. "People Take Up Sports Trading Cards as Hobby in Pandemic, Business Booms," Economic Times (Jul. 19, 2021), http://www.ecoti.in/Ujqfwb.
5. Darren Rovell, "The 10 Most Expensive Sports Trading Card Sales of All Time," Action Network (Mar. 31, 2022), https://www.actionnetwork.com/news/10-most-expensive-sports-trading-cards-sales-ever; Ava Brand, "One-of-a-Kind Steph Curry Trading Card Sells for Record-Breaking $5.9 Million," Brobible (Jul. 7, 2021), https://brobible.com/sports/article/steph-curry-rookie-card-record-sale/; "List of Most Expensive Sports Cards," Wikipedia, https://en.wikipedia.org/wiki/List_of_most_expensive_sports_cards.
6. Rovell, "The 10 Most."
7. Chad Finn, "Sports Card Collecting Is Booming, but It Looks a Lot Different Than You Might Remember," Boston Globe (Aug. 29, 2021), https://www.boston.com/sports/mlb/2021/08/29/sports-card-collecting-boom-panini/.
8. St. John Alexander, "Real Estate So Yesterday? Investing in Old Sports and Game Cards Is Suddenly the Rage," CTV News (Jun. 2. 2021), https://bc.ctvnews.ca

/real-estate-so-yesterday-investing-in-old-sports-and-game-cards-is-suddenly
-the-rage-1.5452492.

9. Jeff Wilser, "Most Influential 2021: Roham Gharegozlou," CoinDesk (Dec. 7, 2021), https://www.coindesk.com/business/2021/12/07/most-influential-2021-roham-gharegozlou/.

10. Ibid.

11. "How Rare Is an NBA Top Shot Moment Collectible," NBA Top Shot (Oct. 17, 2021), https://blog.nbatopshot.com/posts/nba-top-shot-rarity-blog.

12. A. J. Perez, "NBA Top Shot Reaches $1B in Sales Amid NFT Market Downturn," Front Office Sports (May 20, 2022), https://frontofficesports.com/nba-top-shot-reaches-1b-in-sales-amid-nft-market-downturn/.

13. Shaurya Malwa, "Battle of the Ethereum NFTs: CryptoPunk Sales Exceed NBA Top Shots," Cryptoslate (Apr. 11, 2021), https://cryptoslate.com/battle-of-the-ethereum-nfts-cryptopunk-sales-exceed-nba-top-shots/.

14. "NBA Top Shot Sales Volume Data, Graphs & Charts," Cryptoslam, https://cryptoslam.io/nba-top-shot/sales/summary.

15. Inti Pacheco, "Flipping Air Jordans Is No Longer a Slam Dunk" *Wall Street Journal* (July 23–24, 2022), https://www.wsj.com/articles/flipping-air-jordans-is-no-longer-a-slam-dunk-11658548817.

16. Clegainz, "The History of NBA Top Shot: Past, Present, and Future of NBA NFTs," Collective (Mar. 1, 2022), https://collective.xyz/blog/the-history-of-nba-top-shot-past-present-and-future-of-nba-nfts.

17. This Week in Startups, "Dapper Labs CEO Roham Gharegozlou on powering NFTs, NBA Top Shot, & CryptoKitties," YouTube (Apr. 13, 2021), https://youtu.be/ebPpxu5U-Fg?t=1275.

18. Michael Scotto, "How Players Make Money off NBA Top Shot," Hoopshype (Mar. 4, 2021), https://hoopshype.com/lists/nba-top-shot-money/; Tim Levin, "NBA Top Shot Maker Dapper Labs Just Nabbed Another $305 Million Investment from the Likes of Michael Jordan and Will Smith," Business Insider (Mar. 30, 2021), https://www.businessinsider.com/top-shot-nba-nft-dapper-labs-investment-funding-round-valuation-2021-3.

19. "Terms of Use," NBA Top Shot (last updated Feb. 2, 2022), https://nbatopshot.com/terms.

20. "What to Expect: Welcome to the Beta," NBA Top Shot (Jun. 14, 2020), https://blog.nbatopshot.com/posts/welcome-to-the-beta.

21. "New Findings from Deloitte Canada Reveal Minting an NFT on Flow Takes Less Energy Than a Google Search or Instagram Post," Onflow (Feb. 11, 2022), https://www.onflow.org/post/flow-blockchain-sustainability-energy-deloitte-report-nft.

22. Nicole LaPorte, "How Dapper Labs Is Making Web3 Safe for Normies with Help from the NBA, UFC, and La Liga," *Fast Company* (Mar. 8, 2022), https://www.fastcompany.com/90721921/dapper-labs-web3-safe-with-help-nba-ufc-and-la-liga.

23. Ibid.

24. Ibid.

25. Jabari Young, "People Have Spent More Than $230 Million Buying and Trading Digital Collectibles of NBA Highlights," CNBC (Mar. 2, 2021), https://www.cnbc.com/2021/02/28/230-million-dollars-spent-on-nba-top-shot.html.

26. Clegainz, "The History of NBA Top Shot."

27. Elizabeth Lopatto, "NBA Top Shot Seemed Like a Slam Dunk—So Why Are Some Collectors Crying Foul?," The Verge (Jun. 7, 2022), https://www.theverge.com/23153620/nba-top-shot-nft-bored-ape-yacht-club.

28. Jaspreet Kalra, "Dapper's NBA Top Shot Launches out of Beta with Samsung Galaxy Store Deal," CoinDesk (Oct. 1, 2020), https://www.coindesk.com/business/2020/10/01/dappers-nba-top-shot-launches-out-of-beta-with-samsung-galaxy-store-deal/.

29. Alex Flippin, "Sports Card Fraud Rampant During Pandemic," KWCH (Apr. 5, 2021), https://www.kwch.com/2021/04/06/sports-card-fraud-rampant-during-pandemic/.

30. "NBA Top Shot," Dapp Radar, https://dappradar.com/flow/collectibles/nba-top shot.

31. Finn, "Sports Card Collecting."

32. Lopatto, "NBA Top Shot."

33. Ibid.

34. Jessica Rizzo, "The Future of NFTs Lies with the Courts," *Wired* (Apr. 3, 2022), https://www.wired.com/story/nfts-cryptocurrency-law-copyright/.

35. Michael McCann and Jacob Feldman, "NBA Top Shot Fights NFT Securities Label in 'Moments' Case," Sportico (Sept. 7, 2022), https://www.sportico.com/law/analysis/2022/nba-top-shot-securities-lawsuit-1234687545.

36. Andrea Tinianow, "No Slam Dunk for Plaintiffs in NBA Top Shot Moments Class Action Lawsuit," *Forbes* (May 17, 2021), https://www.forbes.com/sites/andreatinianow/2021/05/17/no-slam-dunk-for-plaintiffs-in-nba-top-shot-moments-class-action-lawsuit/.

37. NBA Top Shot, Twitter (Jul. 12, 2022), https://twitter.com/nbatopshot/status/1546869816736108546?s=20&t=Mm1lnVAAv-nk0mCLkbY3vw.

38. "Removed from Circulation: The New Look NBA Top Shot Locker Room and Upcoming Stress Tests," NBA Top Shot (Mar. 3, 2022), https://blog.nbatopshot.com/posts/removed-from-circulation-new-look-nba-top-shot-locker-room.

39. Clegainz, "The History of NBA Top Shot."

40. Weston Blasi, "NFL Top Shot? NFL Makes NFT Bet in Latest Deal with Dapper Labs," MarketWatch (Sep. 30, 2021), https://www.marketwatch.com/story/nfl-top-shot-nft-platform-dapper-labs-agrees-to-a-deal-with-the-nfl-11632926260.

41. Michael LoRé, "Major League Soccer Partners with Sorare for NFT-Based Fantasy Game," *Forbes* (Mar. 29, 2022), https://www.forbes.com/sites/michaellore/2022/03/29/major-league-soccer-partners-with-sorare-for-nft-based-fantasy-game/?sh=2807a17b66c2.

42. David Adler, "MLB, Candy Digital Agree on NFT Partnership," MLB (Jun. 1, 2021), https://www.mlb.com/news/mlb-strikes-long-term-deal-as-first-nft-partner-of-candy-digital.

43. Zvonimir Potocki, "DraftKings and NFLPA Team Up for Unique Gamified NFL Player NFT Collections," US Gaming Review (Dec. 13, 2021), https://usgamingreview.com/news/216818-draftkings-nfl-nfts-marketplace-football/.

44. "Reignmakers," Draftkings, https://www.draftkings.com/reignmakers-football.

45. Zara Stone, "Inside Autograph, Tom Brady's NFT Startup," *Fast Company* (Apr. 18, 2022), https://www.fastcompany.com/90729336/autograph-tom-brady-nft-startup.

46. Cameron Thompson, "Tom Brady's Autograph, ESPN Launch Network's First NFT Collection," CoinDesk (Apr. 6, 2022), https://www.coindesk.com/business/2022/04/07/tom-bradys-autograph-espn-launch-networks-first-nft-collection/.

47. "Welcome to the Huddle," Autograph, https://autograph.io/tom-brady.

48. "Hall of Honor Inductee: Adolphus Busch," U.S. Department of Labor, https://www.dol.gov/general/aboutdol/hallofhonor/2007_busch.

49. Budweiser, "Budverse Cans—Heritage Edition," OpenSea, https://opensea.io/collection/budverse-cans-heritage-edition.
50. Ibid.
51. Ibid.
52. "Budweiser NFT Collection Sells Out in an Hour. 75% up for Resale," Ledger Insights (Nov. 30, 2021), https://www.ledgerinsights.com/budweiser-nft-sells-out-in-an-hour-75-up-for-resale/.
53. Sara Karlovitch, "Bud Light Brews Up Limited-Edition NFTs to Launch Zero-Carb Beer," Marketing Dive (Jan. 27, 2022), https://www.marketingdive.com/news/bud-light-brews-up-limited-edition-nfts-to-launch-zero-carb-beer/617858/.
54. Ibid.
55. Austin Huguelet, "A-B Says Its Latest NFT Collection Sold Out, Making $4.5M," Stltoday (Feb. 22, 2022), https://www.stltoday.com/business/local/a-b-says-its-latest-nft-collection-sold-out-making-4-5m/article_dc5eb4f0-c30f-526f-84cf-71c2c73f6095.html.
56. Alex White-Gomez, "How the Budweiser Royalty NFT Project Uplifts Emerging Musicians," ONE37pm (Jan. 20, 2022), https://www.one37pm.com/nft/what-is-the-budweiser-royalty-nft-project.
57. Langston Thomas, "Budweiser Partners with 22 Emerging Music Artists on New NFT Collection," NFTnow (Jan. 14, 2022), https://nftnow.com/news/budweiser-emerging-music-artists-nft-drop/.
58. Jonah Krueger, "Fresco Trey Signs with Warner Records, Unleashes Video for 'Need You': Exclusive," Consequence (Feb. 24, 2022), https://consequence.net/2022/02/fresco-trey-need-you-video-signs-warner-records/.
59. Andrew Hayward, "Bud Light Super Bowl Ad Includes Nouns Ethereum NFT Imagery," Decrypt (Feb. 7, 2022), https://decrypt.co/92239/bud-light-super-bowl-ad-includes-nouns-ethereum-nft-imagery.
60. Alex White-Gomez, "What Is the Nouns DAO and Why Is It Important?," ONE37pm (Jan. 20, 2022), https://www.one37pm.com/nft/what-is-the-nouns-dao
61. Neal Stephenson, *Snow Crash* (New York: Del Rey, 2017), 45.
62. Helen Papagiannis, "Zoom + Digital Fashion," XR Goes Pop (Mar. 30, 2020), https://xrgoespop.com/home/zoomfashion.
63. Jessica Golden, "Nike Teams Up with Roblox to Create a Virtual World Called Nikeland," CNBC (Nov. 19, 2021), https://www.cnbc.com/2021/11/18/nike-teams-up-with-roblox-to-create-a-virtual-world-called-nikeland-.html.
64. Kevin Tran, "Justin Bieber Illustrates the Limits of Virtual Concerts," *Variety* (Nov. 22, 2021), https://variety.com/vip/justin-bieber-illustrates-the-limits-of-virtual-concerts-1235116379/.
65. Dean Takahashi, "Newzoo: U.S. Gamers Are in Love with Skins and In-Game Cosmetics," VentureBeat (Dec. 18, 2020), https://venturebeat.com/2020/12/18/newzoo-u-s-gamers-are-in-love-with-skins-and-in-game-cosmetics/.
66. Ibid.
67. Ibid.
68. Anjali Sriniwasan, "How NFTs Compare to Rare In-Game Skins and Items," Ambcrypto (Apr. 22, 2021), https://ambcrypto.com/how-nfts-compare-to-rare-in-game-skins-and-items/.
69. Ibid.
70. Philip Maughan, "RTFKT Is the Creator-Led Studio Bringing Art, Fashion, & Nike into the Metaverse," Highsnobiety, https://www.highsnobiety.com/p/rtfkt-interview/.

71. Ibid.
72. Ibid.
73. Ibid.
74. "Who Is FEWOCiOUS?—The Digital Artist with a Powerful Story," NFT Explained, https://nftexplained.info/who-is-fewocious-the-digital-artist-with-a-powerful-story/.
75. "RTFKT Studios Set to Drop the Meta-Pigeon NFT & Physical Sneakers with Jeff Staple," Nicekicks (May 5, 2021), https://www.nicekicks.com/jeff-staple-rtfkt-studios-meta-pigeon-nft-physical-sneakers/.
76. Jennifer Alsever, "Avatars Are Influencers Now," *Utah Business* (Feb. 11, 2022), https://www.utahbusiness.com/avatars-are-influencers-now/.
77. Owen Fernau, "CloneX NFTs Sell Out in Auction Roiled by Attacks and Controversy," The Defiant (Dec. 1, 2021), https://thedefiant.io/clonex-nfts-rtfkt/.
78. "NFT Collection Rankings by Sales Volume (All-time)," Cryptoslam, https://www.cryptoslam.io/ (visited Sep. 25, 2022); "CloneX Sales Volume Data, Graphs & Charts," Cryptoslam, https://cryptoslam.io/clonex/sales/summary (visited Sep. 25, 2022).
79. Daz 3D, "Daz 3D X RTFKT—CloneX Shatters Boundaries Across the Metaverse," YouTube (Nov. 4, 2021), https://www.youtube.com/watch?v=nGpL6Jpdyvg.
80. "Digital Collectible Limited Commercial Use License Terms (RTFKT-Owned Content—CloneX Avatars)," RTFKT, https://rtfkt.com/legal-2C (no Murakami trait).
81. "Digital Collectible Terms (RTFKT-Owned Content)," RTFKT, https://rtfkt.com/legal-2A (Murakami trait).
82. Maughan, "RTFKT."
83. Ibid.
84. "NIKE, Inc. Acquires RTFKT," Nike (Dec. 13, 2021), https://news.nike.com/news/nike-acquires-rtfkt.
85. Maughan, "RTFKT."
86. Ibid.
87. Andrew Rossow, "RTFKT's 'Space Drip' Is Turning NFT Designs into Real-World Sneakers," Hypebeast (Jun. 28, 2022), https://hypebeast.com/2022/6/rtfkt-space-drip-sneaker-creation-artists.
88. Matthew Beedham, "Nike Now Holds Patent for Blockchain-Based Sneakers Called 'CryptoKicks,'" The Next Web (Dec. 10, 2019), https://thenextweb.com/news/nike-blockchain-sneakers-cryptokick-patent.
89. Maghan McDowell, "Why Nike's Next Web3 Move Is a Black Hoodie: Rtfkt's Founders Tell All," *Vogue Business* (Jul. 18, 2022), https://www.voguebusiness.com/technology/why-nikes-next-web3-move-is-a-black-hoodie-rtfkts-founders-tell-all.
90. Ibid.
91. Rudy Fares, "RTFKT Nike Hoodie—Sold OUT and People Angry, What Happened?," Cryptoticker (Jul. 22, 2022), https://cryptoticker.io/en/rtfkt-nike-hoodie-sold-out-people-angry-what-happened/.
92. Joseph Genest, "RTFKT's CloneX Collection Ushers in Forging SZN," Highsnobiety (Aug. 30, 2022), https://www.highsnobiety.com/p/rtfkt-clonex-drop-avatar-nft-lookbook/.
93. "Digital Fashion You Can Create. Trade. Wear," The Fabricant, https://www.thefabricant.studio/; Samantha Conti, "Metaverse Symposium: Design in the Metaverse Should Be About Democracy and Cocreation," *WWD* (Jul. 13, 2022), https://wwd.com/business-news/technology/metaverse-symposium-design-metaverse-democracy-cocreation-1235248264/.

94. "Sarabande: The Lee Alexander McQueen Foundation," Sarabande Foundation, https://sarabandefoundation.org/en-us/blogs/whats-on/sarabande-the-lee-alex ander-mcqueen-foundation.

95. "AUROBOROS presents Biomimicry Digital Ready-to-Wear Collection," London Fashion Week, https://londonfashionweek.co.uk/designers/auroboros.

96. Alice Finney, "Auroboros' 'Living' Biomimicry Dress Crystalises and Changes Shape in Real Time," Dezeen (Nov. 15, 2021), https://www.dezeen.com/2021 /11/15/auroboros-biomimicry-dress-crystalises-transforms-real-time/.

97. Kelly Lim, "How Tech Couture House Auroboros Is Paving the Way for Digital Fashion," Buro247 (Jul. 29, 2021), https://www.buro247.my/fashion/insiders /auroboros-digital-fashion-interview.html.

98. "AUROBOROS presents."

99. Daniel Rodgers, "Inside AUROBOROS and Grimes' Riotous Metaverse Fashion Week Collaboration," Dazed Digital (Mar. 25, 2022), https://www.dazeddigital .com/fashion/article/55769/1/auroboros-grimes-metaverse-fashion-week-mvfw -nft-decentraland-unxd-avatars.

100. Joelle Diderich, "Metaverse Symposium: Fashion Is a Long Way from Understanding Gaming," *WWD* (Jul. 13, 2022), https://wwd.com/business-news /business-features/rtkft-benoit-pagotto-says-fashion-a-long-way-from-under standing-gaming-metaverse-1235250187/.

101. "Gen Z Is Already in the Metaverse," Ypulse (Mar. 7, 2022), https://www.ypulse .com/article/2022/03/07/gen-z-is-already-in-the-metaverse/.

102. "Our Next Great Chapter," Ralph Lauren, https://corporate.ralphlauren.com /strategy.

103. Martine Paris and Bloomberg, "Ralph Lauren Ventures into the Metaverse Again by Debuting Digital Fashion Line on Roblox," *Fortune* (Dec. 8, 2021), https:// fortune.com/2021/12/08/ralph-lauren-digital-fashion-line-roblox-metaverse/; "Ralph Lauren Creates Expansive Holiday-Themed Experience on Roblox," Ralph Lauren (Dec. 8, 2021), https://corporate.ralphlauren.com/pr_211208_Roblox .html.

104. "Ralph Lauren Reports Third Quarter Fiscal 2022 Results and Raises Fiscal 2022 Outlook," Yahoo! (Feb. 3, 2022), https://www.yahoo.com/now/ralph-lauren -reports-third-quarter-130100984.html.

105. Ralph Lauren Corporation (RL) CEO Patrice Louvet on Q3 2022 Results— Earnings Call Transcript, Seeking Alpha (Feb. 3, 2022), https://seekingalpha.com /article/4484085-ralph-lauren-corporation-rl-ceo-patrice-louvet-on-q3–2022 -results-earnings-call-transcript

106. "Ralph Lauren Creates."

107. Melissa Repko, "Ralph Lauren CEO Says Metaverse Is Way to Tap into Younger Generation of Shoppers," CNBC (Jan. 17, 2022), https://www.cnbc .com/2022/01/17/ralph-lauren-ceo-says-metaverse-is-way-to-tap-into-younger -shoppers.html.

108. Isabelle Lee, "Luxury NFTs Could Become a $56 Billion Market by 2030 and Could See 'Dramatically' Increased Demand Thanks to the Metaverse, Morgan Stanley Says," Business Insider (Nov. 16, 2021), https://markets.businessinsider .com/news/currencies/luxury-nfts-metaverse-56-billion-market-revenue-2030 -morgan-stanley-2021–11.

109. Ibid.

110. "Number of Gamers Worldwide 2022/2023: Demographics, Statistics, and Predictions," Finances Online, https://financesonline.com/number-of-gamers-world wide/.

111. Entertainment Software Association, "2022 Essential Facts About the Video Game

Industry," ESA, 2, https://www.theesa.com/wp-content/uploads/2022/06/2022
-Essential-Facts-About-the-Video-Game-Industry.pdf.

112. Ibid., 3.
113. "Number of Gamers."
114. Frank Gogol, "Study: 94% of Crypto Buyers Are Gen Z/Millennial, but Gen X Is Outspending Them," Stilt (Apr. 26, 2022), https://www.stilt.com/blog/2021/03 /vast-majority-crypto-buyers-millennials-gen-z/.
115. Ibid.
116. Zack Butovich, "Are NFTs the Next Wave of Collector's Items? Most Still Unsure What They Are," Civic Science (Apr. 27, 2021), https://civicscience.com/are-nfts -the-next-wave-of-collectors-items-most-still-unsure-what-they-are/; "Millennials, Gen Z Want NFTs in Investment Portfolios," My Startup World (Apr. 4, 2022), https://mystartupworld.com/millennials-gen-z-want-nfts-in-investment -portfolios/.
117. Shantanu David, "Gen Alpha: How Brands Are Using Immersive Games to Connect with Their Newest Consumers," exchange4media (Jun. 9, 2022), https://www .exchange4media.com/digital-news/gen-alpha-how-brands-are-using-immersive -games-to-connect-with-their-newest-consumers-120724.html.
118. Brian Dean, "Roblox User and Growth Stats 2022," Backlinko (Jan. 5, 2022), https://backlinko.com/roblox-users.
119. Ibid.

Chapter 4: Tokenism

1. "Gelett Burgess Bio," Mypoeticside, https://mypoeticside.com/poets/gelett-bur gess-poems; "Burgess, Gelett," Circasomething, https://www.circasomething.com /burgess-gelett.
2. "Gelett Burgess Bio."
3. "Editor Burgess Kills 'The Lark,'" *San Francisco Call* (Mar. 31, 1897), 14.
4. "The Lark and the Cow," *Little Magazine Collection at UW-Madison Memorial Library* (Apr. 30, 2021), https://uwlittlemags.tumblr.com/post/649913317388877824 /the-lark-and-the-cow.
5. Anita Silvey, *Children's Books and Creators* (New York: Houghton Mifflin Harcourt, 1995), 103.
6. "The Lark and the Cow."
7. Max Kozloff, *Cubism/Futurism* (New York: CharterHouse, 1973), 3.
8. Ibid., 5.
9. Mark Antilff and Patricia Leighten, *Cubism and Culture* (New York: Thames & Hudson, 2001), 24.
10. "The 'Cubists' Dominate Paris' Fall Salon," *New York Times* (Oct. 8, 1911), 13.
11. Gelett Burgess, "The Wild Men of Paris," *Architectural Record* (New York: Architectural Record, 1910), 401, https://www.architecturalrecord.com/ext/resources /news/2016/02-Feb/wild-men-of-paris-architectural-record-may-1910.pdf.
12. Ibid.
13. Ibid.
14. Ibid.
15. Ibid., 408.
16. "Cubism," Tate, https://www.tate.org.uk/art/art-terms/c/cubism.
17. Albert Gleizes and Jean Metzinger, *Cubism* (London: T. Fisher Unwin, 1913) (English translation), 33.
18. Burgess, "The Wild Men," 414.
19. Gleizes and Metzinger, *Cubism*, 46.
20. Ibid., 12.

21. Douglas Cooper, *The Cubist Epoch* (London: Phaidon, 1971), 263.
22. Kozloff, *Cubism/Futurism*, 11.
23. "Cubism," Tate.
24. Park West Gallery, "These Early Reviews of Picasso's Art Are Adorably Hysteric," Medium (Aug. 23, 2019), https://medium.com/@parkwestgallery/park-west-gallery-review-picasso-147efeccdf31.
25. "It Requires an Odd Sort of Taste to Appreciate Their Crazy Drawing, but One Parisian Faction Hails Them as Geniuses Regardless of What Another Set Calls Them," *Salt Lake Tribune* (Magazine Section), (Nov. 19, 1911), 6.
26. Ibid.; Kevin Buist, "Lolo the Donkey and Avant-Garde That Never Was: Part 1," *Michigan Quarterly Review* (Mar. 2016), https://sites.lsa.umich.edu/mqr/2016/03/lolo-the-donkey-and-the-avant-garde-that-never-was-part-1/.
27. "Women Growing Less Beautiful?," *Ogden Standard-Examiner* (Aug. 13, 1922), 6.
28. Ibid.
29. Hugh Eakin, *Picasso's War* (New York: Penguin Random House, 2022), 52 (citing *Chicago Daily Tribune*, Apr. 17, 1913).
30. Ibid.
31. "The Armory Show," Art Institute of Chicago, https://archive.artic.edu/armoryshow/finale (citing *Chicago Evening Post*, Apr. 17, 1913).
32. Ibid.
33. "Cubists of All Sorts," *New York Times* (Mar. 16, 1913), 6, https://timesmachine.nytimes.com/timesmachine/1913/03/16/issue.html.
34. Eakin, *Picasso's War*, 144.
35. "Medical Science's Protest Against New 'Art,'" *Washington Times* (Oct. 9, 1921), 4.
36. Eakin, *Picasso's War*, 145.
37. Ibid.
38. "Medical Science's Protest."
39. Ibid.
40. Ibid.
41. Dina A. Pate and Kenneth G. Swan, "Francis Xavier Dercum: A Man for All Seasons," *Annals of Clinical and Translational Neurology* (Mar. 2014): 233–37, https://pubmed.ncbi.nlm.nih.gov/33755344/.
42. "Medical Science's Protest."
43. Ibid.
44. Ibid.
45. Eakin, *Picasso's War*, 147–48.
46. Ibid., 147.
47. "Nazification of German Culture," Holocaust Encyclopedia, https://encyclopedia.ushmm.org/content/en/article/degenerate-art-1.
48. "Hitler's Speech at the Opening of the House of German Art in Munich (July 18, 1937)," German History Documents, 1, https://germanhistorydocs.ghi-dc.org/pdf/eng/English87_.pdf.
49. Suzanne Muchnic, "Hitler's Sordid Little Art Show," *Los Angeles Times* (Feb. 10, 1991), https://www.latimes.com/archives/la-xpm-1991-02-10-ca-1401-story.html.
50. "'Entartete Kunst': The Nazis' Inventory of 'Degenerate Art,'" Victoria and Albert Museum, https://www.vam.ac.uk/articles/entartete-kunst-the-nazis-inventory-of-degenerate-art; Stephanie J. Beach, "Nazi-Confiscated Art: Eliminating Legal Barriers to Returning Stolen Treasure," *Loyola of Los Angeles Law Review* 53, no. 4 (Summer 2020): 855.
51. "Hitler's Speech."
52. Janet Maslin, "Film Festival Review: Pulp Fiction; Quentin Tarantino's Wild Ride on Life's Dangerous Road," *New York Times* (Sep. 23, 1994), https://www.nytimes

.com/1994/09/23/movies/film-festival-review-pulp-fiction-quentin-tarantino-s
-wild-ride-life-s-dangerous.html.

53.   Cassie Hill, "Why Quentin Tarantino Uses Non-Linear Storytelling and Small
       Talk Dialogue," Medium (Dec. 3, 2019), https://medium.com/@casscassbug
       /why-quentin-tarantino-uses-non-linear-storytelling-and-small-talk-dialogue
       -c59305f3a35b; "*Pulp Fiction*: Narrative Structure," Wikipedia, https://en.wikipe
       dia.org/wiki/Pulp_Fiction#Narrative_structure.

54.   Afzal Ibrahim, "Futurism," The Artist (Apr. 16, 2022), https://www.theartist.me
       /art-movement/futurism/; see, e.g., Svetozara Saykova, "The Asynchronous Sto-
       rytelling of Machevski," AUBG, https://today.aubg.edu/news/the-asynchronous
       -storytelling-of-manchevski/.

55.   John Berger, *The Success and Failure of Picasso* (New York: Vintage Books, 1967), 70.

56.   Bob Cotton, "Cubism Perception and Experimental Film," ZeitEYE (Jan. 25,
       2012), https://zeiteye.wordpress.com/2012/01/25/cubism-perception-and-exper
       imental-film/.

57.   NFT now, "Quentin Tarantino, Tom Bilyeu, Mike Novogratz & More on NFTs
       & Art," YouTube (Nov. 3, 2021), https://youtu.be/QD61k5R7X7c?t=260.

58.   Ibid., https://youtu.be/QD61k5R7X7c?t=745.

59.   Venetia Jolly and Ed Peter Traynor, "NFTs in Digital Art: Tokens or Tokenism,"
       Agora Digital (Apr. 28, 2021), https://agoradigital.art/blog-nfts-in-digital-art
       -tokens-or-tokenism/; Dream McClinton, "Non-Fungible Tokenism: Where Is the
       Diversity in Cryptoart?," Dazed (Nov. 26, 2021), https://www.dazeddigital.com
       /science-tech/article/54869/1/non-fungible-tokenism-diversity-in-cryptoart-nft.

60.   "ERC-721 Non-Fungible Token Standard," Ethereum (Jun. 23, 2022), https://
       ethereum.org/en/developers/docs/standards/tokens/erc-721/.

61.   Lodewijk Petram, "The World's First IPO," World's First Stock Exchange
       (Oct. 15, 2020), https://www.worldsfirststockexchange.com/2020/10/15/the
       -worlds-first-ipo/.

62.   Lodewijk Petram, "The Oldest Share," World's First Stock Exchange (Nov. 2,
       2020), https://www.worldsfirststockexchange.com/2020/11/02/the-oldest-share/.

63.   Lee, "The Cryptic Case," 6.

64.   Edward Lee, "Why the CryptoPunks 2022 License Is Better for Owners than
       the Bored Ape License, on Paper, Setting a New Standard for Decentralized
       Collaboration," NouNFT (Aug. 18, 2022), https://nounft.com/2022/08/18/why
       -the-cryptopunks-2022-license-is-better-for-owners-than-the-bored-ape-license
       -on-paper-setting-a-new-standard-for-decentralized-collaboration/.

65.   "Terms of Use," NBA Top Shot, https://nbatopshot.com/terms.

66.   "Terms & Conditions," Deadfellaz, https://www.deadfellaz.io/terms.

67.   Branyce Wong, "The History of NFTs & How They Got Started," Portion, https://
       blog.portion.io/the-history-of-nfts-how-they-got-started/; Shanti Escalante–
       De Mattei, "Sotheby's, Artist Kevin McCoy Sued over Sale of $1.5. NFT," *ARTnews*
       (Feb. 7, 2022), https://www.artnews.com/art-news/news/sothebys-kevin-mccoy
       -quantum-nft-sale-lawsuit-1234618249/.

68.   Satoshi Nakamoto, "Bitcoin: A Peer-to-Peer Electronic Cash System," Bitcoin,
       https://bitcoin.org/bitcoin.pdf.

69.   Arthur I. Miller, *Einstein, Picasso: Space, Time, and the Beauty That Causes Havoc*
       (New York: Basic Books, 2001), 2–3.

70.   Ibid., 3.

71.   *Picasso and Braque Go to the Movies* (2008) (1:50).

72.   Kim Parker, Juliana Menasche Horowitz, and Rachel Minkin, "How the Coro-
       navirus Outbreak Has—and Hasn't—Changed the Way Americans Work," Pew
       Research Center (Dec. 9, 2020), https://www.pewresearch.org/social-trends/20

20/12/09/how-the-coronavirus-outbreak-has-and-hasnt-changed-the-way
-americans-work/.

73. Mathias Sablé-Meyera, Joël Fagot, Serge Caparos, Timo van Kerkoerle, Marie
Amalric, and Stanislas Dehaene, "Sensitivity to Geometric Shape Regularity in
Humans and Baboons: A Putative Signature of Human Singularity," 118 PNAS
(Apr. 12, 2011), https://doi.org/10.1073/pnas.2023123118; Siobhan Roberts, "Is
Geometry a Language That Only Humans Know?," *New York Times* (Mar. 22, 2022),
https://www.nytimes.com/2022/03/22/science/geometry-math-brain-primates
.html.

74. Louis Wise, "The Real Problem with NFTs? They're Ugly," *Financial Times*
(Mar. 13, 2022), https://www.ft.com/content/583f9601-a45d-43c1–94d4–8c19d5
f5299f; Amy Francombe, "Why Does NFT Art Look So Bad?," Vice (Feb. 1,
2022), https://www.vice.com/en/article/qjbz5m/why-does-nft-art-look-so-bad;
Andy Storey, "5 Reasons Why Some NFTs Are So Ugly," Postergrind (May 12,
2022), https://postergrind.com/5-reasons-why-some-nfts-are-so-ugly/.

75. Ryan Cooper, "The NFT Craze Has Stopped Being Funny: These Hideous Cartoon Apes Will Not Be Worth Half a Million Dollars for Long," *The Week* (Jan.
4, 2022), https://theweek.com/culture/arts/1008539/the-nft-craze-has-stopped
-being-funny.

76. Kayleigh Donaldson, "All These NFTs Are So Effing Ugly and That's Kind of the
Point," Pajiba (Feb. 11, 2022), https://www.pajiba.com/miscellaneous/all-these
-nfts-are-so-effing-ugly-and-thats-kind-of-the-point.php.

77. "Pablo Picasso Line Drawings," PabloPicasso.net, https://www.pablopicasso.net
/drawings/; Janet Flanner, "Pablo Picasso's Idiosyncratic Genius," *New Yorker*
(Mar. 2, 1957), https://www.newyorker.com/magazine/1957/03/09/the-surprise
-of-the-century-i.

78. Nikki Griffin, "The Monkey Artist Hoax," Today I Found Out (Mar. 20, 2013),
http://www.todayifoundout.com/index.php/2013/03/the-monkey-artist-hoax/.

79. Evan Armstrong, "NFT Projects Are Just MLMs for Tech Elites," Every (Sep. 30,
2021), https://every.to/napkin-math/nft-projects-are-just-mlms-for-tech-elites;
Andy Day, "NFTs Are a Pyramid Scheme and People Are Already Losing Money,"
Fstoppers (Mar. 18, 2021), https://fstoppers.com/opinion/nfts-are-pyramid-scheme
-and-people-are-already-losing-money-554869; Amanda Marcotte, "NFTs Aren't
Art—They're Just the Cult of Crypto's Latest Scam," Salon (Feb. 16, 2022),
https://www.salon.com/2022/02/16/nfts-arent-art—theyre-just-the-of-cryptos
-latest-scam/.

80. Rachel Wolfson, "NFT Philanthropy Demonstrates New Ways of Giving Back,"
Cointelegraph (Jan. 31, 2022), https://cointelegraph.com/news/nft-philanthropy
-demonstrates-new-ways-of-giving-back.

81. Samantha Hissong, "NFT Scams Are Everywhere. Here's How to Avoid Them,"
Rolling Stone (Jan. 24, 2022), https://www.rollingstone.com/culture/culture
-features/nft-crypto-scams-how-to-not-get-scammed-1286614/; Tim Copeland,
"Supposed 17-Year-Old Artist Sells $138,000 Worth of Fake NFTs and Dis-
appears," The Block Crypto (Sept. 30, 2021), https://www.theblockcrypto.com
/post/119150/supposed-17-year-old-artist-sells-138000-worth-of-fake-nfts
-and-disappears; "Two Defendants Charged in Non-Fungible Token ('NFT') Fraud
and Money Laundering Scheme," U.S. Department of Justice (Mar. 24, 2022),
https://www.justice.gov/usao-sdny/pr/two-defendants-charged-non-fungible
-token-nft-fraud-and-money-laundering-scheme-0.

82. Arijit Sarkar, "How to Identify and Avoid a Crypto Pump-and-Dump Scheme?"
Cointelegraph (Jul. 16, 2022), https://cointelegraph.com/news/how-to-identify
-and-avoid-a-crypto-pump-and-dump-scheme.

83. Joseph Johnson, "Global Spam Volume as Percentage of Total E-mail Traffic from January 2014 to March 2021, by Month," Statista (Jul. 20, 2021), https://www.statista.com/statistics/420391/spam-email-traffic-share/.

84. Ana Gajić, "Spam Statistics," 99firms, https://99firms.com/blog/spam-statistics/.

85. Ibid.

86. OpenSea, Twitter (Jan. 27, 2022), https://twitter.com/opensea/status/1486843204062236676.

87. Jeff Yeung, "OpenSea Implements New Measures to Better Detect Fake NFTs," Hypebeast (May 12, 2022), https://hypebeast.com/2022/5/opensea-fake-nfts-copy mints-detection-measures.

88. Christopher Mims, "NFTs, Cryptocurrencies and Web3 Are Multilevel Marketing Schemes for a New Generation," *Wall Street Journal* (Feb. 19, 2022), https://www.wsj.com/articles/nfts-cryptocurrencies-and-web3-are-multilevel -marketing-schemes-for-a-new-generation-11645246824; Kyle Chayka, "Why Bored Ape Avatars Are Taking Over Twitter," *New Yorker* (July 30, 2021), https://www.newyorker.com/culture/infinite-scroll/why-bored-ape-avatars-are-taking -over-twitter.

89. "Multi-Level Marketing Businesses and Pyramid Schemes," FTC, https://consumer.ftc.gov/articles/multi-level-marketing-businesses-pyramid-schemes.

90. Ibid.

91. Cassio Gusson, "The NFT Sector Is Projected to Move Around $800 Billion over Next 2 Years: Report," Cointelegraph (Apr. 28, 2022), https://cointelegraph.com /news/the-nft-sector-is-projected-to-move-around-800-billion-over-next-2 -years-report.

92. Katie Notopoulos, "17 Celebrities Just Got Warning Letters About Shilling NFTs," *BuzzFeed News* (Aug. 8, 2022), https://www.buzzfeednews.com/article /katienotopoulos/celebrities-warning-letters-nft-ftc.

93. Federal Trade Commission, "CSGO Lotto Owners Settle FTC's First-Ever Complaint Against Individual Social Media Influencers," FTC (Sep. 7, 2017), https://www.ftc.gov/news-events/news/press-releases/2017/09/csgo-lotto-owners-settle -ftcs-first-ever-complaint-against-individual-social-media-influencers.

94. "Two Celebrities Charged with Unlawfully Touting Coin Offerings," SEC (Nov. 29, 2018), https://www.sec.gov/news/press-release/2018-268.

95. Christine Smythe, "The Backlash Against NFTs: Why One Artist Says They're a 'Classic Ponzi Scheme,'" Business of Business (Dec. 12, 2021), https://www.busi nessofbusiness.com/articles/the-backlash-against-nfts-one-artist-says-theyre -a-classic-ponzi-scheme-fraud-theft-crypto/; @thatkimparker, Twitter (Mar. 12, 2021), https://twitter.com/thatkimparker/status/1370579822213173248?s=20&t =ngQBrYfYBfrZgj71utgyfw.

96. John R. Emshwiller, "One Man's Bid to Clear His Name Online: 4 Years, $3 Million and Some Dead Turtles," *Wall Street Journal* (Feb. 24, 2017), https://www.wsj.com/articles/3-million-dead-turtles-and-a-sex-website-inside-one-mans -bid-to-clear-his-name-on-the-internet-1487949319; Robert D. Mitchell, "The Perils of Internet Defamation: $38.3 Million Jury Verdict," Mitchell Attorneys, https://web.archive.org/web/20201121212954/http://mitchell-attorneys.com /internet-defamation; *Cohen v. Hansen*, 748 Fed. Appx. 128, 129 (9th Cir. 2019) (upholding jury verdict finding defendant committed defamation by creating website that compared plaintiff "to Bernie Madoff and his Ponzi scheme"). Ironically, the United States later convicted the same losing defendant for running a Ponzi-like scheme. "Pair Who Went on the Run after Being Found Guilty of Fraud at a Now Defunct Precious Metals Firm, Sentenced to Prison," U.S. Department of Justice (Jun. 6, 2022), https://www.justice.gov/usao-wdwa/pr/pair

-who-went-run-after-being-found-guilty-fraud-now-defunct-precious-metals
-firm.

97. Mims, "NFTs."

98. Nathan J. Robinson, "Why CryptoCurrency Is a Giant Fraud," *Current Affairs*
(Apr. 20, 2021), https://www.currentaffairs.org/2021/04/why-cryptocurrency-is
-a-giant-fraud.

99. Saifedean Ammous, *The Bitcoin Standard: The Decentralized Alternative to Central
Banking* (Hoboken, N.J.: John Wiley & Sons, 2018).

100. Paul Krugman, "Technobabble, Libertarian Derp and Bitcoin," *New York Times*
(May 20, 2021), https://www.nytimes.com/2021/05/20/opinion/cryptocurrency
-bitcoin.html.

101. Paul Krugman, "Why Most Economists' Predictions Are Wrong," *Red Herring*
(Jun. 10, 1998), https://web.archive.org/web/19980610100009/http:/www.redher
ring.com/mag/issue55/economics.html.

102. Ibid.

103. David Emery, "Did Paul Krugman Say the Internet's Effect on the World Economy Would Be 'No Greater Than the Fax Machine's'?," Snopes (June 7, 2018),
https://www.snopes.com/fact-check/paul-krugman-internets-effect-economy/.

104. Ibid.

105. Manoj Singh, "The 2007–2008 Financial Crisis in Review," Investopedia (May
17, 2022), https://www.investopedia.com/articles/economics/09/financial-crisis
-review.asp.

106. "Fidelity Will Start Offering Bitcoin as an Investment Option in 401(k) Accounts," NPR (Apr. 26, 2022), https://www.npr.org/2022/04/26/1094798564
/fidelity-will-start-offering-bitcoin-as-an-investment-option-in-401-k-accounts.

107. Kevin Roose, "The Latecomer's Guide to Crypto," *New York Times* (Mar. 18, 2022),
https://www.nytimes.com/interactive/2022/03/18/technology/cryptocurrency
-crypto-guide.html.

108. Yuliya Chernova, "Venture Capitalists Flock to Crypto While Deals in Other
Sectors Slow," *Wall Street Journal* (Apr. 26, 2022), https://www.wsj.com/art
icles/venture-capitalists-flock-to-crypto-while-deals-in-other-sectors-slow
-11650967201.

109. Hannah Miller, "Crypto Startup Funding Falls to a One-Year Low," Bloomberg
(July 12, 2022), https://www.bloomberg.com/news/articles/2022–07–12/crypto
-startup-funding-in-q2-falls-to-a-one-year-low.

110. "Today's Cryptocurrency Prices by Market Cap," Coinmarketcap (Aug. 10, 2022),
https://coinmarketcap.com/.

111. William Power, "U.S.-Stock Funds Are Down 17.3% So Far in 2022," *Wall Street
Journal* (Sept. 4, 2022), https://www.wsj.com/articles/u-s-stock-funds-down-17
–3-in-2022–11662146408.

112. Kif Leswing, "Tim Cook Says He Owns Cryptocurrency and He's Been 'Interested in It for a While,'" CNBC (Nov. 9, 2021), https://www.cnbc.com/2021/11/09
/apple-ceo-tim-cook-says-he-owns-cryptocurrency.html.

113. Tae Kim, "Jamie Dimon Says He Regrets Calling Bitcoin a Fraud and Believes in the Technology Behind It," CNBC (Jan. 9, 2018), https://www.cnbc
.com/2018/01/09/jamie-dimon-says-he-regrets-calling-bitcoin-a-fraud.html.

114. JP Morgan, "Opportunities in the Metaverse," 2, https://www.jpmorgan.com
/content/dam/jpm/treasury-services/documents/opportunities-in-the-metaverse
.pdf.

115. Ibid., 12.

116. Ibid., 2.

117. Edward Lee, "List of Businesses Adopting or Developing NFTs," NouNFT

(Feb. 1, 2022), https://nounft.com/2022/02/01/list-of-businesses-adopting-or-de veloping-nfts/.

118. Citi GPS: Global Perspectives & Solutions, "Metaverse and Money: Decrypting the Future" (March 2022), 12, https://icg.citi.com/icghome/what-we-think /citigps/insights/metaverse-and-money_20220330.

119. P. Smith, "Global Apparel Market—Statistics & Facts," Statista (Aug. 17, 2022), https://www.statista.com/topics/5091/apparel-market-worldwide/; Mathilde Carlier, "Global Automotive Manufacturing Industry Revenue Between 2020 and 2022," Statista (Aug. 9, 2022), https://www.statista.com/statistics/574151/global -automotive-industry-revenue/.

120. Eamon Barrett, "Even After Berkshire Hathaway Sank $1 Billion into Crypto-Friendly Bank, Vice Chairman Charlie Munger Calls Coins Like Bitcoin a 'Venereal Disease,'" Fortune (Feb. 17, 2022), https://fortune.com/2022/02/17/cha rlie-munger-calls-crypto-venereal-disease-bitcoin-warren-buffett-nubank/.

121. Yashu Gola, "Warren Buffett Invests $1B in Bitcoin-Friendly Neobank, Dumps Visa and Mastercard Stocks," Cointelegraph (Feb. 15, 2022), https://cointelegraph .com/news/warren-buffett-invests-1b-in-bitcoin-friendly-neobank-dumps-visa -and-mastercard-stocks; Jesse Pound, "Warren Buffett's Berkshire Hathaway Makes $500 Million Investment in Brazilian Digital Bank," CNBC (Jun. 8, 2021), https://www.cnbc.com/2021/06/08/warren-buffetts-berkshire-hathaway -makes-500-million-investment-in-brazilian-digital-bank.html.

122. Tae Kim, "Warren Buffett Says Bitcoin Is 'Probably Rat Poison Squared,'" CNBC (May 6, 2018), https://www.cnbc.com/2018/05/05/warren-buffett-says-bitcoin -is-probably-rat-poison-squared.html; Tristan Rove, "Years After Calling Bitcoin 'Rat Poison,' Warren Buffett Just Invested $1 Billion in a Crypto-Friendly Bank," Fortune (Feb. 16, 2022), https://fortune.com/2022/02/16/warren-buffett -invested-1-billion-crypto-bank/.

123. David Lawder, "Yellen Says U.S. Crypto Rules Should Support Innovation, Manage Risks," Reuters (Apr. 7, 2022), https://www.reuters.com/business/finance/yellen -says-us-crypto-rules-should-support-innovation-manage-risks-2022–04–0 7/; Joseph Biden, "Executive Order on Ensuring Responsible Development of Digital Assets," White House (Mar. 9, 2022), https://www.whitehouse.gov /briefing-room/presidential-actions/2022/03/09/executive-order-on-ensuring -responsible-development-of-digital-assets/.

124. Alex Gailey, "Biden's New Executive Order on Crypto Is a Big Step in the Right Direction, Experts Say. Here's What Investors Should Know," Time (Mar. 11, 2022), https://time.com/nextadvisor/investing/cryptocurrency/biden-executive -order-crypto-expert-reaction/.

125. Jonathan Ponciano, "Crypto Winter Watch: All the Big Layoffs, Record Withdrawals and Bankruptcies Sparked by the $2 Trillion Crash," Forbes (Jul. 14, 2022), https://www.forbes.com/sites/jonathanponciano/2022/07/14/crypto-winter -watch-all-the-big-layoffs-record-withdrawals-and-bankruptcies-sparked-by-the -2-trillion-crash/.

126. Fatima Hussein and Ken Sweet, "New Cryptocurrency Oversight Legislation Arrives as Industry Shakes," PBS (Aug. 3, 2022), https://www.pbs.org/news hour/economy/new-cryptocurrency-oversight-legislation-arrives-as-industry -shakes.

127. Arjun Kharpal, "Ukraine Legalizes Crypto Sector as Digital Currency Donations Continue to Pour In," CNBC (Mar. 17, 2022), https://cnb.cx/3wfxdhR; Amitoj Singh, "Ukraine Has Received Close to $100M in Crypto Donations," CoinDesk (Mar. 9, 2022), https://www.coindesk.com/business/2022/03/09/ukraine-has -received-close-to-100-million-in-crypto-donations/.

128. Olga Kharif, "Ukraine Buys Military Gear with Donated Cryptocurrencies," *Time* (Mar. 5, 2022), https://time.com/6155209/ukraine-crypto/.

129. Cristina Criddle and Joshua Oliver, "How Ukraine Embraced Cryptocurrencies in Response to War," *Financial Times* (Mar. 19, 2022), https://www.ft.com /content/f3778d00–4c9b-40bb-b91c-84b60dd09698; Adi Robertson, "Ukraine Is Selling a Timeline of the Russian Invasion as NFTs: Proceeds Will Go Towards Ukraine's Army and Civilians," The Verge, (Mar. 25, 2022), https://www .theverge.com/2022/3/25/22996168/ukraine-ministry-digital-transformation -nft-crypto-drop-fundraising-war-timeline.

130. Neomi, "Artists and Activists Turn to NFT Sales to Support the Ukrainian People," Bitcoin (Mar. 14, 2022), https://news.bitcoin.com/artists-and-activists-turn -to-nft-sales-to-support-the-ukrainian-people/; Erika Lee, "How Reli3f Raised Over $1 Million for Ukraine in 30 Seconds Selling NFTs," ONE37pm (Mar. 21, 2022), https://www.one37pm.com/nft/tech/how-the-nft-community-raised -over-1-million-for-ukraine.

131. "Greenback movement," Britannica, https://www.britannica.com/event/Green back-movement.

132. Craig K. Elwell, "Brief History of the Gold Standard in the United States," *CRS Report for Congress* (June 23, 2011), 5–6, https://sgp.fas.org/crs/misc/R41887.pdf.

133. Ibid., 7, 13.

134. Gabriel T. Rubin, "U.S. Inflation Hits New Four-Decade High of 9.1%," *Wall Street Journal* (July 13, 2022), https://www.wsj.com/articles/us-inflation-june-2022 -consumer-price-index-11657664129.

135. Andrew Lisa, "What Do Banks Do with Your Money After You Deposit It?," Yahoo! (Aug. 17, 2021), https://www.yahoo.com/now/banks-money-deposit -110024642.html.

136. Andrew Lisa, "Which Countries Are Using Cryptocurrency the Most?," Yahoo! (Jun. 28, 2021), https://www.yahoo.com/video/countries-using-cryptocurrency -most-210011742.html.

137. I. Mitic, "A Modern-Day Gold Rush: 30 Eye-Opening Cryptocurrency Statistics for 2022," Fortunly (Feb. 25, 2022), https://fortunly.com/statistics/cryptocurrency- statistics/.

138. Seth I. Rosen, "Are Diamonds Really Rare? Diamond Myths and Misconceptions," International Gem Society, https://www.gemsociety.org/article/are-diamonds -really-rare/; Jaya Saxena, "Diamonds Aren't Special and Neither Is Your Love," *Atlantic* (Jan. 29, 2021), https://www.theatlantic.com/family/archive/2021/01 /diamonds-arent-special-and-neither-is-your-love/617859/.

139. "Picasso: Art Periods," Pablo Ruiz Picasso, https://www.pablo-ruiz-picasso.net /periods.php.

140. Gelett Burgess, *Goop Tales* (New York: Dover Publications, 1973).

141. "Goopdoods by Goopdude," Goopdoods, https://www.goopdoods.io/.

142. Gelett Burgess, "The Charms of Imperfection," *The Romance of the Commonplace* (San Francisco: Stanley-Taylor Co., 1902), 77.

Chapter 5: Interactive Ownership

1. *The Late Show with Stephen Colbert*, "Stephen Colbert Presents: 'NFT Heist' - The First Blockbuster Movie About NFTs!" YouTube (Mar. 12, 2022), https://youtu .be/boWHBjHkPSo?t=58.

2. "The Creator Economy Comes of Age as a Market Force," Valuewalk (Jun. 23, 2021), https://www.valuewalk.com/creator-economy-comes-age-asmarket-force/.

3. Clara Lindh Bergendorff, "Participatory Capitalism: The Ownership Economy and the Macro Trend of Micro Organizations," *Forbes* (Mar. 7, 2022), https://www

.forbes.com/sites/claralindhbergendorff/2022/03/07/participatory-capitalism—the-ownership-economy-and-the-macro-trend-of-micro-organizations/.

4.   Ibid.

5.   "NFT Staking Guide—What Is NFT Staking," Esports, https://www.esports .net/crypto/nft-staking/.

6.   *Jacque v. Steenberg Homes, Inc.*, 563 N.W.2d 154, 156 (Wis. 1997).

7.   Ibid., 157.

8.   Ibid., 160.

9.   *Loretto v. Teleprompter Manhattan CATV Corp.*, 458 U.S. 419, 435 (1982).

10. *Lingle v. Chevron U.S.A. Inc.*, 544 U.S. 528, 539 (2005).

11. William Blackstone, *Commentaries on the Laws of England* (1765–69), 2:2.

12. Carol M. Rose, "Canons of Property Talk, or, Blackstone's," *Yale Law Journal* 108 (1998): 601, 603–605.

13. Chris Sirise, "How NFTs Are Building Communities Online," Tech in Asia (Jan. 10, 2022), https://www.techinasia.com/nfts-giving-community-builders -ways-scale-authenticity-online.

14. "15 Top NFTs with Utility Projects with Potential (June 2022)," NFTkeshi (May 1, 2022), https://nftkeshi.com/best-nft-utility-projects-with-potential/.

15. Charles B. Sheppard, "Land Use Covenants: A Summary of Aspects of California Law Regarding Land Use Covenants with Comparison to the Restatement (Third) of Property," *Western State University Law Review* 37 (2009): 40–41.

16. *Montoya v. Barreras*, 473 P.2d 363, 365 (N.M. 1970) (emphasis added).

17. See, e.g., "Terms & Conditions," Deadfellaz, https://www.deadfellaz.io/terms (re-sale clause).

18. *Anthony v. Brea Glenbrook Club*, 58 Cal. App. 3d 506, 512 (Ct. App. 1976); Jay Weiser, "The Real Estate Covenant as Commons: Incomplete Contract Remedies Over Time," *Southern California Interdisciplinary Law Journal* 13 (2004): 284–85.

19. See Elinor Ostrom, *Governing the Commons: The Evolution of Institutions for Collective Action* (Cambridge: Cambridge University Press, 1990), 29–57.

20. "Doodles SXSW," VT Pro Design, https://vtprodesign.com/work/doodles-sxsw.

21. Chris Katje, "Doodles Brings Experiences to SXSW, Collabs with Behr, Shopify: How You Can Win a NFT," Benzinga (Mar. 15, 2022), https://www.benzinga .com/markets/cryptocurrency/22/03/26150048/doodles-brings-experiences-to -sxsw-collabs-with-behr-shopify-how-you-can-win-a-nft.

22. Marc Ferrero, "Doodles NFT Party at SXSW 2022," YouTube (Mar. 15, 2022), https://www.youtube.com/watch?v=NkOqzSEaf70.

23. Ryan Singel, "Are You Ready for Web 2.0?," *Wired* (Oct. 6, 2005), https://www .wired.com/2005/10/are-you-ready-for-web-2-0/.

24. Lawrence Lessig, *Remix: Making Art and Commerce Thrive in the Hybrid Economy* (New York: Penguin Press, 2008), 36–83.

25. Zuboff, *The Age of Surveillance Capitalism*, 54–55.

26. MK Manoylov, "A Mutant Ape Yacht Club Serum Sold for Nearly $6 Million—Here's What That Means for the Bored Ape Ecosystem," The Block Crypto (Jan. 3, 2022), https://www.theblockcrypto.com/post/129023/a-mutant-ape-yacht-club -serum-sold-for-nearly-6-million-heres-what-that-means-for-the-bored-ape-eco system.

27. Theo, "Check Out This 1:1 Mutant Ape NFT Popped Live on Twitch Last Night," NFT Evening (Dec. 29, 2021), https://nftevening.com/check-out-this-11-mutant -ape-nft-popped-live-on-twitch-last-night/.

28. NFTstatistics.eth (@punk9059), Twitter (Apr. 28, 2022), https://twitter.com/punk 9059/status/1519688088116551680.

29. Edward Lee, "Bored Ape Owners Share Life-Changing Experience from APE

COIN Drop from BAYC," NouNFT (Mar. 18, 2022), https://nounft.com /2022/03/18/bored-ape-owners-share-life-changing-experience-from-apecoin -drop-from-bayc/; Kyle Swenson, "This Bored Ape Yacht Club Whale Became the Club's Largest Holder This Weekend," The Bored Ape Gazette (Feb. 8, 2022), https://www.theboredapegazette.com/post/this-bored-ape-yacht-club-whale -became-the-club-s-largest-holder-this-weekend.

30. "ApeCoin," CoinMarketCap, https://coinmarketcap.com/currencies/apecoin-ape/; "Bored Ape Yacht Club," NFTpricefloor, https://nftpricefloor.com/bored-ape -yacht-club.

31. Nellie Bowles, "CryptoKitties, Explained . . . Mostly," *New York Times* (Dec. 28, 2017), https://www.nytimes.com/2017/12/28/style/cryptokitties-want-a-block chain-snuggle.html?_r=0.

32. Xin-Jian Jiang and Xiao Fan Liu, "CryptoKitties Transaction Network Analysis: The Rise and Fall of the First Blockchain Game Mania," *Frontiers in Physics* 9 (Mar. 3, 2021): 7–8, https://doi.org/10.3389/fphy.2021.631665.

33. NFTstatistics.eth (@punk9059), Twitter (Apr. 28, 2022), https://twitter.com /punk9059/status/1519788221554700288.

34. Nike Inc., "System and Method for Providing Cryptographically Secured Digi-tal Assets," US Pat. No. 10505726B1, https://patents.google.com/patent/US1050 5726B1.

35. Ibid.

36. Ibid.

37. Shanti Escalante–De Mattei, "Mysterious Pak NFT Project Generates $91.8 M. in Sales on Nifty Gateway," *ARTnews* (Dec. 6, 2021), https://www.artnews.com /art-news/news/pak-merge-nft-sale-nifty-gateway-1234612436/; Rupal Sharma, "Decoding the Smart Contract of Pak's Merge NFT Project," Cryptotimes (Sept. 6, 2022), https://www.cryptotimes.io/decoding-smart-contract-of-pak -merge-nft/.

38. "merge," Nifty Gateway, https://niftygateway.com/collections/pakmerge.

39. Makena Rasmussen, "Meet Alice: The Artificially Intelligent Human Who Sold for $500,000 at Sotheby's," Virtualhumans (July 26, 2021), "https://www.virtual humans.org/article/meet-alice-the-artificially-intelligent-virtual-human-who -sold-for-500–000-in-a-sothebys-nft-auction."

40. Larry Dvoskin, "Why Community Is the Secret of NFT Success," *Rolling Stone* (Jan. 17, 2022), https://www.rollingstone.com/culture-council/articles/commu nity-secret-nft-success-1283244/.

41. Lucas Matney, "The Cult of CryptoPunks," TechCrunch (Apr. 8, 2021), https:// techcrunch.com/2021/04/08/the-cult-of-cryptopunks/.

42. Arianne Gift, "Collector punk6529 Announces Metaverse Museum of 'Most High-End Art NFTs,'" Micky (Apr. 15, 2022), https://micky.com.au/collector -punk6529-announces-metaverse-museum-of-most-high-end-art-nfts/.

43. "6529 Mission," 6529, https://6529.io/about/mission/.

44. "Open Metaverse," 6529, https://6529.io/about/open-metaverse/.

45. "Varvara Alay, About," Varvara Alay, https://www.varvaraalay.com/about/.

46. Ibid.

47. Varvara Alay, Twitter (Dec. 4, 2021), https://twitter.com/VarvaraAlay/status /1467321728909127683.

48. "The Flower Girls," Flower Girls NFT, https://www.flowergirlsnft.com/.

49. Varvara Alay, Twitter (Nov. 25, 2021), https://twitter.com/VarvaraAlay/status /1463933047464730628.

50. Ibid.

51. "Special Editions," Flower Girls NFT, https://www.flowergirlsnft.com/.

52. *The Flower Girls Newsletter*, no. 6 (Jun. 9, 2022), https://www.getrevue.co/profile /flowergirlsnft/issues/the-flower-girls-newsletter-issue-6–1186753.
53. The Flower Girls, Twitter (Mar. 6, 2022), https://twitter.com/FlowerGirlsNFT /status/1507918266991316995.
54. *The Flower Girls Newsletter*, no. 6.
55. "Flower Girls Children," Flower Girls NFT, https://www.flowergirlsnft.com/.
56. Ibid.; Ian Dean, "Are NFTs Art? We Ask Award-Winning Graphic Designer Varvara Alay," Creativebloq (Aug. 2, 2022), https://www.creativebloq.com/features /are-nfts-art-flower-girls-interview.
57. The Flower Girls, Twitter (Apr. 16, 2022), https://twitter.com/FlowerGirlsNFT /status/1515363387105964037.
58. "The Dolphin Partnership," Flower Girls NFT, https://www.flowergirlsnft.com/.
59. Rosie Perper, "Chicago Bulls to Release NFT Artwork Reimagining Its Iconic Logo," Decrypt (Sep. 8, 2022), https://www.coindesk.com/business/2022/09/08 /chicago-bulls-to-release-nft-artwork-reimagining-its-iconic-logo/; Varvara Alay x Bulls: The Flower Bull, Coinbase, https://nft.coinbase.com/nft/ethereum/0 x0a394942c0bd33232639c03448e6daf15157092e/21.
60. Dean, "Are NFTs Art?"
61. Ryan Mac, "Meet 3LAU, the DJ That Turned Down Wall Street," *Forbes* (Aug. 24, 2015), https://www.forbes.com/sites/ryanmac/2015/08/24/meet-3lau-the-dj that-turned-down-wall-street/?sh=28c7fd921a57.
62. Abram Brown, "Largest NFT Sale Ever Came from a Business School Dropout Turned Star DJ," *Forbes* (Mar. 3, 2021), https://www.forbes.com/sites/abram brown/2021/03/03/3lau-nft-nonfungible-tokens-justin-blau/.
63. Mac, "Meet 3LAU."
64. Emma Newberry, "How the Winklevoss Twins Amassed a $6 Billion Bitcoin Fortune," Fool (Apr. 13, 2022), https://www.fool.com/the-ascent/buying-stocks/arti cles/how-the-winklevoss-twins-amassed-a-6-billion-bitcoin-fortune/.
65. Brown, "Largest NFT."
66. Morgan Chittum, "Exclusive: DJ Justin '3LAU' Blau on NFTs and Music Royalties as an Asset Class," Blockworks (Jan. 7, 2022), https://blockworks.co/exclusive -dj-justin-3lau-blau-on-nfts-and-music-royalties-as-an-asset-class/.
67. Nick, "3LAU Brings In Over $11.6 Million in Crypto Art NFT Auction," This Song Is Sick (Mar. 2, 2021), https://thissongissick.com/post/3lau-11-million-nft -auction/.
68. Brown, "Largest NFT."
69. Royal, https://royal.io/; Helen Partz, "3LAU Introduces Blockchain Music Platform Royal with $16M Raise," Cointelegraph (Aug. 26, 2021), https:// cointelegraph.com/news/3lau-introduces-blockchain-music-platform-royal-with -16m-raise.
70. Jeff Rumage, "Royal Raises $55M for Platform That Sells Music Royalties as NFTs," Built in Austin (Nov. 23, 2021), https://www.builtinaustin.com /2021/11/23/royal-raises-55m-music-nfts.
71. Andrew Rossow, "Justin Blau and 'Royal' Create First Artist-Fan Monetization Pipeline with Initial Round of Payouts," Hypemoon (Jul. 28, 2022), https:// hypemoon.com/2022/7/nft-music-platform-royal-airdrops-first-fan-royalty -payouts.
72. Ibid.
73. Ben Sisario, "Musicians Say Streaming Doesn't Pay. Can the Industry Change?," *New York Times* (May 10, 2021), https://www.nytimes.com/2021/05/07/arts /music/streaming-music-payments.html.
74. Glenn Peoples, "Who Gets Paid for a Stream?," *Billboard* (Feb. 24, 2022), https://

www.billboard.com/pro/music-streaming-royalty-payments-explained-song
-profits.

75. Emily Blake, "Data Shows 90 Percent of Streams Go to the Top 1 Percent of Artists," *Rolling Stone* (Sept. 9, 2020), https://www.rollingstone.com/pro/news /top-1-percent-streaming-1055005.

76. Amy X. Wang, "The Paltry Sum Paid to a Writer for 178 million Streams of His Hit Song." *QZ* (Oct. 14, 2015), https://qz.com/510004/the-paltry-sum-paid-to-a -writer-for-178-million-streams-of-his-hit-song.

77. Andrew R. Chow, "Independent Musicians Are Making Big Money from NFTs. Can They Challenge the Music Industry?" *Time* (Dec. 2, 2021), https://time .com/6124814/music-industry-nft/.

78. Sisario, "Musicians."

79. Tim Ingham, "Sony Generated $7.5BN Across Recorded Music and Publishing Last Year, Up 34 percent YOY," Music Business Worldwide (Feb. 2, 2022), https:// www.musicbusinessworldwide.com/sony-generated-7-5bn-across-recorded -music-and-publishing-last-year-up-24-yoy/; Tim Ingham, "Universal Music Group Surpassed $10 Billion in Revenues Last Year. It's Now Double the Size It Was a Decade Ago," Music Business Worldwide (Mar. 3, 2022), https://www .musicbusinessworldwide.com/universal-music-group-crashed-past-10-billion -in-revenue-last-year-its-now-double-the-size-it-was-a-decade-ago; Tim Ingham, "Warner Music Group Revenues Up 12.1 Percent in Calendar Q2; Recorded Music Streaming Up 2.7 percent," Music Business Worldwide (Aug. 9, 2022), https:// www.musicbusinessworldwide.com/warner-music-group-revenues-up-12-1-in -calendar-q2-recorded-music-streaming-up-2-7.

80. "Music Industry Investigation Report: Key Challenges, Collective Insights, and Possible Futures for the Music Industry," Creative Independent Report (2020), https://thecreativeindependent.com/music-industry-report/.

81. "The Song Goes On Forever; Can the Copyright End?," Kelly-IP (Apr. 2, 2020), https://www.kelly-ip.com/copyright/the-song-goes-on-forever-can-the-copy right-end/.

82. Taylor Swift, Tumblr (June 30, 2019), https://taylorswift.tumblr.com/post/1859 58366550/for-years-i-asked-pleaded-for-a-chance-to-own-my.

83. Kate Irwin, "Steve Aoki Says He's Made More Money with NFTs Than from 10 Years of Music Advances," Decrypt (Feb. 14, 2022), https://decrypt.co/92938 /steve-aokimore-money-nfts-decade-music.

84. Andrew Hayward, "DJ Steve Aoki Launches Ethereum NFT Membership Club: 'I Am Building My Own World,'" Decrypt (Jan. 27, 2022), https://decrypt .co/91317/dj-steve-aoki-launches-ethereum-nft-membership-club-i-am-building -my-own-world.

85. Ibid.

86. Stephanie Prange, "New NFTs of Anthony Hopkins Feature 'Zero Contact' Available," Media Play News (Feb. 22, 2022), https://www.mediaplaynews.com /new-nfts-of-anthony-hopkins-feature-zero-contact-available/.

87. Mitch Eiven, "NFT Communities Greenlight Web3 Films: A Decentralized Future for Fans and Hollywood," Cointelegraph (Aug. 3, 2022), https://cointele graph.com/magazine/2022/08/03/nft-communities-greenlight-web3-films -decentralized-future-fans-hollywood.

88. "The Medici. Artistic Patrons of the Renaissance," Italian Renaissance Art, https://www.italian-renaissance-art.com/The-Medici.html.

89. Metakovan and Twobadour, "NFTs: The First 5000 Beeples," Metapurser (Mar. 18, 2021), https://metapurser.substack.com/p/nfts-the-first-5000-beeples?s=r.

90. Chris Berg, "Opinion: Non-Fungible Tokens and the New Patronage Economy,"

CoinDesk (Sep. 14, 2021), https://www.coindesk.com/business/2021/03/22/non-fungible-tokens-and-the-new-patronage-economy/.

91. *2021 and Done with Snoop Dogg and Kevin Hart*, Peacock (Dec. 28, 2021).

92. Snoop Dogg, Twitter (Sep. 20, 2021), https://twitter.com/SnoopDogg/status/14400384604174574567.

93. Chris Eggertsen, "Sia Says She's Behind Popular Snoop Dogg–Affiliated NFT Twitter Account." *Billboard* (Mar. 8, 2022), https://www.billboard.com/business/tech/sia-nfts-snoop-dogg-bianca-medici-1235041414/.

94. Michelai Graham, "Champ Medici Is Making a Name of His Own in Web3," Boardroom (Jun. 22, 2022), https://boardroom.tv/watch/champ-de-medici-nft-nyc/.

95. Nitish Pahwa, "If Snoop Dogg Isn't This Secret NFT Trader, Who Is?," Slate (Sept. 23, 2021), https://slate.com/technology/2021/09/snoop-dogg-nft-crypto-cozomo-medici-twitter.html.

96. Chris Morris, "Snoop Dogg Is Converting Death Row Records into the First NFT Music Label," *Fortune* (Feb. 16, 2022), https://fortune.com/2022/02/16/snoop-dogg-death-row-records-nfts/.

97. Murray Stassen, "Snoop Dogg Sells Over $44M Worth of 'Stash Box' NFTs in Just Five Days," Music Business Worldwide (Feb. 15, 2022), https://www.musicbusinessworldwide.com/snoop-dogg-sells-over-44m-worth-of-stash-box-nfts-in-just-five-days123/.

98. DeathRowNFT, "Dogg on It: Death Row Mixtape Vol. 1," OpenSea, https://opensea.io/collection/dogg-on-it-death-row-mixtape-vol-1.

99. London Jennn, "Snoop Dogg & Wiz Khalifa Drop NFT Mixtape Ft. Xzibit, Daz Dillinger, Juicy J & More," Allhiphop (Mar. 24, 2022), https://allhiphop.com/news/snoop-dogg-wiz-khalifa-drop-nft-mixtape-ft-xzibit-daz-dillinger-juicy-j-more/.

100. Dean Takahashi, "The Sandbox Metaverse Hits 2M Users and Launches Alpha Season 2," VentureBeat (Mar. 3, 2022), https://venturebeat.com/2022/03/03/the-sandbox-metaverse-hits-2m-users-and-launches-alpha-season-2/.

101. Kate Irwin, "Someone Paid $450K to Be Snoop Dogg's Metaverse Neighbor," Decrypt (Dec. 2, 2021), https://decrypt.co/87524/someone-paid-450k-snoop-dogg-metaverse-neighbor.

102. Neomi, "Playable Sandbox Avatar NFTs—Mint a Unique Doggie and Explore the Metaverse in Style," Bitcoin (Feb. 21, 2022), https://news.bitcoin.com/snoop-dogg-drops-10000-playable-sandbox-avatar-nfts-mint-a-unique-doggie-and-explore-the-metaverse-in-style/.

103. "Snoop Dogg," Sandbox, https://www.sandbox.game/en/snoopdogg/.

104. @Supreme14kt, Twitter (Apr. 2, 2022), https://twitter.com/Supreme14kt/status/1510287047457751043.

105. Darlene Aderoju, "Snoop Dogg Releases First Metaverse Music Video with 'House I Built': 'It's About Keeping It Real,'" *Billboard* (Apr. 1, 2022), https://www.billboard.com/music/rb-hip-hop/snoop-dogg-releases-first-ever-metaverse-music-video-with-house-i-built-1235053365/.

106. Will Lavin, "Snoop Dogg Confirms He Now Owns the Masters to Dr. Dre's 'The Chronic,'" *NME*, https://www.nme.com/news/music/snoop-dogg-confirms-he-now-owns-the-masters-to-dr-dres-the-chronic-3176302.

107. SnoopDoggTV, "Snoop Dogg - House I Built (Official Music Video)," YouTube (Apr. 1, 2022), https://youtu.be/AzwLybCKlzc (comment of Micah B.).

108. Reese Witherspoon, Twitter (Feb. 21, 2021), https://twitter.com/ReeseW/status/1495888247616315396.

109. "Value Creation in the Metaverse: The Real Business of the Virtual World," Mc-

Kinsey (June 2022), 5–6, 37, 40–41, https://www.mckinsey.com/business-functions/growth-marketing-and-sales/our-insights/value-creation-in-the-metaverse.

110. Matt Wille, "Meta Won't Build a Dedicated Metaverse After All, Exec Says," Input Mag (May 19, 2022), https://www.inputmag.com/culture/meta-wont-build-metaverse-nick-clegg-facebook.

111. Rebecca Moody, "Screen Time Statistics: Average Screen Time in US vs. the Rest of the World," Comparitech (Mar. 21, 2022), https://www.comparitech.com/tv-streaming/screen-time-statistics/.

112. Kim Joo-heon, "Seoul Launches Metaverse-Based Science Education Program for 2,100 Students," *Ajudaily* (Mar. 3, 2022), https://www.ajudaily.com/view/20210826105856637.

113. Morgan Chittum, "South Korea to Pour $187M into 'World-Class Metaverse Ecosystem,'" Blockworks (Feb. 28, 2022), https://blockworks.co/south-korea-to-pour-187m-into-world-class-metaverse-ecosystem/.

114. Ibid.

115. Oluwapelumi Adejumo, "LG Copies Samsung, to Launch Own NFT-Enabled Smart TV," Yahoo! Finance (Jan. 6, 2022), https://finance.yahoo.com/news/lg-copies-samsung-launch-own-124539779.html.

116. Byun Hye-Jin, "Korean Retailers Jump into NFT Craze," *Korea Herald* (Jan. 25, 2022), http://www.koreaherald.com/view.php?ud=20220125000796.

117. Brian Newar, "Why NFT Adoption Is So High in South Korea," Cointelegraph (Mar. 29, 2022), https://cointelegraph.com/news/why-nft-adoption-is-so-high-in-south-korea.

118. Emma Marris, "K-pop Fans Have a New Nemesis," *Atlantic* (Dec. 22, 2021), https://www.theatlantic.com/technology/archive/2021/12/nft-kpop-environmental-problems/621091/.

119. Jiyoung Sohn, "BTS's NFT Venture Hits Sour Note with Fans," *Wall Street Journal* (Dec. 30, 2021), https://www.wsj.com/articles/btss-nft-venture-hits-sour-note-with-fans-11640871772?st=70mzrqgijux6kys&reflink=desktopwebshare_permalink.

Chapter 6: De-IP

1. Hover Pictures, "Justin Aversano for Canon—Equally Obsessed," Vimeo (2019), https://vimeo.com/294096039; Charlie Kolbrenner, "Justin Aversano's Twin Flames Demonstrates the Potential of NFT Photo Projects," ONE37pm (Aug. 9, 2021), https://www.one37pm.com/nft/justin-aversano-twin-flames-nft-photography.

2. Taylor Locke, "This 28-Year-Old Artist Made Over $130,000 Selling NFTs in Just 5 Months," CNBC (July 9, 2021), https://www.cnbc.com/2021/07/09/millennial-artist-made-over-130000-selling-nfts-in-about-5-months.html; Bankless, "Twin Flames NFT Photographer Justin Aversano | Layer Zero," YouTube (Dec. 7, 2021), https://youtu.be/HIyMiXRYSOI?t=4227.

3. Locke, "This 28-Year-Old Artist."

4. Taylor Locke, "'Covid Alien' CryptoPunk NFT Sells for Over $11.7 Million to Billionaire Buyer in Sotheby's Auction," CNBC (Jun. 10, 2021), https://www.cnbc.com/2021/06/10/covid-alien-cryptopunk-nft-sells-for-11point7-million-in-sothebys-auction.html.

5. Bankless, "Twin Flames NFT Photographer Justin Aversano | Layer Zero," YouTube (Dec. 7, 2021), https://youtu.be/HIyMiXRYSOI?t=4267.

6. Andrew Hayward, "How NFT Photo Sensation Twin Flames Landed at Christie's," Decrypt (Oct. 6, 2021), https://decrypt.co/82730/how-nft-photo-sensation-twin-flames-landed-at-christies.

7. "Justin Aversano, Twin Flames #49, Alyson & Courtney Aliano," Sotheby's, https://www.sothebys.com/en/buy-auction/2021/natively-digital-a-curated-nft-sale-2/announced-soon.

8. Charlie Kolbrenner, "Justin Aversano and Twin Flames #49 Make History with 871 ETH Sale," ONE37pm (Nov. 30, 2021), https://www.one37pm.com/nft/justin-aversano-twin-flames-49-nft-photography.

9. Ibid.; "List of Most Expensive Photographs," Wikipedia, https://en.wikipedia.org/wiki/List_of_most_expensive_photographs.

10. @theRAWdao, Twitter (Dec. 11, 2021), https://twitter.com/theRAWdao/status/1469689224786026503?s=20.

11. John Scott Lewinski, "How Non-Fungible Tokens Are Transforming the Art World," *Barrons* (Mar. 12, 2021, 3:38 pm), https://www.barrons.com/articles/how-non-fungible-tokens-are-transforming-the-art-world-01615581494.

12. "Five Reasons Why Public Art Matters," Save Art Space, https://www.saveartspace.org/.

13. Bankless, "Twin Flames," https://youtu.be/HIyMiXRYSOI?t=2217.

14. Hauser, "The French Droit de Suite: The Problem of Protection for the Underprivileged Artist Under the Copyright Law," *Copyright Law Symposium (ASCAP)* 11 (1962): 1.

15. Frank McNally, "Jean-François Millet—an Artist Who Moved the Market," *Irish Times* (Oct. 4, 2014), https://www.irishtimes.com/culture/heritage/jean-fran%C3%A7ois-millet-an-artist-who-moved-the-market-1.1951447; Maria Boicova-Wynants, "The Two Sides of a Coin. A Write-Up on Artists' Resale Rights," Artlaw (Jun. 20, 2019), https://artlaw.club/en/artlaw/the-two-sides-of-a-coin-a-write-up-on-artists-resale-rights.

16. Catherine Jewell, "The Artist's Resale Right: A Fair Deal for Visual Artists," *WIPO* (Jun. 2017), https://www.wipo.int/wipo_magazine/en/2017/03/article_0001.html.

17. Vanessa Giorgo, "DACS hits £100m paid out in Artist's Resale Right Royalties," DACS (Jun. 9, 2021), https://www.dacs.org.uk/latest-news/dacs-hits-%C2%A3100m-artist-s-resale-right-royalties-pa.

18. Berne Convention for the Protection of Literary and Artistic Works, Sept. 9, 1886, revised July 24, 1971 and amended Sept. 28, 1979, art. 14ter(2), 1161 U.N.T.S. 18338, https://wipolex.wipo.int/en/text/283698.

19. Anna J. Mitran, "Royalties Too?: Exploring Resale Royalties for New Media Art," *Cornell Law Review* 101 (2016): 1354 n4.

20. Ibid., 1363–64.

21. Office of the Register of Copyrights, "Resale Royalties: An Updated Analysis," (Dec. 2013), 65–66.

22. *Close v. Sotheby's, Inc.*, 894 F.3d 1061, 1072 (9th Cir. 2018).

23. Kent Thune, "What Are NFT Royalties & How Do They Work?," Seeking Alpha (Mar. 20, 2022), https://seekingalpha.com/article/4483346-nft-royalties.

24. Locke, "This 28-Year-Old Artist."

25. "Twin Flame #2. Jessica & Joyce Gayo," OpenSea, https://opensea.io/assets/0x495f947276749ce646f68ac8c248420045cb7b5e/55009236754177688704712285819362994549214138196257374091251074528856481202177.

26. Bankless, "Twin Flames," https://youtu.be/HIyMiXRYSOI?t=4657.

27. "Twin Flames #83. Bahareh & Farzaneh, accompanied by Twin Flames Full Physical Collection, 2017–2018," Christie's (Oct. 5, 2021), https://www.christies.com/lot/lot-6336923.

28. Andrew Hayward, "Justin Aversano's Quantum Art Ethereum NFT Platform

Raises $7.5M," Decrypt (Feb. 9, 2022), https://decrypt.co/92463/justin-aversano
-quantum-art-ethereum-nft-platform-7–5m.

29. Ben Munster, "Justin Aversano Announces Plan for Physical NFT Gallery in
Santa Monica," Decrypt (Apr. 4, 2022), https://decrypt.co/96845/justin-aversano
-announces-plan-for-physical-nft-gallery-in-santa-monica; "Quantum Space LA,"
Quantum.art, https://quantum.art/space/la.

30. Office of the Register of Copyrights, "Resale," 65, 72.

31. Developers are devising smart contracts with different standards to enable resale
royalties to be automatically collected across all marketplaces. "CXIP Guaran-
tees NFT Creators Receive Their Royalties with New PA1D Feature," Hypebeast
(Sept. 14, 2021), https://hypebeast.com/2021/9/cxip-nft-pa1d-royalties-payment
-solution.

32. James Beck, "Can NFTs Crack Royalties and Give More Value to Artists?," Con-
sensys (Mar. 2, 2021), https://consensys.net/blog/blockchain-explained/can-nfts
-crack-royalties-and-give-more-value-to-artists/.

33. Aleksandar Gilbert, "Artists Say NFT Markets Betray Web3 by Nixing Royalty
Payments," Defiant (Sept. 8, 2022), https://thedefiant.io/how-web3-social-media
-will-takeover-web2; Langston Thomas, "Here's What You Need to Know About
the NFT Creator Royalty Debate," nftnow (Aug. 26, 2022), https://nftnow.com
/features/nft-community-is-split-over-creator-royalties/.

34. "Are Blockchains the Second Coming of Napster? (Perspective)," Bloomberg
Law (Jan. 18, 2017), https://news.bloomberglaw.com/business-and-practice/are
-blockchains-the-second-coming-of-napster-perspective.

35. Ben Mezrich, *Bitcoin Billionaires* (New York: Flatiron Books, 2019), 45 (describing
money as "the oldest social network").

36. Satoshi Nakamoto, "Bitcoin: A Peer-to-Peer Electronic Cash System," Bitcoin
(2008), https://bitcoin.org/bitcoin.pdf.

37. Ibid., 5, 8.

38. Curtis Miles, "Blockchain Security: What Keeps Your Transaction Data Safe?,"
IBM (Dec. 12, 2017), https://www.ibm.com/blogs/blockchain/2017/12/block
chain-security-what-keeps-your-transaction-data-safe/; Techskill Brew, "Merkle
Tree in Blockchain (Part 5—Blockchain Series)," Medium (Jan. 10, 2022), https://
medium.com/techskill-brew/merkle-tree-in-blockchain-part-5-blockchain
-basics-4e25b61179a2.

39. Primavera De Filippi and Aaron Wright, *Blockchain and the Law* (Cambridge,
MA: Harvard University Press, 2018), 21–27; Techskill Brew, "Hash Functions
in Blockchain (Part 3—Blockchain Series)," Medium (Dec. 31, 2021), https://
medium.com/techskill-brew/hash-functions-in-blockchain-part-3-blockchain-
basics-c3a0286064b6.

40. Satoshi Nakamoto, "Bitcoin Open Source Implementation of P2P Currency,"
P2P Foundation (Feb. 11, 2009), http://p2pfoundation.ning.com/forum/topics
/bitcoin-open-source.

41. Ammous, *Bitcoin Standard*, 136–42; Fabian Schar, "Decentralized Finance: On
Blockchain- and Smart Contract-Based Financial Markets," Economic Research
Federal Reserve Bank of St. Louis (Feb. 5, 2021), https://research.stlouisfed
.org/publications/review/2021/02/05/decentralized-finance-on-blockchain-and
-smart-contract-based-financial-markets.

42. Matthew O'Brien, "How the Fed Let the World Blow Up in 2008," *Atlantic* (Feb.
26, 2014), https://www.theatlantic.com/business/archive/2014/02/how-the-fed
-let-the-world-blow-up-in-2008/284054/.

43. Lewis Gudgeon et al., *The Decentralized Financial Crisis*, arXiv.org, (Feb. 19,
2020), https://arxiv.org/pdf/2002.08099.pdf. But see Brian Brooks, "Don't Fear

'DeFi': It Could Be Less Risky Than Traditional Finance," *Fortune* (Aug. 3, 2021), https://fortune.com/2021/08/03/what-is-defi-risks-crypto-regulation-decent ralized-finance/.

44. Sam Cooling, "National Bureau of Economic Research: Top 1% of Bitcoin Hold-ers Own 27% of BTC Supply," Yahoo! (Dec. 31, 2021), https://finance.yahoo .com/news/national-bureau-economic-research-top-134932791.html.

45. "Crypto Meltdown: 7 Companies that Were Worst Hit by the Crunch," *Business Today* (Jul. 7, 2022), https://www.businesstoday.in/crypto/story/crypto-meltdown -7-companies-that-were-worst-hit-by-the-crunch-340714–2022–07–07.

46. James Royal, "How Fed Rate Hikes Could Impact Stocks, Crypto and Other Investments," Bankrate (Apr. 27, 2022), https://www.bankrate.com/investing /federal-reserve-impact-on-stocks-crypto-other-investments/.

47. Jocelyn Yang, "Bitcoin's Correlation with Stocks Comes Back as Economic Factors Roil Markets," CoinDesk (Sep. 9, 2022), https://www.coindesk.com /markets/2022/09/09/bitcoins-correlation-with-stocks-comes-back-as-economic -factors-roil-markets.

48. Alex Veiga and Stan Choe, "From the Stock Market to Crypto, a Punishing Six Months for Investors," PBS (Jun. 30, 2022), https://www.pbs.org/newshour/eco nomy/from-the-stock-market-to-crypto-a-punishing-six-months-for-investors.

49. Adriana Hamacher, "Who Are Ethereum's Co-founders and Where Are They Now?," Decrypt (Jul. 8, 2020), https://decrypt.co/36641/who-are-ethereums-co -founders-and-where-are-they-now.

50. Filippi and Wright, *Blockchain*, 27–28.

51. Max Antony Rapkin, "CEO of WAX Blockchain: Every Industry Will Have NFTs," NFT News Today (Apr. 4, 2022), https://nftnewstoday.com/2022/04/04 /ceo-of-wax-blockchain-every-industry-will-have-nfts/.

52. Ibid.

53. Edward Lee, "NFTs as Decentralized Intellectual Property," *University of Illi-nois Law Review* 2023 (forthcoming), https://papers.ssrn.com/sol3/papers.cfm? abstract_id=4023736.

54. Ibid., 28–48.

55. "What Is Intellectual Property?," *WIPO*, https://www.wipo.int/about-ip/en/.

56. Ibid.

57. Ibid.

58. "Nouns (NOUN)," Coingecko (floor price $93,881.14), https://www.coingecko .com/en/nft/nouns (last visited Oct. 26, 2022); "Moonbirds (MOONBIRD)," Coingecko (floor price $13,021.26), https://www.coingecko.com/en/nft/moo nbirds (last visited Oct. 26, 2022).

59. *ETW Corp. v. Jireh Publishing, Inc.*, 332 F.3d 915, 930 (6th Cir. 2003).

60. At a preliminary stage, the High Court of Justice in London ruled that "there is at least a realistically arguable case that such tokens [NFTs] are to be treated as property as a matter of English law." *Osbourne v. (1) Persons Unknown* [2022], EWHC 1021 [13].

61. Eric Paul Rhoades, "CryptoPunks and Copyrights: What's All the Fuss About?," The Outer Realm (July. 12, 2021), https://www.theouterrealm.io/blog /cryptopunks-copyrights; Lachlan Keller, "'All Eyes Are on It:' CryptoPunks at Center of Copyright Legal Dispute," Forkast (Feb. 14, 2022), https://forkast .news/all-eyes-cryptopunks-center-copyright-legal-dispute/; BowTied SizeLord, "Let's Get Phunky: CryptoPhunks and Web3 Censorship," Bowtied Island (Dec. 27, 2021), https://bowtiedisland.com/lets-get-phunky-cryptophunks-and-web3 -censorship/.

62. "Unofficial Punks Sub-Genre List (Community Maintained)," Google Docs,

https://docs.google.com/spreadsheets/d/1FqG9cjSOJp-XNBve4tQx6eeG8kw4 EFKNSrlkMS2TN3U/edit#gid=1631079339.

63. Amy Adler, "Why Art Does Not Need Copyright," *George Washington Law Review* 86 (2018), 322–23.

64. Ibid., 323, 330.

65. Lessig, *Remix*, 100.

66. "Unit 1: What Is Creative Commons," Creative Commons, https://certificates .creativecommons.org/cccertedu/chapter/1–1-the-story-of-creative-commons/.

67. "About CC Licenses," Creative Commons, https://creativecommons.org/about/cc licenses/.

68. Miles Jennings and Chris Dixon, "The Can't Be Evil NFT Licenses," a16zcrypto (Aug. 31, 2022), https://a16zcrypto.com/introducing-nft-licenses/.

69. Ibid.

70. *Kimble v. Marvel Entm't, LLC*, 576 U.S. 446, 465 (2015); *Brulotte v. Thys Co.*, 379 U.S. 29, 32–33 (1965).

71. A similar question occurs with the assertion of trademark for a character whose copyright has expired. Kathryn M. Foley, "Protecting Fictional Characters: Defining the Elusive Trademark-Copyright Divide," *Connecticut Law Review* 41 (2009), 954–59.

72. Lee, "NFTs as," 52.

73. *Close v. Sotheby's, Inc.*, 894 F.3d 1061, 1070–71 (9th Cir. 2018).

74. *Capitol Records, LLC v. Redigi Inc.*, 910 F.3d 649, 656 (2d Cir. 2018).

75. *ProCD, Inc. v. Zeidenberg*, 86 F.3d 1447, 1454 (7th Cir. 1996) (no preemption by contracts); *Wrench LLC v. Taco Bell Corp*, 256 F.3d 446, 47–58 (6th Cir. 2001) (no preemption unless the contracts are tantamount to a promise not to violate the exclusive rights of copyright).

76. Office of the Register of Copyrights, "Resale," 65, 71–72.

Chapter 7: The Decentralized Disney

1. Neil Gabler, *Walt Disney: The Triumph of American Imagination* (New York: Vintage Books, 2006), 117–18.

2. Ibid., 116–17.

3. Ibid., 117–19.

4. Keith Gluck, "Selling Mickey: The Rise of Disney Marketing," Walt Disney Family Museum (June 8, 2012), https://www.waltdisney.org/blog/selling-mickey-rise -disney-marketing.

5. Ibid.

6. Gabler, *Walt Disney*, 196.

7. Ibid., 197.

8. L. H. Robbins, "Mickey Mouse Emerges as Economist," *New York Times Magazine* (Mar. 10, 1935), 8.

9. Ibid.

10. Gabler, *Walt Disney*, 139.

11. Ibid.

12. Ibid.

13. Ibid.

14. Ibid., 140.

15. Ibid., 195.

16. Robbins, "Mickey."

17. Ibid., 22.

18. Gluck, "Selling Mickey."

19. Roger Ebert, "Snow White and the Seven Dwarfs" (Oct. 14, 2001), https://www .rogerebert.com/reviews/great-movie-snow-white-and-the-seven-dwarfs-1937.

20. Gabler, *Walt Disney*, 198.
21. Matthew Johnston, "How Disney Makes Money," Investopedia (Feb. 17, 2022), https://www.investopedia.com/how-disney-makes-money-4799164.
22. Brandon Gaille, "Explanation of the Hub and Spoke Business Model" (Mar. 16, 2015), https://brandongaille.com/explanation-of-the-hub-and-spoke-business-model/.
23. Gabler, *Walt Disney*, 196.
24. Ibid., 197.
25. "Top Global Licensors 2021," License Global, https://www.licenseglobal.com/rankings-and-lists/top-global-licensors-2021.
26. Phil Hall, "The Crisis at Disney: Part 4, Can Disney Conquer NFTs and the Metaverse?," Benzinga (June 24, 2022), https://www.benzinga.com/news/22/06/27840714/the-crisis-at-disney-part-4-can-disney-conquer-nfts-and-the-metaverse.
27. Lauren Forristal, "Disney+ Releases Its First AR-Enabled Short Film, 'Remembering,' Starring Brie Larson," TechCrunch (Sept. 8, 2022), https://techcrunch.com/2022/09/08/disney-plus-new-ar-short-film-starring-brie-larson/.
28. Dawn Chmielewski, "Disney CEO Lays out Early Plan for Digital Future," Reuters (Sep. 11, 2022), https://www.reuters.com/business/media-telecom/disney-ceo-lays-out-early-plan-digital-future-2022-09-11/.
29. James Ellis, "Disney Is Hiring a Lawyer for Their Move into the Metaverse," NFT Evening (Sep. 30, 2022), https://nftevening.com/disney-is-hiring-a-lawyer-for-their-move-into-the-metaverse/.
30. Samantha Hissong, "How Four NFT Novices Created a Billion-Dollar Ecosystem of Cartoon Apes," *Rolling Stone* (Nov. 1, 2021), https://www.rollingstone.com/culture/culture-news/bayc-bored-ape-yacht-club-nft-interview-1250461/.
31. "NFT Collection Rankings by Sales Volume (All-time)," Cryptoslam, https://cryptoslam.io/ (visited on Aug. 11, 2022).
32. Shirley Halperin, "Bored Ape Yacht Club Creators Yuga Labs Sign Representation Deal with Madonna, U2 Manager Guy Oseary (EXCLUSIVE)," *Variety* (Oct. 12, 2021), https://variety.com/2021/digital/news/bored-ape-yacht-club-yuga-labs-sign-with-madonna-u2-manager-guy-oseary-1235086011/.
33. Bored Ape Yacht Club, Twitter (Nov. 28, 2021), https://twitter.com/BoredApeYC/status/1465002596742144004.
34. Edward Lee, "Bored Ape Yacht Club, Adidas, Punks Comic, Gmoney Announce Partnership for the Metaverse," NouNFT (Dec. 21, 2021), https://nounft.com/2021/12/02/bored-ape-yacht-club-adidas-punks-comic-announce-partnership-for-the-metaverse/.
35. Jay Peters, "Adidas Sold More Than $22 Million in NFTs, but It Hit a Few Snags Along the Way," The Verge (Dec. 17, 2021), https://www.theverge.com/2021/12/17/22843104/adidas-nfts-metaverse-sold-bored-ape.
36. Kyle Swenson, "Adidas Is Set to Drop Its 'Into the Metaverse' NFT Tomorrow. Here's What We Know So Far," The Bored Ape Gazette (Dec. 16, 2021), https://www.theboredapegazette.com/post/adidas-is-set-to-drop-its-into-the-metaverse-nft-tomorrow-here-s-what-we-know-so-far.
37. "NIKE, Inc. Acquires RTFKT," Nike (Dec. 13, 2021), https://news.nike.com/news/nike-acquires-rtfkt.
38. Joseph Genest, "RTFKT's CloneX Collection Ushers in Forging SZN," Highsnobiety (Aug. 30, 2022), https://www.highsnobiety.com/p/rtfkt-clonex-drop-avatar-nft-lookbook/.
39. Chris Dixon, "Why Web3 Matters," Future (Oct. 7, 2021), https://future.com/why-web3-matters/.

40.   Todd Spanger, "Bored Ape Yacht Club NFT Creator Yuga Labs Raises $450 Million in Seed Round, Valuing Company at $4 Billion," *Variety* (Mar. 22, 2022), https://variety.com/2022/digital/news/bored-ape-yacht-club-nft-yuga-funding-round-1235211728/.

41.   BAYC, "Terms and Conditions," Bored Ape Yacht Club, https://boredapeyacht club.com/#/terms (emphasis added).

42.   Hashmasks, "Terms and Conditions," Hashmasks (Jan. 27, 2021), https://www.thehashmasks.com/terms.

43.   Kingship, Twitter (Apr. 19, 2022), https://twitter.com/therealkingship/status/1516470657214664704.

44.   EminemMusic, "Eminem & Snoop Dogg—from the D 2 the LBC [Official Music Video]," YouTube (Jun. 23, 2022), https://www.youtube.com/watch?v=RjrA-slMoZ4.

45.   See Deconomist, "Bored Ape Yacht Club: The Case for Licensed Commercial Use Rights," Medium (Sept. 17, 2021), https://medium.com/@deconomist/bored-ape-yacht-club-the-case-for-licensed-commercial-use-rights-b1bbd463d189.

46.   Daito, "Jenkins the Valet: The Bored and Dangerous Book and Beyond," ONE 37pm (Jul. 26, 2022), https://www.one37pm.com/nft/jenkins-valet-bored-dangerous.

47.   "The Writer's Room: How It Works," Jenkins the Valet, https://www.jenkinsthevalet.com/how-it-works.

48.   Jenkins the Valet, "How We're Bringing Web3's First Community-Generative Novel to Market," Medium (Jun. 17, 2022), https://jenkinsthevalet.medium.com/how-were-bringing-web3-s-first-community-generative-novel-to-market-117c0596b82e.

49.   Tom Farren, "Tally Labs Strives to Expand Decentralized Content Ecosystem with $12M Funding," Cointelegraph (May 18, 2022), https://cointelegraph.com/news/tally-labs-strive-to-expand-decentralized-content-ecosystem-with-12m-funding.

50.   Ibid.

51.   A preview of the Azurian characters didn't go well. Fans panned the artwork. Tally Labs immediately responded by hosting a Twitter Space to entertain the criticisms and then figure out a plan to address them. Ross Wardop, "Azurbala Azurians Art Preview Receives Terrible Feedback," NFT Evening (Oct. 1, 2022), https://nftevening.com/azurbala-azurians-art-preview-receives-terrible-feedback/.

52.   Hissong, "How Four NFT."

53.   Chayka, "Why Bored Ape."

54.   Ibid.

55.   "An Introduction to the Bored Ape Yacht Club," NFTtech (Jan. 11, 2022), https://www.nfttech.com/insights/an-introduction-to-the-bored-ape-yacht-club.

56.   Katie Notopoulos, "We Found the Real Names of Bored Ape Yacht Club's Pseudonymous Founders," *BuzzFeed News* (Feb. 4, 2022), https://www.buzzfeednews.com/article/katienotopoulos/bored-ape-nft-founder-identity.

57.   Ibid.

58.   David Yaffe-Bellany, "Millions for Crypto Start-Ups, No Real Names Necessary," *New York Times* (Mar. 2, 2022), https://www.nytimes.com/2022/03/02/technology/cryptocurrency-anonymity-alarm.html.

59.   Amy Castor, "Bored Ape Yacht Club: Unanswered Questions," (Apr. 26, 2022), https://amycastor.com/2022/04/26/bored-ape-yacht-club-unanswered-questions/.

60.   Chayka, "Why Bored Ape Avatars."

61. Samantha Hissong, "The NFT Art World Wouldn't Be the Same Without This Woman's 'Wide-Awake Hallucinations,'" *Rolling Stone* (Jan. 26, 2022), https://www.rollingstone.com/culture/culture-features/seneca-bored-ape-yacht-club-digital-art-nfts-1280341/.

62. Ibid.

63. Notopoulos, "We Found."

64. Farokh, "The Bored Ape Yacht Club Reached a Historical 100 ETH Floor, a Q&A with the Founders!" Medium (Jan. 31, 2022), https://medium.com/@farokhh/the-bored-ape-yacht-club-reached-a-historical-100-eth-floor-a-q-a-with-the-founders-a78bd52113c1.

65. Gabler, *Walt Disney*, 113–14, 143–44.

66. Seneca, "Little One," SuperRare, https://superrare.com/artwork-v2/little-one-32663.

67. "Studio Visits All Seeing Seneca," Hypebeast (Mar. 25, 2022), https://hypebeast.com/2022/2/studio-visits-all-seeing-seneca-coinbase.

68. Eric Paul Rhoades, "A Short History of Alt-Punks NFTs," OuterRealm (Aug. 13, 2021), https://www.theouterrealm.io/blog/a-short-history-of-alt-punks-nfts (cataloguing alternatives of CryptoPunks); Max Parasol, "NFT Clone Punks: Right or Wrong?," Cointelegraph (Dec 17, 2021), https://cointelegraph.com/magazine/2021/12/10/can-someone-explain-to-me-why-nft-clones-are-selling-for-so-much; Adi Robertson, "Two NFT Copycats Are Fighting Over Which Is the Real Fake Bored Ape Yacht Club," Verge (Dec. 20, 2021, 2:29 pm), https://www.theverge.com/2021/12/30/22860010/bored-ape-yacht-club-payc-phayc-copycat-nft; Shlomo Sprung, "The Bored Ape NFT Family Tree," Boardroom (Jan. 16, 2022), https://boardroom.tv/bored-ape-yacht-club-family-nft/.

69. "Expansion Punks," Expansion Punks, https://expansionpunks.com/; "0xApes Trilogy," OpenSea, https://opensea.io/collection/0xapes-trilogy.

70. Andrew Hayward, "'No Current Plans' for Scrapped V1 CryptoPunks NFTs, Says Yuga Labs," Decrypt (Aug. 18, 2022), https://decrypt.co/107740/no-current-plans-for-v1-cryptopunks-nfts-yuga-labs.

71. "RR/BAYC," RRBAYC, https://rrbayc.com/; Claire Voon, "'No Mere Monkey Business': Creators of Bored Apes NFTs Sue Artist Ryder Ripps for Trademark Infringement," The Art Newspaper (July 1, 2022), https://www.theartnewspaper.com/2022/07/01/bored-ape-yacht-club-yuga-labs-lawsuit-ryder-ripps-infringement. The complaint also identifies Jeremy Cahen as a defendant, who allegedly took part in the production of the RR/BAYC NFTs with Ripps.

72. Dorian Batyckz, "Artist Ryder Ripps Called the Bored Ape Yacht Club NFTs Racist. Now, Yuga Labs Is Suing Him for Trademark Infringement and Harassment," Artnet news (Jun. 29, 2022), https://news.artnet.com/art-world/yuga-labs-v-ryder-ripps-bayc-2137737.

73. Ryder-Ripps.eth, Twitter, https://twitter.com/ryder_ripps (visited Aug. 12, 2022).

74. Sander Lutz, "Bored Ape Yacht Club's Creators Declared War on a Vocal Critic. Could It Backfire?," Decrypt (Jul. 3, 2022), https://decrypt.co/104366/bored-ape-yacht-clubs-creators-declared-war-on-a-vocal-critic-could-it-backfire.

75. *Rockwell Graphic Sys., Inc. v. DEV Indus., Inc.*, 925 F.2d 174, 179 (7th Cir. 1991).

76. Andrew Hayward, "Arizona Iced Tea's Bored Ape NFT Brand Use Was 'Inappropriate,' Creators Warn," Decrypt (Aug. 23, 2021), https://decrypt.co/79231/arizona-iced-tea-bored-ape-nft-brand-use-inappropriate.

77. Ryder Ripps, "Bored Ape Yacht Club Is Racist and Contains Nazi Dog Whistles," Gordon Goner, https://gordongoner.com/; Tom Waite, "Breaking Down the Conspiracy Theory About Bored Ape Yacht Club's Nazi Ties," Dazed Digital (Jan. 12,

2022), https://www.dazeddigital.com/art-photography/article/55223/1/breaking
-down-conspiracy-theory-bored-ape-yacht-club-nazi-ties-ryder-ripps.

78. Ripps, "Bored Ape Yacht Club."

79. Adrian Chen, "Ryder Ripps: An Artist of the Internet," *New York Times* (July 8,
2014), https://www.nytimes.com/2014/07/10/fashion/ryder-ripps-an-artist-of-the
-internet.html.

80. "Ryder Ripps Takes On Our Clickbait Culture with 50,000 Tiny Images," Artsy
(Nov. 2, 2016), https://www.artsy.net/article/artsy-ryder-ripps-takes-on-our-click
bait-culture-with-50–000-tiny-images.

81. Ryder Ripps (@ryder_ripps), Instagram (Jun. 30, 2021), https://www.instagram
.com/p/CQwdw5XLLwk/; Daniel Kuhn, "CryptoPunks Get Punked," Yahoo! Life
(Jul. 6, 2021), https://www.yahoo.com/lifestyle/cryptopunks-punked-181112751
.html.

82. "RR/BAYC," RRBAYC.

83. Gordon Goner (Wylie Aronow), "A Letter from the Founders," Medium (Jun. 24,
2022), https://medium.com/@team_69582/a-letter-from-the-founders-678e5a3
431e7.

84. Ibid.

85. Jessica Klein, "Planet of the Bored Apes: Inside the NFT World's Biggest Success Story," Input Mag (Aug. 3, 2022), https://www.inputmag.com/features/bored
-ape-yacht-club-greg-solano-wylie-aronow-profile.

86. Ibid.

87. The original motion was stricken due to procedural infirmities made by Ripps's
attorney in the filing, but the court permitted a corrected filing. Notice of Motion;
Anti-SLAPP Motion to Strike and Motion to Dismiss, *Yuga Labs, Inc. v. Ripps*
(Oct. 3, 2022), https://storage.courtlistener.com/recap/gov.uscourts.cacd.855658
/gov.uscourts.cacd.855658.48.0.pdf.

88. Jerry Christopher, "Ryder Ripps' Anti-SLAPP Lawsuit Against Bored Ape Yacht
Club Authors: Here's What Happened," Today NFT News (Aug. 19, 2022), https://
www.todaynftnews.com/ryder-ripps-anti-slapp-lawsuit-against-bored-ape-yacht
-club-authors-heres-what-happened/; Cal. Civ. Proc. Code § 425.16 (2019).

89. *Mindys Cosmetics, Inc. v. Dakar*, 611 F.3d 580, 598 (9th Cir. 2010).

90. It's worth noting that Walt Disney faced allegations of anti-Semitism and racist
stereotypes in Disney films. The allegation of anti-Semitism has been roundly disputed, however. Lynn Elber, "Walt Disney Experts Rebut Dogged Anti-Semitic
Allegations," AP News (Aug. 2, 2015), https://apnews.com/article/4716906a97f
c4952b297151aaafd9131. The Disney company acknowledged the latter criticism
in 2020, when the company said it would add warning labels to some prior Disney movies that used racist stereotypes, including *Dumbo, Peter Pan*, and *Alad-
din*. Bryan Pietsch, "Disney Adds Warnings for Racist Stereotypes to Some Older
Films," *New York Times* (Oct. 18, 2020), https://www.nytimes.com/2020/10/18
/business/media/disney-plus-disclaimers.html.

91. Bryan Pietsch, "Maker of Bored Ape NFTs Sues Artist for Profiting off 'Copycat'
Images," *Washington Post* (June 29, 2022), https://www.washingtonpost.com/busi
ness/2022/06/29/bored-ape-nft-sues-ryder-ripps/.

92. Ibid.

93. Shradha Jain, "Popular Copyright Infringement Cases Highlighting How Disney Is Protective of Its Intellectual Property Rights," IP Leaders (July 10, 2021),
https://blog.ipleaders.in/popular-copyright-infringement-cases-highlighting
-disney-protective-intellectual-property-rights/.

94. "Disney in Copyright Spats with Day Care Center, Restaurant," AP News (Apr.
30, 1989), https://apnews.com/article/4d98c8dee1c72fa5ac42ce01dff143fd.

95. David Mikkelson, "Did Disney Demand the Removal of Cartoon Murals from Daycare Center Walls?" Snopes (Dec. 29, 1996), https://www.snopes.com/fact-check/daycare-center-murals.

96. "ApeCoin Is for the Web3 Economy," Apecoin, https://apecoin.com/about.

97. Olga Kharif, "ApeCoin Owners Consider Locking Up Coins to Keep NFT Mania Going," Bloomberg (May 6, 2022), https://www.bloomberg.com/news/articles/2022–05–06/apecoin-owners-consider-locking-up-coins-to-keep-nft-mania-going.

98. "A Strange New World," Otherside, https://otherside.xyz/world.

99. "Enter the Otherside," Otherside, https://otherside.xyz/.

100. Jamie Redman, "The Largest NFT Mint in History—Bored Ape's Otherside Virtual Land Sale Raises $320 Million," Bitcoin (May 1, 2022), https://news.bitcoin.com/the-largest-nft-mint-in-history-bored-apes-otherside-virtual-land-sale-raises-320-million/.

101. Kate Irwin, "Yuga Labs Sees $561 Million in Otherside Ethereum NFT Sales Within 24 Hours," Decrypt (May 1, 2022), https://decrypt.co/99156/yuga-labs-sees-561-million-in-otherside-ethereum-nft-sales-within-24-hours.

102. Kyle Swenson, "Over 34,000 Unique Wallets Now Hold an Otherdeed. Find More About the Otherside Here," The Bored Ape Gazette (May 7, 2022), https://www.theboredapegazette.com/post/over-34–000-unique-wallets-now-hold-an-otherdeed-find-more-about-the-otherside-here.

103. Yogita Khatri, "Yuga Labs' Otherdeed Virtual Land NFT Sells for Record $1.5 Million," The Block Crypto (May 9, 2022), https://www.theblockcrypto.com/post/145818/yuga-labs-otherdeed-virtual-land-nft-sells-for-record-1–5-million?utm_source=rss&utm_medium=rss.

104. Arijit Sarkar, "ETH Gas Price Surges as Yuga Labs Cashes in $300M Selling Otherside NFTs," Cointelegraph (May 1, 2022), https://cointelegraph.com/news/eth-gas-price-surges-as-yuga-labs-cashes-in-300m-selling-otherside-nfts.

105. Ibid.

106. Ifeanyi Jesse, "NFT Mint That Broke Ethereum, Worst Gas War That Wasted $180 Million in Fees," Coinscreed (May 4, 2022), https://coinscreed.com/nft-mint-that-broke-ethereum-sparked-gas-war.html.

107. Chris Katje, "Bored Ape Otherside Deed Land Sale Sells Out, Burns Over $100M in Ethereum: Why Are Many Upset?," Benzinga (May 1, 2022), https://www.benzinga.com/markets/cryptocurrency/22/05/26920672/bored-ape-otherside-deed-land-sale-sells-out-burns-over-100-million-in-ethereum-heres-the-.

108. Ibid.

109. Edward Lee, "Yuga Labs Drops Another Bombshell Late Friday Night: Video of 'Otherside' Featuring Not Just Bored Apes, but CryptoPunks, Meebits, World of Women, Cool Cats, Nouns, Toadz, and Music from the Doors," NouNFT (Mar. 19, 2022), https://nounft.com/2022/03/19/yuga-labs-drops-another-bombshell-late-friday-night-video-of-otherside-featuring-not-just-bored-apes-but-cryptopunks-meebits-world-of-women-cool-cats-nouns-toadz-and-music-from-the-doors/.

110. "Come as You Are," Otherside, https://otherside.xyz/.

111. "Game-Changing Tech," Otherside, https://otherside.xyz/.

112. Brian Quarmby, "Otherside Metaverse Demo Kicks Off with 4,500 Participants: Highlights," Cointelegraph (Jul. 18, 2022), https://cointelegraph.com/news/otherside-metaverse-demo-kicks-off-with-4–500-participants-highlights.

113. Dean Takahashi, "Herman Narula: How Improbable Put 4,500 Bored Apes in the Same Metaverse Space," Venturebeat (Aug. 3, 2022), https://venturebeat.com/2022/08/03/herman-narula-how-improbable-put-4500-bored-apes-in-the-same-metaverse-space/.

114. "The Otherside Litepaper," Otherside, https://otherside.xyz/litepaper.

115. Annie2Fun, "Everything You Need to Know About Otherdeed for Otherside and Kodas," Medium (May 3, 2022), https://medium.com/nswap/everything-you -need-to-know-about-otherdeed-for-otherside-and-kodas-16108ba13849; "The World," Otherrside, https://otherside.xyz/world.

116. "Create for the Otherside," Otherside, https://otherside.xyz/.

117. "Koda License Agreement," Otherside.xyz, https://otherside.xyz/license.

118. "NFT Purchase Agreement," Otherside, https://otherside.xyz/nft-purchase-agree ment.

119. J. Clement, "Number of Video Gamers Worldwide in 2021, by region," Statista, https://www.statista.com/statistics/293304/number-video-gamers/.

120. "Number of Gamers Worldwide 2022/2023: Demographics, Statistics, and Pre- dictions," Finances Online, https://financesonline.com/number-of-gamers-world wide/.

121. Alyssa Celatti, "Study: 69% of Gamers Hate NFTs," Fandomspot, https://www .fandomspot.com/gamers-hate-nfts-study/.

122. Casey Newton, "Why Gamers Hate Crypto, and Music Fans Don't," The Verge (Feb. 4, 2022), https://www.theverge.com/22917126/nfts-crypto-gamers-music -fans-fandoms.

123. Chris Morris, "After Player Backlash, Video Game Companies Are Quietly Scrapping Their NFT Plans," *Fast Company* (Feb. 3, 2022), https://www.fastcom pany.com/90718590/after-player-backlash-video-game-companies-are-quietly -scrapping-their-nft-plans.

124. Dean Takahashi, "Ubisoft Ends Making NFTs and Other Updates for Ghost Recon: Breakpoint," Venturebeat (Apr. 6, 2022), https://venturebeat.com /2022/04/06/ubisoft-ends-making-nfts-and-other-updates-for-ghost-recon -breakpoint/.

125. Joseph Young, "Metaverse Heats Up: How Axie Infinity's $3B Valuation Led Crypto Game Frenzy," *Forbes* (Oct. 6, 2021), https://www.forbes.com/sites /youngjoseph/2021/10/06/metaverse-heats-up-how-axie-infinitys-30b-valuation -led-crypto-game-frenzy/?sh=7c4961af25c6.

126. Stephen Graves and Andrew Hayward, "What Is Axie Infinity? The Play-to-Earn NFT Game Taking Crypto by Storm," Decrypt (Mar. 30, 2022), https://decrypt .co/resources/what-is-axie-infinity-the-play-to-earn-nft-game-taking-crypto-by -storm.

127. "Axie Growth Data," Google Docs, https://docs.google.com/spreadsheets/d/1g 4d2lzBytC-Wo4_rKGHjR3vGeJHb8hd1jb55qRf_S2g/edit#gid=0.

128. Jacquelyn Melinek, "Why Axie Infinity's Co-founder Thinks Play-to-Earn Games Will Drive NFT Adoption," TechCrunch (May 4, 2022), https://techcrunch .com/2022/05/04/why-axie-infinitys-co-founder-thinks-play-to-earn-games -will-drive-nft-adoption/.

129. Prashant Jha, "The Aftermath of Axie Infinity's $650M Ronin Bridge Hack," Cointelegraph (Apr. 12, 2022), https://cointelegraph.com/news/the-aftermath -of-axie-infinity-s-650m-ronin-bridge-hack.

130. Jack Kelly, "Axie Infinity's Play-To-Earn 'Smooth Love Potion' Gaming Has Changed Lives and Lifted People out of Poverty," *Forbes* (Mar. 6, 2022), https:// www.forbes.com/sites/jackkelly/2022/03/06/axie-infinity-play-to-earn-smooth -love-potion-gaming-has-changed-lives-and-lifted-people-out-of-poverty/.

131. "The Philippines Economy and the Impact of COVID-19," FutureLearn (Aug. 18, 2021), https://www.futurelearn.com/info/futurelearn-international/philippines -economy-covid-19.

132. Vittoria Elliott, "Workers in the Global South Are Making a Living Playing the

Blockchain Game Axie Infinity," Rest of World (Aug. 19, 2021), https://restof world.org/2021/axie-infinity/.

133. Matthew Smith, "Not Everyone Wants NFTs to Be the Future of Gaming," *Wired* (Mar. 15, 2022), https://www.wired.com/story/nfts-gaming-tim-morten-frost -giant-starcraft-interview/.

134. "WTF?," Nouns, https://nouns.wtf/.

135. Ibid.

136. Stephen Graves, "Nouns DAO Backs NFT Crowdfunding Effort for Indie Film 'Calladita,'" Decrypt (Apr. 14, 2022), https://decrypt.co/97862/nouns-dao-backs -nft-crowdfunding-effort-for-indie-film-calladita.

137. Andrew Hayward, "Bud Light Super Bowl Ad Includes Nouns Ethereum NFT Imagery," Decrypt (Feb. 7, 2022), https://decrypt.co/92239/bud-light-super -bowl-ad-includes-nouns-ethereum-nft-imagery; "Bud Light commercial pro- motes Nouns NFTs," Investing (Feb. 7, 2022), https://www.investing.com/news /cryptocurrency-news/bud-light-commercial-promotes-nouns-nfts-2758795.

138. "Summary," Nouns, https://nouns.wtf/.

139. MrClean, "CC0 NFT Projects: The Power of Public Domain in Web3," Mirror (Dec. 21, 2021), https://mirror.xyz/0x148089038088cC49CDcF26e0f96776c25e 5CfACd/LyW1nstrKXvW22PD-QMOndzx_-hQnzJYXeRj6e28vkM.

140. Andrew Hayward, "How Ethereum NFT Project Nouns Is Building Open- Source IP," Decrypt (Nov. 24, 2021), https://decrypt.co/86795/how-ethereum -nft-project-nouns-is-building-open-source-ip.

141. Lessig, *Remix*, 228–31.

142. "Projects," Nouns, https://nouns.center/projects.

143. Ola, "Lil Nouns: The Collection Dropping One NFT Every 15 Minutes, Forever," NFT Evening (May 11, 2022), https://nftevening.com/lil-nouns-the-collection -dropping-one-nft-every-15-minutes-forever/.

144. Tortita.eth, Twitter (May 20, 2022), https://twitter.com/TortitaTrades/status /1527669231256580098.

145. "Prop House: Scaling Ecosystem Funding," Nouni, https://nouni.sh/8t35zq839c.

146. "Nouns DAO: Treasury," Etherscan, https://etherscan.io/tokenholdings?a=0x0B C3807Ec262cB779b38D65b38158acC3bfedE10.

147. Garfield Miller, "Fund BlockbusterDAO Studios to Develop the Nouns Narrative Universe," Discourse, https://discourse.nouns.wtf/t/fund-blockbusterdao-studios -to-develop-the-nouns-narrative-universe/837.

148. "Proposal: Nouns Studio1," Nouns, https://discourse.nouns.wtf/t/proposal-nouns -studio1/390.

149. Flashrekt and Scott Duke Kominers, "Why NFT Creators Are Going CC0," a16 zcrypto (Aug. 3, 2022), https://a16zcrypto.com/cc0-nft-creative-commons-zero -license-rights/.

150. Gabler, *Walt Disney*, 170.

151. Chayka, "Why Bored Ape."

152. Ibid.

153. Ibid.

154. Tim Wu, "Intellectual Property, Innovation, and Decentralized Decisions," *Vir- ginia Law Review* 92 (2006): 127.

155. Marjory S. Blumenthal and David D. Clark, "Rethinking the Design of the Inter- net: The End-to-End Arguments vs. the Brave New World," *ACM Transactions on Internet Technology* 1 (2001): 71–72.

156. Lawrence Lessig, *The Future of Ideas* (New York: Random House, 2001), 37.

157. For the new CryptoPunks license adopted in 2022, Yuga Labs included a restric- tion in the commercial license against using the CryptoPunks in hate speech.

"CryptoPunks Terms," CryptoPunks, https://licenseterms.cryptopunks.app/. That type of provision is becoming more widely adopted.

158. "BrandFinance Global 500 (100) | 2022," RankingtheBrands, https://www.rankingthebrands.com/The-Brand-Rankings.aspx?rankingID=83&year=1397 (No. 19).

Chapter 8: FOMO and NFT Bubbles

1. Langston Thomas, "A Guide to Moonbirds: What Are These PFP Owl NFTs?," nftnow (Apr. 29, 2022), https://nftnow.com/guides/a-guide-to-moonbirds-what-are-these-pfp-owl-nfts/.

2. "Floor Price Charts—by @punk9059," Google Docs, https://docs.google.com/spreadsheets/d/1vh8Q8wSoI6kTOeVZWVLThVUrtHFMhBFv3HcoeTbrdpg/edit#gid=0 .

3. Albert Costill, "Average Retirement Savings by Age," Due (May 11, 2022), https://due.com/blog/average-retirement-savings-by-age/#Fiftysomethings.

4. "Floor Price Charts—by @punk9059," Google Docs; "Bored Ape Yacht Club OpenSea Price Floor," Dune, https://dune.com/queries/114895/232903.

5. "Historical Sales / April, 2022 / Moonbirds," Cryptoslam, https://cryptoslam.io/moonbirds/sales/summary/?month=2022–04; "Historical Sales / May, 2021 / Bored Ape Yacht Club," Cryptoslam, https://www.cryptoslam.io/bored-ape-yacht-club/sales/summary/?month=2021–05.

6. Phil Mackintosh, "Trends in IPO Pops," NASDAQ (Mar. 4, 2021), https://www.nasdaq.com/articles/trends-in-ipo-pops-2021–03–04.

7. Ibid.

8. Ibid.

9. Mike Murphy, "Beyond Meat Soars 163% in Biggest-Popping U.S. IPO Since 2000," MarketWatch (May 5, 2019), https://www.marketwatch.com/story/beyond-meat-soars-163-in-biggest-popping-us-ipo-since-2000–2019–05–02.

10. Renaissance Capital, "nCino Jumps 195% in Biggest IPO Pop for a US Tech Company Since the Internet Bubble," NASDAQ (July 15, 2020), https://www.nasdaq.com/articles/ncino-jumps-195-in-biggest-ipo-pop-for-a-us-tech-company-since-the-internet-bubble-2020–07.

11. Ibid.

12. "Median Time from Initial Venture Capital Funding to IPO Exit in the United States from 2000 to 2021," Statista (May 6, 2022), https://www.statista.com/statistics/320793/median-time-venture-capital-exit-usa/.

13. Will Gottsegen, "Moonbird NFTs Are a Bet on Kevin Rose's Rep," CoinDesk (Apr. 18, 2022), https://www.coindesk.com/layer2/2022/04/18/moonbird-nfts-are-a-bet-on-kevin-roses-rep/.

14. Ibid.

15. Matt Lynley, "The Inside Story on Why Kevin Rose Never Had a Big Hit," Business Insider (July 17, 2012), https://www.businessinsider.com/digg-kevin-rose-untold-history-2012-7.

16. Ibid.

17. Ibid.

18. Alexia Tsotsis, "Digg Sold to LinkedIn AND the Washington Post and Betaworks," TechCrunch (July 12, 2012), https://techcrunch.com/2012/07/12/digg-sold-to-linkedin-and-the-washington-post-and-betaworks/; Viktor, "What Happened to Digg? Why Did It Fail?," Productmint (Jan. 1, 2022), https://productmint.com/what-happened-to-digg/.

19. Proof, "Moonbirds Launch—CEO, Kevin Rose," YouTube (Apr. 16, 2022), https://youtu.be/MskiNZUScqk?t=273.

20. Lucas Matney, "Kevin Rose on Crypto Winters, Pseudonymous Founders and His Buzzy Moonbirds NFT Project," TechCrunch (May 16, 2022), https://tech crunch.com/2022/05/15/kevin-rose-on-crypto-winters-pseudonymous-founders -and-his-buzzy-moonbirds-nft-project/.

21. Gottsegen, "Moonbird NFTs."

22. Eduardo Prospero, "Blue Chip NFTs 101—What Is the Proof Collective and Who's Behind It?," Newsbtc (May 10, 2022), https://www.newsbtc.com/nft/blue -chip-nfts-101-what-is-the-proof-collective-and-whos-behind-it/.

23. Chris Williams, "Days After $66M NFT Drop, Moonbirds Executive Unveils Fund," Crypto Briefing (Apr. 25, 2022), https://cryptobriefing.com/days-after -66m-drop-moonbirds-executive-unveils-fund/.

24. Eli Tan, "Moonbirds COO Leaves Project for New Fund—with $1M in NFTs in Tow," CoinDesk (Apr. 24, 2022), https://www.coindesk.com/business /2022/04/25/moonbirds-coo-leaves-project-for-new-fund-with-1m-in-nfts-in -tow/.

25. Elizabeth Napolitano, "NFT Collective Proof Raises $50M in Funding Round Led by a16z," CoinDesk (Aug. 30, 2022), https://www.coindesk.com/business /2022/08/30/nft-collective-proof-raises-50m-in-funding-round-led-by-a16z/.

26. Tim Wu, *The Master Switch* (New York: Vintage Books, 2011), 318.

27. Stephanie Landsman, "'Bubble' Hitting 50% of Market, Top Investor Warns as Fed Gets Ready to Meet," CNBC (May 2, 2022), https://www.cnbc.com /2022/05/02/50percent-of-market-is-in-a-bubble-dan-suzuki-warns-as-fed-gets -ready-to-meet.html; Bernhard Warner, "The $1 Trillion Crypto Collapse Is Crippling Digital Coin Bulls. But the Rest of Us Will Hardly Notice, Says Goldman Sachs," *Fortune* (May 20, 2022), https://fortune.com/2022/05/20/trillion-crypto -collapse-btc-eth-binance-goldman-sachs/; Elizabeth Howcroft, "Cryptoverse: NFT Bubble Gets That Shrinking Feeling," Reuters (Apr. 13, 2022), https:// www.reuters.com/technology/cryptoverse-nft-bubble-gets-that-shrinking -feeling-2022–04–05/.

28. "@sealaunch / Moonbirds Proof NFT Analytics Floor Price Holders Nesting," Dune, https://dune.com/sealaunch/Proof-Moonbirds (reviewed on May 13, 2022).

29. "NFT Collections," Dappradar, https://dappradar.com/nft/collections (viewed on May 16, 2022).

30. Kevin Rose, Twitter (Aug. 4, 2022), https://twitter.com/kevinrose/status/15552 62099093200896.

31. "Terms of Sale," Moonbirds (Jul. 5, 2022), available at https://web.archive.org /web/20220705145700/https://www.moonbirds.xyz/terms.

32. "Moonbirds DAO," Proof, https://docs.proof.xyz/dao.

33. Edward Lee, "MoonBirds Owners Get 'Full Commercial Art Rights for the Moonbird They Own,' Apparently Similar to Bored Ape License," NouNFT (Apr. 22, 2022), https://nounft.com/2022/04/22/moonbirds-owners-get-full-com mercial-art-rights-for-the-moonbird-they-own-apparently-similar-to-bored-ape -license/.

34. King BlackBored, Twitter (Aug. 4, 2022), https://twitter.com/KingBlackBored /status/1555364977179082753; Melvincapital, Twitter (Aug. 5, 2022), https:// twitter.com/melvincapital__/status/1555657183815139330.

35. Steve (@NFTbark), Twitter (Aug. 7, 2022), https://twitter.com/NFTbark/status /1556270331937038336.

36. "Terms," Moonbirds, https://www.moonbirds.xyz/terms.

37. *Citizens Telecomms. Co. of WV v. Sheridan*, 799 S.E.2d 144, 149 (W.V. S. Ct. 2017); *Douglas v. U.S. District Court ex rel Talk America*, 495 F.3d 1062, 1066 (9th Cir. 2007); *Cullinane v. Uber Technologies, Inc.*, 893 F.3d 53, 62–63 (1st Cir. 2018).

38. Gary Vaynerchuk, Twitter (Feb. 27, 2021), https://twitter.com/garyvee/status/1365883296064954370.

39. CoinDesk, Twitter (May 23, 2021), https://twitter.com/CoinDesk/status/1396411819389079554.

40. Phil Rosen, "Gary Vaynerchuk Says 98% of NFT Projects Will Fail After the Gold Rush Fades. Here's Why 2 Experts Think He Might Be Right," Yahoo! (Feb. 13, 2022), https://news.yahoo.com/gary-vaynerchuk-said-98-nft-131500442.html.

41. Libby Kane and Alyson Shontell, "The CEO of a Multimillion-Dollar Company Explains What He Did in His 20s to Set Himself Up for Success in His 30s," Business Insider (May 4, 2017), https://www.businessinsider.com/how-gary-vaynerchuk-set-himself-up-for-success-in-his-30s-2017-5; Tim Morrison, "Q&A: Internet Wine Guru Gary Vaynerchuk," *Time* (Oct. 13, 2009), http://content.time.com/time/arts/article/0,8599,1929929,00.html.

42. Laurie Dunn, "Gary Vee King of the NFTs Thinks They Are Going to Zero," Cryptodaily (Feb. 14, 2022), https://cryptodaily.co.uk/2022/02/gary-vee-king-of-the-nfts-thinks-they-are-going-to-zero.

43. Brent Goldfarb, David Kirsch, and David Miller, "Was There Too Little Entry During the Dot Com Era?," *Journal of Economics and Finance* 86 (2007), https://doi.org/10.1016/j.jfineco.2006.03.009; Brent Goldfarb, David Kirsch, and Michael D. Pfarrer, "Searching for Ghosts: Business Survival, Unmeasured Entrepreneurial Activity and Private Equity Investment in the Dot-com Era," Robert H. Smith School Research Paper No. RHS 06–027, 3, http://dx.doi.org/10.2139/ssrn.825687.

44. Brian McCullough, "A Revealing Look at the Dot-com Bubble of 2000—and How It Shapes Our Lives Today," Ideas (Dec. 4, 2018), https://ideas.ted.com/an-eye-opening-look-at-the-dot-com-bubble-of-2000-and-how-it-shapes-our-lives-today/.

45. TradeSmith, "Revisiting the Great British Bicycle Bubble of 1896," NASDAQ (Dec. 8, 2020), https://www.nasdaq.com/articles/revisiting-the-great-british-bicycle-bubble-of-1896–2020–12–08.

46. Yashu Gola, "Looks Bare: OpenSea Turns into NFT Ghost-Town after Daily Volume Plunges 99% from Peak," Cointelegraph (Aug. 29, 2022), https://cointelegraph.com/news/looks-bare-opensea-turns-into-nft-ghost-town-after-volume-plunges-99-in-90-days.

47. McCullough, "A Revealing Look."

48. Charles Mackay, *Extraordinary Popular Delusions and the Madness of Crowds* (London: Richard Bentley, 1841).

49. William Quinn and John D. Turner, *Boom and Bust: A Global History of Financial Bubbles* (Cambridge, UK: Cambridge University Press, 2020), 11.

50. "You Can't Spot a Bubble, So Don't Even Try, Says Eugene Fama," ai-cio (Nov. 11, 2019), https://www.ai-cio.com/news/cant-spot-bubble-dont-even-try-says-eugene-fama/.

51. Robin Wigglesworth, *Trillions* (New York: Portfolio, 2021), 280–81.

52. Quinn and Turner, *Boom and Bust*, 11.

53. Ibid.

54. Ibid., 5–7.

55. Ibid., 7.

56. Ibid., 4.

57. Ibid., 58–59, 98–102, 152–57.

58. Chris Morris, "The NFT Bubble Is Showing Clear Signs of Bursting," *Fortune* (Mar. 4, 2022), https://fortune.com/2022/03/04/nft-bubble-market-crash-price-value/; Elizabeth Howcroft, "Cryptoverse: NFT Bubble Gets That Shrinking Feel

ing," Reuters (Apr. 13, 2022), https://www.reuters.com/technology/cryptoverse -nft-bubble-gets-that-shrinking-feeling-2022-04-05/; Erin Prater, "'The NFT Thingy Is Starting to Burst,' Warns Guru Whose 'Black Swan' Theory Foresaw 2007 Financial Crisis," *Fortune* (Apr. 16, 2022), https://fortune.com/2022/04/16 /nft-thingy-starting-burst-warns-author-the-black-swan-predictor-2007–2008 -financial-crisis-nassim-nicholas-taleb-cryptocurrency/.

59. Robert J. Shiller, *Irrational Exuberance* (Princeton, N.J.: Princeton University Press, 3rd ed., 2015), 175–79.

60. Michael Hiltzik, "Column: Bitcoin, NFTs, SPACs, Meme Stocks—All Those Pandemic Investment Darlings Are Crashing," *L.A. Times* (May 12, 2022), https://www.latimes.com/business/story/2022-05–12/bitcoin-nfts-crypto-spacs -meme-stocks-struggling.

61. Jon Hilsenrath, "If the U.S. Is in a Recession, It's a Very Strange One," *Wall Street Journal* (Jul. 4, 2022), https://www.wsj.com/articles/recession-economy -unemployment-jobs-11656947596; Ben Casselman, "How This Economic Moment Rewrites the Rules," *New York Times* (Aug. 6, 2022), https://www.nytimes .com/2022/08/06/business/economy/economy-jobs-inflation.html.

62. Quinn and Turner, *Boom and Bust*, 3.

63. Ibid., 166.

64. William Quinn and John Turner, "Are We in the Middle of a Tech Bubble?," Economics Observatory (May 24, 2021), https://www.economicsobservatory.com /are-we-in-the-middle-of-a-tech-bubble.

65. Quinn and Turner, *Boom and Bust*, 113.

66. Ibid., 76.

67. Shira Ovide, "What's Good About Tech Bubbles," *New York Times* (Apr. 5, 2021), https://www.nytimes.com/2021/04/05/technology/tech-bubbles.html.

68. Dominic Chalmers, Christian Fisch, Russell Matthews, William Quinn, and Jan Recker, "Beyond the Bubble: Will NFTs and Digital Proof of Ownership Empower Creative Industry Entrepreneurs?," *Journal of Business Venturing Insights* 17 (2022), 10.1016/j.jbvi.2022.e00309.

69. Julien Pénasse and Luc Renneboog, "Speculative Trading and Bubbles: Evidence from the Art Market," *Articles in Advance* (2021), 4944, https://doi.org/10.1287 /mnsc.2021.4088.

70. Helen Barrett, "NFTs Transform the Art Market for Young Novice Buyers," *Financial Times* (Sep. 1, 2021), https://www.ft.com/content/39c5ef2b-c69c-4611 –88f5-f5a7f611d8c8.

71. "6 Key Factors Driving Art Collectors—from Aesthetics to Investment," Artsy (Sep. 23, 2019), https://www.artsy.net/article/artsy-editorial-drives-art-buyers.

72. Ibid.

73. "Hiscox Online Art Trade Report 2021—Part Two," 2, 20, Hiscox, https://www .hiscox.co.uk/sites/default/files/documents/2022–04/21674b-Hiscox_online_art _trade_report_2021-part_two_1.pdf.

74. Ibid., 20.

75. Ibid.

76. Robert Stevens, "What Is Tokenomics and Why Is It Important?," CoinDesk (Apr. 11, 2022), https://www.coindesk.com/learn/what-is-tokenomics-and-why- is-it-important/.

77. The Moonstream team, "An Analysis of 7,020,950 NFT Transactions on the Ethereum Blockchain," Github (Oct. 22, 2021), 8, https://github.com/bugout-dev/ moonstream/blob/main/datasets/nfts/papers/ethereum-nfts.pdf.

78. Hristina Yordanova, "Meebits NFTs Attract Whale Activity, Floor Price Jumps

93%," Dappradar (Mar. 11, 2022), https://dappradar.com/blog/meebits-nfts-attract-whale-activity-floor-price-jumps-93.

79. Chris Katje, "EXCLUSIVE: Unusual Whales Creates 'Nancy Pelosi ETF' So You Can Track Her Trades," Benzinga (Jan. 12, 2022), https://www.benzinga.com/news/22/01/25015596/exclusive-unusual-whales-creates-nancy-pelosi-etf-so-you-can-track-her-trades.

80. "Whale Tracking," NFTgo, https://nftgo.io/whale-tracking/trade.

81. Gary Vaynerchuk, *The Thank You Economy* (New York: Harper Business, 2011), 51–52.

82. Ibid., 65.

83. "Daily Time Spent on Social Networking by Internet Users Worldwide from 2012 to 2022," Statista, https://www.statista.com/statistics/433871/daily-social-media-usage-worldwide/.

84. Ibid.

85. Alexa Herman, "How Gen Z Is Driving the Future of Retail," NRF (Jul. 20, 2021), https://nrf.com/blog/how-gen-z-driving-future-retail.

86. Robin Murdoch et al., "Why the Future of Shopping Is Set for a Social Revolution," Accenture (Jan. 2, 2022), https://www.accenture.com/us-en/insights/software-platforms/why-shopping-set-social-revolution.

87. Mayank Gupta and Aditya Sharma, "Fear of Missing Out: A Brief Overview of Origin, Theoretical Underpinnings and Relationship with Mental Health," *World Journal of Clinical Cases* 9 (19) (2021): 4881, 10.12998/wjcc.v9.i19.4881.

88. Tara Siegel Bernard, "Everyone Has Crypto FOMO, but Does It Belong in Your Portfolio?," *New York Times* (Mar. 25, 2022), https://www.nytimes.com/2022/03/24/your-money/bitcoin-investing-cryptocurrency.html.

89. Abbruzzese, "This Ethereum-Based Project."

90. Upson, "The 10,000 Faces."

91. Ibid.

92. Investor Archive, "Warren Buffett/Bill Gates/Lecture/University of Nebraska/2005," YouTube (Nov. 11, 2020), https://youtu.be/1AlPTiJrJnE?t=1811.

93. Chayka, "Why Bored Ape Avatars."

94. Lionel Laurent, "The FOMO Economy: Is Everyone Making Money but You?," Bloomberg (Jun. 9, 2021), https://www.bloomberg.com/news/articles/2021–06–10/is-everyone-making-money-but-you-the-fomo-economy-of-memes-crypto-housing.

95. Shiller, *Irrational Exuberance*, 240.

96. John Authers, "Don't Call Bitcoin a Bubble. It's an Epidemic," Bloomberg (Jun. 8, 2021), https://www.bloomberg.com/opinion/articles/2021–06–09/don-t-call-bitcoin-a-bubble-it-s-an-epidemic.

97. Ibid.

98. Ibid.

99. Robert J. Shiller, *Narrative Economics: How Stories Go Viral & Drive Major Economic Stories* (Princeton, N.J.: Princeton University Press, paperback ed., 2020), xvii–xxv.

100. Ibid., xxi.

101. Ibid., xv.

102. Ibid., quoting Frederick Lewis Allen, *Only Yesterday: An Informal History of the 1920's* (New York: Perennial Classics, 2000), 273.

103. Ibid., 11.

104. Nassim Nicholas Taleb, *The Black Swan: The Impact of the Highly Improbable* (New York: Random House Trade Paperbacks, 2nd ed., 2010), xxxi.

105. Ibid.
106. Hissong, "NFT Scams."
107. Lucas Matney, "Justin Kan's NFT Platform Suffers Rocky Debut as Scammer Makes Off with $150K in User Funds," TechCrunch (Dec. 21, 2021), https://tcrn .ch/32rLqLq.
108. Julia Arvelaiz, "Could Musk Fix This? Blue Checked NFT Scams Swamp Twitter," Bitcoinist (Apr. 2022), https://bitcoinist.com/could-musk-fix-this-blue-checked -nft-scams-twitter/.
109. Corin Faife, "Thief Steals $1 Million of Bored Ape Yacht Club NFTs with Insta gram Hack," Verge (Apr. 25, 2022), https://www.theverge.com/2022/4/25/230 41415/bored-ape-yacht-club-nft-hack-instagram.
110. Ezra Reguerra, "Community Calls out Bots Spamming Crypto Twitter Threads," Cointelegraph (Sep. 8, 2022), https://cointelegraph.com/news/community-calls -out-bots-spamming-crypto-twitter-threads.
111. Turner Wright, "Elon Musk's 'Top Priority' for Twitter Includes Cutting Down on Crypto Scam Tweets," Cointelegraph (Apr. 14, 2022), https://cointelegraph.com /news/elon-musk-s-top-priority-for-twitter-includes-cutting-down-on-crypto -scam-tweets.
112. Muhammad Shadab Iqbal and Lin Li, "Does COVID-19 Really Make Peo ple Risk Averse in Investment Decision-Making?," *SHW Web of Conferences* 132 (2022), https://doi.org/10.1051/shsconf/202213201021.
113. Priya Raghubir and Joydeep Srivastava, "Effect of Face Value on Product Valua tion in Foreign Currencies," *Journal of Consumer Research* 29 (Dec. 2002): 335–47, 10.1086/344430.
114. Ibid., 341, 344.
115. Later in 2022, OpenSea dropped the parentheses from its USD listings. For clar ity, I have used the old format for this example.
116. Kingpickle.eth, Twitter (May 5, 2022), https://twitter.com/KingpickIe/status /1522285776179916800.
117. Ibid.
118. Ibid.
119. Andrew Chow, "The Man Behind Ethereum Is Worried About Crypto's Fu ture," *Time* (Mar. 18, 2022), https://time.com/6158182/vitalik-buterin-ethereum -profile/.
120. Ibid.
121. Andrew Hayward, "Ethereum Creator Vitalik Buterin: I Don't Hate Bored Ape Yacht Club NFTs," Decrypt (Mar. 22, 2022), https://decrypt.co/95683/ethereum -vitalik-buterin-dont-hate-bored-ape-nfts.
122. Will Gottsegen, "What Is ApeCoin and Who Is Behind It?," CoinDesk (Mar. 18, 2022), https://www.coindesk.com/layer2/2022/03/18/what-is-apecoin-and-who -is-behind-it/.

Chapter 9: Regulating Web3?
1. John Perry Barlow, "A Declaration of the Independence of Cyberspace," Electronic Frontier Foundation (Feb. 8, 1996), https://www.eff.org/cyberspace-independence.
2. Ibid.
3. Ibid.
4. Andy Greenberg, "It's Been 20 Years Since This Man Declared Cyberspace In dependence," *Wired* (Feb. 8, 2016), https://www.wired.com/2016/02/its-been-20 -years-since-this-man-declared-cyberspace-independence/.
5. Ibid.
6. "A Look Back in Time . . . at the Most Visited Web Domains of 1996!," Com-

score (July 21, 2011), https://www.comscore.com/Insights/Blog/A-Look-Back-in -Time-at-the-Most-Visited-Web-Domains-of-1996.

7. Rebecca Klar, "Zuckerberg: 'Facebook Shouldn't Be the Arbiter of Truth of Everything That People Say Online,'" *The Hill* (May 27, 2020), https://thehill.com /policy/technology/499852-zuckerberg-face.

8. Senate Select Committee on Intelligence, 116th Congress, Rep. on Russian Active Measures Campaigns and Interference in the 2016 U.S. Election, Volume 2: *Russia's Use of Social Media with Additional Views* 4, 6, 48 (Comm. Print 2019).

9. Edward Lee, "Moderating Content Moderation: A Framework for Nonpartisanship in Online Governance," *American University International Law Review* 70 (2021): 913, 932–37.

10. HB 20, https://capitol.texas.gov/tlodocs/872/billtext/html/HB00020F.HTM.

11. *Netchoice, LLC v. Paxton*, 49 F.4th 439, 2022 WL 4285917 (5th Cir. Sept. 16, 2022), reversing 573 F. Supp. 3d 1092, 1099 (W.D. Tex. Dec. 1, 2021).

12. Isaac Chotine, "Why Elon Musk Bought Twitter," *New Yorker* (Apr. 26, 2022), https://www.newyorker.com/news/q-and-a/why-elon-musk-bought-twitter.

13. Brian Fung and Clare Duffy, "Elon Musk Says He Would Reverse Twitter's Trump Ban," CNN (May 10, 2022), https://edition.cnn.com/2022/05/10/tech /elon-musk-twitter-trump-ban/index.html; Brakkton Booker, "House Democrats Use Trump's Own Words to Argue He Showed No Remorse After Attack," NPR (Feb. 11, 2021), https://www.npr.org/sections/trump-impeachment-trial-live-up dates/2021/02/11/967034292/house-democrats-use-trumps-own-words-to -argue-he-showed-no-remorse-after-attack.

14. "Elon Musk to Acquire Twitter," PR Newswire (Apr. 25, 2022), https://www .prnewswire.com/news-releases/elon-musk-to-acquire-twitter-301532245.html.

15. Lauren Feiner, "Twitter Sues Elon Musk to Enforce Original Merger Agreement," CNBC (Jul. 12, 2022), https://www.cnbc.com/2022/07/12/twitter-sues-elon -musk-to-enforce-original-merger-agreement.html.

16. Jon Brodkin, "Musk Says Twitter Must Show Data Behind Spam Estimate or He'll Kill the Deal," Arstechnica (May 17, 2022), https://arstechnica.com/tech -policy/2022/05/musk-says-twitter-must-show-data-behind-spam-estimate-or -hell-kill-the-deal/.

17. Jef Feeley, Ed Hammond, and Kurt Wagner, "Musk Proposes to Buy Twitter for Original Price of $54.20 a Share," Bloomberg (Oct. 4, 2022), https://www .bloomberg.com/news/articles/2022–10–04/musk-proposes-to-proceed-with -twitter-deal-at-54–20-a-share.

18. Adrienne LaFrance, "The Largest Autocracy on Earth," *Atlantic* (Sep. 27, 2021), https://www.theatlantic.com/magazine/archive/2021/11/facebook-authoritarian -hostile-foreign-power/620168/.

19. Michael Posner, "Why Elon Musk Would Be Bad for Twitter," *Forbes* (Apr. 20, 2022), https://www.forbes.com/sites/michaelposner/2022/04/20/why-elon-musk -would-be-bad-for-twitter/.

20. Edward Lee, "Virtual Governments," *UCLA Journal of Law and Technology* 27 (2022): 13.

21. Ibid. (dictionary definition of "virtual").

22. "About Verified Accounts," Twitter, https://help.twitter.com/en/managing-your -account/about-twitter-verified-accounts.

23. Angie, "How to Beat the 2022 Instagram Algorithm," The Lovely Escapist, https://thelovelyescapist.com/2018-instagram-algorithm/; Jack Stanley, "Instagram Denies Limiting Your Posts' Reach," Hypebeast (Jan. 23, 2019), https:// hypebeast.com/2019/1/instagram-post-reach-limit-denial-details.

24. Kif Leswing, "Facebook Says Apple iOS Privacy Change Will Result in

$10 Billion Revenue Hit This Year," CNBC (Feb. 3, 2022), https://www.cnbc.com/2022/02/02/facebook-says-apple-ios-privacy-change-will-cost-10-billion-this-year.html.

25. Lawrence Lessig, *Code and Other Laws of Cyberspace* (New York: Basic Books, 1999), 6.

26. Lee, "Virtual Governments," 27–28.

27. *AT&T Corp. v. City of Portland*, 216 F.3d 871, 876 (9th Cir. 2000).

28. Michael Gariffo, "What Is Web3? Everything You Need to Know About the Decentralized Future of the Internet," ZDnet (Jan. 18, 2022), https://www.zdnet.com/article/what-is-web3-everything-you-need-to-know-about-the-decentralised-future-of-the-internet/.

29. Chris Dixon, "Why Decentralization Matters" (Feb. 18, 2018), cdixon, https://cdixon.org/2018/02/18/why-decentralization-matters.

30. Lee, "Virtual Governments," 22–23.

31. "Web2 Vs Web3," Ethereum (Sep. 16, 2022), https://ethereum.org/en/developers/docs/web2-vs-web3/.

32. Vitalik Buterin, "The Meaning of Decentralization," Medium (Feb. 6, 2017), https://medium.com/@VitalikButerin/the-meaning-of-decentralization-a0c92b76a274; Miles Jennings, "Decentralization for Web3 Builders: Principles, Models, How," a16z (Apr. 7, 2022), https://future.a16z.com/web3-decentralization-models-framework-principles-how-to/; Divya Siddarth, Danielle Allen, and E. Glen Weyl, "The Web3 Decentralization Debate Is Focused on the Wrong Question," *Wired* (May 12, 2022), https://www.wired.com/story/web3-blockchain-decentralization-governance/.

33. Kevin Roose, "What Is Web3?," *New York Times* (Mar. 18, 2022), https://www.nytimes.com/interactive/2022/03/18/technology/web3-definition-internet.html; "What Is Web 3.0: A Beginner's Guide to the Decentralized Internet of the Future," Cointelegraph, https://cointelegraph.com/blockchain-for-beginners/what-is-web-3-0-a-beginners-guide-to-the-decentralized-internet-of-the-future.

34. Alyssa Blackburn et al., "Cooperation Among an Anonymous Group Protected Bitcoin During Failures of Decentralization," arXiv:2206.02871 (2022): 10 (unpublished paper); Siobhan Roberts, "How 'Trustless' Is Bitcoin, Really?," *New York Times* (Jun. 6, 2022), https://www.nytimes.com/2022/06/06/science/bitcoin-nakamoto-blackburn-crypto.html.

35. Emily Graffeo and Bloomberg, "Just 0.1% of Bitcoin Miners Control Half of All Mining Capacity, According to a New Study," *Fortune* (Oct. 25, 2021), https://fortune.com/2021/10/26/bitcoin-mining-capacity-ownership-concentration-top-investors-nber-study/.

36. "Ethereum," Miningpoolstats, https://miningpoolstats.stream/ethereum; Steven Buchko, "The 3 Best Ethereum Mining Pool Options," CoinCentral (Mar. 7, 2021), https://coincentral.com/best-ethereum-mining-pool/.

37. Brian Njuguna, "Ethereum's Top 5 Mining Pools Account for 65.4% of ETH Blocks," Blockchain (Nov. 8, 2021), https://blockchain.news/analysis/ethereum-top-5-mining-pools-account-for-65.4-percent-eth-blocks.

38. David Pan, "World's Biggest Ether Mining Firm Turns Off Servers After Merge," Bloomberg (Sept. 15, 2022), https://www.bloomberg.com/news/articles/2022-09-14/world-s-biggest-ether-mining-firm-to-shut-down-after-the-merge.

39. "Proof-Of-Stake (POS)," Ethereum, https://ethereum.org/en/developers/docs/consensus-mechanisms/pos/.

40. Stacy Elliott, "Ethereum Staking Pools: Who Runs the Largest Ones?," Decrypt (Sep. 3, 2022), https://decrypt.co/108906/ethereum-staking-pools-who-runs-the-largest-ones.

41. Tech Desk, "Facebook and Instagram May Allow Users to Create, Showcase, and Sell NFTs: Report," *Indian Express* (Jan. 28, 2022), https://indianexpress.com/article/technology/crypto/facebook-and-instagram-may-allow-users-to-create-showcase-and-sell-nfts-report-7740581/.

42. Meta, "Horizon Mature Worlds Policy," Facebook, https://store.facebook.com/help/quest/articles/horizon/create-in-horizon-worlds/restrictions-to-worlds-in-horizon/.

43. Casey Newton, "Facebook's Big New Experiment in Governance," Platformer (Sep. 20, 2022), https://www.platformer.news/p/facebooks-big-new-experiment-in-governance/.

44. "NFT Marketplace Competition Heats Up," Forkast (Q1 2022), https://forkast.news/state-of-the-nft-market/nft-marketplace-competition-heats-up/.

45. Lee, "Virtual Governments," 11–12.

46. Samuel Falkon, "The Story of the DAO—Its History and Consequences," Medium (Dec. 24, 2017), https://medium.com/swlh/the-story-of-the-dao-its-history-and-consequences-71e6a8a551ee.

47. "Gutter Cat Gang Terms & Conditions," Guttercatgang, https://guttercatgang.com/gutter-cat-gang-terms-conditions/.

48. Mark Sullivan, "Tim O'Reilly Helped Bring Us Web 1.0 and 2.0. Here's Why He's a Web3 Skeptic," *Fast Company* (Feb. 3, 2022), https://www.fastcompany.com/90716841/tim-oreilly-on-web3.

49. Jakob Steinschaden, "Bored Ape Yacht Club Founder Yuga Labs Raises $450M in a Seed Investment," Trendingtopics (Mar. 23, 2022), https://www.trendingtopics.eu/bored-ape-yacht-club-founder-yuga-labs-raises-450m-in-a-seed-investment/.

50. "The Otherside Litepaper," Otherside, https://otherside.xyz/litepaper.

51. Patrick Hansen, "Europe's Third Way Is Web3: Why the EU Should Embrace Crypto," SLSblogs (Nov. 12, 2021), https://law.stanford.edu/2021/11/12/europes-third-way-is-web3-why-the-eu-should-embrace-crypto/.

52. Md Sadek Ferdous, Farida Chowdhury, and Madini O. Alassafi, "In Search of Self-Sovereign Identity Leveraging Blockchain Technology," *IEEE Access* 7 (2019), 10.1109/ACCESS.2019.2931173.

53. Ibid.

54. "Open Metaverse," 6529, https://6529.io/about/open-metaverse/.

55. Yat Siu, Twitter (Apr. 30, 2022), https://twitter.com/ysiu/status/1520482225292070912; Kyle Swenson, "Animoca Brands Chairman and BAYC Member Yat Siu," The Bored Ape Gazette (Mar. 11, 2022), https://www.theboredapegazette.com/post/anicoma-brands-chairman-and-bayc-member-yat-siu-explains-why-he-kyc-s-are-important-for-the-space.

56. Bored Ape Yacht Club, Twitter (Mar. 10, 2022), https://twitter.com/BoredApeYC/status/1502056862639923202.

57. Yuga Labs, Twitter (Apr. 30, 2022), https://twitter.com/yugalabs/status/1520612359991336961.

58. Ornella Hernandez, "Yuga Labs Faces User Backlash for Under Wraps KYC-Restricted Project," Cointelegraph (Mar. 11, 2022), https://cointelegraph.com/news/yuga-labs-faces-user-backlash-for-under-wraps-kyc-restricted-project.

59. Edward Lee, "Caked Apes NFTs Turn Sour. Nasty Lawsuits Embroil Creators of Caked Apes Who Sue Each Other over Ownership. Taylor Whitley (taylorwtf) Sues Jake Nygard (Cake Nygard), Clare Maguire, Antonius Wiriadjaja, Donglee Han, Who Countersue TaylorWTF," NouNFT(Mar. 25, 2022), https://nounft.com/2022/03/25/caked-apes-nfts-turn-sour-nasty-lawsuits-embroil-creators-of-caked-apes-who-sue-each-other-over-ownership-taylor-whitley-taylorwtf-sues-jake-nygard-cake-nygard-clare-maguire-antonius-wiriadjaj/.

60. Roose, "What Is Web3"; "Introduction to Web3," Ethereum (May 26, 2022), https://ethereum.org/en/web3/.

Chapter 10: Legal Controversies

1. *Denver Area Educ. Telecommuns. Consortium, Inc. v. F.C.C.*, 518 U.S. 727, 778 (1996) (Souter, J., concurring).
2. *SEC v. W. J. Howey Co.*, 328 U.S. 293, 294–97 (1946).
3. Adee Braun, "Misunderstanding Orange Juice as a Health Drink," *Atlantic* (Feb. 6, 2014), https://www.theatlantic.com/health/archive/2014/02/misunderstanding-orange-juice-as-a-health-drink/283579/.
4. *Howey*, 328 U.S. at 300.
5. Ibid., 298; SEC, "Framework for 'Investment Contract' Analysis of Digital Assets," SEC (Apr. 3, 2019), https://www.sec.gov/corpfin/framework-investment-contract-analysis-digital-assets.
6. "What Is a Registration Statement," SEC, https://www.sec.gov/education/smallbusiness/goingpublic/registrationstatement.
7. The Praetorian Group, "Form S-1 Registration Statement Under the Securities Act of 1933," SEC (Mar. 6, 2018), https://www.sec.gov/Archives/edgar/data/1721980/000137647418000045/pr_s1.htm.
8. Morgan Chittum, "SEC Reportedly Targets NFT Market over Potential Violations of Securities Law," Blockworks (Mar. 3, 2022), https://blockworks.co/sec-reportedly-targets-nft-market-over-potential-violations-of-securities-law/.
9. Andrea Tinianow, "No Slam Dunk for Plaintiffs in NBA Top Shot Moments Class Action Lawsuit," *Forbes* (May 17, 2021), https://www.forbes.com/sites/andreatinianow/2021/05/17/no-slam-dunk-for-plaintiffs-in-nba-top-shot-moments-class-action-lawsuit/; Gargi Chadhuri and James V. Masella III, "Are NFTs Securities? Analysis of the NBA Top Shot Litigation and Other NFT-Related Actions," PBWT (Mar. 29, 2022), https://www.pbwt.com/securities-litigation-insider/are-nfts-securities-analysis-of-the-nba-top-shot-litigation-and-other-nft-related-actions.
10. William Hinman, "Digital Asset Transactions: When Howey Met Gary (Plastic)," SEC (June 14, 2018), https://www.sec.gov/news/speech/speech-hinman-061418.
11. Ibid.
12. SEC Strategic Hub for Innovation and Financial Technology, "Framework for 'Investment Contract' Analysis of Digital Assets," SEC (Apr. 3, 2019), https://www.sec.gov/corpfin/framework-investment-contract-analysis-digital-assets#_edn1.
13. "SEC Commissioner Hester Peirce Says Some Crypto Sales May Be Illegal in the US—Here's Why," Dailyhodl (Mar. 28, 2021), https://dailyhodl.com/2021/03/28/sec-commissioner-hester-peirce-says-some-crypto-sales-may-be-illegal-in-the-us-heres-why/.
14. *Howey*, 328 U.S. at 298.
15. Ibid., 299 (emphasis added).
16. *SEC v. SG Ltd.*, 265 F.3d 42, 55 (1st Cir. 2001).
17. *United Housing Foundation, Inc. v. Forman*, 421 U.S. 837, 852–53 nn.16–17 (1975).
18. Opulous, "Why Opulous Is Offering Music Security NFTs on Republic," Medium (Oct. 6, 2021), https://opulous.medium.com/why-opulous-is-offering-music-security-nfts-on-republic-a4e27e8fa70f.
19. Murray Stassen, "Lil Pump Royalty Shares Sell Out in Two Hours Via Opulous Partnership, Raising $500,000," Music Business Worldwide (Nov. 4, 2021), https://www.musicbusinessworldwide.com/lil-pump-royalty-shares-sell-out-in-two-hours-via-crowdfunding-opulous-raising-500000/.
20. Polybius, "S-NFTs Make Their Debut: Lil Pump on Republic," Polybiussquare

(Nov. 9, 2021), https://www.polybiussquare.com/s-nfts-make-their-debut-lil-pump-on-republic/.

21. GRM Daily, "Premiere: Ard Arz Drops Off Visuals for 'Patek Myself,'" GRM Daily (May 19, 2022), https://grmdaily.com/ard-adz-patek-myself/.

22. "SEC Nearly Doubles Size of Enforcements's Crypto Assets and Cyber Unit," SEC (May 3, 2022), https://www.sec.gov/news/press-release/2022–78.

23. Paul Kiernan and Vicky Ge Huang, "Ether's New 'Staking' Model Could Draw SEC Attention," *Wall Street Journal* (Sep. 15, 2022), https://www.wsj.com/articles/ethers-new-staking-model-could-draw-sec-attention-11663266224.

24. Kevin Helms, "3 Bills Introduced in US to Make CFTC Primary Regulator of Crypto Spot Markets," Bitcoin (Aug. 8, 2022), https://news.bitcoin.com/3-bills-introduced-in-us-to-make-cftc-primary-regulator-of-crypto-spot-markets/.

25. Alys Key, "SEC Chair Gensler: Crypto Bill Could 'Undermine' Existing Protections," Decrypt (June 15, 2022), https://decrypt.co/102972/sec-chair-gensler-crypto-bill-could-undermine-existing-protections; Andrew Ackerman, "SEC's Gensler Signals Support for Commodities Regulator Having Bitcoin Oversight," *Wall Street Journal* (Sept. 8, 2022), https://www.wsj.com/articles/secs-gensler-supports-commodities-regulator-having-bitcoin-oversight-11662641115?st=4jdtjdmwpx7ogrx&reflink=desktopwebshare_permalink.

26. "Securities Act of 1933," SEC, https://www.investor.gov/introduction-investing/investing-basics/role-sec/laws-govern-securities-industry#secact1933.

27. "Securities Exchange Act of 1934," SEC, https://www.investor.gov/introduction-investing/investing-basics/role-sec/laws-govern-securities-industry#secexact1934.

28. *In re. Donald J. Trump Casino Sec. Litig.–Taj Mahal Litig.*, 7 F.3d 357, 371 (3d Cir. 1993).

29. Donald C. Langevoort, "Selling Hope, Selling Risk: Some Lessons for Law from Behavioral Economics About Stockbrokers and Sophisticated Consumers," *California Law Review* 84 (1996): 682.

30. Hadar Y. Jabotinsky, "The Regulation of Cryptocurrencies: Between a Currency and a Financial Product," *Fordham Intellectual Property Media and Entertainment Law Journal* 31 (2020): 159.

31. SEC Staff, "Study Regarding Financial Literacy Among Investors," SEC (Aug. 2012), viii–viii, https://www.sec.gov/files/917-financial-literacy-study-part1.pdf.

32. Stephen J. Choi and A. C. Pritchard, "Behavioral Economics and the SEC," *Stanford Law Review* 56 (2003): 7–14.

33. Stephen J. Choi, "Behavioral Economics and the Regulation of Public Offerings," *Lewis & Clark Law Review* 10 (2006): 113.

34. Susanna Kim Ripken, "Predictions, Projections, and Precautions: Conveying Cautionary Warnings in Corporate Forward-Looking Statements," *University of Illinois Law Review* (2005): 984; Christoph Engel, Sinika Timme, and Andreas Glockner, "Coherence-Based Reasoning and Order Effects in Legal Judgments," *Psychology Public Policy and Law* 26 (2020): 334.

35. Doodles, "Terms of Service," Doodles, https://docs.doodles.app/terms-of-service.

36. Cheyenne Ligon and Jack Schickler, "NFT Collections Will Be Regulated Like Cryptocurrencies Under EU's MiCA Law, Official Says," CoinDesk (Aug. 10. 2022), https://www.coindesk.com/policy/2022/08/10/nft-collections-will-be-regulated-like-cryptocurrencies-under-eus-mica-law-official-says/; Jack Schickler and Helene Braun, "EU's MiCA Crypto Law Text Ready Within 6 Weeks, Lead Lawmaker Says," CoinDesk (Sep. 1, 2022), https://www.coindesk.com/policy/2022/09/01/eus-mica-crypto-law-text-ready-within-6-weeks-lead-lawmaker-says/.

37. Diego Ballon Ossio, "MiCA—EU Reaches Agreement on the Crypto-Assets

Regulation," Clifford Chance (July 1, 2022), https://www.cliffordchance.com /insights/resources/blogs/talking-tech/en/articles/2022/07/MiCA-EU-reaches -agreement-on-the-crypto-assets-regulation.html.

38. 17 CFR § 240.10b5–1; Akhilesh Ganti, "Insider Trading," Investopedia (Mar. 7, 2022), https://www.investopedia.com/terms/i/insidertrading.asp.

39. Liam Vaughan, "'Most Americans Today Believe the Stock Market Is Rigged, and They're Right,'" Bloomberg (Sep. 28, 2021), https://www.bloomberg.com/news /features/2021–09–29/is-stock-market-rigged-insider-trading-by-executives -is-pervasive-critics-say; Thomas Franck, "Insider Trading Is Still Rampant on Wall Street, Two New Studies Suggest," CNBC (Feb. 14, 2018), https://www .cnbc.com/2018/02/14/insider-trading-is-still-rampant-on-wall-street-two-news -studies-suggest.html.

40. Ekin Genç, "Insider Trading 'Common' in NFTs, Investors Say After First Arrest," Vice (June 3, 2022), https://www.vice.com/en/article/akewdz/insider -trading-common-in-nfts-investors-say-after-first-arrest.

41. Edward Lee, "How Is Insider Trading of NFTs a Felony if It Doesn't Involve a 10b-5 Securities Violation? The Wire Fraud Theory in *U.S. v. Nate Chastain*, Former OpenSea Employee.," NouNFT (June 2, 2022), https://nounft.com /2022/06/02/how-is-insider-trading-of-nfts-a-felony-if-it-doesnt-involve-a-10b -5-securities-violation-the-wire-fraud-theory-in-u-s-v-nate-chastain-former -opensea-employee/.

42. Jeff Kauflin of *Forbes* examined what he called "circumstantial" evidence of possible insider NFT trading, although the individuals allegedly involved denied it. Jeff Kauflin, "Did the Son of the World's Third-Richest Person Trade NFTs with Inside Information?," *Forbes* (Mar. 30, 2022), https://www.forbes.com/sites/jeff kauflin/2022/03/30/did-the-son-of-the-worlds-third-richest-man-trade-nfts -with-inside-information/.

43. Andrey Sergeenkov, "What Is NFT Wash Trading?," CoinDesk (Aug. 23, 2022), https://www.coindesk.com/learn/what-is-nft-wash-trading/.

44. "NFT Transaction Activity Stabilizing in 2022 After Explosive Growth in 2021," Chainalysis (May 5, 2022), https://blog.chainalysis.com/reports/chainalysis-web3 -report-preview-nfts/; Thomas McGovern, "How Many People Own NFTs in 2022," Earthweb (Sept. 11, 2022), https://earthweb.com/how-many-people-own -nfts/.

45. U.S. Attorney's Office, Southern District of New York, "Two Defendants Charged in Non-Fungible Token ('NFT') Fraud and Money Laundering Scheme," U.S. Department of Justice (Mar. 24, 2022), https://www.justice.gov/usao-sdny/pr/ two-defendants-charged-non-fungible-token-nft-fraud-and-money-laundering- scheme-0.

46. Ibid.

47. Edward Lee, "*US v. Le Ahn Tuan*: Second Criminal Indictment for Rug Pull Involving Baller Ape Club NFTs," NouNFT (July 5, 2022), https://nounft .com/2022/07/05/us-v-le-ahn-tuan-second-criminal-indictment-for-rug-pull -involving-baller-ape-club-nfts/.

48. "The Biggest Threat to Trust in Cryptocurrency: Rug Pulls Put 2021 Crypto- currency Scam Revenue Close to All-time Highs," Chainalysis (Dec. 16, 2021), https://blog.chainalysis.com/reports/2021-crypto-scam-revenues/.

49. "Confirmed Rug Pulls," Rug Pull Finder, https://www.rugpullfinder.io/services /confirmed-rug-pulls.

50. Rug Pull Finder, Twitter (May 11, 2022), https://twitter.com/rugpullfinder /status/1524465653738053632 ("Rug pull—any project which either a) shuts down a project, closing all socials, and abandoning the project; b) drains the liquidity out

of a project, in a way that makes the project unsustainable, or drains the project funds without detailed insight as to the whereabouts of the funds and financial plans; c) multiple direct wallet transactions to previous rug pulls; d) is active over a period of time, while failing to deliver on any component of its roadmap") (first attached photo).

51. Kyril Kotashev, "Startup Failure Rate: How Many Startups Fail and Why?," Failory (Jan. 9, 2022), https://www.failory.com/blog/startup-failure-rate.

52. Zagabond, "A Builder's Journey," Mirror (May 9, 2022), https://mirror.xyz/0x 1Cb8332607fba6A780DdE78584AD3BFD1eEB1E40/yG8rI1lpQGLPhZch0kj xYRjKTtA9rAL51zg-ZrURyAc.

53. Zagabond.eth, Twitter (May 10, 2022), https://twitter.com/ZAGABOND /status/1524189056225013761; Reethu Ravi, "Azuki NFT Founder Releases An Apology Statement After Nightmare Space," NFT Evening (Aug. 21, 2022), https://nftevening.com/azuki-nft-founder-releases-an-apology-statement-after -nightmare-space/.

54. Jex Exmundo, "Azuki Creator in Hot Water Amidst Rug Pull Allegations: Here Are the Facts," NFTnow (May 10, 2022), https://nftnow.com/news/azuki-creator -in-hot-water-amidst-rug-pull-allegations/.

55. Jason Levin, "Shapeshifting Azuki Founder Outfoxes Himself with Strange Confession," The Defiant (May 12, 2022), https://thedefiant.io/azuki-floor-price -collapses-founder-confession/.

56. Meanix.eth, "The End of NFT Rug Pulls?," CoinDesk (Apr. 19, 2022), https:// www.coindesk.com/layer2/2022/04/19/the-end-of-nft-rug-pulls/; Kalli Wang, "Reversible Transactions on Ethereum: ERC-20R and ERC-721R," Mirror (Sep. 24, 2022), https://mirror.xyz/kaili.eth/gB-rx89sNAT3CVuxWo6xVFS5pt NcllW7cVWVCfcFa6k.

57. Karl Taro Greenfield, "Meet the Napster," *Time* (Oct. 2, 2000), https://content .time.com/time/subscriber/article/0,33009,998068–1,00.html.

58. Ibid.

59. Nate Anderson, "Has the RIAA Sued 18,000 People . . . or 35,000?," Arstechnica (July 8, 2009), https://arstechnica.com/tech-policy/2009/07/has-the-riaa-sued -18000-people-or-35000/.

60. Jessica Litman, *Digital Copyright* (Amherst, N.Y.: Prometheus Books, 2001), 151; Lessig, *Remix*, xv–xvi.

61. Amy Harmon, "Black Hawk Download; Moving Beyond Music, Pirates Use New Tools to Turn the Net Into an Illicit Video Club," *New York Times* (Jan. 17, 2022), https://www.nytimes.com/2002/01/17/technology/black-hawk-download -moving-beyond-music-pirates-use-new-tools-turn-net-into.html.

62. Ernesto Van der Sar, "BitTorrent Is Still the King of Upstream Internet Traf- fic, but for How Long?," TorrentFreak (Mar. 4, 2022), https://torrentfreak.com /bittorrent-is-still-the-king-of-upstream-internet-traffic-but-for-how-long -220304/.

63. Damjan Jugovic Spajic, "Piracy Is Back: Piracy Statistics for 2022," Dataprot (May 17, 2022), https://dataprot.net/statistics/piracy-statistics/.

64. Van der Sar, "BitTorrent."

65. Eriq Gardner, "Malibu Media, Litigious Porn Studio, Sued for Allegedly Cheat- ing Financiers," *Hollywood Reporter* (Aug. 13, 2019), https://www.hollywood reporter.com/business/business-news/malibu-media-litigious-porn-studio-sued -allegedly-cheating-financiers-1231192/; Gabe Friedman, "The Biggest Filer of Copyright Lawsuits? This Erotica Web Site," *New Yorker* (May 14, 2014), https:// www.newyorker.com/business/currency/the-biggest-filer-of-copyright-lawsuits -this-erotica-web-site.

66. Jeffrey J. Antonelli, "Torrent Wars: Copyright Trolls, Legitimate IP Rights, and the Need for New Rules Vetting Evidence and to Amend the Copyright Act," *Illinois State Bar Association* 53 (2013): 1, 3, https://www.isba.org/sections/ip/news letter/2013/10/torrentwarscopyrighttrollslegitimat.

67. Matthew Sag and Jake Haskell, "Defense Against the Dark Arts of Copyright Trolling," *Iowa Law Review* 103 (2018): 577.

68. *Malibu Media, LLC, v. Doe* (S.D.N.Y. July 6, 2015), No. 15 Civ. 4369 (AKH), 2015 WL 4092417, *3.

69. Timothy Geigner, "Malibu Media Finally Paid Wrongfully Accused Six Figures . . . Via Collections Agency," techdirt (May 11, 2022), https://www.tech dirt.com/2022/05/11/malibu-media-finally-paid-wrongfully-accused-six-figures -via-collections-agency/.

70. 17 U.S.C. § 512.

71. Karyn Temple Claggett, "Session II: The Impact of International Copyright Trea- ties and Trade Agreements on the Development of Domestic Norms," *Columbia Journal of Law and the Arts* 40 *(2017)*: 350.

72. Shreya Tewari, "Evolution of DMCA Notices: Trends and a Timeline," Lumen Database (July 2, 2021), https://www.lumendatabase.org/blog_entries/evolution -of-dmca-notices-trends-and-a-timeline.

73. Joe Karganis and Jennifer Urban, "The Rise of Robo Notice," *Communications of ACM* 58 (2015): 28–30, https://cacm.acm.org/magazines/2015/9/191182-the -rise-of-the-robo-notice/fulltext.

74. Daniel Seng, "Copyrighting Copywrongs: An Empirical Analysis of Errors with Automated DMCA Takedown Notices," *Santa Clara High Technology Law Jour- nal* 37 (2021): 126.

75. Directive 2019/790 of the European Parliament and of the Council of April 17, 2019, on Copyright and Related Rights in the Digital Single Market and Amend ing Directives 96/9/EC and 2001/29/EC, art. 17, 2019 O.J. (L 130).

76. Case C-401/19, *Republic of Poland v. European Parliament*, ECLI:EU:C:2022: 297, 94.

77. Seng, "Copyrighting Copywrongs," 127–28, 164.

78. Julia Collins, "The Intrepid Crew of the Berkman Center for Internet and Soci- ety," Harvard Law Today (June 24, 1999), https://today.law.harvard.edu/feature /building-cyberspace/.

79. Madana Prathap, "NFTs Are the New Crypto Wild West—Artists and Brands with Big Pockets Are the Only Ones Who Can Afford to Fight Back," Business Insider (Feb. 17, 2022), https://www.businessinsider.in/investment/news/nfts-are -the-new-crypto-wild-west-artists-and-brands-with-big-pockets-are-the-only -ones-who-can-afford-to-fight-back/articleshow/89613624.cms.

80. Ibid.

81. Edward Lee, "Mason Rothschild Invokes First Amendment Right to Create Meta- Birkins NFTs, Rejects Hermes' Cease and Desist Letter," NouNFT (Jan. 5, 2022), https://nounft.com/2022/01/05/mason-rothschild-invokes-first-amendment -right-to-create-metabirkins-nfts-rejects-hermes-ceast-and-desist-letter/.

82. Dominic Patten, "Quentin Tarantino Wants 'Offensively Meritless' Miramax NFT Suit Tossed Out; Studio Sued Oscar Winner over 'Pulp Fiction' Script Auc- tion," Deadline (Dec. 9, 2021), https://deadline.com/2021/12/quentin-tarantino -nft-lawsuit-dismissal-motion-pulp-fiction-miramax-1234888031/.

83. Lewis A. Kaplan, "Keynote Address: Resolving Tensions Between Copyright and the Internet," *American University Law Review* 50 (2000): 409, 414–15.

84. Ibid., 419.

85. Wahid Pessarlay, "Chinese Court Makes First Public Ruling Involving NFTs,"

Coingeek (Apr. 30, 2022), https://coingeek.com/chinese-court-makes-first
-public-ruling-involving-nfts/.

86. Ann Fauvre-Willis, "Authenticity on OpenSea: Updates to Verification and Copy-
     mint Prevention," OpenSea (May 11, 2022), https://opensea.io/blog/announc
     ements/improving-authenticity-on-opensea-updates-to-verification-and-copy
     mint-prevention/.

87. Ibid.

88. Eileen Brown, "New Platform Uses NFTs as a Gateway for Digital Rights Man-
     agement," ZDNet (Mar. 4, 2021), https://www.zdnet.com/finance/blockchain
     /new-platform-uses-nfts-as-a-gateway-for-digital-rights-management/.

89. Sarah Emerson, "Someone Stole Seth Green's Bored Ape, Which Was Supposed
     to Star in His New Show," *BuzzFeed News* (May 24, 2022), https://www.buzz
     feednews.com/article/sarahemerson/seth-green-bored-ape-stolen-tv-show.

90. Sarah Emerson, "The Owner of Seth Green's Stolen Bored Ape Said They Have
     No Plans to Return It," *BuzzFeed News* (May 25, 2022), https://www.buzzfeed
     news.com/article/sarahemerson/seth-green-bored-ape-owner.

91. "Transaction Details," Etherscan, https://etherscan.io/tx/0x8e456f0b4b42e9bd
     bc9be050c547f0a748ade6046c9fbca2f07e98f21a4b419d.

92. Arnold Kirimi, "NFT Owners Reminded to Be Vigilant After 29 Moonbirds
     Were Stolen by Clicking a Bad Link," Cointelegraph (May 25, 2022), https://coin
     telegraph.com/news/nft-owners-reminded-to-be-vigilant-after-29-moonbirds
     -were-stolen-by-clicking-a-bad-link.

93. Eileen Kinsella, "'All My Apes Gone': An Art Dealer's Despondent Tweet About
     the Theft of His NFTs Went Viral . . . and Has Now Become an NFT," Art-
     net (Jan. 5, 2022), https://news.artnet.com/market/kramer-nft-theft-turned-nft
     -2056489.

94. Ibid.

95. Emerson, "Someone Stole"; OpenSea, "Why Was My NFT Reported for Sus-
     picious Activity?" OpenSea, https://support.opensea.io/hc/en-us/articles/4409
     456298515-Why-was-my-NFT-reported-for-suspicious-activity-.

96. "Anatomy of an NFT Phishing Scam," TRMlabs (Mar. 24, 2022), https://www
     .trmlabs.com/post/anatomy-of-an-nft-phishing-scam.

97. "So Your Stuff Got Stolen: What Do You Do?," NFTtorney (Dec. 28, 2021),
     https://nfttorney.com/2021/12/28/so-your-shit-got-stolen-what-do-you-do/.

98. Wataru Suzuki, "FBI Links North Korean Hackers to Axie Infinity Crypto Theft,"
     Nikkei Asia (Apr. 15, 2022), https://asia.nikkei.com/Spotlight/Cryptocurrencies
     /FBI-links-North-Korean-hackers-to-Axie-Infinity-crypto-theft.

99. Ibid.

100. Sarah Emerson, "Seth Green's Stolen Bored Ape Is Back Home," *BuzzFeed News*
     (June 9, 2022), https://www.buzzfeednews.com/article/sarahemerson/seth-green
     -bored-ape-nft-returned.

101. Seth Green, Twitter (May 30, 2022), https://twitter.com/SethGreen/status/1531
     267330725974016.

102. Stallion, Twitter (May 31, 2022), https://twitter.com/atcontino/status/15318
     19765160783874.

103. Shawn Ghassemitari, "Collection of Bored Ape NFTs Worth Millions Sto-
     len from Art Gallery Owner," Hypebeast (Jan. 4, 2022), https://hypebeast
     .com/2022/1/bored-ape-yacht-club-nfts-stolen-todd-kramer-ross-kramer
     -gallery-owner-opensea.

104. Seth Green, Twitter (May 24, 2022), https://twitter.com/SethGreen/status/1529
     191356660215808.

105. Alan Schwartz and Robert E. Scott, "Rethinking the Law of Good Faith Purchase,"

Columbia Law Review 111 (2011): 1335–57; Giuseppe Dari-Mattiaci and Carmine Guerriero, "Divergence and Convergence at the Intersection of Property and Contract," *Southern California Law Review* 92 (2019): 816–23.

106. "Overview of 2022 Amendments to the Uniform Commercial Code—Emerging Technologies,"Uniformlaws, 2, https://www.uniformlaws.org/HigherLogic/System/DownloadDocumentFile.ashx?DocumentFileKey=a116549b-6067-5f82-83ac-3501c7ad882d&forceDialog=0.

107. Edwin E. Smith and Steven O. Weise, "The Proposed 2022 Amendments to the Uniform Commercial Code: Digital Assets," Business Law Today (Mar. 25, 2022), https://businesslawtoday.org/2022/03/proposed-2022-amendments-uniform-commercial-code-digital-assets/.

108. Karen Theresa Burke, "International Transfers of Stolen Cultural Property: Should Thieves Continue to Benefit from Domestic Laws Favoring Bona Fide Purchasers?," *Loyola of Los Angeles International and Comparative Law Review* 13 (1990): 445–46.

109. Uniform Commercial Code § 2–403(1).

110. Katie Schoolov, "Stolen Goods Sold on Amazon, eBay and Facebook Are Causing Havoc for Major Retailers," CNBC (June 17, 2022), https://www.cnbc.com/2022/06/17/the-fight-against-stolen-products-on-amazon-and-facebook-marketplace.html; eBay, "Stolen Property Policy," https://www.ebay.com/help/policies/prohibited-restricted-items/stolen-property-policy?id=4334; Facebook, "What Should I Do if I See a Stolen Item on Facebook Marketplace?," Facebook, https://www.facebook.com/help/312500235963976.

111. Schoolov, "Stolen Goods."

112. OpenSea, "What Is a Verified Account or Badged Collection?," OpenSea, https://support.opensea.io/hc/en-us/articles/360063519133-What-is-a-verified-account-or-badged-collection-; Anne Fauvre-Willis, "An Update on Verification and Copymint Prevention," OpenSea (Aug. 9, 2022), https://opensea.io/blog/announcements/an-update-on-verification-and-copymint-prevention/.

113. James Ellis, "OpenSea Faces Lawsuit Over 'Broken' Stolen NFT Feature," NFT Evening (Aug. 21, 2022), https://nftevening.com/opensea-faces-lawsuit-over-broken-stolen-nft-feature/.

114. Gregin8er, Twitter (Aug. 2, 2022), https://twitter.com/Gregin8er/status/1554585519773945858.

115. OpenSea, Twitter (Aug. 10, 2022), https://twitter.com/opensea/status/1557487545876762625.

116. "What Is OpenSea's Stolen Item Policy?," OpenSea (Jul. 15, 2022), https://web.archive.org/web/20220715105458/https://support.opensea.io/hc/en-us/articles/4815371492499-What-is-OpenSea-s-stolen-item-policy-.

117. OpenSea, "Why Was My NFT."

118. Ibid.

119. Karen Hoffman, "This Tracker Lists and Ranks the Biggest Heists of NFT Cryptocurrency," SC Magazine (Aug. 13, 2022), https://www.scmagazine.com/analysis/threat-intelligence/this-tracker-lists-and-ranks-the-biggest-heists-of-nft-cryptocurrency.

120. Ryan Browne, "Bored Ape NFT Reportedly Sells for $3,000 Instead of $300,000 Due to 'Fat-Finger' Mistake," CNBC (Dec. 14, 2021), www.cnbc.com/2021/12/14/bored-ape-nft-accidentally-sells-for-3000-instead-of-300000.html.

121. Weilun Soon, "A researcher's avatar was sexually assaulted on a metaverse platform owned by Meta, making her the latest victim of sexual abuse on Meta's platforms, watchdog says," Business Insider (May 30, 2022), https://www.businessinsider.com/researcher-claims-her-avatar-was-raped-on-metas-metaverse-platform-2022-5.

Chapter 11: Diversity and Sustainability

1. Gavin Wood, "Why We Need Web 3.0," Medium (Sep. 12, 2018), https://gav ofyork.medium.com/why-we-need-web-3–0–5da4f2bf95ab; Dixon, "Why Decentralization."
2. Wood, "Why We Need."
3. Scott Smith and Lina Srivastava, "Web3 and the Trap of 'For Good,'" *Stanford Social Innovation Review* (Mar. 8, 2022), https://ssir.org/articles/entry/web3_and _the_trap_of_for_good.
4. Ibid.
5. Peter Howson, "Climate Crises and Crypto-Colonialism: Conjuring Value on the Blockchain Frontiers of the Global South," *Front. Blockchain* (May 13, 2020), https://doi.org/10.3389/fbloc.2020.00022.
6. Deloitte, "Striving for Balance, Advocating for Change: The Deloitte Global 2022 Gen Z & Millennial Survey," 38, https://www2.deloitte.com/content/dam /Deloitte/global/Documents/deloitte-2022-genz-millennial-survey.pdf.
7. Ibid., 7.
8. Ibid., 4.
9. Ibid., 23.
10. Ibid., 14.
11. Richard Carufel, "Gen Z Goes to Work: Just 1 in 5 Would Work for a Company that Doesn't Share Their Values," Agilitypr (Jul. 16, 2021), https://www.agilitypr .com/pr-news/public-relations/gen-z-goes-to-work-just-1-in-5-would-work-for -a-company-that-doesnt-share-their-values/.
12. Alec Tyson, Brian Kennedy, and Cary Funk, "Gen Z, Millennials Stand Out for Climate Change Activism, Social Media Engagement with Issue," Pew Research (May 26, 2021), https://www.pewresearch.org/science/2021/05/26/gen -z-millennials-stand-out-for-climate-change-activism-social-media-engagement -with-issue/.
13. Ibid.
14. Kim Parker, Nikki Graf, and Ruth Igielnik, "Generation Z Looks a Lot Like Millennials on Key Social and Political Issues," Pew Research (Jan. 17, 2019), https:// www.pewresearch.org/social-trends/2019/01/17/generation-z-looks-a-lot-like -millennials-on-key-social-and-political-issues/.
15. Jennifer Miller, "For Younger Job Seekers, Diversity and Inclusion in the Workplace Aren't a Preference. They're a Requirement.," *Washington Post* (Feb. 18, 2021), https://www.washingtonpost.com/business/2021/02/18/millennial-genz -workplace-diversity-equity-inclusion/.
16. Hansi Lo Wang, "Generation Z Is the Most Racially and Ethnically Diverse Yet," NPR (Nov. 15, 2018), https://www.npr.org/2018/11/15/668106376/generation-z -is-the-most-racially-and-ethnically-diverse-yet.
17. Smith and Srivastava, "Web3 and the Trap."
18. National Center for Women & Information Technology, "By the Numbers," NCWIT (Mar. 1, 2022), https://ncwit.org/resource/bythenumbers/; Gemini, "2021 State of U.S. Crypto Report," Gemini (2021), 8, https://www.gemini.com /state-of-us-crypto; Taylor Whitten Brown, "Why Is Work by Female Artists Still Valued Less Than Work by Male Artists?," Artsy (Mar. 8, 2019), https://www .artsy.net/article/artsy-editorial-work-female-artists-valued-work-male-artists.
19. Chad M. Topaz et al., "Diversity of Artists in Major U.S. Museums," *PLOS One* 14(3) (2019), https://doi.org/10.1371/journal.pone.0212852.
20. Nancy Minty, "Genius Has No Gender*: Rethinking the Old Master Moniker," Artstor (Mar. 1, 2022), https://www.artstor.org/2022/03/01/genius-has-no -gender1-rethinking-the-old-master-moniker/.

21. Julia Halperin and Charlotte Burns, "Museums Claim They're Paying More Attention to Female Artists. That's an Illusion," Artnet (Sep. 19, 2019), https://news.artnet.com/womens-place-in-the-art-world/womens-place-art-world-museums-1654714 (research by Julia Vennitti).

22. Fabian Y. R. P. Bocart, Marina Gertsberg, and Rachel A. J. Pownall, "An Empirical Analysis of Price Differences for Male and Female Artists in the Global Art Market," *Journal of Cultural Economics* 46 (2021): 545–46, https://doi.org/10.1007/s10824–020–09403–2.

23. Ibid., 546.

24. "Artist Demographics and Statistics in the US," Zippia, https://www.zippia.com/artist-jobs/demographics/.

25. Topaz, "Diversity" (overall data from Table 2).

26. Artist James Case-Leal oversaw the project. Some corrections were made to the original figures based on crowd-sourcing. An archived version of the study can be found in the Internet Archive. "Art Statistics," Haven for the Dispossessed (Sept. 16, 2018), available at https://web.archive.org/web/20180926081208/http://www.havenforthedispossessed.org/.

27. Sinduja Rangarajan, "How We Created a Baseline for Silicon Valley's Diversity Problem," Reveal News (June 25, 2018), https://revealnews.org/blog/how-we-created-a-baseline-for-silicon-valleys-diversity-problem/; Sinduja Rangarajan, "Here's the Clearest Picture of Silicon Valley's Diversity Yet: It's Bad. But Some Companies Are Doing Less Bad," Reveal News (June 25, 2018), https://revealnews.org/article/heres-the-clearest-picture-of-silicon-valleys-diversity-yet/. The Center for Investigative Reporting and the Center for Employment Equity make their data available under an Open Database License: "Silicon Valley Diversity Data," Github, https://github.com/cirlabs/Silicon-Valley-Diversity-Data.

28. Donald Tomaskovic-Devey and JooHee Han, "Is Silicon Valley Tech Diversity Possible Now?," Center for Employment Equity (Jan. 2018) (data from Table 1), https://www.umass.edu/employmentequity/silicon-valley-tech-diversity-possible-now-0.

29. EEOC, "Diversity in High Tech," EEOC, https://www.eeoc.gov/special-report/diversity-high-tech; see also JooHee Han and Donald Tomaskovic-Devey, Center for Employment Equity (Jan. 2022), https://www.umass.edu/employmentequity/tech-sector-diversity-improving.

30. Kate Rooney and Yasmin Khorram, "Tech Companies Say They Value Diversity, but Reports Show Little Change in Last Six Years," CNBC (Jun. 12, 2020), https://www.cnbc.com/2020/06/12/six-years-into-diversity-reports-big-tech-has-made-little-progress.html; "Diversity Tracker," Protocol, https://www.protocol.com/workplace/diversity-tracker/.

31. Claire Williams, "Black Innovators Did Some of the Earliest Work in Cryptocurrency. What Happens Now That It's Mainstream?," Morning Consult (Dec. 9, 2021), https://morningconsult.com/2021/12/09/black-cryptocurrency-influencers-polling/.

32. Andrew Perrin, "16% of Americans Say They Have Ever Invested in, Traded or Used Cryptocurrency," Pew Research (Nov. 11, 2021), https://www.pewresearch.org/fact-tank/2021/11/11/16-of-americans-say-they-have-ever-invested-in-traded-or-used-cryptocurrency/.

33. Charisse Jones and Jessica Menton, "Black, Latino, LGBTQ Investors See Crypto Investments Like Bitcoin as 'a New Path' to Wealth and Equity," Yahoo! (Aug. 15, 2021), https://finance.yahoo.com/news/black-latino-lgbtq-investors-see-100412051.html.

34. Ibid.

35. Will Gottsegen, "At Least 77% of NFT Art Sales Going to Male Creators: Study," Coindesk (Nov. 10, 2021), https://www.coindesk.com/business/2021/11/10/at least-77-of-nft-art-sales-going-to-male-creators-study/.
36. Ibid.
37. Werner Vermaak, "The Top 20 Most Expensive NFTs," Finder (May 16, 2022), https://www.finder.com/most-expensive-nfts.
38. Ola, "The 10 Best-Selling."
39. Anushree Dave, "NFT Art Market Boom Is Overwhelmingly Benefiting Male Creators," Bloomberg (Nov. 9, 2021), https://www.bloomberg.com/news/articles /2021–11–09/nft-crypto-art-market-boom-biggest-sales-going-to-male-artists -women-lag.
40. Justin Roberti, "Exclusive: NFT.NYC CEO Touts Landmark Event with 1,500 Speakers and 15,000 Attendees," Benzinga (June 10, 2022), https://www.ben zinga.com/fintech/22/06/27644065/exclusive-nft-nyc-2022-is-bigger-than-ever -with-1–500-speakers-giving-voice-to-the-nft-community.
41. "Hiscox Online Art Trade Report 2021," 22; Mike Proulx and Martha Bennet, "NFTs Are Having a Bromance with US Males," Forrester (Nov. 4, 2021), https:// www.forrester.com/blogs/nfts-are-having-a-bromance-with-us-males/.
42. Julia Maltby, "Where Are the Female NFT Investors and Creators?," Medium (Jan. 7, 2022), https://jvmaltby.medium.com/the-metaverse-already-has-a-diver sity-problem-where-are-the-female-nft-investors-and-creators-cc96a2f00680.
43. Whitten Brown, "Why Is Work by Female Artists."
44. "How Race Is Playing a Major Role in the NFT Boom," Getwizer (May 11, 2022), https://www.getwizer.com/resources/how-race-is-playing-a-major-role-in-the -nft-boom/.
45. Misyrlena Egkolfopoulou and Akayla Gardner Misyrlena, "Even in the Metaverse, Not All Identities Are Created Equal," Bloomberg (Dec. 6, 2021), https://www .bloomberg.com/news/features/2021–12–06/cryptopunk-nft-prices-suggest-a -diversity-problem-in-the-metaverse.
46. "How Race Is Playing," Getwizer.
47. "Leo Hendrik Baekeland," Science History (Dec. 1, 2017), https://www.science history.org/historical-profile/leo-hendrik-baekeland.
48. "History and Future of Plastics," Science History, https://www.sciencehistory.org /the-history-and-future-of-plastics.
49. Roland Geyer, Jenna R. Jambeck, and Kara Lavender Law, "Production, Use, and Fate of All Plastics Ever Made," *Science Advances* (2017): 3, 10.1126/sciadv.1700782.
50. Ali Chamas et al., "Degradation Rates of Plastics in the Environment," *ACS Sustainable Chemical Engineering* 8 (2020): 3494, https://doi.org/10.1021/acssusche meng.9b06635.
51. Ibid., 3494–95; Laura Parker, "Plastic Trash Flowing into the Seas Will Nearly Triple by 2040 Without Drastic Action," *National Geographic* (Jul. 23, 2020), https://www.nationalgeographic.com/science/article/plastic-trash-in-seas-will -nearly-triple-by-2040-if-nothing-done.
52. Alyssa Hertig, "What Is Proof-of-Work?," CoinDesk (Mar. 9, 2022), https:// www.coindesk.com/learn/2020/12/16/what-is-proof-of-work/.
53. Jeremy Hinsdale, "Cryptocurrency's Dirty Secret: Energy Consumption," Columbia University (May 4, 2022), https://news.climate.columbia.edu/2022/05/04 /cryptocurrency-energy/; Jon Huang, Claire O'Neill, and Hiroko Tabuchi, "Bitcoin Uses More Electricity Than Many Countries. How Is That Possible?," *New York Times* (Sep. 3, 2021), https://www.nytimes.com/interactive/2021/09/03/climate /bitcoin-carbon-footprint-electricity.html.
54. A carbon dioxide equivalent "is a metric measure used to compare the emissions

from various greenhouse gases on the basis of their global-warming potential (GWP) by converting amounts of other gases to the equivalent amount of carbon dioxide with the same global warming potential." Eurostat, "Glossary: Carbon dioxide equivalent," Europa, https://ec.europa.eu/eurostat/statistics-explained /index.php/Glossary:Carbon_dioxide_equivalent.

55.   For Bitcoin and Ethereum pre-merge, I used estimates of CO_2 footprint for a single transaction in January 2022 by Digiconomist. For Ethereum post-merge, I used an estimate by Digiconomist on October 4, 2022. "Ethereum Energy Consumption," Digiconomist, https://digiconomist.net/ethereum-energy-consumption (last visited on Oct. 4, 2022). For simplicity, I did not include the Digiconomist's estimate of Bitcoin's footprint on that day, which was lower (775.25 $kgCO_2$) than January's estimate. "Bitcoin Energy Consumption," Digiconomist, https://digiconomist .net/bitcoin-energy-consumption (last visited on Oct. 4, 2022). The airplane figure was from Our World in Data's estimate based on UK government data. "Which Form of Transport Has the Smallest Carbon Footprint?," Our World in Data (2018), https://ourworldindata.org/travel-carbon-footprint. The estimates for vehicles, ICE and EVs, were based on figures for the United States. Mandira Roy, Hamed Ghoddusi, and Jessika E. Trancik, "Supporting Information Evaluating Low-Carbon Transportation Technologies When Demand Responds to Price," ACS Publications (2022), S6, https://pubs.acs.org/doi/suppl/10.1021/acs .est.1c02052/suppl_file/es1c02052_si_001.pdf (ICEV and EVUSAavg). EVs do not emit CO_2, but require electricity for charging; the EV estimate is based on the U.S. average for electric power to charge the EV based on 41 percent use of coal.

56.   Jake Frankenfield, "Proof-of-Stake (PoS)," Investopedia (June 9, 2022), https:// www.investopedia.com/terms/p/proof-stake-pos.asp.

57.   Taylor Locke, "Ethereum Developers Suggest 'Merge' on Track for September 15," *Fortune* (Aug. 11, 2022), https://fortune.com/2022/08/11/ethereum-merge-date -estimate-developers-september/.

58.   "Ethereum Energy Consumption," Digiconomist.

59.   Andrew Hayward, "Ethereum Energy Usage, Carbon Footprint Down 99.99% After Merge: Report," Decrypt (Sept. 15, 2022), https://decrypt.co/109848 /ethereum-energy-carbon-footprint-down-99-percent-merge.

60.   Krisztian Sandor, "Ethereum Proof-of-Work Fork Stumbles as Justin Sun's Poloniex Supports Rival Fork," CoinDesk (Sept. 16, 2022), https://www.coindesk .com/markets/2022/09/16/ethereum-proof-of-work-fork-crashes-as-justin-suns -poloniex-supports-rival-fork/.

61.   Moritz Platt et al., "The Energy Footprint of Blockchain Consensus Mechanisms Beyond Proof-of-Work," 2021 IEEE 21st International Conference on Software Quality, Reliability and Security Companion (QRS-C):1135, 1139, 10.1109/ QRS-C55045.2021.00168; "New Findings from Deloitte Canada Reveal Minting an NFT on Flow Takes Less Energy Than a Google Search or Instagram Post," Onflow (Feb. 11, 2022), https://www.onflow.org/post/flow-blockchain-sus tainability-energy-deloitte-report-nft.

62.   Barlow, "A Declaration."

63.   Ibid.

64.   Mary Anne Franks, "Beyond the Public Square: Imagining Digital Democracy," *Yale Law Journal Forum* (Nov. 16, 2021): 453.

65.   Halperin and Burns, "Museums."

66.   Caroline Goldstein, "Reality Star and Crypto Evangelist Paris Hilton Is Spearheading a Digital Art Acquisition Fund at LACMA," Artnet (June 9, 2022), https://news.artnet.com/market/lacma-acquisition-fund-paris-hilton-2127802.

67.   Rachel Wolfson, "NFTs of Empowered Women Aim to Drive Female Engage-

ment in Crypto," Cointelegraph (Oct. 19, 2021), https://cointelegraph.com/news /nfts-of-empowered-women-aim-to-drive-female-engagement-in-crypto.

68. Daniela Avila, "Boss Beauties' Lisa Mayer Releases NFT Role Models Collection for International Women's Day," *People* (Mar. 8, 2022), https://people.com /human-interest/lisa-mayer-boss-beauties-releases-nft-womens-collection/.

69. Emma Hinchliffe and Nimah Quadri, "Exclusive: Boss Beauties Raises $4.4 Million to Turn Its NFT Collection into Media IP," *Fortune* (Apr. 20, 2022), https://fortune.com/2022/04/20/boss-beauties-raises-4-4-million-to-turn-nft -collection-into-media-ip/.

70. "About the Artist," Metaangelsnft, https://www.metaangelsnft.com/artist.

71. "Meta Angels Lending Program," Metaangelsnft, https://www.metaangelsnft .com/lending.

72. Taylor Locke, "This 29-Year-Old Launched a Business to Support Black NFT Artists—and It Made $140,000 in 10 Months: I See It as a Way to 'Rebalance Power,'" CNBC (Jan. 14, 2022), https://www.cnbc.com/2022/01/14/iris-nevins -launched-business-umba-daima-to-uplift-black-nft-artists.html.

73. Demetrius Simms, "How the World's Largest Collection of LGBTQ-Inspired NFT Art Is Raising Money for Good Causes," *Robb Report* (June 1, 2022), https:// robbreport.com/lifestyle/news/pride-icons-nft-artworks-1234681588/.

74. Ibid.

75. Abigail Covington, "Meet FEWOCiOUS, the Teenager Who Crashed Christie's Auction House," *Esquire* (June 29, 2021), https://www.esquire.com/entertain ment/a36878931/fewocious-crypto-nft-art-christies-profile/.

76. Rob Nowill, "A Sale of Virtual Sneakers Raised $3.1 Million USD in Seven Minutes," Hypebeast (Mar. 3, 2021), https://hypebeast.com/2021/3/rtfkt-studios -fewocious-sale-nfts.

77. Marco Quiroz-Gutierrez, "NFT Artist FEWOCiOUS Sold Nearly $20 Million of His Digital Work in 24 Hours," *Fortune* (Apr. 7, 2022), https://fortune .com/2022/04/07/nft-artist-fewocious-sells-20-million-24-hours-art-crypto/.

78. "Bowie by FEWOCiOUS," OpenSea, https://opensea.io/assets/ethereum/0xfe7d 465d8c420ee4aead45d54d32defc4e3cff2c/1.

79. Unblocked, Twitter (Aug. 3, 2022), https://twitter.com/onunblocked/status/1554 983621227712513.

80. Tat Bellamy-Walker, "Meet the Trans Teen Whose Crypto Artwork Has Earned Him Nearly $50 Million," NBC News (June 1, 2022), https://www.nbcnews.com /nbc-out/nbc-out-proud/meet-trans-teen-whose-crypto-artwork-earned-nearly -50-million-rcna28810.

81. Adele, "Blind Singer Lachi X Teams Up with Disabled Artists for Charitable NFTs," NFT Evening (Dec. 3, 2021), https://nftevening.com/blind-singer-lachi -x-teames-up-with-disabled-artists-for-charitable-nfts/.

82. "ARTXV—NFTs to Celebrate Diversity and Support Neurodiverse Artists," Crypto Altruism (Jan. 11, 2022), https://www.cryptoaltruism.org/blog/project -showcase-artxv-nfts-to-celebrate-diversity-and-support-neurodiverse-artists.

83. "Two Sisters Challenging the Traditional Art World," ARTXV, https://www .artxv.org/about.

84. "NFTs," ARTXV, https://www.artxv.org/nfts.

85. "Building a Better NFT: Making Your NFTs Climate Positive with Klima DAO," Klima DAO (May 5, 2022), https://www.klimadao.finance/blog/climate -positive-nft-guide.

86. Brian Newar, "Klima DAO Accumulates $100M of Carbon Offsets, Aims to Drive Up Price," Cointelegraph (Nov. 12, 2021), https://cointelegraph.com/news /klima-dao-accumulates-100m-of-carbon-offsets-aims-to-drive-up-price.

87. "What Is a Carbon Offset?," Offsetguide, https://www.offsetguide.org/under standing-carbon-offsets/what-is-a-carbon-offset/.

88. Sarah Murray, "Environmentalists Cast Doubt on Carbon Offsets," *Financial Times* (July 12, 2021), https://www.ft.com/content/81d436c2–79f1–4a43-ab52 -cbbcddb149df.

89. Newar, "Klima DAO."

90. "CO2_Compound: A Carbon Compounding Artwork," Klima DAO, https://co 2compound.klimadao.finance/.

91. "Recent Study Reveals More Than a Third of Global Consumers Are Willing to Pay More for Sustainability as Demand Grows for Environmentally-Friendly Alternatives," Businesswire (Oct. 14, 2021), https://www.businesswire.com /news/home/20211014005090/en/Recent-Study-Reveals-More-Than-a-Third-of -Global-Consumers-Are-Willing-to-Pay-More-for-Sustainability-as-Demand -Grows-for-Environmentally-Friendly-Alternatives; Shelby Jordan, "Why Is Diversity Marketing Important," Top Design Firms (Nov. 11, 2020), https://top designfirms.com/web-design/blog/diversity-marketing.

92. Gary Gensler, "Statement on Proposed Mandatory Climate Risk Disclosures," SEC (Mar. 21, 2022), https://www.sec.gov/news/statement/gensler-climate -disclosure-20220321.

93. Ibid.

94. VeeFriends, https://veefriends.com/faqs.

95. "WoW Community: One of a Kind," World of Women, https://worldofwomen .art/our-community.html; "Manifesto," Azuki, https://www.azuki.com/mani festo; Pudgy Penguins, "Terms of Use," Pudgy Penguins, https://pudgypenguins .com/terms-and-conditions.

96. "Realizing a Better Future for All Its Inhabitants," FTX, https://www.ftx-climate .com/; "The FTX Foundation Group Launches the FTX Climate Program," PRnewswire (July 27, 2021), https://www.prnewswire.com/news-releases/the-ftx -foundation-group-launches-the-ftx-climate-program-301342380.html.

97. "We Commit to Diversity, Inclusiveness and an Engaging Environment," Soft-bank, https://group.softbank/en/about/compliance/code_of_conduct/respect.

98. "Our Mission," Opportunity Fund, https://theopportunityfund.com/.

99. Yuliya Chernova, "SoftBank, Andreessen Horowitz Set Up Funds to Back Diverse Founders," *Wall Street Journal* (June 4, 2020), https://www.wsj.com/art icles/softbank-andreessen-horowitz-set-up-funds-to-back-diverse-founders -11591298091.

100. Natasha Mascarenhas, "SoftBank Turns Fund for Diverse Entrepreneurs into an 'Evergreen' Opportunity," TechCrunch (Mar. 14, 2022), https://techcrunch .com/2022/03/14/softbank-opportunity-evergreen-fund/.

101. Kenrick Cai, "SoftBank to Turn Its Fund for Underrepresented Founders into Evergreen Vehicle," *Forbes* (Mar. 14, 2022), https://www.forbes.com/sites/ken rickcai/2022/03/14/softbank-opportunity-fund-for-underrepresented-founders -evergreen/?sh=42c80cde5338; Ben Dooley, "SoftBank Reports $23 Billion Loss as Tech Investments Plummet," *New York Times* (Aug. 8, 2022), https://www.ny times.com/2022/08/08/business/softbank-vision-funds-loss.html.

102. Naithan Jones, "Announcing TxO's First Cohort," a16z (Oct. 30, 2020), https:// a16z.com/2020/10/30/announcing-txos-first-cohort/; Jeff Jordan, Kofi Ampadu, and Tauri Laws Phillips, "Meet TxO Cohort Two," a16z (Jan. 25, 2022), https:// a16z.com/2022/01/25/meet-txo-cohort-2/.

103. Alex Konrad, "A16z Crypto's Record New $4.5 Billion Fund Doubles Down on Web3 Amid Market Crash," *Forbes* (May 25, 2022), https://www.forbes.com /sites/alexkonrad/2022/05/25/a16z-crypto-record-4th-fund-doubles-down-on

-web3-amid-market-crash/?sh=3bb0292d34ff; Camomile Shumba, "Venture-Capital Firm Northzone Raises $1B Fund for Fintech, Web3 Investments," CoinDesk (Sep. 15, 2022), https://www.coindesk.com/business/2022/09/13/vc-firm -northzone-raises-1b-fund-for-fintech-web3-investments/.

104. "CreatorDAO Raises $20M Seed Round from a16z Crypto and Initialized Capital to Invest in Creators," PRnewswire (Aug. 9, 2022), https://www.prnewswire .com/news-releases/creatordao-raises-20m-seed-round-from-a16z-crypto-and -initialized-capital-to-invest-in-creators-301602543.html.

Chapter 12: The Flight for the Future

1. "Strange Ships That Sail in the Skies," *St. Paul Globe* (May 9, 1897), 20.
2. Ibid.
3. David McCullough, *The Wright Brothers* (New York: Simon & Schuster Paperbacks, 2015), 27.
4. Ibid., 28–29.
5. Ibid., 29.
6. "Wilbur Wright Letter Dated May 30, 1899," Smithsonian Institution Archives, https://siarchives.si.edu/history/featured-topics/stories/letter-dated-may-30 –1899.
7. Ibid.
8. Ibid.
9. "Richard Rathbun Launched Wright Brothers' Research," Smithsonian Institution Archives, https://siarchives.si.edu/collections/siris_sic_3900; Tom Crouch, *The Bishop's Boys: A Life of Wilbur and Orville Wright* (New York: W. W. Norton & Co., paperback 2003), 162.
10. McCullough, *Wright Brothers*, 36–37.
11. Ibid., 105–106.
12. Ibid., 38.
13. Ibid.; Crouch, *Bishop's Boys*, 165–68.
14. Crouch, *Bishop's Boys*, 167.
15. Ibid., 169–70; "Aircraft Control," NASA, https://wright.nasa.gov/airplane/con trol.html.
16. "The 1902 Glider," National Air and Space Museum, https://airandspace.si.edu /exhibitions/wright-brothers/online/fly/1902/glider.cfm.
17. Danica Lo, "Tech Workers Are Fleeing FAANG for Web3, Here's Why," *Fast Company* (Apr. 8, 2022), https://www.fastcompany.com/90739257/leaving-faang -web3-jobs; Ryan Browne, "Crypto Companies Are Tempting Top Talent Away from Big Tech to Build 'Web3,'" CNBC (Feb. 23, 2022), https://www.cnbc .com/2022/02/23/crypto-companies-tempt-top-talent-away-from-big-tech-to -build-web3.html.
18. Bessie Lu, "Are People Leaving Their Tech Jobs for Web3?," Blockworks (Jun. 2, 2022), https://blockworks.co/are-people-leaving-their-tech-jobs-for-web3/.
19. Marco Quiroz-Gutierrez, "Companies Like Nike and Disney Are Hiring Like Crazy for the Metaverse—and It's Just the Start," *Fortune* (Feb. 2, 2022), https:// fortune.com/2022/02/02/nike-disney-meta-companies-hiring-spree-metaverse/.
20. "55k Metaverse-Based Jobs on Offer as IT Cos and Startups Chalk Out Plans," *Economic Times* (July 24, 2022), https://m.economictimes.com/tech/technol ogy/demand-for-tech-professionals-for-it-cos-metaverse-startups-surge/article show/93094252.cms.
21. Marco Quiroz-Gutierrez, "The Crown Prince of Dubai Says He Has a 'Metaverse Strategy' That Will Add 40,000 Jobs and $4 Billion to the Economy in 5 Years," *Fortune* (July 19, 2022), https://fortune.com/2022/07/19/dubai-metaverse-

strategy-crypto-emerging-tech-web3/; Cheyenne Ligon, "Why Is South Korea Throwing Money at the Metaverse?," CoinDesk (May 25, 2022), https://www.coindesk.com/layer2/metaverseweek/2022/05/25/why-is-south-korea-throwing-money-at-the-metaverse/.

22. "'Find the Smartest Technologist in the Company and Make Them CEO,'" McKinsey (June 22, 2022), https://mck.co/3xIACop.

23. Ibid.

24. Willis Harman, "Humanistic Capitalism: Another Alternative," *Journal of Humanistic Psychology* 14, no. 1 (Winter 1974): 31.

25. Mark Serrels, "Facebook and Instagram Are Making Changes to 'Nudge' Teens Away from Harmful Content," CNET (Oct 11, 2021), https://www.cnet.com/news/politics/facebook-and-instagram-are-making-changes-to-nudge-teens-away-from-harmful-content/.

26. Burgess, "Wild Men of Paris," 401.

27. Crouch, *Bishop's Boys*, 128.

INDEX

ABOUT THE AUTHOR

EDWARD LEE is a leading legal expert on NFTs and intellectual property. He is a professor of law and codirector of Illinois Institute of Technology Chicago-Kent College of Law's Center for Design, Law, and Technology, the first U.S. institution devoted to the research of creativity, technology, design, and the law. His website, nouNFT.com, analyzes the latest developments in NFTs. He founded The Free Internet Project, a nonprofit whose mission is to protect Internet freedoms. Lee is a former contributor to the *Huffington Post*. His work has been featured in outlets such as the *Washington Post* and *Billboard*. He worked on public interest litigation as an attorney for Stanford Law School's Center for Internet and Society. Lee graduated from Williams College and Harvard Law School. An accomplished photographer, he has shown his works in group exhibitions and art fairs in New York City, Chicago, Miami, Amsterdam, and Dubai.